Great Novels

Great Novels

The world's most remarkable fiction explored and explained

Consultant

John Mullan

DK LONDON
Senior Editor Angela Wilkes
Senior Art Editor Gillian Andrews
Editors Rose Blackett-Ord, Jo Edwards, Andy Szudek
Project Art Editor Katie Cavanagh
Picture Researchers Sarah Smithies, Sarah Hopper
Managing Editor Gareth Jones
Senior Managing Art Editor Lee Griffiths
Production Editor Rob Dunn
Senior Production Controller Rachel Ng
Jacket Design Development Manager Sophia M.T.T.
Associate Publishing Director Liz Wheeler
Art Director Karen Self
Publishing Director Jonathan Metcalf

DK DELHI
Senior Editor Janashree Singha
Project Editor Nandini D. Tripathy
Editor Ankita Gupta
Senior Art Editors Chhaya Sajwan, Ira Sharma
Project Art Editor Shipra Jain
Art Editor Anukriti Arora
Managing Editor Soma B. Chowdhury
Senior Managing Art Editor Arunesh Talapatra
Senior DTP Designers Jagtar Singh,
Vishal Bhatia, Harish Aggarwal
Production Manager Pankaj Sharma
Pre-production Manager Balwant Singh
Senior Jacket Designer Suhita Dharamjit
Senior Jackets Coordinator Priyanka Sharma Saddi
Editorial Head Glenda Fernandes
Design Head Malavika Talukder

First published in Great Britain in 2022 by
Dorling Kindersley Limited
DK, One Embassy Gardens, 8 Viaduct Gardens,
London, SW11 7BW

Copyright © 2022 Dorling Kindersley Limited
A Penguin Random House Company
10 9 8 7 6 5 4 3 2 1
001–325058–Oct/2022

A CIP catalogue record for this book
is available from the British Library.
ISBN: 978-0-2415-1584-6

Printed and bound in China

For the curious
www.dk.com

MIX
Paper from
responsible sources
FSC™ C018179

This book was made with Forest
Stewardship Council ™ certified
paper – one small step in DK's
commitment to a sustainable future.
For more information go to
www.dk.com/our-green-pledge

Contents

CHAPTER 1
BEFORE 1800

CONSULTANT

John Mullan is Lord Northcliffe Professor of Modern English Literature at University College London. He has published widely on 18th- and 19th-century literature. His most recent book is *The Artful Dickens*. His other books include *What Matters in Jane Austen?* and *Anonymity: A Secret History of English Literature*. He is also a broadcaster and journalist, writing on contemporary fiction for *The Guardian*. He is the author of *How Novels Work* and in 2009 was one of the judges for the Man Booker Prize.

CONTRIBUTORS

Mark Collins Jenkins has a Master's degree in English from the University of Virginia, US. His publications include *Worlds to Explore* and *The Book of Marvels*. He also co-authored *A Man of the World: The Memoirs of Gilbert M. Grosvenor*.

B.J. Epstein Woodstein is a translator, writer, editor, and an associate professor in literature and translation at the University of East Anglia. She translated *The Book That Did Not Want to be Read* by David Sundin, and edited *International LGBTQ+ Literature for Children and Young Adults*.

R.G. Grant has written extensively in the fields of history, biography, and culture. He contributed to *1001 Books You Must Read Before You Die*, *500 Great Writers*, *Writers: Their Lives and Works*, and *Great Diaries*.

Autumn Green studied religion and history of art at Smith College, US, before receiving a Master's in art history at Oxford University. She contributed to DK's *Banned Books* and *Women: A Visual History*.

Tianyun Hua is a Ph.D. student in Comparative Literature at the University of California, Davis, US. She contributed to *Banned Books* and has translated Bertolt Brecht into Chinese.

Andrew Kerr-Jarrett is a writer and editor who specializes in literature and history. He read English at Cambridge University and taught English before becoming an editor at Toucan Books. He contributed to DK's *Banned Books*.

Richard Niland is a lecturer in literature and has published on a range of 19th- and 20th-century writers. The author of *Conrad and History*, he has taught at the University of Oxford and the University of Strathclyde. He also currently teaches at the City Literary Institute in London.

Esther Ripley is a writer and editor, who began her career in journalism and was a managing editor at DK. She writes on a range of cultural subjects and contributed to *Writers: Their Lives and Works* and *Great Diaries*.

Rachel Sykes is senior lecturer in contemporary literature and culture at the University of Birmingham. Their publications include *The Quiet Contemporary American Novel* and *Marilynne Robinson*, and they regularly write on contemporary American fiction and television.

Iain Zaczek studied at Oxford University, and the Courtauld Institute in London. He has written more than 30 books on various aspects of literature, history, and art, and contributed to DK's *Great Diaries*.

Introduction

Novels grip readers like no other kind of book. How often does someone speak of staying up late at night, unable to put their novel down until they have finished it? In the 18th century, when the novel first became the bestselling type of book throughout Europe, critics and moralists warned about its power to possess readers. Novels were just too exciting; they gave young people (especially young women) dangerous ideas and distracted them from their duties. In her novel *Northanger Abbey*, Jane Austen records some of the "common cant" of her day about them: "I am no novel-reader – I seldom look into novels – Do not imagine that *I* often read novels". She, of course, laughs at all this.

Thanks in part to great novelists such as Austen herself, novels survived all the suspicion and condescension, and, around the world, the novel as a genre remains in the rudest health. This is a book designed to make you want to read (or reread) more novels. We have tried something impossible: to select around 80 great novels from all those ever written, and to give you an idea of what is so "great" about them. Any reader who loves fiction will have his or her disagreements with our selection, but the choice is not just a matter of taste or opinion. Some novels have survived the fashions of their time, while others have not. Certain novels have influenced

or inspired other novelists. Above all, readers have kept returning to certain great novels – books that prove to repay rereading. Some of these have always been popular and accessible. Novels such as *Jane Eyre* and *Great Expectations*, *To Kill a Mockingbird,* and *Portnoy's Complaint*, were bestsellers in their own day and are easy books to enjoy. Other great novels can be more challenging. Works such as Laurence Sterne's *Tristram Shandy* or James Joyce's *Ulysses* set out to unsettle the reader's expectations of what a story should be like. Yet books like these were written to entertain as well as perplex us, and gave generations of future novelists new ideas about what fiction was able to do.

This book tries to tell you why each novel is interesting and to say something about the writer who created it. The main entries tell you about the great novels we have chosen, but each section also has a directory at the end of it, with briefer entries on novels that did not quite make it into the main part. The selection is arranged chronologically because novels have developed over time, influenced by those before them.

It was difficult to know where to start. From ancient times, there have been fictional narratives written in prose. The earliest novels, such as *Journey to the West* or *Don Quixote*, tend to be collections of stories and episodes. Some would

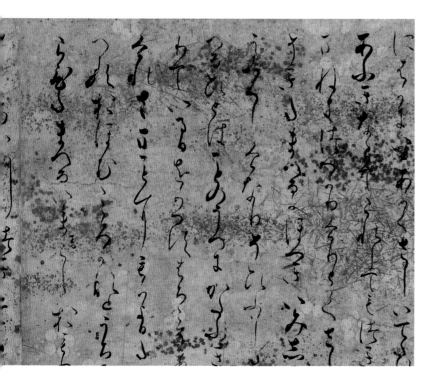

▲ **JAPANESE FORERUNNER** This is part of a 12th-century restored scroll of *The Tale of Genji*, widely considered to be the world's first novel. It was written by 11th-century Japanese noblewoman Murasaki Shikibu.

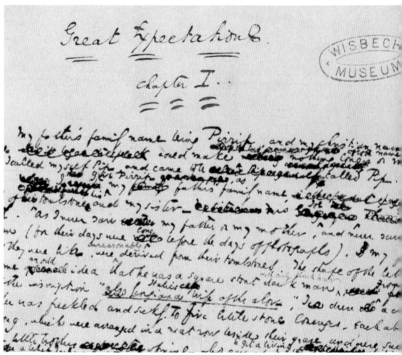

▲ **FAMOUS BEGINNING** The first page of Charles Dicken's manuscript of *Great Expectations* (1861) is dense with corrections. The story starts in a churchyard and sets the scene for one of the most evocative openings of any novel.

> Every novel says to the reader: 'Things are not as simple as you think.' That is the novel's eternal truth.

MILAN KUNDERA, *THE ART OF THE NOVEL*, 2005

argue that these are really "proto-novels": fascinating preludes to "true" novels. It was in the 18th century, with works such as *Robinson Crusoe* and *Pamela*, that English readers became conscious of a wholly new kind of story and started using the word "novel" to describe it. This new kind of book was not just a long prose narrative – it had to have other characteristics, too. It had to be believable ("probable" was the usual word in English). It also had to feature ordinary characters (not princes and princesses). And it had to focus on the individual, exploring their state of mind and emotions.

The novels in this collection come from all around the world, but all of them are easy to obtain in other languages. The availability of translations, especially in recent decades, has made the novel an international genre. The selection is particularly international as we move closer to the present day. The main entries in Chapter 6 (1980–Present) feature 21 novels, by authors from 17 different countries. These books from all over the world come together and can be compared and contrasted with each other.

In this guide to the history of fiction, images matter as well as words. We have featured pictures of pages from the original manuscripts of most of the novels in our main entries. These books may now be considered "classics", neatly arranged in bookshops and libraries, but they often began life as hesitant experiments. The manuscripts and marked-up page proofs will give you an insight into how writers revised and corrected their writing as they went along. We have also shown many first-edition jackets, especially from the 20th and 21st centuries, so that you can also see just how these novels first announced themselves. And our contextual images illustrate the places and events, social changes, and literary movements that inspired the novels. We hope that they make this book a pleasure not just for the mind, but also for the eye.

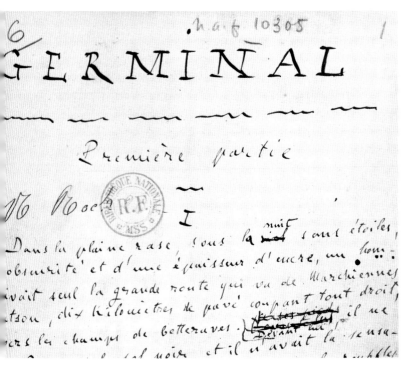

▲ **SEMINAL WORK** This is the first page of Émile Zola's handwritten draft of *Germinal* (1885). One of his most political novels, it tells the story of a young migrant worker swept up in a coal strike in northern France.

▲ **MAIN CHARACTER** This is a lithograph that author Günter Grass made by combining a picture that he had drawn of Oskar Matzerath, the protagonist of *The Tin Drum* (1959), with his text for the opening of the book.

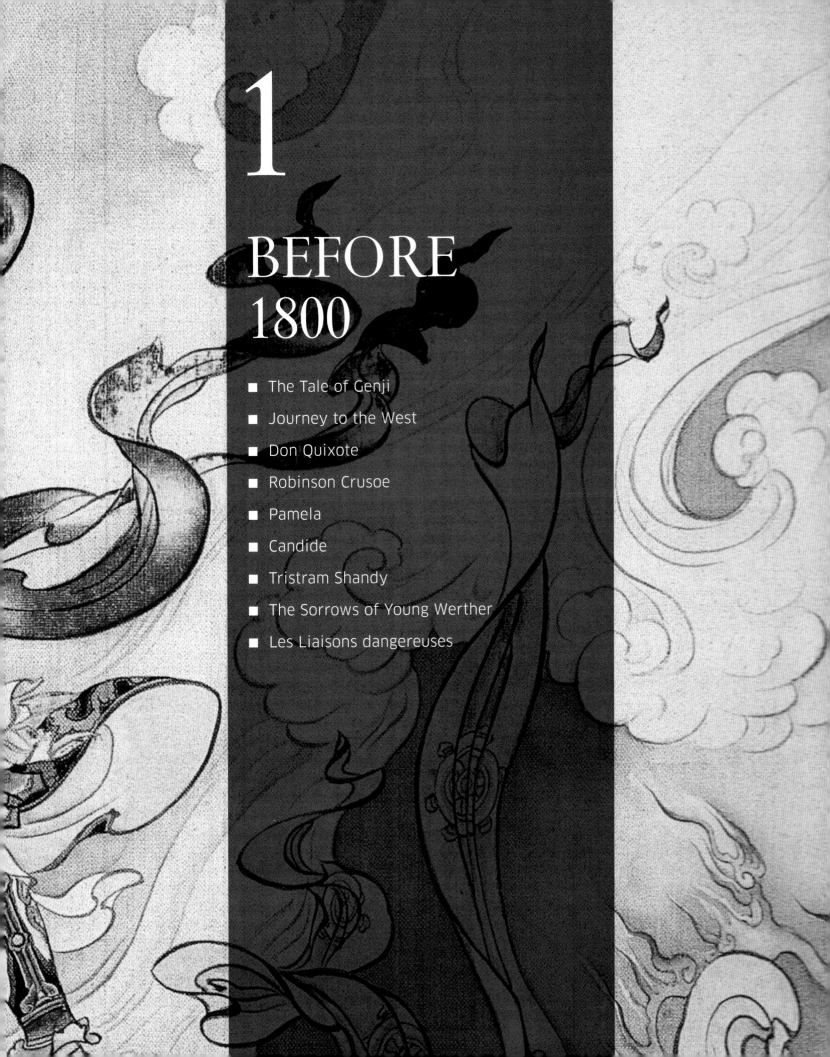

1

BEFORE 1800

The Tale of Genji

c.1021 ▪ HAND SCROLL ▪ JAPAN

MURASAKI SHIKIBU (c.978–1031)

Widely considered to be the world's first novel, *The Tale of Genji* was written by Japanese noblewoman Murasaki Shikibu in the early 11th century, at a time when fiction was seen as a low form of art in Japan. It is set in the capital Heian-kyō (now Kyoto) during the Heian period (794–1185), and focuses on the lives of the nobility. Murasaki's hero, Genji, is the son of the emperor but is unable to inherit the title because his mother is not of sufficiently high birth. The story follows Genji's unhappy arranged marriage, as well as his many love affairs, including an affair with one of the emperor's wives, Fujitsubo – which produces a son who eventually becomes emperor himself – and another with Fujitsubo's niece, Murasaki, who is the main female character.

The novel paints an intimate portrait of the very formal, hierarchical life of the Japanese court. In this world, language is highly restrained and lovers are not allowed to express themselves openly, often communicating via intermediaries. Yet feelings may be expressed through poetry, and the novel contains hundreds of poems. Murasaki writes with profound psychological insight into her characters, and this is what makes *The Tale of Genji* seem most like a modern novel.

Medieval Japanese women were not usually well educated. Unlike men, who wrote in Chinese (the scholarly language of court), literate women usually wrote in Japanese, which was thought unfit for literary works. Murasaki's completion of a sophisticated text of more than 1,100 pages was therefore a remarkable feat. Highly proficient at writing in her own tongue, in addition to being well versed in Chinese, Murasaki was also the author of a book of poems and a notable diary, but *The Tale of Genji* is considered her greatest achievement.

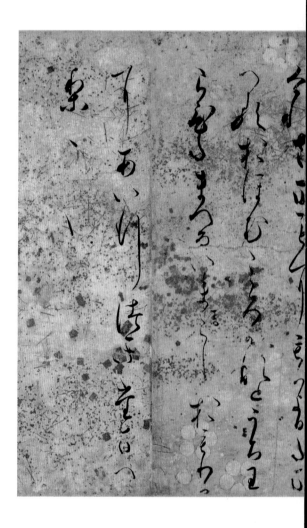

In context

◀ **HEIAN LIFE** The Heian imperial court is intricately depicted in Murasaki's novel: life for the nobility followed set patterns, and a strict etiquette was observed. This section of the 12th-century handscroll on which a later copy of the novel was written shows an outdoor scene in a traditional arbour where a noblewoman sits with her maids.

▶ **THE FUJIWARA CLAN** The Heian emperor's role was largely ceremonial; power lay with the Fujiwara family, a clan of regents who controlled the government. Fujiwara no Michinaga (see right) was the most powerful of these regents, and is said to have inspired the character of Genji.

▼ **MANUSCRIPT COPIES** The original 11th-century manuscript of *Genji* no longer exists, but there are surviving sections of the book dating from the 12th century, such as this manuscript page from an illustrated, restored hand scroll. Copies vary in their accuracy. Scholars collect and compare the different versions, in order to create an authentic text of the entire book.

" In a certain reign (whose can it have been?) someone of no very great rank, among all His Majesty's Consorts and Intimates, enjoyed exceptional favour. Those others who had always assumed that pride of place was properly theirs despised her as a dreadful woman, while the lesser Intimates were unhappier still. The way she waited on him day after day only stirred up feeling against her... but His Majesty, who could less and less do without her, ignored his critics until his behavior seemed bound to be the talk of all. "

THE TALE OF GENJI, CHAPTER 1, "KIRITSUBO"

◄ **AKIKO YOSANO** *The Tale of Genji* uses a medieval form of Japanese that people today struggle to read. To make the novel more accessible, the pioneering feminist and poet Akiko Yosano produced the first translations into modern Japanese early in the 20th century. These included both an abridgement of the novel and a complete version.

NARRATIVE STYLE

Murasaki's novel has a distinctive narrative style, with a rich variety of digressions, subplots, and shifts of perspective. Rather than the single, overarching narrative structure favoured by many modern novelists, *The Tale of Genji* is made up of a series of separate episodes in which new characters often appear. These episodes are linked in several ways: by their settings, for example; by a general concern with themes, such as love and family loyalties; and also by the need to fit in with the manners and customs of the courtly life of the period.

The final section of the novel is slightly different in tone because the story's two main characters, Genji and Murasaki, have both died and live on only in the memories of others. This divergence has led some scholars to suggest that this part of the novel was written by someone else, after the original author had died, but most people still accept that it is the work of Murasaki Shikibu alone.

Journey to the West

C.1592 ▪ 100 CHAPTERS ▪ CHINA

WU CHENG'EN (c.1505–1580)

The origins of *Journey to the West* lie in the 7th-century travels of the Chinese monk, Xuanzang. In 629CE, he set off on a 17-year pilgrimage to India to learn true Buddhism and collect precious scriptures. Xuanzang's travelogue became the starting point for a collection of fantasy tales, including encounters with deities and demons, that has remained popular for more than 1,000 years. The story was originally passed down by word of mouth, by Buddhist preachers or theatrical performances, for example. As it evolved, some elements became constant, including the monk's disciples (such as Sun Wukong the Monkey King, and the White Dragon Horse), the 81 challenges that Xuanzang faces, and the demons he meets on the road. Eventually, during the Ming Dynasty, a 100-chapter book of this legendary story was printed. Although experts dispute its true authorship, it is widely attributed to the scholar Wu Cheng'en.

Deeply rooted in Chinese culture, *Journey* depicts a world that fuses together aspects of Buddhist, Taoist, and Confucian traditions. The interplay between these religions is central to the text, but presented without piety. The novel often makes fun of the lofty gods, especially through the rebellious spirits

▶ **PILGRIMAGE TO INDIA** The scene from *Journey to the West* depicted in this mural shows the monk Xuanzang (or Tang Sanzang, as he is called in the book) on his pilgrimage to India. He is shown on the back of a white horse, which is the son of Yulong, the Dragon King, in disguise. Walking alongside the horse is Sun Wukong, the Monkey King, one of Tang Sanzang's key disciples and a major character in the story. Zhu Bajie, another disciple, follows behind.

of the Monkey. In this story, the deities are not perfect. The highest god, Jade Emperor, is petty and cruel, inflicting a three-year drought on an entire region. Later, upon their final arrival at the "West Heaven", the pilgrims fail to offer gifts to two disciples of the Buddha, and so initially receive only blank scriptures in return. In this way, the author weaves both profound satire and humour into an epic adventure story.

Journey mixes reality with fantasy and metaphor to explore the Chinese philosophy of the heart-and-mind. The Monkey gains his power in the Cave of "Slanting Moon and Three Stars", represented by the Chinese character for "heart" (心). Most demons come from Heaven (symbolizing the heart), and the Monkey's double – the Sixth-Ear Macaque – shows that the ultimate enemy is a mirror of the self. To defeat your demon is to tame the heart-and-mind. As such, *Journey* is an exploration of the relationship between human and self – a journey within the realm of the heart-and-mind – rather than the pure adventure story it appears to be.

In context

◀ **XUANZANG** Historical figure Xuanzang was a 7th-century Chinese Buddhist monk, known for the vast collection of Buddhist texts that he acquired on his travels to India: he translated many of them from Sanskrit into Chinese. His travelogue is used as a historical document, and became the inspiration for *Journey*. In the book, Xuanzang is given the name Tang Sanzang.

▶ **THE MONKEY KING** Known in China as Sun Wukong, the Monkey King is a mythical figure who gains supernatural powers. He is imprisoned for 500 years for causing trouble in the Heavens, but is rescued by Tang Sanzang and joins the pilgrimage. Although the Monkey King is mischievous by nature, he attains enlightenment by the end of the story. He is widely loved in Chinese culture for his rebellious spirit.

THE **FOUR GREAT NOVELS**

Romance of the Three Kingdoms (c.1522), *Water Margin* (c.1524), *Journey to the West* (c.1592), and *Dream of the Red Chamber* (c.1791) are four extensive works of fiction, revered across China by adults and children alike. Known as the Four Great Novels, they form the core of Chinese classical literature and still influence modern Chinese culture.

The novels date from the Ming dynasty (1368–1644) and the Qing dynasty (1644–1911). The writing and dissemination of these four works marked the emergence of the novel form in China, which acted as a counterpart to the traditional and more refined philosophical and poetic works. Historically, fiction and drama were not highly regarded in the Chinese or East Asian literary hierarchy. However, in these four texts, the form of the novel proved more flexible, making it possible to blend the historical and the mythological, and to merge the vernacular language with classical Chinese.

▶ **Japanese artist** Utagawa Kuniyoshi depicted a scene from *Water Margin* in this 19th-century painting, *Yang Lin, Hero of the Suikoden*.

> A pointed mouth and hollow cheeks; Two diamond pupils and fiery eyes. Lichens had piled on his head; Wisteria grew in his ears. By his temples was more green grass than hair; Beneath his chin, moss instead of a beard. With mud on his brow, And earth in his nose, He looked most desperate! His fingers coarse And calloused palms Were caked in filth and dirt! Luckily, his eyes could still roll about, And the apish tongue, articulate. Though in speech he had great ease, His body he could not move. He was the Great Sage Sun of five hundred years ago. Today his ordeal ends, he leaves Heaven's net.

JOURNEY TO THE WEST, CHAPTER 14

EL INGENIOSO HIDALGO DON QVI-XOTE DE LA MANCHA.

Compuesto por Miguel de Ceruantes Saauedra.

DIRIGIDO AL DVQVE DE BEIAR,
Marques de Gibraleon, Conde de Benalcazar, y Bañares, Vizconde de la Puebla de Alcozer, Señor de las villas de Capilla, Curiel, y Burguillos.

Año, 1605.

Con priuilegio de Castilla, Aragon, y Portugal.
EN MADRID, Por Iuan de la Cuesta.

Vendese en casa de Francisco de Robles, librero del Rey nro señor.

> In a village of La Mancha, the name of which I have no desire to call to mind, there lived not long since one of those gentlemen that keep a lance in the lance-rack, an old buckler, a lean hack, and a greyhound for coursing... You must know, then, that the above-named gentleman whenever he was at leisure (which was mostly all the year round) gave himself up to reading books of chivalry with such ardour and avidity that he almost entirely neglected the pursuit of his field-sports, and even the management of his property...

DON QUIXOTE OF LA MANCHA, PART 1, CHAPTER 1

In this note, addressed to the Chamber of Castile, Cervantes asks the king's permission to publish his book *The Ingenious Gentleman of La Mancha*

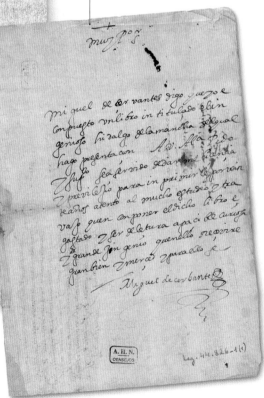

▲ ▶ **FIRST EDITION AND NOTE** Cervantes had been a soldier, a tax collector, a poet, and a playwright before publishing his first novel, *Galatea*, in 1585. He published nothing more until *Don Quixote* in 1605, which was an immediate success, and was translated into several languages. He later wrote: "I am the first who has written *novelas* in the Spanish language... neither imitated nor stolen from anyone". At the time, however, "*novelas*" meant "short works of fiction", rather than "novels" in the modern sense.

Don Quixote

1605, 1615 ■ TWO VOLUMES ■ SPAIN

MIGUEL DE CERVANTES (1547–1616)

Published in two parts, in 1605 and 1615, and considered the first major modern novel, Cervantes' *Don Quixote* follows the exploits of a Spanish *hidalgo* (country gentleman) named Alonso Quixano, who loses his sense of reality by obsessively reading books about medieval chivalry. Inspired by tales of knights and maidens from Spanish, French, and Italian literature, Quixano, who lives in a village in La Mancha, Spain, renames himself Don Quixote de la Mancha, and sets forth to right the world's wrongs and to bring glory to the name of his beloved Dulcinea del Toboso (in reality, a plain country girl he has never met). Accompanied by his peasant squire, Sancho Panza, whom he has promised to make the governor of an island for his services, and borne along by his trusty steed, a malnourished horse named Rocinante, Don Quixote mistakes the everyday world of 16th-century Spain for scenes taken from chivalric romance.

Part 1 of the novel is a loose account of Don Quixote's initial adventures, and draws on the Spanish "picaresque" tradition of accompanying ordinary characters on their travels in a contemporary setting. Originally planned as a *cuento* (short story), the novel expanded to become a series of episodes recounting the modern knight's misreading of reality – he mistakes windmills for giants, frees dangerous criminals from a chain-gang, regards country inns as castles, and insists that a barber's shaving basin is the fabulous helmet of the

THE GOLDEN CENTURY IN SPAIN

During a period known as *El Siglo de Oro* (the Golden Century), Spain flourished both economically and artistically. The period began in 1492, when the Spanish regained southern Spain from the Moors, and sponsored Christopher Columbus to cross the Atlantic. Over the next 150 years, writers such as Lope de Vega, Garcilaso de la Vega, Francisco de Quevedo, Luis de Góngora, and St John of the Cross produced an extraordinary range of drama and poetry. During this period, artists such as El Greco, Diego Velázquez, Bartolomé Esteban Murillo, and Francisco de Zurbarán also created major paintings that celebrated aspects of Spanish culture, including its members of the aristocracy and the country's Catholic traditions.

▲ **Count-Duke of Olivares,** by Diego Velázquez, depicts Spanish military prowess during the mid-17th century.

Moorish king Mambrino. The earthy, proverbial statements of Sancho Panza, bemused by Don Quixote's peculiar ideas and language, provide a sceptical running commentary on his master's actions, most of which soon make bad situations worse. In the early chapters, the narrator also introduces a recurring element of irony – he informs us that we are reading a transcription of a translation of an original Arabic document by one Cide Hamete Benegeli, recounting the real life of Don Quixote.

In context

▶ **BATTLE OF LEPANTO** In Europe, the 16th century was a time of political and religious upheaval. Cervantes fought alongside his countrymen at the Battle of Lepanto (1571), in which the Ottomans were defeated in the biggest naval engagement of the era. During the battle, Cervantes suffered a permanent injury to his left hand. In his later travels, he was taken prisoner and held captive in Algiers from 1575–80. This experience features in the Captive's Tale in Part 1 of *Don Quixote*.

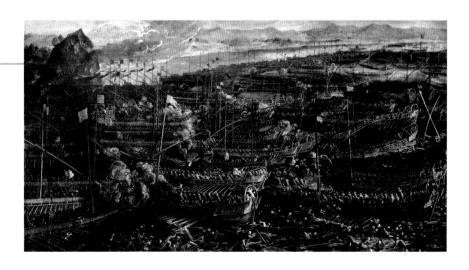

" ... I am Don Quixote of La Mancha, who hath filled the world with his achievements. "

DON QUIXOTE OF LA MANCHA, PART 2, CHAPTER 60

Don Quixote's quest, which frequently involves beatings, defeats, and humiliations, is interspersed with the tales of characters he encounters on the road, which explore love, fidelity, captivity, and madness. At the end of the first volume of comical escapades, Don Quixote, whom by now Sancho Panza has dubbed the *Caballero de la Triste Figura* (the Knight of the Sad Face), speaks of his intention to travel to Saragossa for further adventures, but is finally persuaded to return to his village and abandon his "quixotic" (imaginative but unrealistic) behaviour.

In 1615, Cervantes published his long-awaited sequel to the story, elaborating on Don Quixote's further travels, and allowing Sancho Panza to finally realize, albeit briefly, his dream of ruling an island. More tightly structured and more philosophical, but still freewheeling in the style of Part 1, the sequel extended Cervantes' playful discussion of the subject of literature. The narrator frequently comments on the sources of the story and continues to make inflated claims about the significance of the adventures described. This self-referential aspect of the novel influenced many later writers, as did the idea of focusing on two companions on the road, and the comical clash of medieval and modern ways of thinking.

While Cervantes was writing Part 2, an unauthorized sequel to Part 1 was published in 1614 by a writer with the pseudonym Alonso Fernández de Avellaneda. This version of the tale took the characters to Saragossa, as suggested towards the end of Part 1, and Cervantes incorporated many of the negative reviews of this book into his own authentic Part 2. In particular, instead of going to Saragossa, as outlined in the spurious sequel, Cervantes has Don Quixote suddenly decide to travel to Barcelona instead, after which he returns home and declares that his days of reading books of chivalry are over for good.

FICTION VERSUS REALITY

Don Quixote satirizes the tales of chivalry that feed the imagination of its hero. Don Quixote refers to many of these works, especially his favourite, *Amadís de Gaula*, by Garcia Rodríguez de la Montalvo. Others include a range of stories dealing with figures from the worlds of King Arthur and Charlemagne. These books make up Don Quixote's library, which is later destroyed by his priest and barber in an attempt to bring him to his senses. Don Quixote usually explains events by insisting that "enchanters" have transformed reality, and Cervantes enhances this by making many of his minor characters aware that Don Quixote is a literary character. In Part 2, for instance, several characters tell him that they have read about his adventures, and Don Quixote even comes across a copy of the unauthorized sequel to Cervantes' original novel.

▲ **Don Quixote sits at his desk** in this illustration, brandishing his sword, while reading about medieval knights and chivalry.

◄ **INSPIRATION FOR THE BATTLE WITH THE GIANTS**
Don Quixote famously attacks a group of windmills, which he mistakes for giants. The scene exemplifies Cervantes' approach of presenting Don Quixote's exploits in unremarkable settings. The novel replaces the typical pastoral environment of chivalric tales with the common, everyday landscape of 16th-century Spain. The battle with the giants is brief, but it lives on in the expression "tilting at windmills", which means "taking on imaginary foes".

▲ **DON QUIXOTE AND SANCHO PANZA** The relationship between Don Quixote and Sancho Panza forms the crux of the novel and shapes many of the episodes. The dialogue between the two characters highlights the difference between Don Quixote's idealism and Sancho Panza's commonsense approach to life. Although Cervantes never strays from the comic, the emotional heart of the novel is the companionship of the master and his squire.

Robinson Crusoe

1719 ■ THREE VOLUMES ■ ENGLAND

DANIEL DEFOE (1660–1731)

With *Robinson Crusoe,* Daniel Defoe helped to invent the modern novel. He wrote it when he was almost 60, having already spent decades pouring out journalism, political pamphlets, satires, poems, and works of religious controversy. The son of a chandler, he wrote for money and only began to write novels late in life.

Like all of Defoe's later novels, *Robinson Crusoe* presents itself as a real memoir, written by its protagonist. Defoe's name did not appear on the title page. No novels existed for Defoe to imitate, so he combined elements of voyage narratives and spiritual autobiographies. He produced a book that was hugely popular from its publication in 1719: there were over 200 different editions and abridgements of *Robinson Crusoe* in the 18th century alone.

Even people who have never read the novel might think that they know this story of an Englishman shipwrecked on a bountiful desert island. In the original novel, however, Crusoe has many adventures before he ever reaches his island. Despite the pleas of his parents, he cannot resist going to sea. He is shipwrecked on one voyage and captured by pirates on another. He is sold into slavery in Morocco, escaping after two years in a daring voyage down the coast of Africa in a small boat.

Yet his wanderlust sends him to sea again. This time he is the sole survivor of another shipwreck, and is marooned for the next 27 years on an island south of Trinidad. His account, supposedly written after his return to civilization, describes in gripping detail the adversities he conquers and the resourcefulness that enables him to survive.

> " At the Approach of Night, I slept in a Tree for fear of wild Creatures. "
>
> ***ROBINSON CRUSOE***

This engraving by Clark and Pine shows Crusoe on his island, bearing two flintlock muskets and a cutlass

> ❝ I walk'd about on the Shore, lifting up my Hands, and my whole Being, as I may say, wrapt up in the Contemplation of my Deliverance, making a Thousand Gestures and Motions which I cannot describe, reflecting upon all my Comerades that were drown'd, and that there should not be one Soul sav'd but my self; for, as for them, I never saw them afterwards, or any Sign of them, except three of their Hats, one Cap, and two Shoes that were not Fellows… I cast my Eyes to the stranded Vessel… Lord! how was it possible I could get on Shore? ❞

ROBINSON CRUSOE

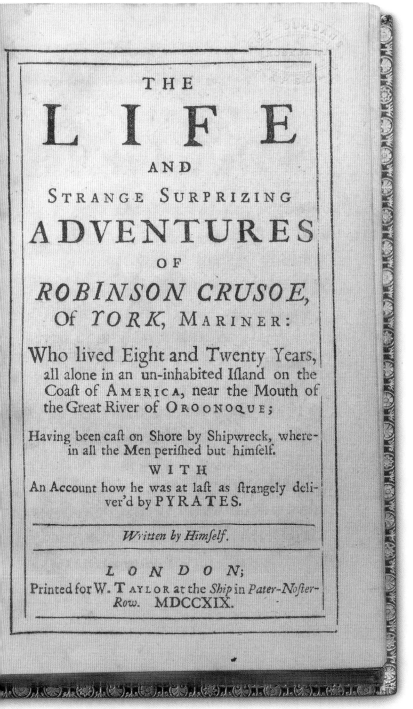

◄ **MAP OF THE JUAN FERNANDEZ ISLANDS**
This group of Pacific islands is some 645km (400 miles) off the coast of Chile. Alexander Selkirk, the likely model for Robinson Crusoe, was marooned on the largest of the islands in 1704. In 1966, to encourage tourism, the Chilean government renamed this large island Robinson Crusoe Island, and one of the other islands Alejandro Selkirk Island.

VOYAGE LITERATURE

Supposed first-hand accounts of daring sea voyages to distant lands became popular in England in the late 17th century. The demand for such narratives followed the publication of the *New Voyage around the World* (1697), written by the roguish William Dampier. Dampier later sailed to the Pacific with fellow buccaneers, including a Scotsman, Alexander Selkirk, intending to raid Spanish possessions on the South American coast.

Selkirk was left behind on the uninhabited island of Juan Fernandez, after a violent quarrel with his fellow sailors, and remained there for four years. His ordeals became widely known through another voyage narrative: Woodes Rogers' *Cruising Voyage Round the World* (1712). Rogers was the captain of the ship that rescued Selkirk. Defoe almost certainly read this account and was inspired by Selkirk's story.

▲ **Illustration of Scottish privateer** Alexander Selkirk, one of the real-life inspirations for *Robinson Crusoe*

▲ **TITLE PAGE OF THE FIRST EDITION** Although the spine of the first edition simply reads "Defoe's Robinson Crusoe", the title page gives the book's full title, which summarizes the entire story. The fashion for such long titles ended during the 19th century, when novels were serialized.

> " ... the Evil which in itself we seek most to shun...
> is oftentimes the very means... of our Deliverance. "

ROBINSON CRUSOE

Crusoe is a model of self-reliance, proving that "by stating and squaring every thing by Reason, and by making the most rational Judgment of things, every Man may be in time Master of every mechanic Art". He teaches himself to make pots and furniture, to grow crops, and to make a dwelling. He takes a similar approach with Christianity: having arrived as a young man, with no thought of God's will, he learns religion from introspection and from reading a Bible that has survived the wreck.

When he is shipwrecked, Crusoe is sailing to Guinea to enslave people to work on his newly established sugar plantation in Brazil. Looking back, he condemns himself for the stupidity of the venture, but never questions its

▶ **MAP OF CRUSOE'S ISLAND** This engraving by Clark and Pine is from *Serious Reflections During the Life and Surprising Adventures of Robinson Crusoe*, a sequel by Defoe published in 1720. It shows a map of Crusoe's island and illustrates various scenes from the book, including a man being eaten by cannibals at the bottom left. Crusoe stands to the right, with Friday behind him, addressing some newly marooned sailors.

morality. This is not the only moment that might set the novel at odds with the attitudes of modern readers: later, Crusoe rescues a "savage" from "cannibals", who have landed on the island, and takes it for granted that the man will become his servant. "I made him know that his Name should be *Friday*, which was the Day I sav'd his Life." He teaches the man to call him "Master".

However, as he learns to speak English, Friday often baffles Crusoe with questions about his European habits and Christian beliefs. Friday becomes a challenge to Crusoe as well as his support, and Crusoe is forced to recognize that this "savage" possesses all the same moral faculties and "the same Reason" as himself.

We are often invited to hear the older Crusoe, looking back on his life and trying to make better sense of it than he ever did at the time. "How strange a Chequer Work of Providence is the Life of Man!" As he tells his story, he keeps admitting to his inadequacy as a narrator: "I cannot explain… Nothing can describe…". In the past, these admissions were taken as showing Defoe's clumsiness as a novelist. Now, they seem true to Defoe's creative purpose – not just to give the reader "strange surprizing adventures", but also to show us a man's attempts to describe and make sense of his life.

▲ **CRUSOE DISCOVERS A FOOTPRINT IN THE SAND** After 15 years alone on his island, Crusoe makes an astounding discovery: a single footprint on the sand, larger than his own. He is not pleased, but "terrify'd". At first, he thinks that "the Devil" is playing tricks on him – then he lives in fear that "savages" from the mainland might have landed.

> " It happen'd one Day about Noon going towards my Boat, I was exceedingly surpriz'd with the Print of a Man's naked Foot on the Shore, which was very plain to be seen in the Sand: I stood like one Thunder-struck, or as if I had seen an Apparition; I listen'd, I look'd round me, I could hear nothing, nor see any Thing, I went up to a rising Ground to look farther, I went up the Shore and down the Shore, but it was all one, I could see no other Impression but that one. "

ROBINSON CRUSOE

◄ **PROVIDENCE** Crusoe learns to see the signs of God's purposes, or "Providences", in everything that happens to him. Dates, which he records in notches on "a great Cross", become especially significant. Important events seem to happen on the same dates. He becomes convinced that there is "a strange Concurrence of Days, in the various Providences which befell me".

ROBINSONADES

Robinson Crusoe shaped a great deal of subsequent fiction. Recognizing its influence, Johann Gottfried Schnabel coined the word "Robinsonade", in the 1731 preface to his utopian fiction *Die Insel Felsenburg*. Robinsonades are updated versions of Defoe's story of a resourceful castaway. The most famous Robinsonade is probably *The Swiss Family Robinson*, published by a Swiss pastor, Johann Wyss, in 1812. From R.M. Ballantyne's Victorian bestseller *The Coral Island* to William Golding's *Lord of the Flies* and J.M. Coetzee's *Foe*, Defoe's myth-like tale has been adapted anew time after time. The desert-island narrative, the survival tale, and the adventure story itself are all the offspring of *Robinson Crusoe*.

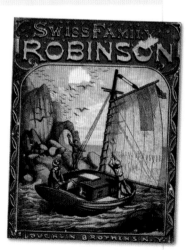

▲ In *The Swiss Family Robinson,* an entire family is shipwrecked upon an island in the East Indies.

Pamela

1740 ▪ TWO VOLUMES ▪ ENGLAND

SAMUEL RICHARDSON (1689–1761)

The author of Pamela was an unlikely literary figure. Samuel Richardson, a successful London printer, was 51 years old when the novel was published. A carpenter's son, with little formal education, he had begun life as a printer's apprentice. He married his boss's daughter and set up his own printing business, just off Fleet Street, in London. *Pamela*, his first novel, seems to have originated with a book that he was asked to compile by two booksellers. This was his *Letters Written to and for Particular Friends* (see opposite), a collection of model correspondence demonstrating how readers could best address a range of moral and domestic issues in their letters. He interrupted the composition of this to write *Pamela*, and insisted that the latter was based on a true story.

Richardson's novel is told entirely in letters, almost all of which are written by Pamela herself. She is a 15-year-old servant girl, who has to fend off the advances of her young master, Mr B. He tries flattery, bribery, and even bullying, assuming that his rank and wealth give him the right to possess her. When she continues to refuse him, he has her abducted and kept in a secluded country house, where he continues to try to wear down her resistance. All of this time, Pamela is writing letters to her parents, and although she is rarely able to send them, she continues writing in order to record her ordeal. Often, she has to write in secret and conceal the letters. The fate of these letters is an essential part of the story.

Richardson brilliantly used the potential of letters to capture events and emotions as they are unfolding. He called this "writing to the moment". Sometimes the very writing is interrupted: "–But I must break off, here's some-body coming!–". Sometimes we are to imagine Pamela's writing "all bathed and blotted with my Tears".

In context

◀ **SERVANTS IN FOCUS** *Pamela* was arguably the first English literary work to have a servant as its main character – indeed, its narrator. 18th-century novels were innovative in their depictions of characters who belonged to different social classes. The art of Richardson's contemporary, William Hogarth, had a similar range. His group portrait *Servants* (from the mid-1750s) gives each person the dignity of individuality.

▲ **PAMELA WRITING A LETTER** Although she is a servant girl, Pamela is literate: her father was a schoolteacher, and she was further tutored by her mistress. She often tries to find the time to write letters to her parents, although her master is suspicious of this activity, always wanting to know what she is writing. In this illustration, made by Joseph Highmore in 1740, Mr B. is seen interrupting her in mid-flow.

LETTER WRITING

As literacy rates increased, letter writing became an important part of fashionable life. This was particularly true for women, who usually had far fewer opportunities to mix socially outside the home. In Richardson's day, the so-called "bluestocking" circle of female intellectuals relied on their letters, in which they discussed books and ideas with each other.

Several also corresponded with Richardson. He was an energetic letter-writer, and had a circle of mostly female friends with whom he discussed his fiction, often while it was still in progress. Like many authors, he wrote with an eye on posterity; he collected and sometimes made copies of his letters, knowing that they might be published after his death.

Letter writing was so central to refined life in the 18th century that many kinds of literature were cast in the form of letters. After Richardson, the epistolary novel became the fashion throughout Europe.

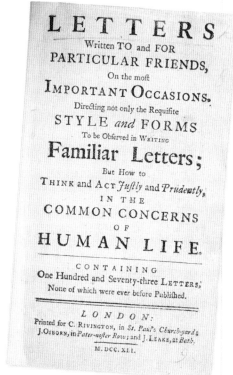

▲ **Richardson's letter-writing manual** contains model letters that show readers how to deal with moral dilemmas.

> ❝ ... I cannot hold my Pen!... I must leave off, till I can get quieter Fingers! ❞

***PAMELA*, LETTER: "SEVEN O'CLOCK"**

KEY CHARACTERS

```
MR ANDREWS          MRS ANDREWS      former        LADY B.
Labourer            Housewife      employer of   Gentlewoman (deceased)

        parents of                                    mother of

    PAMELA ANDREWS      employer and       MR B.              LADY DAVERS
    Maidservant          pursuer of      Country squire        Gentlewoman

                employer of          illegitimate    takes          aunt of
                                     father of   responsibility for

MRS JERVIS      JOHN ARNOLD    MRS JEWKES     MISS GOODWIN        JACKEY
Housekeeper      Footman       Housekeeper    Young lady       Young gentleman
(Bedfordshire)                 (Lincolnshire)
```

When it was first published, *Pamela* was a sensation among the genteel classes, who could afford to buy books. There is some evidence that it also reached a lower-class audience, often by being read aloud. By the standards of the day, its sales figures were impressive. Its popularity was marked by many spin-offs – not just imitations, sequels, and dramatizations, but also paintings, fans, and even waxworks. The many "Anti-Pamela" publications, including Henry Fielding's *Shamela*, were themselves evidence of the novel's extraordinary success (Fielding's own first novel, *Joseph Andrews*, was the story of Pamela's supposed brother). Sceptics argued that the book's descriptions of attempted seductions were "inflaming", but as its subtitle, "Virtue Rewarded", indicates, *Pamela* is a highly moral work. The heroine's virtue is rewarded: eventually, Mr B. reforms and marries her, having intercepted and read many of her letters, and been converted by them. Indeed, *Pamela* was the book that made the novel a respectable genre.

A teenage servant girl was an unlikely heroine, and some mocked *Pamela* as "low" and vulgar. Richardson was extremely sensitive to criticism, and was always making changes to meet

> ❝ ... you are *Lucifer* himself in the **Shape of my Master,** or you could not use me thus. ❞
>
> **PAMELA, LETTER: "WEDNESDAY MORNING"**

objections. As its printer, he was in an unusually good position to fiddle with the text. His rewriting went on over the course of 20 years. There were nine authorized editions of the novel, each one different from its predecessor as a result of Richardson's amendments. Gradually, he "improved" his heroine's prose and made her more refined. Where critics had faulted her conduct in any way, he supplied her with new justifications of her behaviour. As a consequence, by the end, he had almost robbed her of her original verve and freshness.

> ❝ AND no young Ladies! – So that, I fansy – But, hold, I hear their Coach, I believe. I'll step to the Window. – I won't go down to them, I am resolv'd. – Good Sirs! good Sirs! What will become of me! Here is my Master come in his fine Chariot! – Indeed he is! – What shall I do? Where shall I hide myself! – Oh! what shall I do! – Pray for me! But Oh! you'll not see this! – Now, good Heaven preserve me! ❞
>
> **PAMELA, LETTER: "FIVE O'CLOCK IS COME"**

CONDUCT BOOKS

The title page of *Pamela* declared that it was published "In order to cultivate the Principles of VIRTUE and RELIGION in the Minds of the YOUTH of BOTH SEXES". This aligned it with the tradition of "conduct books", which rose to prominence in the 18th century. These were mostly targeted at girls and young women. With titles such as *The Whole Duty of Woman and Female Conduct*, they instructed their readers in manners, social conventions, and morals. Several were written in the form of letters, allowing the reader to overhear "familiar" advice from an experienced parent. Some, such as Hester Chapone's *Letters on the Improvement of the Mind*, written for her 15-year-old niece, were indeed created for young family members.

▶ *Young Girl Reading* by Jean-Honoré Fragonard, 1770, shows a demure young woman intent on a book.

Page 115.

AN
APOLOGY
FOR THE
LIFE
OF
Mrs. SHAMELA ANDREWS.

In which, the many notorious FALSHOODS and MISREPRESENTATIONS of a Book called

PAMELA,

Are exposed and refuted; and all the matchless ARTS of that young Politician, set in a true and just Light.

Together with

A full Account of all that passed between her and Parson *Arthur Williams*; whose Character is represented in a manner something different from that which he bears in *PAMELA*. The whole being exact Copies of authentick Papers delivered to the Editor.

Necessary to be had in all FAMILIES.

By Mr. CONNY KEYBER.

LONDON:
Printed for A. DODD, at the *Peacock*, without *Temple-bar*.
M. DCC. XLI.

▲ **HENRY FIELDING'S *SHAMELA***
Richardson's novel was mocked and parodied as much as it was admired. The best burlesque of *Pamela* was *Shamela*, published anonymously, although we now know it was written by Henry Fielding. His heroine is a cynical and calculating minx who uses her attractions, and feigned demureness, to trick her master, Squire Booby, into marrying her.

◄ **ILLUSTRATION FROM THE 1741 EDITION** This image is from the first of several illustrated editions of *Pamela* that appeared in the 18th century. Pamela believes that she has persuaded Mr B. to allow her to return to her parents. He even kindly provides his own "chariot" to conduct her home. Before boarding, she bids a tearful farewell to all of her fellow servants. However, she is being deceived - the coachman is going to drive her to Mr B.'s isolated Lincolnshire estate instead.

Candide

1759 ■ 299 PAGES ■ FRANCE

VOLTAIRE (1694–1778)

The novella Candide, by French writer and philosopher Voltaire, is one of the most influential books ever published. It tells the story of a young man, Candide, who is brought up in the household of a Westphalian baron. He is taught a philosophy of incontrovertible optimism by his tutor, Dr Pangloss, but when he falls in love with the baron's daughter, Cunégonde, Candide is banished from the household. He ends up on a series of adventures that expose him to various disasters – including war, the catastrophic Lisbon earthquake of 1755, and Cunégonde's abduction – and these transform his view of life.

Voltaire tells his tale in the third person, but some characters, such as Cunégonde and the Old Lady who becomes her servant, tell part of their stories in the first person, adding additional viewpoints to the author's distanced, often ironic, narrative. The diverse characters that Candide meets on his travels, both in Europe and South America, enable Voltaire to take satirical aim at all kinds of people and institutions. These include the Roman Catholic inquisition in Portugal, which organizes an *auto-da-fé* (mass execution) after the Lisbon earthquake; the worldly Jesuits in Paraguay; and the British authorities who execute Admiral Byng for cowardice, "to encourage the others". Voltaire also targets dogmatic philosophers, and Cunégonde's various lovers or would-be lovers, who range from a Bulgar captain to the Grand Inquisitor himself. However, Candide also

◄ **CANDIDE AND CUNÉGONDE** This illustration shows Candide's uncle, Baron Thunder-ten-Tronckh, creeping up on the hero as he kisses Cunégonde's hand when the pair are behind a screen. The Baron disapproves of Candide's behaviour, and brutally banishes him from his castle. This sends Candide on the adventures that make up the rest of the novel.

meets many loyal, charitable, and hard-working people who help him along the way. Among these are Martin, his travelling companion; Jacques, who saves him from being lynched; and the faithful servants Cacambo and the Old Lady. In the end, the characters who survive their troubles learn that it is better to stay at home and focus on a quiet life "cultivating your garden" than to espouse grand but unrealistic philosophies.

THE *CONTE PHILOSOPHIQUE*

Candide belongs to a genre of fiction known as the *conte philosophique* (philosophical tale), which was created by Voltaire. In this kind of fiction, as exemplified by Voltaire's *Micromégas*, *Zadig*, and *Candide*, philosophy provides a context for the story, and enables the author to satirize impractical or hardline ideas. Although the stories themselves may be unrealistic, containing unlikely plot twists and coincidences, the satire is biting. Voltaire used it to take aim at various views that were commonly held in his time – for example, that the Earth exists solely for the benefit of human beings (in *Micromégas*), or that everything that happens turns out for the best (in *Candide*). Two other great writers of the *conte philosophique* were the Anglo-Irish satirist Jonathan Swift and the French Enlightenment writer Denis Diderot.

► *A Philosophers' Dinner,* by 18th-century artist Jean Huber, shows Voltaire (with his arm raised) dining with fellow philosophers.

Each chapter title summarizes the story, without spoiling the plot. Here, Voltaire writes: "How Candide was brought up in a beautiful castle, and how he was driven away"

Voltaire emphasizes the philosophical theme of the novel by including a subtitle, "L'optimisme" (optimism)

> Pangloss taught metaphysico-theologo-cosmolo-nigology. He proved incontestably that there is no effect without a cause, and that in this best of all possible worlds, his lordship's country seat was the most beautiful of mansions and her ladyship the best of all possible ladyships. 'It is proved,' he used to say, 'that things cannot be other than they are, for since everything was made for a purpose, it follows that everything is made for the best purpose. Observe: our noses were made to carry spectacles, so we have spectacles... It follows that those who maintain that all is right talk nonsense; they ought to say that all is for the best.'

CANDIDE, CHAPTER 1

▲ **ORIGINAL MANUSCRIPT** Voltaire's manuscript was thought lost until it was discovered by the American scholar Owen Wade in 1957. Its pages contain several passages that the author cut from the published book, including a chapter about Paris, which he called a "city of all hells". The text is neatly written, but there are surprising spelling errors, including a misplaced "s" in the book's subtitle, "L'optimisme".

Tristram Shandy

1759-67 ▪ NINE VOLUMES ▪ ENGLAND

LAURENCE STERNE (1713-1768)

Laurence Sterne was an obscure Yorkshire clergyman until, in his late 40s, he became famous almost overnight when the first two volumes of his novel *The Life and Opinions of Tristram Shandy, Gentleman* were published in London in 1759. His brilliantly unorthodox novel was a mock autobiography. Tristram tries to describe his own character and tell the story of his own life, but he keeps having to go back in time to explain how his fortunes were shaped. Some novels start with the birth of the protagonist, but the opening chapter of this novel takes us back to the very moment of Tristram's conception. Tristram has so much to tell us about the eccentric members of the Shandy household, that, by the end of Volume 2, he is "not yet born".

Sterne would go on to publish seven more volumes of the novel at intervals over the next seven years, often teasing his readers about what they might get in future volumes. When reviewers were negative, their responses were promptly parodied in the next instalment of the book. Sterne used many elements from his own life: his own travels, his own friends (and foes), and even his own house. Instalment by instalment, his fiction kept up with his life, or perhaps it was the other way around. "Time wastes too fast: every letter I trace tells me with what rapidity Life follows my pen." Sterne's distinctive punctuation – long, stretching dashes that show the narrator changing his mind, pausing to digress, reaching for the next surprise – enacts this liveliness.

Sterne loved books, and his novel is full of mock learning: quotations and misquotations; real and invented allusions. It is also informal, even chatty. Tristram converses with us, the novel's readers. He also nudges us to understand his innuendoes. Some contemporary critics condemned the novel for being "bawdy", but this seemed to help its sales. *Tristram Shandy* made Sterne the first celebrity author. "I wrote not to be *fed*, but to be *famous*," he cheerfully declared.

> [16]
> affair has nothing to do with them an further than this, That if Tom ha not married the widow——or had pleafed God after their marriage, tha they had but put pork into their faufa ges, the honeft foul had never been take out of his warm bed, and dragg'd t the inquifition——'Tis a curfed place— added the Corporal, fhaking his heac —when once a poor creature is ir he is in, an' pleafe your honour, fc ever.
>
> 'Tis very true ; faid my uncle Tob looking gravely at Mrs. Wadman's houf as he fpoke.
>
> Nothing, continued the Corporal, ca be fo fad as confinement for life—or fweet, an' pleafe your honour, as liberty
>
> Nothin
>
> 3

> " In a word, my work is **digressive,** and it is progressive too,– and at the same time. "

TRISTRAM SHANDY, VOLUME 1, CHAPTER 22

> Writing, when properly managed (as you may be sure I think mine is) is but a different name for conversation. As no one, who knows what he is about in good company, would venture to talk all;- so no author, who understands the just boundaries of decorum and good-breeding, would presume to think all: The truest respect which you can pay to the reader's understanding, is to halve this matter amicably, and leave him something to imagine... For my own part, I am eternally paying him compliments of this kind and do all that lies in my power to keep his imagination as busy as my own.

TRISTRAM SHANDY, VOLUME 2, CHAPTER 11

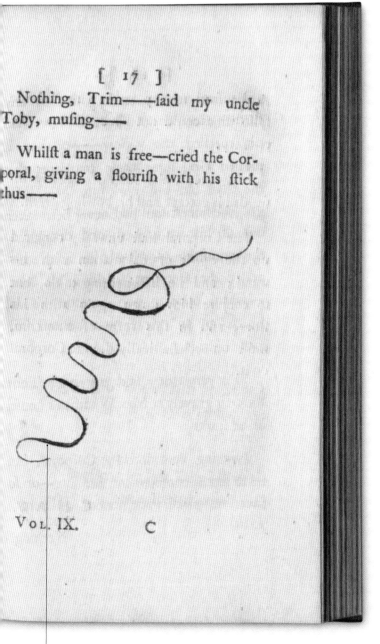

Corporal Trim's "flourish" is one of the novel's many daring pictographic devices

▲ **THE SIEGE OF NAMUR** In *Tristram Shandy*, every character has a "hobby-horse", or compulsion. Tristram's gentle uncle Toby, for example, is obsessed with the battles of the Nine Years' War, in which he fought against the French. With his manservant, Corporal Trim, he reenacts the Siege of Namur (during which he was wounded in the groin) in miniature on his bowling green.

DEATH AND COMEDY

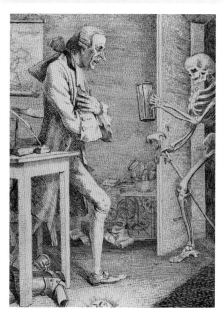

▲ *And When Death Himself Knocked on My Door,* an engraving by Thomas Patch, takes its title from a line in *Tristram Shandy*, referring to Tristram's symptoms of tuberculosis.

▲ **FIRST EDITION** Appearing in five instalments over the course of seven years, *Tristram Shandy* was unlike any previous novel. It surprised and delighted its first readers with its digressive narrative. It also explored the visual tricks of print as never before. Sterne used expressive loops, squiggles, and asterisks, black or marbled pages, and blank spaces. Even the punctuation, especially the distinctive long dashes, was thoroughly idiosyncratic.

One of the characters in *Tristram Shandy* is Parson Yorick, who takes his name from the jester to whose skull Hamlet speaks in Shakespeare's play. Death and comedy go together in the novel. When Yorick dies, we get two black pages – the novel goes into mourning. When the death of Tristram's brother, Bobby, is announced, the other characters' different responses are funny, as well as affecting. Tristram, like Sterne himself, has the symptoms of tuberculosis. His time is short; his story must hurry on, "curvetting and frisking it away". For his health, Tristram travels to warmer climes, as Sterne did. As he "scampers" south through France, he hears Death "clattering at my heels".

The Sorrows of Young Werther

1774 ▪ 160 PAGES ▪ GERMANY

JOHANN WOLFGANG VON GOETHE (1749–1832)

In 1828, when this portrait (see left) was painted, Goethe was the leading literary figure in Germany, if not all of Europe. But some 44 years earlier, in the spring of 1774, he had been a distraught 24-year-old lawyer pouring his heart into a novel that mirrored his own unhappy experience of unrequited love. Young Werther's "sorrows" had been Goethe's own (although the novel was published anonymously). Lotte, whom Werther adores, was based on Charlotte Buff: a young woman with whom Goethe was besotted, but who, like Lotte, was engaged to another man. Werther's despair drew on Goethe's own breakdown. Goethe learned that an acquaintance embroiled in a similarly impossible passion had shot himself. In the novel, Werther ultimately dies by suicide.

Readers devoured this epistolary tale – written as letters from Werther to his friend Wilhelm. Although it was a simple story of a man unable to endure his emotional suffering, Goethe's straightforward language and acute psychological insight were an exciting departure from sentimental and moralistic epistolary fiction. "Werther Fever" swept across Europe and there were reportedly copycat suicides – the bodies of young men were apparently being found dressed as Werther, with a copy of the novel in their pockets.

The impact of this book has endured. It has influenced writers such as Friedrich Nietzsche and Franz Kafka, and Thomas Mann even wrote a sequel, *Lotte in Weimar*. Modern German literary language is often traced back to this small volume. Crucially, it vaulted Goethe to the front rank of German literature, where he remains to this day.

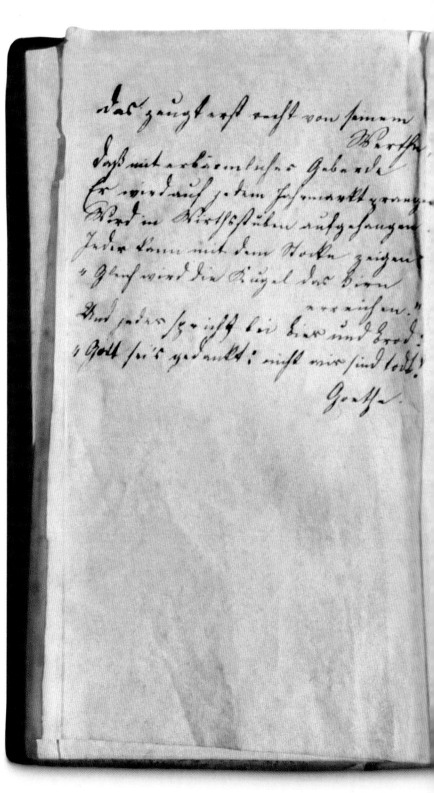

▶ **TITLE PAGE OF THE FIRST EDITION** Written in a four-month blaze of creativity, the novel was finished in May 1774 and sent to the publisher in Leipzig. It was in the bookstalls by late September of that year, and caused such a sensation that it was banned in 1775 by the School of Divinity in Leipzig because of its supposed advocacy of suicide, a mortal sin.

> " Here, Lotte, without a shudder I take up the cold and fearful cup from which I am to drink intoxicating death. You handed it to me and I am not afraid... If only I could have had the happiness of dying for you, Lotte, of sacrificing myself for you. I would die bravely, I would die joyfully, if I could give your life its peace and its delight again. But alas, it is given to only a few of the noblest to spill their blood for their loved ones and to quicken by their death new life for their friends a hundredfold. "

THE SORROWS OF YOUNG WERTHER, LETTER: "AFTER 11"

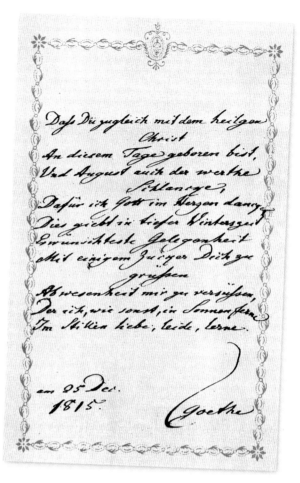

▲ **LETTER FROM GOETHE** This handwritten poem to Charlotte Buff is just one of many letters that Goethe sent her. He did not try hard to disguise his loved one in *The Sorrows of Young Werther*, although he did give her the dark eyes of another married woman with whom he had also fallen in love.

STURM UND DRANG

The period from 1765-85 in German literature is often called Sturm und Drang, meaning "Storm and Stress". This literary movement sought to overthrow the values of the Enlightenment, such as rationalism, balance, classicism, and moderation, in favour of imagination, genius, individualism, and the sublime in both nature and art. Sturm und Drang also fostered a new nationalism, harking back to German myth and folktale, and was the first stage of the Romantic Era that swept across Europe and America in the late 18th and early 19th centuries. Its German exponents included the philosophers Friedrich Schiller and Johann Gottfried Herder, as well as Goethe, and its primary literary expression was *The Sorrows of Young Werther*. The term "Sturm und Drang" came from the title of a play written by an early Romantic, Friedrich Klinger, yet the movement was already alive in spirit by then.

◄ **Johann Gottfried Herder** was a mentor to Goethe, and advocated the literary diction that Goethe employed in writing *Werther*.

Les Liaisons dangereuses

1782 ▪ FOUR VOLUMES ▪ FRANCE

PIERRE CHODERLOS DE LACLOS (1741–1803)

Les Liaisons dangereuses has always been impossible to ignore. In its day, it was seen as a threat to public morals, but it is now recognized as one of the greatest novels of the 18th century, and perhaps the finest epistolary novel ever written. Its author, Pierre de Laclos, spent most of his career as a soldier, although his record was unremarkable. He left the army on the eve of the French Revolution and was imprisoned twice during the Terror. After this, the army may have seemed a safer option, and so he resumed his military career and became one of Napoleon's generals.

Les Liaisons is Laclos' only significant literary achievement. He did also write the libretto for an indifferent comic opera, which was booed off the stage on its opening night, and did not return, and a number of factual studies. Ironically, in view of the actions of some of his characters, one of these was a treatise on the education of women. However, when Les Liaisons was published, it proved to be a phenomenal success. Even Marie-Antoinette, the Queen of France, is said to have owned a copy. Readers were delighted by the scandalous correspondence of the novel's two leading characters, the

> ❝ Nothing amuses me so much as a lover's despair. ❞
>
> **LES LIAISONS DANGEREUSES, LETTER 5**

Vicomte de Valmont and the Marquise de Merteuil. The pair are former lovers, but their letters are filled with schemes for new amorous adventures. The Vicomte wants to seduce a virtuous married woman, while Merteuil wishes to take revenge on a man who has spurned her, by getting Valmont to deflower his innocent future bride, Cécile.

Valmont and Merteuil egg each other on, teasing and provoking, until their adventures become as dangerous as the title of the novel implies. Later generations have been unsure how to view all this. Was the book meant as a searing criticism of the Ancien Régime, when idle aristocrats had the leisure time to indulge in such dubious pursuits, or was it simply an enjoyable romp? The answer is still tantalizingly unclear.

In context

◀ **EPISTOLARY NOVELS** In the 18th century, letter writing was an important, everyday activity, both in real life and in literature. Laclos was not the only author to find the epistolary format convenient for creating a narrative. Samuel Richardson's *Clarissa* (1748) and Jean-Jacques Rousseau's *La Nouvelle Héloïse* (1761) were important precedents. Letters provided an excellent way of building up a picture of a relationship – or, indeed, of leading a lover astray. As the Marquise advises Cécile: "You must understand that when you write to someone, you are doing it for them, not for yourself. You should therefore try to say not so much what you think, as what he would most like to hear".

◄ **MANUSCRIPT** Laclos wrote *Les Liaisons dangereuses* while he was stationed on the island of Aix, near La Rochelle. Bored, and aware that his career had reached a cul-de-sac, he wrote to a friend: "having penned a few elegies on the dead, who will make nothing of them... I resolved to write a book which would create some stir in the world and continue to do so after I had gone from it". He supervised the printing in Paris in 1781.

Laclos' manuscript runs to 142 pages, written on both sides. The text is densely packed and scattered with corrections

LIBERTINISM

In the 18th century, libertines were – most often – aristocrats who believed that they were above morality. In matters of the heart, pleasure was their ultimate goal, and they considered marriage to be a hypocrisy. Much of the plot of *Les Liaisons* concerns what today we would condemn as the grooming of 15-year-old Cécile by two experienced libertines. Aristocrats often placed their young daughters in convents, where they learned how to be good wives, but were taught nothing about the ways of the world, leaving them with few defences against a libertine's advances.

▲ *Le Verrou (The Bolt,* **1777),** by Jean-Honoré Fragonard, is a classic image of a libertine.

> ❝ Another observation, which I am surprised you have not made for yourself: there is nothing more difficult in love than expressing in writing what one does not feel – I mean expressing it with conviction. It is not a question of using the right words: one does not arrange them in the right way. Or rather one does arrange them, and that is sufficiently damning. Read your letter again. It is so beautifully composed that every phrase betrays you... This is the great defect of all novels. Though the author whips himself up into a passion the reader is left cold. *Heloise* is the sole exception one might be tempted to make. Despite the author's talent, it is for this reason that I have always thought it true. There is not the same difficulty in conversation. Long practice in using the voice has made it a sensitive instrument. ❞

LES LIAISONS DANGEREUSES, LETTER 33

Directory: Before 1800

GARGANTUA AND PANTAGRUEL

FRANÇOIS RABELAIS, 1532–48

A classic of comic literature, the series of books narrating the rambunctious adventures of the giant Gargantua and his son Pantagruel were the masterpiece of French humanist François Rabelais (c.1494–1553). A carnivalesque celebration of what the author called "gaiety of spirit", these rambling texts are scatological, farcical, satirical, absurdist, and supremely rich in verbal invention. Crude humour sits alongside classical erudition and serious debate about education and the reform of the Church.

The first volume, *Pantagruel*, appeared in 1532, followed by a prequel, *Gargantua*, two years later. The third and fourth volumes, published in the 1540s, describe the event-packed journey of Pantagruel and the foolish Panurge in search of the Divine Bottle – which will tell Panurge whether, if he marries, he is to become a cuckold. A purported fifth volume, published long after Rabelais'

death, is often printed as part of the series, but was probably the work of another hand. Rabelais was only able to publish his subversive text, which is both obscene and hostile to religion, because he had friends in high places. It remains an exuberant insult to order and decency.

LÁZARILLO DE TORMES

ANON, 1554

The Life of Lázarillo de Tormes and of his Fortunes and Adversities was a 16th-century bestseller that founded the genre of the picaresque – tales of rogues whose adventures satirize the follies and injustices of society. It was published anonymously, and attempts to identify its author have proved to be a futile guessing game.

The story is narrated by the eponymous antihero in a racy, colloquial style. A child of poverty and misfortune, he finds work as the guide of a wily blind man, who teaches him the ruthless tricks needed for survival in a wicked world. The tales

of his subsequent employment by various mean and dishonest churchmen are vehemently anti-clerical. Lázarillo also works for a penniless Spanish squire, who is keeping up noble appearances while starving for lack of a crust of bread. Eventually, our antihero achieves the status of a town crier and makes a convenient if dishonourable marriage to a priest's mistress. Not surprisingly, the book was banned by the Inquisition for its attacks on the Church, but its irresistible humour and sharp characterization guaranteed it an immediate international readership and lasting fame.

THE PRINCESS OF CLEVES

COMTESSE DE LA FAYETTE, 1678

The Princess of Cleves founded the French tradition of the psychological novel, focusing as it does on the emotional subtleties of love and the moral conflicts it creates. The book was written by the Comtesse de La Fayette (1634–93), a Parisian literary hostess, as a historical novel set more than a century before her time. Arriving at the court of French king Henry II, where adultery and seduction abound, the novel's innocent heroine marries the honourable Prince of Cleves as the best defence for her virtue. This marriage, sustained by mutual respect, is fatally undermined when the Princess encounters the handsome Duc de Nemours and the pair fall passionately in love.

The plot unfolds with much artifice, including overheard conversations and a mislaid letter, but attending closely to the reactions and feelings of its protagonists. The writing is precise and witty, conveying emotions that become heavily charged as the novel proceeds to its denouement.

Published anonymously, it was an instant success, and provoked considerable debate about the compatibility (or otherwise) of passionate love and marriage.

OROONOKO

APHRA BEHN, 1688

The author of *Oroonoko, or the Royal Slave*, Aphra Behn (1640–90), has been described as England's first female professional author. Her novella aimed to feed a public taste for exoticism, sex, and sentimentality.

The hero of the story, Oroonoko, is a West African warrior of the "noble savage" tradition. He comes into disastrous conflict with his king over possession of the beautiful Imoinda. Both Oroonoko and Imoinda are then carried off by English slave traders to Suriname, where they meet the English woman, possibly Behn herself, who is narrating their tale. Initially, the enslavers seem benevolent, but the colonial authorities prove to be far more brutal. When Oroonoko revolts against his enslavers, the uprising that he leads is crushed, and the story ends tragically in a welter of blood.

Oroonoko was the first fiction to describe the nascent Atlantic slave trade and slavery in the English colonies. However, it is not the book's purpose to protest against slavery, but to denounce in general the cruelty and dishonesty that noble natures are fated to endure.

GIL BLAS

ALAIN-RENÉ LESAGE, 1715–35

Prolific French author Alain-René Lesage (1668–1747) was, among other things, a translator of Spanish fiction, and the Hispanic influence is prominent in his best-known work, *The Adventures of Gil Blas of Santillane*. Published in four parts, the first two of which appeared in 1715 and the others in 1724 and 1735, *Gil Blas* is essentially a Spanish picaresque novel written in French.

In classic picaresque style, its Spanish hero is born in poverty, learns to live by his wits, and undergoes a series of unlikely comic adventures that throw a satiric light

A page from a manuscript of *Dream of the Red Chamber*, dating from 1759

upon corruption and wrongdoing at all levels of society. Working as a valet, he imitates the vices of his various masters; serving a quack doctor, he learns to cheat patients of their cash with useless treatments; serving a serial seducer, he learns the art of seduction. However, unlike the traditional heroes of the picaresque, Gil is destined to succeed, surviving many vicissitudes to become a favourite at the royal court and retire a wealthy man. Vivacious and warm-hearted, *Gil Blas* was a key step in the development of the comic novel.

GULLIVER'S TRAVELS

JONATHAN SWIFT, 1727

A dazzlingly inventive blend of fantasy fiction and misanthropic satire, *Gulliver's Travels* was written by Anglo-Irish cleric Jonathan Swift (1667–1745), a wit, poet, and political pamphleteer. It mimicked the popular genre of outlandish travellers' tales, but exaggerated to absurdity. The hero and narrator, Lemuel Gulliver, embarks on four troubled voyages, encountering extraordinary peoples such as the little Lilliputians, the giant Brobdingnagians, and the grotesquely senile Struldbrugs. On the flying island of Laputa, he finds scientists trying to extract sunbeams from cucumbers. In the land of the Houyhnhnms, a wise race of horses rules over the vile, human-like Yahoos.

There is plenty of fantasy in Gulliver's misadventures, which is why they have often been sold as children's fiction, but Swift's underlying satire is dark and multilayered. Some of his targets are specific follies of his (and our) times, such as war and religious conflict, but he also expresses disgust at human beings in general, both for their moral failings and their gross physicality. In the end, Gulliver prefers the company of a cleaner, nobler species – horses.

◀ DREAM OF THE RED CHAMBER

CAO XUEQIN, MID-1700S

A much-loved classic of Qing-dynasty Chinese literature, *Dream of the Red Chamber* was the work of Cao Xueqin

(c.1724–63), a member of an aristocratic family that had fallen on hard times. Although framed by a fantasy tale of a sentient stone (the book was originally known as *The Story of the Stone*), Cao's novel is primarily a realist work, narrating the complex cross-generational saga of a family like his own. The plot centres on the vicissitudes of young love and marriage, presented with sharp psychological insight against a background of social decline.

Among the extensive cast of more than 400 major and minor characters, women and girls stand out for their moral and intellectual superiority to the men and the boys. The action is precisely embedded in everyday life under the Qing Empire, and contains much detail about cooking and medical practices, clothing and religious rites, that is now of great historical interest. The first 80 chapters were circulated privately in manuscript form in Cao's lifetime. The current 120-chapter version, first printed in 1791, may have been completed by other writers.

CLARISSA

SAMUEL RICHARDSON, 1747–48

A successful printer, Samuel Richardson (1689–1761) only began to write fiction in his fifties. He popularized the epistolary novel, which takes the form of letters exchanged by the main characters. In his masterpiece, *Clarissa*, this formal device gives the melodramatic tale immediacy and variety of viewpoint.

Confined by her own family, who are determined to force her into an unwanted marriage, the young Clarissa Harlowe can only escape into the clutches of the heartless libertine Lovelace. Drugged and raped, she still upholds her virtue and refuses to bend to his will, holding out to a tragic conclusion. The characterization has real complexity. Clarissa is a resolute and assertive woman, but lacks self-knowledge. Lovelace is a cruel villain, yet exerts a powerful charm: the heroine is unconsciously drawn towards him, as, perhaps, is the reader.

An immediate international hit, *Clarissa* had even more influence on literature in continental Europe

The foundling Tom Jones, as illustrated in the first edition of the novel

than in England. At almost a million words, it is a long read, but it uses its length fruitfully to explore the inner lives of its characters.

▲ TOM JONES

HENRY FIELDING, 1749

Written by Henry Fielding (1707–54), an English dramatist turned novelist, *The History of Tom Jones, A Foundling* was the first masterpiece in the ebullient tradition of the English comic novel. The story of a penniless young man born out of wedlock who makes his way in a wicked world, it shuns the cynical social satire of the European picaresque, preferring to focus on its hero's vigorous, genial

temperament and lusty sexual adventures. Its tumultuous panorama of English society highlights much hypocrisy and villainy, but also loyalty and good-heartedness.

Formal complexity is provided by the narrator, who may or may not be the author, but who interrupts to comment on the action and hold a dialogue with the reader, defending the book against its critics. The plot is a finely constructed mechanism, springing its ultimate comic surprises with exact timing to the reader's perfect delight. Even though its bawdiness raised some eyebrows when it first appeared, *Tom Jones* on the whole showed England a view of itself as it would like to be seen, and was rewarded with enduring popularity.

2
1800–1870

> After a silence of several minutes, he came towards her in an agitated manner, and thus began: "In vain I have struggled. It will not do. My feelings will not be repressed. You must allow me to tell you how ardently I admire and love you." Elizabeth's astonishment was beyond expression. She stared, coloured, doubted, and was silent. This he considered sufficient encouragement; and the avowal of all that he felt, and had long felt for her, immediately followed. He spoke well; but there were feelings besides those of the heart to be detailed; and he was not more eloquent on the subject of tenderness than of pride. His sense of her inferiority – of its being a degradation – of the family obstacles which had always opposed to inclination, were dwelt on with a warmth which seemed due to the consequence he was wounding, but was very unlikely to recommend his suit.

**PRIDE AND PREJUDICE,
CHAPTER 34**

▲ **THE FIRST EDITION** *Pride and Prejudice* was published, in three volumes, on 28 January 1813 for 18 shillings. All 1,500 copies sold, and a second edition was called for later the same year. Austen had sold the copyright to the publisher, Thomas Egerton, for a one-off payment of £110 and made no further profit. Egerton made four times as much money from the novel as Austen.

Gave him to understand that her sentiments had undergone so material a change—

▲ **MR DARCY PROPOSING TO ELIZABETH** This picture shows Mr Darcy's second proposal to Elizabeth. He seizes his opportunity when they are out walking with Mr Bingley and Jane Bennet, who are now officially engaged and lag behind, interested only in each other, and Kitty Bennet, who leaves them to call on Maria Lucas. They are alone together, and he can tell her, "*My* wishes and affections are unchanged". This time, she reciprocates.

Pride and Prejudice

1813 ■ THREE VOLUMES ■ UK

JANE AUSTEN (1775–1817)

The author of perhaps the best-known literary classic of all time lived a life of obscurity. Born in 1775, Jane Austen was the seventh child of a Hampshire clergyman, George Austen; she had six brothers and one sister, Cassandra, who was two years older than her and became her closest friend. She grew up in a small Hampshire village, called Steventon; village life would be a feature of her fiction. She had little formal schooling, and depended upon her father, and his library, for her education.

In 1797, Austen completed a novel called *First Impressions.* Her father sent it to a London bookseller in the hope that it would be published, but the manuscript (now lost) was returned unread. Fifteen years later, Austen would return to this manuscript and rewrite it completely to produce *Pride and Prejudice.* After her father's death in 1805, Jane and her mother and sister were dependent on her brothers for financial support. Eventually, her brother Edward, who had been adopted by wealthy, childless relatives, found a secure home for them in the Hampshire village of Chawton. Here, over the course of some seven years, she produced all six of her completed novels, which included *Sense and Sensibility* (1811) and *Emma* (1816).

Although *Pride and Prejudice* followed the "courtship" plot of other novels of the time, it was in many ways unconventional. Elizabeth Bennet was a heroine unlike any other in fiction before her: "arch", irreverent, and independent-minded. Austen's readers were used to virtuous, exemplary heroines. Elizabeth is witty and confident; she also gets things wrong. Indeed, the plot relies on her prejudiced misjudgement of both Mr Darcy and the smooth but deceitful Mr Wickham.

Elizabeth's interest in Mr Darcy is all the more believable because she does not recognize it herself. He, meanwhile, is confident that he can overcome his attraction to her. In the first volume of the novel, they fence with and tease each other. Both have to discover their true feelings through their errors.

> ❝ Elizabeth looked archly, and turned away. Her resistance had not injured her with the gentleman... ❞
>
> **PRIDE AND PREJUDICE, CHAPTER 6**

DANCING

In Austen's world, dances were essential to courtship. They were the most important occasions for young men and women to meet and have some physical contact (although both wore gloves). Some dances were open to anyone who bought a ticket, like the Meryton assembly ball in *Pride and Prejudice.* Others were improvised occasions, to a piano accompaniment, like the dance at the Lucases' in the novel, which happens at the end of a party. And some were grand, private affairs, by invitation only, like the Netherfield ball, where Elizabeth finally dances with Mr Darcy. At all of these, dances were undertaken in "sets", or formations, following complicated patterns that had to be learned in advance. As we see with Elizabeth and Mr Darcy, this often allowed partners to speak to each other as they danced.

▶ **A ball like the one** shown in this 1825 engraving might begin at 9pm and continue throughout the night.

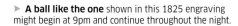

In **Pride and Prejudice,** Austen is alert to the importance of money, and so are all the characters in the novel. Mr Bennet's estate will pass to Mr Collins, a distant cousin, so his five daughters must hope to escape penury through marriage. As the very first chapter reveals, Mrs Bennet is preoccupied with their marriage prospects. Hilariously foolish though she is, many of her hopes are gratified. Even the "wild, noisy, and fearless" Lydia, who elopes, aged just 16, with a rakish seducer, gets a husband in the end. Elizabeth comes to realise that her father, whose "sarcastic humour" she appreciates, is partly to blame for his wife's and daughters' follies.

Marriage for love may be the happy ending towards which *Pride and Prejudice* is headed, but Austen's fiction is clear-eyed about the possible pains of marriage. Mr Bennet has married a woman for whom he has no respect; he takes refuge in his subtle mockery of her and his daughters. The fate of Charlotte Lucas, Elizabeth's closest friend, is unforgettable. Mr Collins, having been refused by Elizabeth, rapidly turns to Charlotte, who accepts for the sake of the financial security this will bring her. When Elizabeth visits her in her new home in Kent, she sees that Charlotte has arranged everything so that she encounters her husband as little as possible. It is a sad prospect for the rest of her life.

▲ **INSPIRATION FOR PEMBERLEY** Jane Austen regularly visited her brother Edward at Godmersham Park, a house that he inherited when his adoptive father, Thomas Knight, died in 1794. It is likely that Austen based Pemberley, Mr Darcy's country estate, on Godmersham Park.

Solemnly self-important, Mr Collins is one of the novel's deliciously comic characters. Another is his patroness, the haughty and bullying Lady Catherine De Bourgh, Mr Darcy's aunt, who has a memorable verbal duel with Elizabeth when she tries to stop her from marrying Mr Darcy. Here, as everywhere in the novel, Austen's dialogue is brilliantly sharp – one of the reasons the novel has proved irresistible to film and TV adaptors.

KEY CHARACTERS: THE BENNET FAMILY

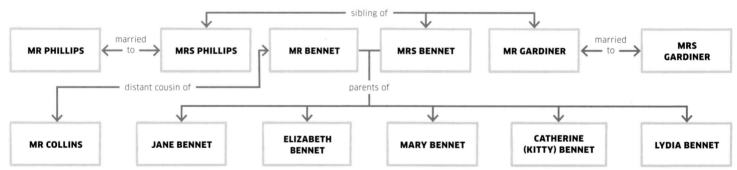

MR PHILLIPS ← married to → MRS PHILLIPS — sibling of — MR BENNET — MRS BENNET — MR GARDINER ← married to → MRS GARDINER

distant cousin of — parents of

MR COLLINS — JANE BENNET — ELIZABETH BENNET — MARY BENNET — CATHERINE (KITTY) BENNET — LYDIA BENNET

PROPOSALS

Strict conventions governed marriage proposals in Austen's day. In her novel *Northanger Abbey*, a character compares matrimony to dancing: "in both, man has the advantage of choice, woman only the power of refusal". The proposal had to come from the man, but once a couple became engaged, only the woman could break off the engagement. Whether made in writing or in speech, any declaration of affection could be taken as a proposal of marriage: Mr Darcy does not explicitly mention marriage in either of his proposals. In Austen's novels, men who propose as if they cannot imagine a negative answer (such as Mr Collins) are turned down: some diffidence is a better sign of true affection.

▶ **In this artwork by Charles Brock,** Mr Collins proposes to Elizabeth, believing that he "will not fail of being acceptable".

> He is a gentleman; I am a gentleman's daughter; so far we are equal.

PRIDE AND PREJUDICE,
CHAPTER 56

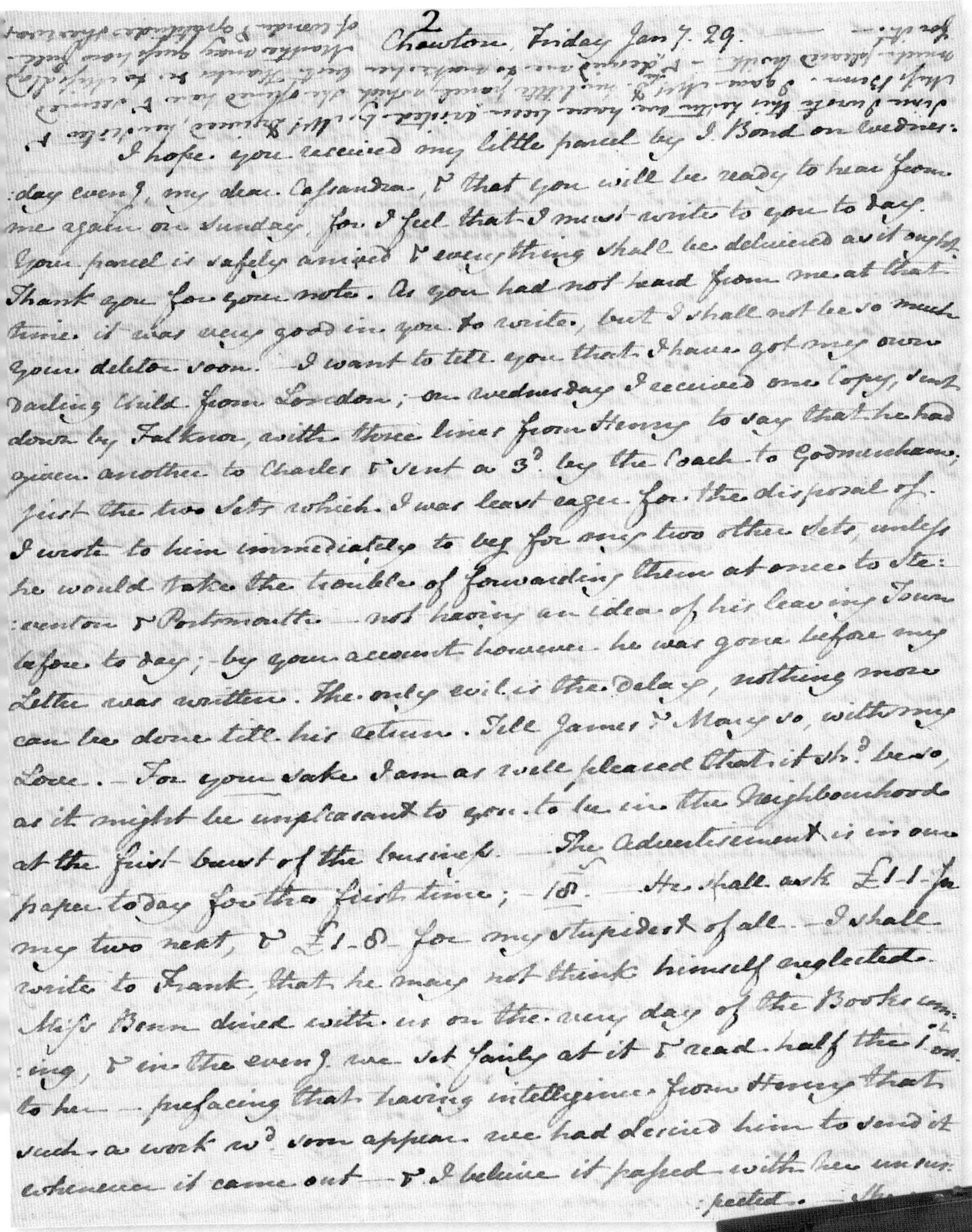

2 Chawton Friday Jany 29.

I hope you received my little parcel by J. Bond on Wednes:day evening, my dear Cassandra, & that you will be ready to hear from me again on Sunday, for I feel that I must write to you to day. Your parcel is safely arrived & everything shall be delivered as it ought. Thank you for your note. As you had not heard from me at that time it was very good in you to write, but I shall not be so much your debtor soon. I want to tell you that I have got my own darling Child from London; on Wednesday I received one Copy, sent down by Falknor, with three lines from Henry to say that he had given another to Charles & sent a 3^d by the Coach to Godmersham; just the two Sets which I was least eager for the disposal of. I wrote to him immediately to beg for my two other Sets, unless he would take the trouble of forwarding them at once to Ste:venton & Portsmouth — not having an idea of his leaving Town before to day; — by your account however he was gone before my Letter was written. The only evil is the delay, nothing more can be done till his return. Tell James & Mary so, with my Love. — For your sake I am as well pleased that it sh^d be so, as it might be unpleasant to you to be in the Neighbourhood at the first burst of the business. — The Advertisement is in our paper to day for the first time; — 18^s. — He shall ask £1-1- for my two next, & £1-8- for my stupidest of all. — I shall write to Frank, that he may not think himself neglected. Miss Benn dined with us on the very day of the Books com:ing, & in the even^g we set fairly at it & read half the 1st vol. to her — prefacing that having intelligence from Henry that such a work w^d soon appear we had desired him to send it whenever it came out — & I believe it passed with her unsus:pected. — She

◄ **AUSTEN'S LETTER DESCRIBING THE NOVEL** Two days after receiving her copy of *Pride and Prejudice*, Jane Austen wrote to her sister Cassandra, her closest confidante, who was staying with their brother Charles, only 15 miles away. She calls the novel "my own darling child". She and her mother have read it aloud to a neighbour, Miss Benn, who never suspects (because the novel is anonymous) that Jane is the author.

> Miss Benn dined with us on the very day of the Books coming, & in the even^g we set fairly at it & read half the 1st vol. to her... I believe it passed with her unsuspected. – She was amused, poor soul! that she c. not help, you know, with two such people to lead the way; but she really does seem to admire Elizabeth. I must confess that I think her as delightful a creature as ever appeared in print, & how I shall be able to tolerate those who do not like her at least, I do not know.

LETTER TO CASSANDRA, 29 JANUARY 1813

▼ **AUSTEN'S WRITING BOX** When Austen was 18, her father gave her this "writing box". As well as being a container for her writing, with a lockable drawer, it was a portable desk. When opened, it became a slope on which to rest paper and write, complete with a place for her ink pot. It is now in the British Library.

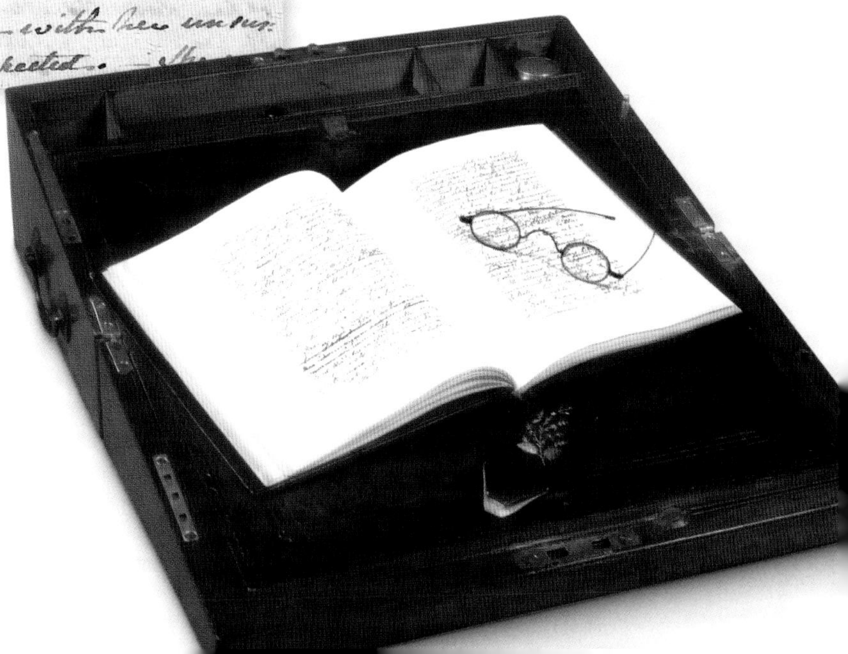

AUSTEN'S OTHER WORKS

Jane Austen completed six novels in her lifetime. *Pride and Prejudice* was the second to be published. It came after *Sense and Sensibility* (1811) – the story of two sisters, the judicious Elinor and the impetuous Marianne – and was followed by *Mansfield Park* (1814), whose heroine, Fanny Price, is as shy as Elizabeth Bennet is outspoken. Next came *Emma* (1815), Austen's longest and most formally ambitious novel, which sees the world through the deluded eyes of its meddling heroine, Emma Woodhouse. Before her death in July 1817, Austen had completed *Persuasion*, the story of a woman, Anne Elliot, who believes that she has lost her one chance of love. This and *Northanger Abbey*, her revision of an early satire of Gothic fiction, were published posthumously.

Frankenstein

1818 ▪ THREE VOLUMES ▪ UK

MARY SHELLEY (1797-1851)

Begun near Lake Geneva in 1816, on a night of telling ghost stories in the company of her future husband Percy Bysshe Shelley; Lord Byron; her half-sister Claire Clairmont; and the young physician John Polidori, Mary Shelley's *Frankenstein; or, the Modern Prometheus* created an enduring literary and cultural myth. Victor Frankenstein, a Swiss student of science and nature, explores forbidden areas of knowledge that come back to haunt him. Seeking "the secrets of heaven and earth", he brings forth a live creature endowed with the power of thought. Horrified by what he has made, Frankenstein flees from his creation and the monster escapes to the mountains to wreak revenge on its maker.

The novel opens near the North Pole, where a weakened Victor Frankenstein is found stranded on the ice by a ship's captain. Frankenstein's story is told within the framework of Captain Walton's letters to his sister. From his cabin bed, Frankenstein recounts the harrowing experiences – including murder – of his family as they became the prey of the monster. He also explains the monster's state of mind, when it confronts Frankenstein high in the Alps and explains why it was intent on evil. Shunned by humanity, it demands that Frankenstein play God once more and create a companion for its solitude.

> " With an anxiety that almost amounted to agony, I collected the instruments of life around me, that I might infuse a spark of being into the lifeless thing that lay at my feet. It was already one in the morning; the rain pattered dismally against the panes, and my candle was nearly burnt out, when, by the glimmer of the half-extinguished light, I saw the dull yellow eye of the creature open; it breathed hard, and a convulsive motion agitated its limbs. How can I describe my emotions at this catastrophe, or how delineate the wretch whom with such infinite pains and care I had endeavoured to form? "

FRANKENSTEIN, CHAPTER 5

Frankenstein explores ambition, community, rejection, the will, and the nature of good and evil, taking us from the sources of life to the darkness of death in a complex story of hunter and hunted. It adopts a distinctly Romantic critique of Promethean themes – its subtitle, "the Modern Prometheus", alludes to the Greek hero who stole fire from the gods and paid the price for doing so. As such, the book continues the committed social engagement of Shelley's parents – the political thinker William Godwin and the feminist Mary Wollstonecraft.

In context

◄ **ALIENATION** In both its themes and its dramatic Alpine setting, *Frankenstein* examines alienation, a common topic in Romantic literature. The theme is found elsewhere in defining works of art of the period, from the paintings of German artist Caspar David Friedrich to the writings of Lord Byron. John Martin's painting *Manfred on the Jungfrau* (left) was inspired by Byron's work *Manfred*. Like *Frankenstein*, it features characters cast out into the sublime grandeur of nature, which diminishes and awes human beings.

Shelley's manuscript was around 300 pages long, and was written in two large notebooks. This page is the opening of Chapter 7

Both Shelley and her husband-to-be, poet Percy Bysshe Shelley, made revisions to the manuscript

Chapter 7th

It was on a dreary night of November that I beheld the frame on my man completed; and with an anxiety that almost amounted to agony. I collected instruments of life around me and endeavoured that I might to infuse a spark of being into the lifeless thing that lay at my feet. It was already one in the morning; the rain pattered dismally against the window panes & my candle was nearly burnt out, when by the glimmer of the half extinguished light I saw the dull yellow eye of the creature open — It breathed hard, and a convulsive motion agitated its limbs.

But how How can I describe my emotion at this catastrophe, or how delineate the wretch whom with such infinite pains and care I had endeavoured to form. His limbs were in proportion and I had selected his features & as beautiful handsome. Handsome; great God! His yellow skin scarcely covered the work of muscles and arteries beneath; his hair of a lustrous black & was flowing and his teeth of a pearly whiteness but these luxuriances only formed a more horrid contrast with his watery eyes that seemed almost of the same colour as the dun white sockets in which they were set,

◄ **HANDWRITTEN MANUSCRIPT** In this part of the manuscript, Frankenstein records his horror at the "catastrophe" of his creature awakening and attempting to approach him. His rejection of the monster, which he calls a "wretch", begins a trail of disaster, moving from Frankenstein's laboratory of scientific creation to the wilderness of pack ice that bookends the novel. This moment has inspired countless efforts to imagine the monster, from cinema and television to graphic novels and advertising.

THE **GOTHIC NOVEL**

The Gothic novel explores the late 18th- and early 19th-century world with an emphasis on subjective experience, the emotions, the obscure corners of the human psyche, and fear of the supernatural. One major influence on the literature of the period was *A Philosophical Enquiry into the Origin of Our Ideas of the Sublime and Beautiful* (1757), by Irish philosopher Edmund Burke, which examined our attraction to "sublime" forces that can overwhelm us. Before *Frankenstein*, the most popular Gothic novels were *The Castle of Otranto* (1764), by Horace Walpole, and *The Mysteries of Udolpho* (1794), by Ann Radcliffe.

▲ *The Nightmare,* ■ painted by Henry Fuseli in 1781, may have been one of the inspirations for Shelley's *Frankenstein*.

▶ **TITLE PAGE OF THE 1831 EDITION**
The Red and the Black was subtitled "A Chronicle of the 19th Century". Along with the work of his compatriot, Honoré de Balzac (see pp.48–51), Stendhal's writing marked a key stage in the development of literary realism, a narrative style that prefers modern social contexts and plausible psychology to historical settings and Gothic plots.

The vignette shows Julien approaching Madame de Rênal near a confessional

> " Julien was indignant at his own cowardice, and said to himself, 'at the exact moment when ten o'clock strikes, I will perform what I have resolved to do all through the day, or I will go up to my room and blow out my brains.'… Finally, when the last stroke of ten was still reverberating, he stretched out his hand and took Madame de Rênal's, who immediately withdrew it. Julien, scarcely knowing what he was doing, seized it again. In spite of his own excitement, he could not help being struck by the icy coldness of the hand which he was taking; he pressed it convulsively; a last effort was made to take it away, but in the end the hand remained in his. "

THE RED AND THE BLACK,
CHAPTER 9

LE ROUGE
ET LE NOIR

CHRONIQUE DU XIXᵉ SIÈCLE,

PAR M. DE STENDHAL.

TOME PREMIER.

PARIS.

A. LEVAVASSEUR, LIBRAIRE, PALAIS-ROYAL.

1831.

The Red and the Black

1830 ▪ TWO VOLUMES ▪ FRANCE

STENDHAL (1783-1842)

The Red and the Black charts the fortunes of a provincial, working-class youth in the years of the Restoration of the Bourbon Monarchy in France (1814-30) after the tumultuous era of the French Revolution and Napoleon Bonaparte. Julien Sorel is intelligent and ambitious, aware that his advancement depends on following either the red uniform of a military career or the black habit of the church, whose colours offer one interpretation of the novel's title. Stendhal, however, never clarified the precise meaning of his resonant and richly symbolic red and black.

Before training for the priesthood, which he abandons, Julien exploits his intellect and skills in Latin to become a tutor to the children of Madame de Rênal and develop his social connections. Overwhelmed by his meeting with the captivating Madame de Rênal, the novel relates Julien's romantic and sexual development through his self-advancing strategies, later charting his arrival in Paris and his pursuits as a private secretary with the wealthy family of the Marquis de la Mole. Amid intrigue, adultery, duels, deception, and delusion, Julien seeks a grand destiny, shaped by his reading of history, in the politically reactionary setting of early 19th-century France.

The Red and the Black tells Julien's story in an ironic yet sympathetic style, revealing his thoughts, while commenting on the nature of fiction: "a novel is a mirror walking along a highway. Sometimes it reflects to your eyes the azures of the heavens, sometimes the mire of the road's mudholes". With Julien, Stendhal explores the path to success, and the social and psychological pitfalls that can lead to failure and defeat. The depiction of character and the psychology of romantic attachment reflects Stendhal's own life and the subjects of his other writings.

In context

◄ **NAPOLEON** Julien is obsessed with the exploits of Napoleon Bonaparte, especially the reports of his military campaigns, and the statements that he recorded towards the end of his life in Emmanuel de las Cases' *The Memorial of Saint Helena* (1823). Julien usually pauses to consider Napoleon's actions and maxims as a guide to his conduct and ambition.

▲ **LIBERTY LEADING THE PEOPLE** *The Red and the Black* was published in the same year as the 1830 revolution in France, in which the reactionary King Charles X was overthrown in favour of the more liberal Louis Philippe. The political energies of the period are captured in this 1830 painting by Eugène Delacroix.

Le Père Goriot

1835 ▪ TWO VOLUMES ▪ FRANCE

HONORÉ DE BALZAC (1799-1850)

One of Honoré de Balzac's best-loved novels, *Le Père Goriot* explores the contrasting but inextricably connected worlds of wealth and poverty in Paris during the early 19th century. Balzac's influential techniques as a chronicler of French society create a multilayered presentation of the social and economic background of his characters and the world in which they live.

Opening in a boarding house run by Madame Vauquer in a shabby quarter of the city, Balzac gathers together a seemingly random collection of individuals whose lives and schemes eventually intersect. Old Goriot has made a fortune as a merchant after the French Revolution of 1789, and has secured the futures of his two daughters, who marry into the elite. However, the restoration of the aristocracy, after the fall of Napoleon in 1815, means that *parvenu* figures such as Goriot can no longer thrive – indeed, they are treated with scorn. Meanwhile, Goriot's status-conscious daughters remain reliant on his wealth to support their profligate but socially acceptable husbands and lovers, and show no gratitude for the sacrifices that he has made for them.

Into the Maison Vauquer steps the provincial Eugène de Rastignac – a student of law who is determined to make his way in Paris, but is still dependent on his family's financial support. Moving between high society, where he feels he will never truly be accepted, and the reality of his limited means as a student, Rastignac encounters Goriot's daughters, after which the novel takes the reader back and forth between the worlds of privilege and privation to reveal a network of secrets and lies. While working out how to be accepted by high society, Rastignac comes under the influence of an enigmatic and unscrupulous boarder named Vautrin. An ex-convict wanted by the police, Vautrin informs Rastignac that there are "no principles, only events", and encourages him to make his way in society by any means possible.

▲ **RASTIGNAC** The character of Rastignac, depicted here by French illustrator Paul Gavarni, is the quintessential Balzacian social climber. Determined to succeed at all costs, he appears in numerous Balzac novels, eventually becoming a minister and a titled member of the nobility.

◄ **THE PARISIAN SOCIAL SCENE** Balzac often explored high society and displays of wealth, notably those of the aristocracy following the return of the French monarchy in 1815. *Le Père Goriot* presents characters whose hold on society is precarious. The Duchesse de Langeais notes: "Society is a mudhole. Let's try to remain up on the heights." This painting shows aristocrats at a ball.

[Manuscript page — handwritten French draft by Honoré de Balzac]

◄ **MANUSCRIPT** Balzac was a prolific writer and was completely immersed in the world of 19th-century French journalism. His novels were regularly serialized in magazines, *Le Père Goriot* initially appearing in the *Revue de Paris*. Fuelled by a legendary coffee habit, Balzac often wrote multiple works at the same time, to strict deadlines. His manuscripts capture the breadth of his imagination and his focused drive. This page includes his vivid introduction of Eugène de Rastignac, which gives context to the character's later social successes.

> " At that time one of the rooms was tenanted by a law student... one of a large family who pinched and starved themselves to spare twelve hundred francs a year for him. Misfortune had accustomed Eugène de Rastignac, for that was his name, to work. He belonged to the number of young men who know as children that their parents' hopes are centred on them, and deliberately prepare themselves for a great career, subordinating their studies from the first to this end, carefully watching the indications of the course of events, calculating the probable turn that affairs will take, that they may be the first to profit by them. "

LE PÈRE GORIOT

REALISM

In the mid-19th century, realism was the dominant artistic style in Europe, in both literature and painting. It responded to the growth of industrialization by examining social, political, and economic fluctuations, especially in cities. Regarding all aspects of the present as worthy of attention, realism focused on characters and their dilemmas, to capture the complexity and unpredictability of the modern world. In his novels, Balzac included precise details of place, clothes, habits, and environmental conditions to help to convey a many-faceted sense of character. He aimed to present a comprehensive look at society and culture by bringing to life a densely populated world animated by his fascination with motivation and personality. Realism was exemplified in painting by Gustave Courbet's famous work *A Burial At Ornans*.

► **A Burial At Ornans,** painted in 1850 by Gustave Courbet, depicted a funeral in a realistic style.

> And with that tear that fell on Father Goriot's grave, Eugène Rastignac's youth ended... He went a few paces further, to the highest point of the cemetery, and looked out over Paris and the windings of the Seine; the lamps were beginning to shine on either side of the river. His eyes turned almost eagerly to the space between the column of the Place Vendôme and the cupola of the Invalides; there lay the shining world that he had wished to reach. He glanced over that humming hive, seeming to draw a foretaste of its honey, and said magniloquently: 'It's between us, now.' And by way of throwing down the glove to Society, Rastignac went to dine with Mme. de Nucingen.

LE PÈRE GORIOT

▲ **PARIS** At a key moment in the book, Rastignac looks down on Paris from the Père Lachaise Cemetery and throws down the gauntlet to French society, declaring: "It's between us, now!" This engraving, based on a 1833 painting by J.M.W. Turner, shows the same view.

◄ **PÈRE GORIOT** This engraving by Alexandre Baulant shows Père Goriot, described as a "grease spot in his daughters' drawing rooms". Neglected "like a lemon peel", his experience of breakdown and the novel's depiction of the suffering of an ageing father rejected by his daughters is often regarded as a 19th-century incarnation of William Shakespeare's King Lear.

The novel is set at the turn of the 1820s. Balzac's intimate knowledge of Paris and its social types drew on his own experience of arriving in the French capital from the regional town of Tours. After studying law for a while, he decided to become a writer. While charting the fluctuating fortunes of Goriot's daughters and the old man's own decline, the novel examines Rastignac's alternating attraction and resistance to Vautrin's schemes, including a plot to murder the brother of a fellow lodger at the Maison Vauquer, Victorine Taillefer, who stands to inherit a fortune. Primed for the role of seducer by Vautrin, Rastignac refuses to sink to such extremes of criminality, but the novel captures his growing awareness of how wealth, class, style, and duplicity function in French society.

In *Le Père Goriot*, Balzac employs his celebrated eye for detail and an often exhaustive descriptive style that established many of the hallmarks of 19th-century fiction. Oscar Wilde once observed that "the 19th century, as we know it, is largely an invention of Balzac's fiction", which offered "imaginative reality". The physical and cultural world portrayed by Balzac is charged by a narrative interest in melodrama and intrigue. *Le Père Goriot* captures a notable feature of 19th-century fiction by exploring the social and personal development of Rastignac, revealing how his eyes are opened to the workings of the world. Behind the façade of hard work and dedication lies the reality of connections, opportunism, and an unsentimental ruthlessness. The novel incorporates aspects of the *Bildungsroman*, a novel of individual development, which charted an individual's induction into the everyday world of work, society, marriage, and status. Tracing the theme of seeing through illusions, the novel alternates between Rastignac's growing understanding of the ways of the world and Goriot's awakening to the callousness of his daughters, which accelerates his eventual demise.

▲ **VAUTRIN** This 1922 illustration shows Vautrin, whose real name is Jacques Collin. A shady figure who goes by the nickname of *Trompe-la-Mort* (Death-dodger), he was based on a famous Parisian criminal-turned-police-chief named Eugène François Vidocq. Vautrin enabled Balzac to explore the darker side of Parisian life.

> " Here is the **crossroads of life,** young man: **choose.** But you **have already chosen.** "
>
> *LE PÈRE GORIOT*

LA **COMÉDIE HUMAINE**

Balzac's vast literary project, *La Comédie humaine (Human Comedy)*, spanned most of his career. Through it, he aimed to depict "all society, sketching it in the immensity of its turmoil". From the early 1830s, Balzac developed the idea that minor characters from previous works would reappear in each new novel, now presented at a crossroads in their lives. *Le Père Goriot* played an important part in this scheme, as Rastignac had already played a minor role in *La Peau de chagrin* (1831). *La Comédie humaine* came to include around 90 different novels and stories, and an estimated 4,000 characters. Over time, Balzac came to see his Human Comedy as a comprehensive and coherent whole, and he placed individual novels into thematic categories, depending on their principal focus, ranging from Studies of Manners and Scenes of Parisian Life to Scenes of Private Life, Provincial Life, and Philosophical Studies. Taken as a whole, Balzac's works offer an unrivalled insight into life in early 19th-century France.

▲ **Balzac and his characters** feature in this sketch of a fan by French designer Grandville.

The Betrothed

1825-27 (FIRST EDITION), 1840-42 (REVISED EDITION) ▪ THREE VOLUMES ▪ ITALY

ALESSANDRO MANZONI (1785-1873)

In a mountain village near Lake Como, in northern Italy, Lucia and her weaver fiancé, Renzo, are due to be married by their parish priest, Don Abbondio. However, Lucia has unintentionally caught the lecherous eye of a tyrannous local nobleman, Don Rodrigo. He sends two of his "bravoes" (henchmen) to intimidate the cowardly priest into not performing the marriage. So begins *I promessi sposi* (*The Betrothed*). First drafted in the 1820s, but set 200 years earlier, at a time when the Thirty Years' War was ravaging Europe, the novel tells the story of how Lucia and Renzo, with Lucia's mother, Agnese, are forced to flee their home village to escape Don Rodrigo's predatory attentions. Events part the betrothed lovers, and both endure many trials, including famine, kidnap for Lucia, and unfair arrest for Renzo. They are eventually reunited in the quarantine station of a plague-stricken Milan.

When it was first published, the novel was a huge bestseller, both in Italy and across Europe. Its author, Alessandro Manzoni, came from a wealthy Milanese family, and had spent much of his childhood on his father's estate near Lake Como. Manzoni's love of his native region and its history, along with his deep Catholic faith, underpins the work, much influenced by the historical fiction of his older, Scottish contemporary, Walter Scott. Essentially a love story, *The Betrothed* has long passages devoted to real historical events and figures, including the poignantly flawed "Nun of Monza" (who shelters, and then betrays Lucia); the fearsome bandit-nobleman, the Unnamed; and the saintly Archbishop of Milan, Cardinal Federigo Borromeo.

A **COMMON LANGUAGE**

One of the issues that preoccupied Italian nationalists in the early 19th century was the "question of the language". At the time, what is now Italy was still a patchwork of kingdoms, duchies, and other states, each with its own dialect. For nationalists, it was important to know what the common language of a united Italy would be. The debate was close to Manzoni's heart. Born in Milan, he spoke the Milanese-Tuscan dialect, which he used for the original edition of *The Betrothed*. However, he came to accept that the dialect of Florence, the native tongue of Italy's great medieval poet, Dante Alighieri, was the natural basis for a standard Italian language.

Putting his belief into practice, Manzoni set about mastering Florentine, and then rewriting his entire novel in it. The result was the revised edition of 1840-42. He described the process as "washing his clothes in the Arno", the river that flows through Florence – and where he led, other writers followed. The united Italy that emerged in 1871 had a generally accepted common language based on the dialect of Florence.

In context

▲ **LAKE COMO** *The Departure of the Betrothed*, Michele Fanoli's 1831 painting, gives a dramatic depiction of Renzo, Lucia, and Lucia's mother, Agnese, escaping across Lake Como by boat. They are fleeing the villainous Don Rodrigo, whose forbidding palace is picked out by moonlight on a cliff above the lake.

▲ **PLAGUE CITY** A late 16th-century map gives a bird's-eye view of Milan, capital of the Duchy of Milan, which at the time of the novel was part of the Spanish Empire. Both Renzo and Lucia find themselves in the city, first during a famine, and then during a plague.

For the second edition, Manzoni rewrote his entire manuscript in Florentine

◄ **RENZO'S ESCAPE** A manuscript page from the archives of Milan's Biblioteca Nazionale Braidense shows a draft of the revised version of *The Betrothed*, published in 1840–42, with (see inset, left) the new edition's elaborately engraved title page. Here, in Chapter 16, Renzo, who has inadvertently fallen foul of the Milanese authorities, has broken free of a police escort and is being encouraged to escape by a friendly crowd.

> ' 'Run for it, lad!' – 'There's a monastery over there!' – 'No, no; over here; run for the church!' – 'That way!' – 'No, this way!' called many voices. As far as running for it was concerned, Renzo did not need any advice... he had been thinking what to do next, and had decided that if he got away he would keep on going until he was safely beyond the city boundaries... 'Somehow or other they've found out my name and got it down in their infernal books,' he said to himself, '... if I've still got a chance of being a bird in the air I won't make myself a bird in a cage.'

***THE BETROTHED*, CHAPTER 16**

▲ **MAN OF GOD** Cardinal Federigo Borromeo, depicted here in a contemporary portrait, was Archbishop of Milan from 1595 to 1631. In the novel, he and the Capuchin friar, Father Cristoforo, both concerned for victims of injustice, stand in contrast to the village priest, Don Abbondio.

Jane Eyre

1847 ▪ THREE VOLUMES ▪ UK

CHARLOTTE BRONTË (1816-1855)

Jane Eyre, Charlotte Brontë's heroine, tells her own story, with great directness and candour, beginning with her childhood. She is an orphan, in the care of an unloving widowed aunt, Mrs Reed, who has three pampered children of her own. Aged 10, Jane is sent away to the brutal Lowood school, which is presided over by the hypocritical and sanctimonious Mr Brocklehurst. Jane's solace in this harsh environment is her friendship with another pupil – the saintly, bookish Helen Burns, who dies of consumption (like Charlotte's own sister Maria, on whom the character is based).

After a terrible typhus outbreak, Mr Brocklehurst is dismissed, and conditions at the school improve. Jane is befriended by a sympathetic teacher, Miss Temple, and eventually she becomes a teacher at Lowood herself. She then travels to Thornfield Hall to be governess in the household of the irascible but fascinating Mr Rochester, with whom she falls in love. The pair become engaged, but Jane discovers that their marriage would be bigamous, because Mr Rochester already has a wife.

Despairing, Jane leaves Thornfield and travels blindly before collapsing on the doorstep of an isolated house. She is taken in by two sisters, Diana and Mary Rivers, whose brother, St John Rivers, finds her work as a teacher in a local school. Admiring Jane's steely integrity, St John Rivers proposes marriage to her, but his coldness repels her – and she seems to hear the voice of Mr Rochester, calling to her. She returns to Thornfield to find the house burnt down, Bertha Rochester dead, and Mr Rochester badly injured. She also learns from St John Rivers that she has inherited a fortune from her uncle. Now, finally, she and Mr Rochester can marry.

> " I desired liberty; for liberty I gasped; for liberty I uttered a prayer; it seemed scattered on the wind... "
>
> **JANE EYRE, CHAPTER 10**

In context

▲ **INSPIRATION FOR LOWOOD SCHOOL** This 19th-century wood engraving shows the Clergy Daughters' School at Cowan Bridge, in Lancashire, where Charlotte, aged 8, was sent with Emily to join their older sisters, Maria and Elizabeth. Conditions were dire, and soon there was an outbreak of typhus. Dangerously ill, Maria was sent home, where she died of tuberculosis, aged 11. Elizabeth died soon after, aged 10.

◄ **GOVERNESSES** At the age of 18, Jane Eyre becomes a governess to Mr Rochester's ward, Adèle. In the 19th century, affluent households often had governesses, who feature a good deal in fiction of the period. The role of governess, a kind of superior servant, was one of the few options open to an educated young woman with little money. Jean-Baptiste Jules Trayer's painting The Lesson (1861) shows a governess teaching a young lady.

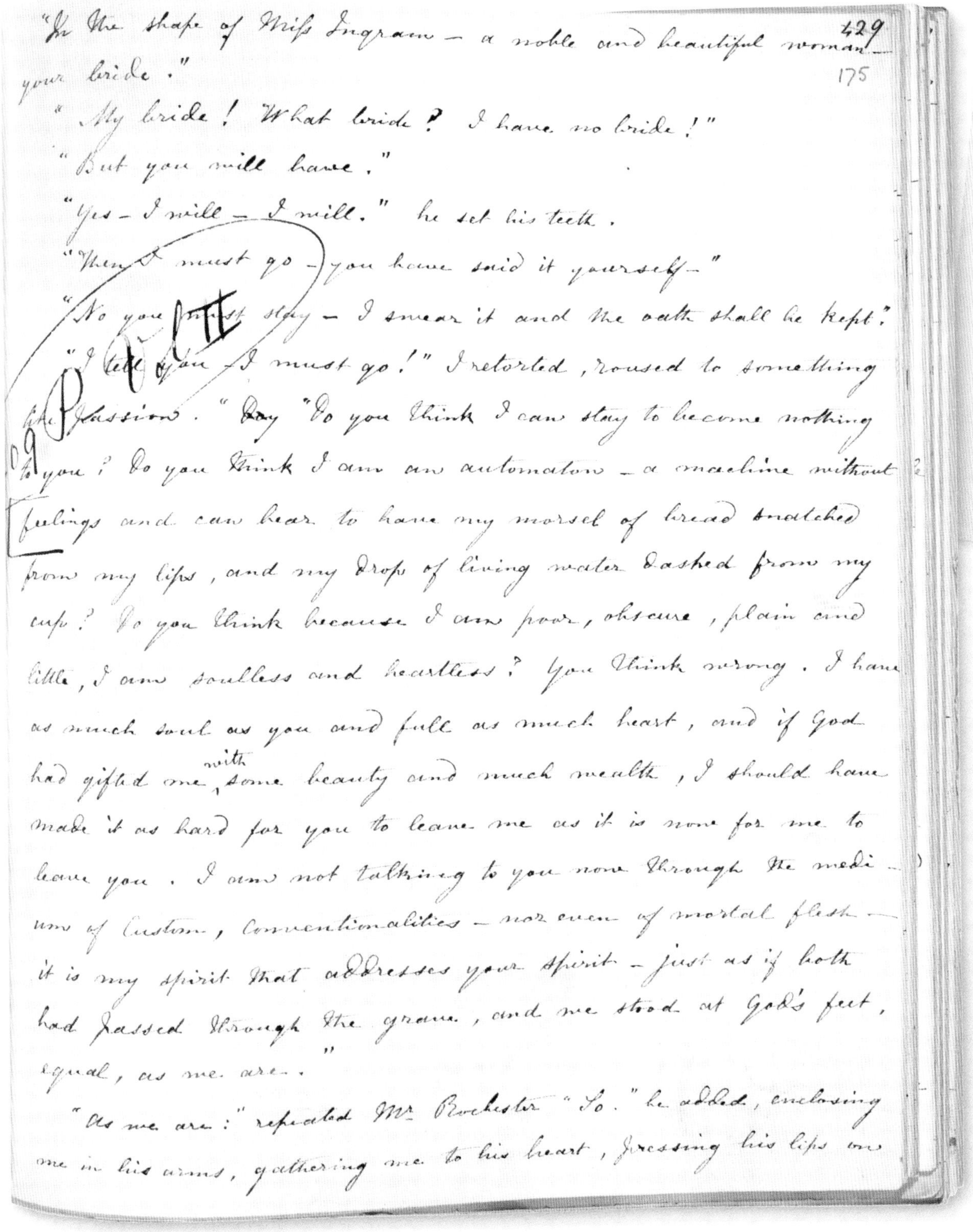

429
175
"In the shape of Miss Ingram — a noble and beautiful woman — your bride."
"My bride! What bride? I have no bride!"
"But you will have."
"Yes — I will — I will." he set his teeth.
"Then I must go — you have said it yourself —"
"No you must stay — I swear it and the oath shall be kept."
"I tell you I must go!" I retorted, roused to something like passion. "Do you think I can stay to become nothing to you? Do you think I am an automaton — a machine without feelings and can bear to have my morsel of bread snatched from my lips, and my drop of living water dashed from my cup? Do you think because I am poor, obscure, plain and little, I am soulless and heartless? You think wrong. I have as much soul as you and full as much heart, and if God had gifted me with some beauty and much wealth, I should have made it as hard for you to leave me as it is now for me to leave you. I am not talking to you now through the medium of Custom, Conventionalities — nor even of mortal flesh — it is my spirit that addresses your spirit — just as if both had passed through the grave, and we stood at God's feet, equal, as we are."
"As we are:" repeated Mr Rochester "So." he added, enclosing me in his arms, gathering me to his heart, pressing his lips on

JANE EYRE.

An Autobiography.

EDITED BY

CURRER BELL.

IN THREE VOLUMES.

VOL. I.

LONDON:
SMITH, ELDER, AND CO., CORNHILL.
1847.

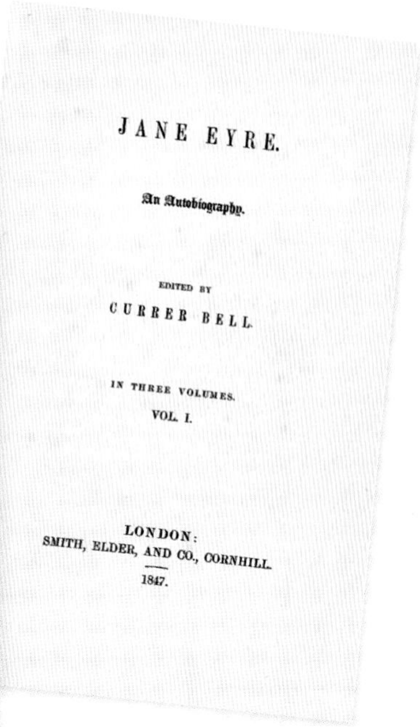

▲ **TITLE PAGE OF THE FIRST EDITION** The Brontë sisters used pseudonyms when they published their novels: Acton (Anne), Currer (Charlotte), and Ellis (Emily) Bell. In the first edition, Charlotte gave *Jane Eyre* the subtitle "An Autobiography", but she removed this from later editions.

◄ **MANUSCRIPT** Only one manuscript of *Jane Eyre* still exists – this fair copy that Charlotte sent to the publisher, Smith, Elder & Co, in August 1847. In this passage, Jane, mistakenly believing that Mr Rochester is going to marry Blanche Ingram, tells him that she is going to leave Thornfield, and passionately describes the force of her feelings.

“Do you think, because I am poor, obscure, plain, and little, I am soulless and heartless? – You think wrong! – I have as much soul as you, – and full as much heart! And if God had gifted me with some beauty, and much wealth, I should have made it as hard for you to leave me, as it is now for me to leave you. I am not talking to you now through the medium of custom, conventionalities, nor even of mortal flesh: – it is my spirit that addresses your spirit; just as if both had passed through the grave, and we stood at God's feet, equal, – as we are!”

***JANE EYRE*, CHAPTER 23**

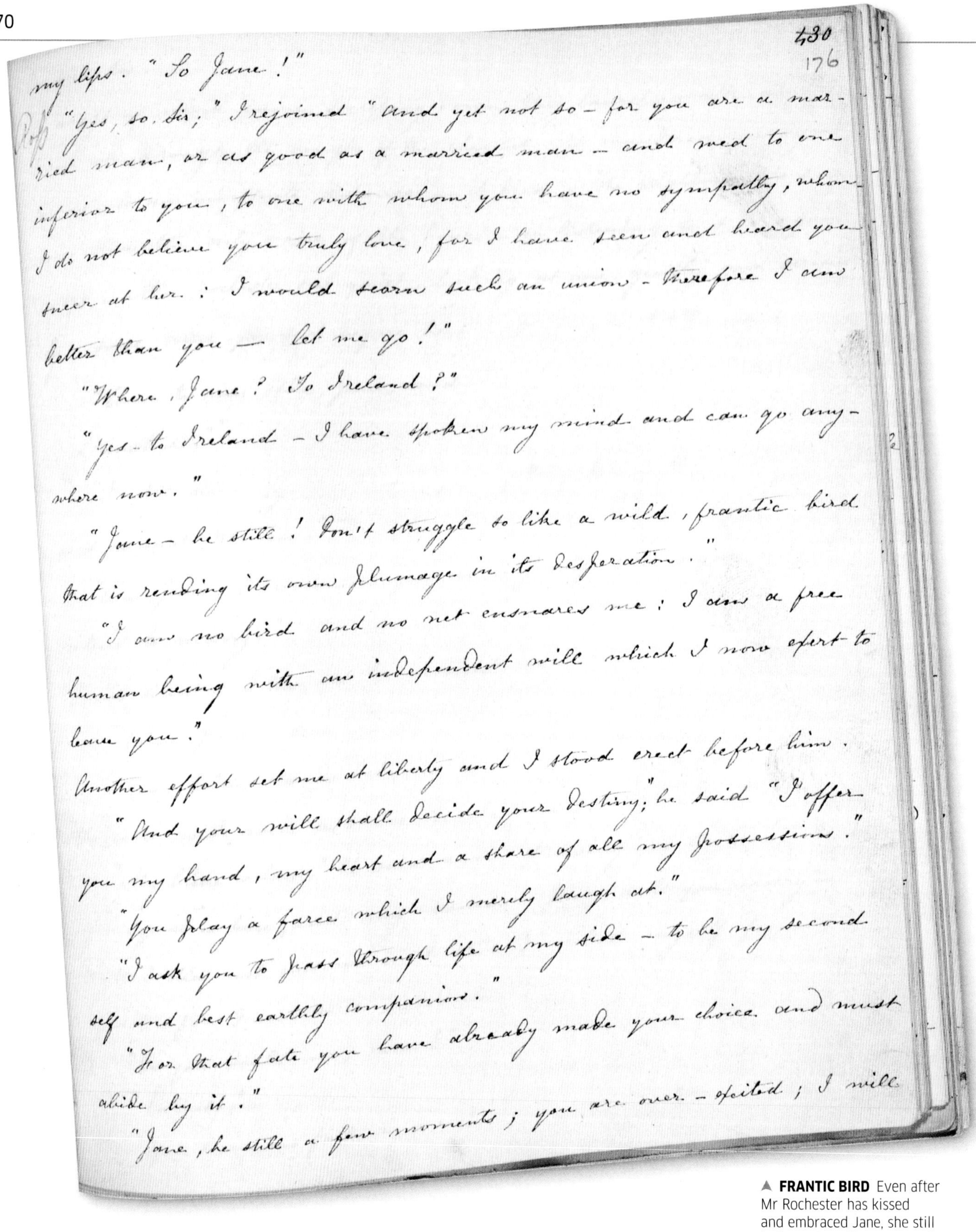

430
176

my lips. "So Jane!"

"Yes, so, Sir;" I rejoined "And yet not so – for you are a married man, or as good as a married man – and wed to one inferior to you, to one with whom you have no sympathy, whom I do not believe you truly love, for I have seen and heard you sneer at her: I would scorn such an union – therefore I am better than you — let me go!"

"Where, Jane? To Ireland?"

"Yes – to Ireland – I have spoken my mind and can go anywhere now."

"Jane – be still! Don't struggle so like a wild, frantic bird that is rending its own plumage in its desperation."

"I am no bird and no net ensnares me: I am a free human being with an independent will which I now exert to leave you."

Another effort set me at liberty and I stood erect before him.

"And your will shall decide your destiny," he said "I offer you my hand, my heart and a share of all my possessions."

"You play a farce which I merely laugh at."

"I ask you to pass through life at my side – to be my second self and best earthly companion."

"For that fate you have already made your choice, and must abide by it."

"Jane, be still a few moments; you are over-excited; I will

> 'Jane, be still; don't struggle so, like a wild, frantic bird that is rending its own plumage in its desperation.' 'I am no bird, and no net ensnares me: I am a free human being with an independent will; which I now exert to leave you.' Another effort set me at liberty, and I stood erect before him. 'And your will shall decide your destiny,' he said: 'I offer you my hand, my heart, and a share of all my possessions.' 'You play a farce, which I merely laugh at.'
> "

JANE EYRE, CHAPTER 23

▲ **FRANTIC BIRD** Even after Mr Rochester has kissed and embraced Jane, she still believes he will marry another woman. He tells her that she is struggling in his arms "like a wild, frantic bird" and she retorts that she is no trapped bird, but "a free human being with an independent will". Even when he offers her his heart and hand, she cannot believe him.

Passionate and forthright, there had never been a narrator like Jane Eyre before. She often addresses the reader directly, sharing thoughts and feelings of which other characters in the novel are unaware. She takes us into her confidence. The novel's most famous sentence, "Reader, I married him", which begins the last chapter, is typical of this. Plain and neglected, Jane hungers for love and for freedom. The novel was indeed deplored by some contemporary critics because of its heroine's rebelliousness. Others, including fellow novelists, admired its original blend of blunt realism and fantastical, Gothic elements. These hark back to the elaborate tales of the imaginary lands of Gondal and Angria that Brontë and her sisters had composed in their youth.

Brontë, then 31, was unknown when the novel was published, but her unconventional love story rapidly became a bestseller. Her pseudonym, "Currer Bell", tantalized readers, and there was much speculation about her true identity. Brontë had hoped to remain anonymous, but had to reveal herself when Thomas Newby, the unscrupulous publisher of *Wuthering Heights* and *Agnes Grey*, also written under pseudonyms, tried to increase their sales by implying that they too had been written by the author of *Jane Eyre*. Despite her reluctance, she became a literary celebrity, but the years that followed were marked by tragedy. Her brother Branwell died at the age of 31, and within a year, her sisters Emily and Anne both died of tuberculosis. Charlotte wrote two more novels – *Shirley* (1849) and then *Villette* (1853). The year after *Villette*'s publication, Charlotte married Arthur Nicholls, her father's former curate. The marriage was happy but short-lived: weakened by pregnancy, she died less than a year later.

▲ **INSPIRATION FOR THORNFIELD HALL** "It was three storeys high, of proportions not vast, though considerable: a gentleman's manor-house, not a nobleman's seat: battlements round the top gave it a picturesque look". Thornfield was probably based on North Lees Hall, near Hathersage, in Derbyshire. Charlotte Brontë knew this well from her visits to her closest friend, Ellen Nussey, who lived in Hathersage.

◄ **BERTHA ROCHESTER** On the point of marrying Mr Rochester, Jane finds out his secret. His wife, Bertha, depicted here by Edmund Henry Garrett, lives confined in rooms on the third storey of Thornfield. Rochester met her, as Bertha Mason, in Jamaica, and married her for her beauty and wealth, not knowing about the mental instability that ran in her family.

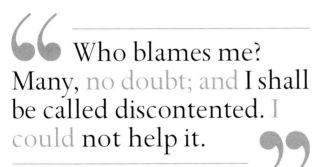

> " Who blames me? Many, no doubt; and I shall be called discontented. I could not help it. "

JANE EYRE, CHAPTER 12

THE **BRONTË FAMILY**

Charlotte Brontë's family history seems tragic, yet her family was also her source of inspiration and encouragement. Her Aunt Branwell, who moved in after Charlotte's mother died, was intelligent and well-read, while Patrick Brontë, although a stern father, was highly educated: both encouraged the bookish interests of his daughters.

From childhood onwards, Charlotte wrote in collaboration and friendly competition with her siblings, including her brother Branwell. Charlotte's first publication was a family one: in 1846, she, Anne, and Emily published a collection of their poems, under the pseudonyms (Acton, Currer, and Ellis Bell) that they later used for their novels. Public awareness of the three sisters as an extraordinary creative group spread rapidly after the publication of Charlotte's "Biographical notice" at the front of the 1850 double-edition of *Wuthering Heights* (written by Emily) and *Agnes Grey* (written by Anne). This gave a vivid picture of the three working alongside each other, sharing their love of reading and their literary ambitions. "We had very early cherished the dream of one day becoming authors."

▶ **This group portrait,** painted by their brother Branwell (whose image has been erased), shows, from left to right, Anne, Emily, and Charlotte Brontë.

Wuthering Heights

1847 ■ 288 PAGES ■ UK

EMILY BRONTË (1818–1848)

"It is moorish, and wild, and knotty as a root of heath." This is how Charlotte Brontë described *Wuthering Heights* in the Biographical Notice that she wrote after her sister Emily's death at the age of just 30, a year after the book's publication. It was Emily Brontë's only novel, although she also wrote a number of powerful, lyrical poems. She spent almost her whole life in Haworth, Yorkshire, eventually taking up many of a housekeeper's duties at her family home, having spent only brief periods away at school, and a short and unhappy time working as a teacher in Halifax. From the dialect spoken by some of the characters to the telling details of weather and of the natural world, this is a novel rooted in a particular setting, inspired by the moorland near her home.

For all the novel's wildness, the narrative structure of *Wuthering Heights* is elaborate and skilfully handled. It opens in 1801, with the narration of Mr Lockwood, who has rented the isolated mansion of Thrushcross Grange. He visits his landlord, Heathcliff, who lives up on the moors at the even more remote hill farm of Wuthering Heights. Lockwood is then given the history of Wuthering Heights by his housekeeper, Nelly Dean. Her narrative takes us back over the preceding three decades to tell a story of bitter rivalries and thwarted passions.

Heathcliff was a foundling child, whom Mr Earnshaw brought to Wuthering Heights. He grew to love Earnshaw's daughter, Catherine, but was treated brutally by his jealous son, Hindley. The Earnshaws become entangled with another family, the Lintons, who were the original owners of Thrushcross Grange. Entranced by their more refined existence, Catherine marries Edgar Linton – and in a scheme of vengeance, Heathcliff wins the heart of Edgar's sister, Isabella. The clashes between these characters are violent and destructive. However, Brontë takes the narrative forward from Lockwood's arrival, to see how a younger generation, Hindley's son Hareton and Catherine's daughter, named after her, are able to escape the furies of an older generation.

In context

▲ **TOP WITHENS** This ruined farmhouse on the moors above Haworth is said to have been the inspiration for Wuthering Heights. Dating from the 16th century, it was still inhabited in the Brontës' day. It bears little resemblance to the house that Lockwood describes in the novel, but its age, remoteness, and exposed situation do match those of Wuthering Heights.

▶ **EMILY BRONTË'S DIARY** Drawn by Emily at the age of 18, this sketch in her diary shows her working at a table opposite her sister Anne, who was then 17 (they are labelled "Anne" and "Emily"). Her entry for 26 June 1837 records that Charlotte is "working" in her aunt's room, while Anne is writing a poem. Emily herself is writing a story about Gondal – an imaginary island, whose history the sisters chronicled.

HEATHCLIFF Depicted here by Clare Leighton in 1931, Heathcliff is one of the most extraordinary characters in all Victorian fiction. Passionate, scornful, and, above all, vengeful, he has what Nelly Dean calls a "violent nature". After being humiliated by Hindley Earnshaw and rejected by Catherine, he leaves Wuthering Heights, only to return three years later, mysteriously affluent, to wreak his revenge.

THE **SUPERNATURAL**

"I have a strong faith in ghosts; I have a conviction that they can, and do, exist among us!" Heathcliff exclaims to Nelly Dean. Several of the characters in *Wuthering Heights*, haunted as they are by the past, seem to share Heathcliff's faith. Brontë uses the supernatural to dramatize her characters' fears and desires, but leaves the reader free to find "natural" explanations for the book's stranger events.

In the opening episode, the unimaginative narrator, Lockwood, has a ghostly vision that may be a nightmare. Likewise, the novel ends with him refusing to believe a shepherd boy's report that he has seen the ghosts of Heathcliff and Cathy out on the moors.

▲ *The Apparition (1942),* by Fritz Eichenberg, shows Lockwood seeing Cathy's ghost at his window.

> ❝ 'My great miseries in this world have been Heathcliff's miseries, and I watched and felt each from the beginning: my great thought in living is himself. If all else perished, and *he* remained, I should still continue to be; and if all else remained, and he were annihilated, the universe would turn to a mighty stranger: I should not seem a part of it. – My love for Linton is like the foliage in the woods: time will change it, I'm well aware, as winter changes the trees. My love for Heathcliff resembles the eternal rocks beneath: a source of little visible delight, but necessary. Nelly, I *am* Heathcliff! He's always, always in my mind: not as a pleasure, any more than I am always a pleasure to myself, but as my own being. So don't talk of our separation again: it is impracticable; and –' She paused, and hid her face in the folds of my gown; but I jerked it forcibly away. I was out of patience with her folly! ❞

WUTHERING HEIGHTS, CHAPTER 9

Moby-Dick

1851 ▪ 635 PAGES ▪ US

HERMAN MELVILLE (1819–1891)

Opening with one of the most famous lines in the history of the novel, "Call me Ishmael", *Moby-Dick* follows the adventures of a wandering seaman who joins the crew of the *Pequod*, a whaling ship. Its enigmatic captain, Ahab, is set upon a quest for personal vengeance against a white whale that had bitten off his leg in the past. Ishmael recounts meeting a Polynesian harpooner, Queequeg, in New Bedford, an important whaling centre on the east coast of the US, before the voyage began.

Ishmael and Queequeg cement their friendship after sharing a bed on a freezing night, and then join the crew of the *Pequod*, which is composed of singular characters, ranging from the American First Mate, Starbuck, to harpooners of various nationalities, including Daggoo, an African, and Tashtego, a Native American. Captain Ahab himself, named after a wicked king in the Old Testament, stands in the shadows in the opening chapters. His appearance on deck unites much of the crew in his pursuit of the legendary whale, Moby Dick. The voyage becomes Ahab's journey of obsession, and the unfolding drama includes stories about the white whale itself, accounts of catching and slaughtering other whales (a more common practice at the time than today), encounters with other ships (both friendly and not), and the everyday work of seamen aboard a 19th-century whaling ship.

After his first book, *Typee,* was published in 1846, Herman Melville became a popular and successful writer of exotic, fictionalized travel stories based on his own experiences as a sailor. In the years leading up to *Moby-Dick*, however, Melville became increasingly frustrated with the demands of his publishers, who wanted him to keep producing more of the same kind of material. As a result, his writing became increasingly philosophical and wide-ranging, as he tried to combine his need to write a compelling story with his desire to take a deeper look at what made the world work.

STORIES OF VENGEFUL WHALES

Moby-Dick is a remarkable feat of literary imagination, but it was also inspired by several real-life cases of vengeful whales. One legendary whale, an albino sperm whale named Mocha Dick, developed a reputation for attacking ships off the coast of Chile, and in 1839 became the subject of an article by J.N. Reynolds entitled "Mocha Dick: or the White Whale of the Pacific: A Leaf from a Manuscript Journal". Melville read the article, which appeared in the New York monthly magazine *The Knickerbocker*. He also drew on a book called *Narrative of the Most Extraordinary and Distressing Shipwreck of the Whale-Ship Essex* (1821), by Owen Chase, which described the sinking of a whaling ship by an irate sperm whale off the coast of South America.

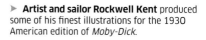
► **Artist and sailor Rockwell Kent** produced some of his finest illustrations for the 1930 American edition of *Moby-Dick*.

► **HUNTING THE WHALE**
Melville had his own personal experience of whaling ships, which were a profitable part of the American economy in the 19th century. He drew on his knowledge to provide a vivid portrait of life on board the *Pequod*, from harpooning whales to how they were butchered. This 1875 painting by French sailor Ambroise Louis Garneray depicts a whaling boat being destroyed by a sperm whale.

66 I'll chase him round Good Hope, and round the Horn...
and round perdition's flames before I give him up. 99

MOBY-DICK, CHAPTER 36

Moby-Dick is an encyclopaedic book, drawing on a wide range of historical, scientific, and fictional sources, many of which are listed in the "Extracts" section at the beginning of the book. On one level, it is a straightforward adventure story that follows Captain Ahab on his quest to destroy a whale. However, it is also an exploration of the natural world, and Ishmael often interrupts the narrative to talk at length about biology, whales, and whaling.

The book also has a visionary aspect, often suggesting that surface appearances conceal a spiritual reality. Both Ishmael and Ahab reflect upon what is real and what is perceived, questioning the role of the mind, the senses, and their own experience. Melville's language is highly literary and draws on a range of styles, from everyday conversation to Shakespeare's soliloquies. He also captures the tone of idiosyncratic 17th-century writers such as Thomas Browne and Robert Burton, giving the narrative a rich, sonorous quality that is both modern and archaic. These elements of the novel have given it a forbidding reputation among readers – like the white whale for the crew of the *Pequod*, it can seem both inscrutable and monstrous.

Following the mixed reception of *Moby-Dick,* which was praised for its power and yet criticized for its excesses, Melville carried on writing novels and short stories, but to an increasingly unresponsive public. It was only in the 1920s, long after Melville's death, that his work was rediscovered and *Moby-Dick* became acknowledged as the finest book of one of America's greatest writers.

KEY CHARACTERS

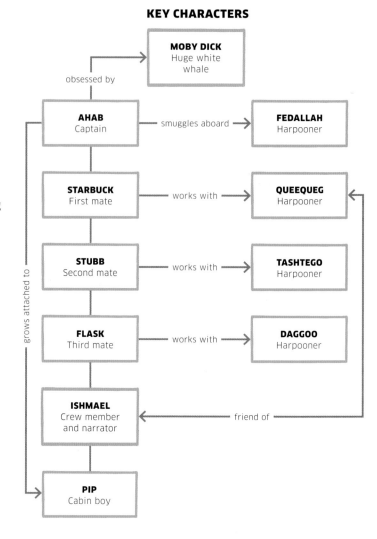

MOBY DICK — Huge white whale

obsessed by

AHAB — Captain — smuggles aboard → FEDALLAH — Harpooner

STARBUCK — First mate — works with → QUEEQUEG — Harpooner

STUBB — Second mate — works with → TASHTEGO — Harpooner

FLASK — Third mate — works with → DAGGOO — Harpooner

ISHMAEL — Crew member and narrator — friend of

grows attached to

PIP — Cabin boy

> " And then it was, that suddenly sweeping his sickle-shaped lower jaw beneath him, Moby Dick had reaped away Ahab's leg, as a mower a blade of grass in the field… Small reason was there to doubt, then, that ever since that almost fatal encounter, Ahab had cherished a wild vindictiveness against the whale, all the more fell for that in his frantic morbidness he at last came to identify with him, not only all his bodily woes, but all his intellectual and spiritual exasperations. The White Whale swam before him as the monomaniac incarnation of all those malicious agencies which some deep men feel eating in them, till they are left living on with half a heart and half a lung. "

MOBY-DICK, CHAPTER 41

MELVILLE'S CONTEMPORARIES

Melville was one of a generation of great American writers whose work has come to define 19th-century American literature. The poet Walt Whitman, the essayists Ralph Waldo Emerson and Henry David Thoreau, and storytellers such as Edgar Allan Poe and Nathaniel Hawthorne, all produced masterpieces that were of their time, yet also went beyond it. Some of these writers, notably Emerson, were associated with a literary and philosophical movement known as American Transcendentalism, which promoted an idealistic and intuitive approach to literature and life, rather than one based on materialism.

At around the time he wrote *Moby-Dick*, Melville struck up a close friendship and correspondence with Nathaniel Hawthorne, author of *The Scarlet Letter* (1850), drawn to both the man and what Melville saw as the darkness in his writing. On reading *Moby-Dick*, Hawthorne wrote to a friend: "What a book Melville has written! It gives me an idea of much greater power than his preceding ones".

▶ **The novelist Nathaniel Hawthorne,** a friend of Melville's, as portrayed by Charles Osgood in 1840

> 66 ... the hidden ways of the Sperm Whale when beneath the surface remain, in great part, unaccountable to his pursuers... 99

MOBY-DICK, CHAPTER 41

▲ PUBLISHING AGREEMENT This is the cover of a two-page contract between Melville and his American publishers, Harper & Brothers. It shows a last-minute change that Melville himself made to the book's title. "Moby Dick" appears as a note beside "The Whale", which was the original title of the book, and which was used for the first UK edition.

◄ FIRST US EDITION Melville's novel was first published in New York and London in 1851. The US edition, published by Harper & Brothers, had what may have been a mistake in the title. The whale is referred to as "Moby Dick" throughout the novel – a name that is only hyphenated once in the text, presumably by mistake. The UK edition, which was published by Richard Bentley, was simply entitled *The Whale*, and, owing to a printer's error, appeared without the final chapter in which Ishmael explains how he survived to tell the tale.

Madame Bovary

1857 ▪ 400 PAGES ▪ FRANCE

GUSTAVE FLAUBERT (1821–1880)

Madame Bovary was the first novel by Gustave Flaubert, a writer who became known for his dedication to an exacting literary style, in which the author's own beliefs and judgments cannot be detected. He began *Madame Bovary* after friends insisted that he apply his evident talent as a writer to a contemporary subject.

Flaubert, who was more interested in classical history and exotic settings, was initially reluctant, but he finally agreed to tackle the story of a provincial woman whose dreams lead her to descend into a downward spiral of debt, deception, and despair. *Madame Bovary* is set in Normandy, which Flaubert knew well, between the 1820s and 1840s. In a clinically detached style that is frequently unsettling, the narrative charts the struggles of a sensuous but also sadly self-deceiving young woman against suffocating bourgeois conventions.

The opening sections of the novel sketch the early life of Charles Bovary, a mediocre and unambitious provincial doctor. After meeting the beautiful daughter of a wealthy local farmer, he marries her, and the novel shifts attention to the aspirations and perceptions of his new wife, Emma. Bored by married life and frustrated by the limitations of her dull-witted husband, Emma hungers for the kinds of experience that she has read about in novels.

The first half of the book charts the mundane early years of Emma's disappointing marriage. It also describes her bedazzlement when she attends the ball of a local aristocrat; the birth of her child, Berthe; her initial foray into an affair with a young student named Léon; and her sudden repentance in a moment of seemingly religious transcendence when she believes she is dying. However, these are just a prelude to the unfolding drama of the second half of the novel, in which Emma embraces her desires and starts to live to the full, whatever the cost to herself.

THE **DETACHED NARRATOR**

Flaubert famously stated that "The artist must be in his work as God is in creation, invisible and all-powerful; one must sense him everywhere but never see him." Unlike Stendhal and Balzac, who often commented on what their characters did, and appeared to take an interest in what happened to them, Flaubert's narrator retains a detached distance.

Although in *Madame Bovary*, Flaubert refines the realist novelists' descriptive eye for detail, his innovation lies in the cool, dispassionate way in which he depicts his characters, and his celebrated method of counterpoint – he sets one image or dialogue alongside another to create a sense of irony. The clichés that Rodolphe trots out while seducing Emma, for example, are interleaved with the platitudes that local dignitaries use in their speeches. Juxtaposing the two ways of speaking highlights how contrived they both are. Flaubert does not use the narrator to tell the reader what to think, but uses his style of writing to convey his opinion more subtly.

▶ **This realist** painting by James Tissot depicts a scene similar to that in which Léon takes Emma for a carriage ride.

> Emma was like all his mistresses; and the charm of novelty, gradually falling away like a garment, laid bare the eternal monotony of passion, that has always the same forms and the same language. He did not distinguish, this man of so much experience, the difference of sentiment beneath the sameness of expression. Because lips libertine and venal had murmured such words to him, he believed but little in the candour of hers; exaggerated speeches hiding mediocre affections must be discounted; as if the fullness of the soul did not sometimes overflow in the emptiest metaphors...

MADAME BOVARY,
CHAPTER 12

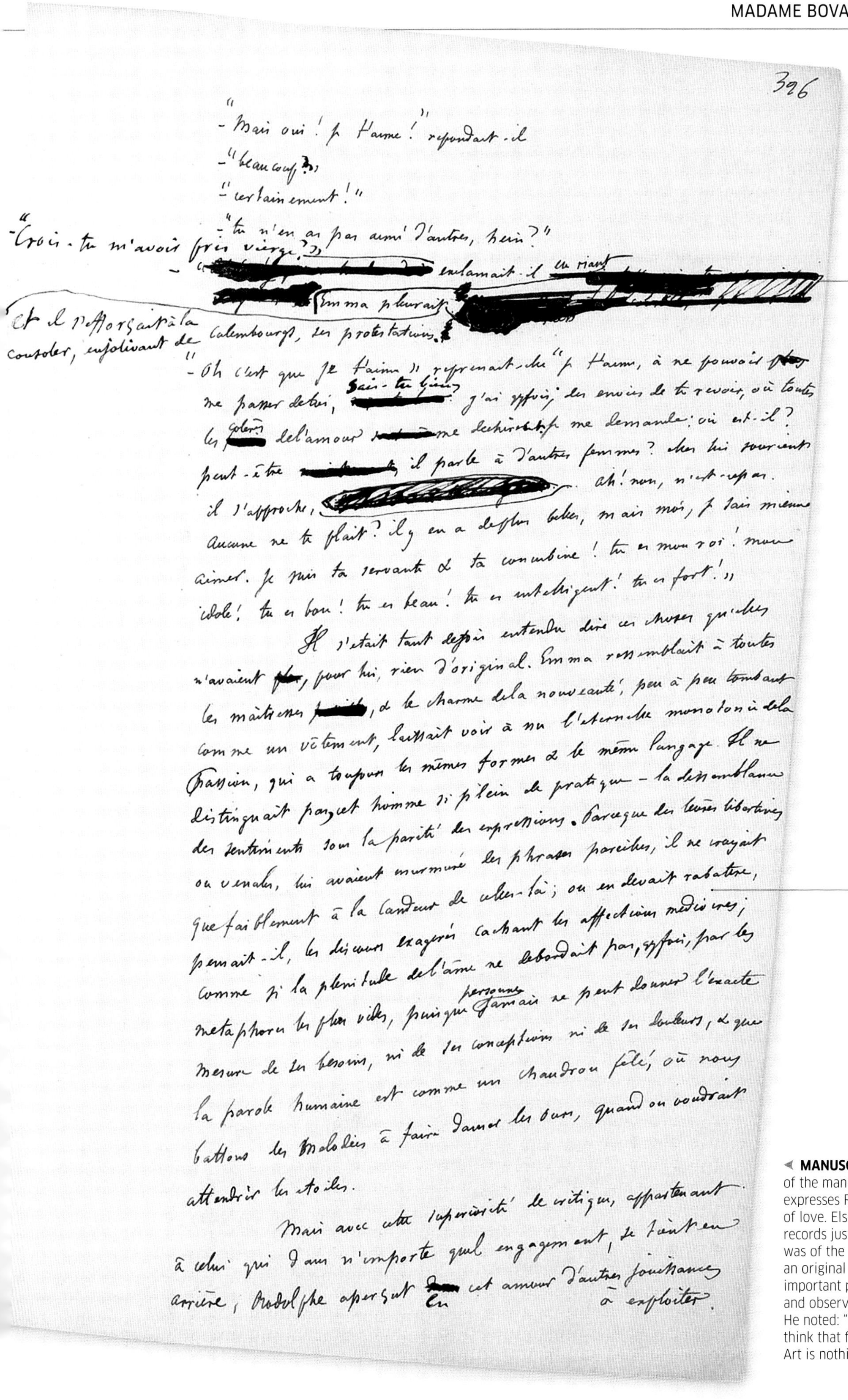

326

"– Mais oui ! je t'aime !" répondait-il

– "beaucoup ?"

– "certainement !"

– "tu n'en as pas aimé d'autres, hein ?"

"Crois-tu m'avoir prise vierge ?" exclamait-il en riant

Emma pleurait, et il s'efforçait à la consoler, enjolivant de calembours ses protestations.

"– Oh ! c'est que je t'aime" reprenait-elle "je t'aime, à ne pouvoir me passer de toi, sais-tu bien ? j'ai parfois des envies de te revoir, où toutes les colères de l'amour me déchirent. je me demande : où est-il ? peut-être il parle à d'autres femmes ? elles lui sourient, il s'approche, ah ! non, n'est-ce pas. aucune ne te plaît ? il y en a de plus belles, mais moi, je sais mieux aimer. Je suis ta servante & ta concubine ! tu es mon roi ! mon idole ! tu es bon ! tu es beau ! tu es intelligent ! tu es fort !"

Il s'était tant de fois entendu dire ces choses qu'elles n'avaient pour lui, rien d'original. Emma ressemblait à toutes les maîtresses ; & le charme de la nouveauté, peu à peu tombant comme un vêtement, laissait voir à nu l'éternelle monotonie de la passion, qui a toujours les mêmes formes & le même langage. Il ne distinguait pas, cet homme si plein de pratique, la dissemblance des sentiments sous la parité des expressions. Parce que des lèvres libertines ou vénales lui avaient murmuré des phrases pareilles, il ne croyait que faiblement à la candeur de celles-là ; on en devait rabattre, pensait-il, les discours exagérés cachant les affections médiocres ; comme si la plénitude de l'âme ne débordait pas, parfois, par les métaphores les plus vides, puisque personne jamais ne peut donner l'exacte mesure de ses besoins, ni de ses conceptions ni de ses douleurs, & que la parole humaine est comme un chaudron fêlé où nous battons des mélodies à faire danser les ours, quand on voudrait attendrir les étoiles.

Mais avec cette supériorité de critique, appartenant à celui qui dans n'importe quel engagement, se tient en arrière, Rodolphe aperçut en cet amour d'autres jouissances à exploiter.

Flaubert wrote and rewrote 4,561 pages of manuscript to produce the 400 pages of the finished novel

The manuscript reveals Flaubert's attention to detail and mastery of rhythmic language

◀ **MANUSCRIPT** In this part of the manuscript, the narrator expresses Rodolphe's jaded view of love. Elsewhere, Flaubert records just how aware he was of the challenge of finding an original way to convey important personal thoughts and observations to the reader. He noted: "One must not always think that feeling is everything. Art is nothing without form".

◄ **BOURGEOIS SOCIAL STATUS** In the 19th century, securing middle-class status was an obsession for many Europeans. In France, as elsewhere, status was shown by acquiring and displaying fashionable goods. Emma, portrayed here by Albert Fourie in 1885, embraces a lavish lifestyle, but soon falls into debt.

▲ **ROUEN** As the capital of Normandy, Rouen, pictured here by J.M.W. Turner in 1834, is the equivalent of Paris for Emma. It is where she and Léon meet at a night at the Opera, and is the setting for one of the novel's most famous sequences: a black horse and carriage is seen crisscrossing the streets of the city as it carries Léon and Emma in the throes of passion.

> " So at last she was to know those joys of love, that fever of happiness of which she had despaired! "
>
> *MADAME BOVARY*, CHAPTER 9

◄ **THE INFLUENCE OF NOVELS**
Emma reads a variety of French and English novels that shape her view of the world. Indeed, the very language of these works alters how she sees things. The novelist Vladimir Nabokov noted that Emma's fate is sealed less by what she reads than by the fact that she is a poor reader, unable to distinguish weaknesses and excesses of literary style. Georges Croegaert's painting *Reading* (1890) captures the abandon of novel-reading in Flaubert's time.

Emma's love affairs make up much of the plot of *Madame Bovary*, and Flaubert's language makes it clear that Emma's romantic ideas, which she believes to be exceptional, are in fact all too conventional. Nevertheless, we are invited to sympathize with Emma's yearnings for something beyond the banality of bourgeois life. Her plight is accentuated by the gallery of small-town characters who shape her life. These include Monsieur Homais, a purveyor of medicines and poisons, and Monsieur Lheureux, who sells luxury items from the finest boutiques, and is eager to ensnare clients in a web of credit. *Madame Bovary* closely observes the language and sometimes absurd customs of provincial life. The subtitle of the book is *"Mœurs de province"* (Provincial manners), and these manners are revealed in a series of grotesquely comic scenes that display the self-interested aspirations and behaviour of the characters.

With detached irony, Flaubert relishes showing the limits of Charles Bovary's abilities, as he botches a medical operation that Emma and Monsieur Homais have encouraged him to perform – she in an attempt to boost her husband's standing, and Homais to promote the reputation of the town. Meanwhile, the novel outlines the main drama of Emma's affair with a local cad named Rodolphe. Having been deceived from the start by this experienced and cynical seducer, Emma is abandoned once again and loses hope, until she re-encounters her now more worldly former lover Léon, leading the novel to its tragic conclusion.

In *Madame Bovary*, Flaubert painted a detailed portrait of 19th-century French provincial life, which he claimed to despise for all its commonplace pettiness and squalor. Yet his descriptions of that life – its weddings, balls, and country fairs, its self-satisfied citizens and self-important priests and doctors – are vividly observed as well as satirical. Flaubert's minor characters give us the sense of a whole society, various and alive even in its prejudices. In the person of Emma Bovary, he created a protagonist who, by design, provokes contradictory responses in the reader. As her impossible dreams give way to tragic reality, we sympathize with her desperation and yet flinch at her deludedness.

THE **OBSCENITY TRIAL**

The *Revue de Paris* serialized *Madame Bovary* in late 1856, and as a result was put on trial for obscenity in January 1857. Later the same year, Charles Baudelaire was also taken to court over his collection of poetry *Les Fleurs du Mal*. Although some of Baudelaire's verse was judged obscene, *Madame Bovary* escaped prosecution after a brief trial. The prosecutor, Ernest Pinard, stated that the novel was an "offence to public and religious morality and to good morals", arguing that it encouraged adulterous conduct while ridiculing the established pillars of bourgeois society. The defence countered that Emma's fate ruled out such a reading. The notoriety created by the trial undoubtedly contributed to the novel's success.

▲ **An 1885 illustration** by Albert Fourie depicts Emma dressing, usually a private moment.

Dickens's writing was very small, so the printer had to be adept at deciphering it

▲ **MANUSCRIPT** Dickens never made fair copies of the manuscripts of his novels: this is the copy that went to the printer. Once he had finished an instalment, it was despatched there, even though he had not yet written the novel's future instalments. Dickens's friend, Chauncey Hare Townshend, gave this manuscript to the Wisbech and Fenland Museum.

The page is dense with corrections. Dickens wrote at great speed, but revised minutely as he went along

Great Expectations

1861 ▪ 544 PAGES ▪ UK

CHARLES DICKENS (1812–1870)

Great Expectations was first published in instalments in Dickens's weekly journal *All the Year Round*. It was only the second of his novels (after *David Copperfield*) to be written entirely in the first person. Its protagonist, Pip, is an orphan who has been brought up by his harsh, ill-natured sister and her kindly husband, Joe Gargery, who is a blacksmith. Pip's story begins with one of the most arresting opening chapters in all fiction. On "a memorable raw afternoon towards evening", he is visiting the churchyard at the edge of the marshes where his parents and five dead brothers are buried, when an escaped convict confronts him. He helps the man with food and a file to remove his leg iron, little knowing how much the encounter will shape his life.

Years pass, and Pip becomes obsessed with the idea of bettering himself. An opportunity seems to present itself when he begins to be cultivated by the wealthy recluse, Miss Havisham, who lives with her ward, Estella, in Satis House. Oblivious to the affection of Biddy, a local girl, Pip grows to love Estella, who is beautiful but cold-hearted. He also meets Herbert Pocket, a boy his own age, who is related to Miss Havisham. Pip becomes Joe's apprentice at the blacksmith's forge, but Mr Jaggers, an intimidating London lawyer, arrives to tell him that a nameless patron has provided money for him to move to London and learn to live like a "gentleman". Meanwhile, Mrs Joe is injured by a mysterious assailant, and Biddy moves into their home to look after her. Pip leaves them all for London, and what he thinks will be a brighter future. Yet his aspirations will be frustrated, as the past, in the form of the convict, Magwitch, returns to claim him.

> ❝ 'Hold your noise!' cried a terrible voice, as a man started up from among the graves at the side of the church porch. 'Keep still, you little devil, or I'll cut your throat!' A fearful man, all in coarse grey, with a great iron on his leg. A man with no hat, and with broken shoes, and with an old rag tied round his head. A man who had been soaked in water, and smothered in mud, and lamed by stones, and cut by flints, and stung by nettles, and torn by briars; who limped, and shivered, and glared, and growled; and whose teeth chattered in his head as he seized me by the chin. ❞

GREAT EXPECTATIONS, CHAPTER 1

In context

▲ **HAUNTING MARSHES** "Ours was the marsh country, down by the river", Pip tells us, in the opening chapter of the novel. Dickens based the haunting landscape on the North Kent marshes near what had been his own childhood home, in Chatham, on the River Medway. He lived there between the ages of 5 and 10.

▲ **NEWGATE PRISON** Pip feels unable to escape the "taint of crime". Mr Jaggers, the lawyer who looks after him when he goes to London, deals with criminals and has premises conveniently close to the walls of Newgate Prison, shown here in an 1888 engraving. Jaggers' clerk, Wemmick, takes Pip to Newgate, to meet his many "clients".

KEY CHARACTERS

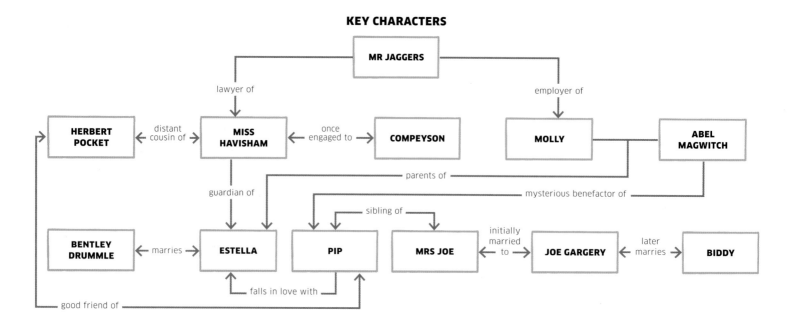

The special quality of Pip's narration comes from the regret and self-criticism with which he recalls his past. His life of "great expectations" has been one of self-delusion. Dickens gives us a painful sense of Pip's failure to understand the feelings of those who really love him – Biddy and Joe. Thinking that he is better than Joe, an illiterate working man, Pip behaves condescendingly towards him. When Estella, destined to break his heart, gets married, Pip realizes that he should have chosen Biddy. He returns to tell her so, only to find that she has married Joe, who became a single man after Mrs Joe's death.

Although *Great Expectations* is sometimes melancholy, Dickens's art is to mingle comedy with darkness. Pip's life is influenced by absurd as well as frightening characters. There is the ridiculous parish clerk, Mr Wopsle, who has theatrical ambitions, and reappears in London as a hilariously bad Shakespearean actor, and the fatuously self-important Mr Pumblechook, a local corn chandler, who bullies the young Pip, and then insists on befriending him once Pip has come into money. Later, Wemmick, Mr Jaggers's worldly clerk, becomes Pip's comic as well as pragmatic guide to the ways of the city. Each character also has their own distinctive way of speaking, which is often highly comic.

Dickens originally gave the novel an unhappy ending, in which Pip, now older and wiser, meets Estella again, but only to part from her for ever. Estella's first husband, the brutish Bentley Drummle, has been killed by a horse that he was mistreating, and Estella has married again. Pip himself remains single. However, Dickens's friend Bulwer Lytton, a far lesser novelist, persuaded him that this ending would outrage his loyal readers. Dickens followed Lytton's advice and wrote a new ending – the only one that was ever published – in which Pip and Estella, now a widow, meet again in the ruins of Satis House. This time, in an equivocal phrase, Pip sees "the shadow of no parting from her".

DICKENS'S OTHER WORKS

Dickens began his first novel, *The Pickwick Papers*, in 1836, when he was 24 years old. It was soon followed by *Oliver Twist* and then *Nicholas Nickleby*, which were hugely popular. By the time he was 30, he had completed two more, *The Old Curiosity Shop* and *Barnaby Rudge*, and had established himself as the bestselling novelist of the age.

In total, Dickens wrote 15 novels and one novella, *A Christmas Carol*. Each novel was written and first published in serial form – some, such as *David Copperfield* and *Bleak House*, monthly and others, such as *A Tale of Two Cities* and *Great Expectations*, weekly. He was just halfway through his last novel, *The Mystery of Edwin Drood*, when he died in 1870. Dickens also wrote travel books, short stories, comic "sketches", and a great deal of journalism. Under the pseudonym "Boz", he wrote numerous articles about life in England, including "A Visit to Newgate", describing the horrors of Newgate Prison, which also features in *Great Expectations*.

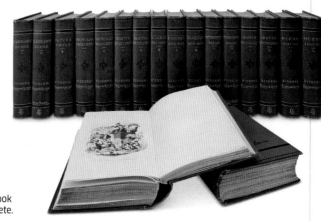

▶ **All of Dickens's novels** were published in book form soon after their magazine runs were complete.

▲ **MISS HAVISHAM** For much of the novel, Pip believes that his benefactor is the rich and reclusive Miss Havisham. Abandoned on her wedding day by the man she was going to marry, she still wears her wedding dress in bitter memory of the fact. She has not allowed anything in her house to be changed since that day. She was portrayed by Helena Bonham Carter (above) in the 2012 film of the book.

> 'The marriage day was fixed, the wedding dresses were bought, the wedding tour was planned out, the wedding guests were invited. The day came, but not the bridegroom. He wrote her a letter –' 'Which she received,' I struck in, 'when she was dressing for her marriage? At twenty minutes to nine?' 'At the hour and minute,' said Herbert, nodding, 'at which she afterwards stopped all the clocks… When she recovered from a bad illness that she had, she laid the whole place waste, as you have seen it, and she has never since looked upon the light of day.'

GREAT EXPECTATIONS, CHAPTER 22

Dickens wrote two to four pages, or "slips", each day, using a goose-quill pen and blue ink

▶ **MANUSCRIPT** In this passage of the novel, Herbert Pocket tells Pip Miss Havisham's story. She was deserted on her wedding day by the man she loved, who was in league with her own half-brother to trick her out of her money. This man, Compeyson, a "gentleman" con man, turns out to have an important role in the novel, as Magwitch's former accomplice and now deadly enemy.

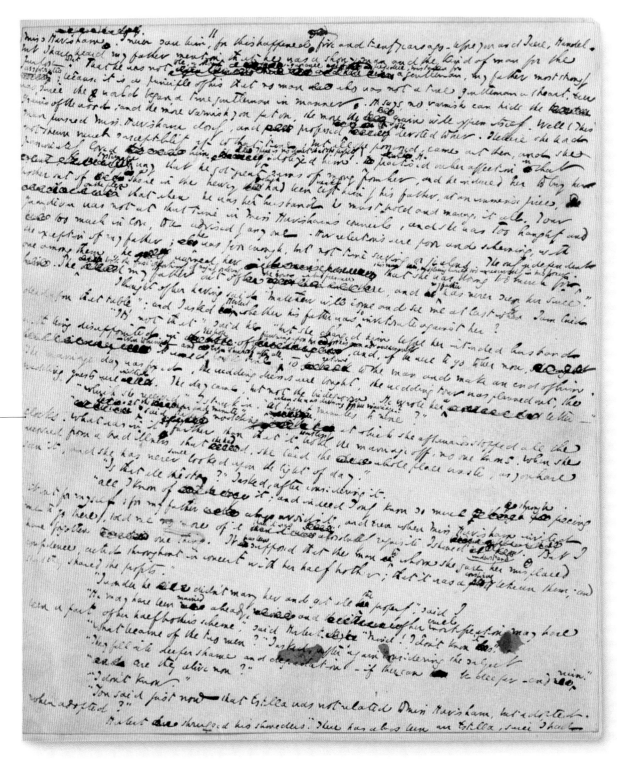

The name "Lizaveta" appears in the margin, several times, showing that Dostoevsky was working on the character who would become Raskolnikov's second victim

Dostoevsky's handwriting ranges from indecipherable scratch marks to elegant calligraphy

> Here a strange thought came into his head: perhaps all his clothes were covered with blood, perhaps there were stains all over them, and he simply did not see, did not notice them, because his reason was failing, going to pieces... Suddenly he remembered that there was also blood on the purse. 'Bah! So then there must be blood inside the pocket as well, because the purse was still wet when I put it in my pocket!' He instantly turned the pocket out and, sure enough, there were traces, stains on the lining.

CRIME AND PUNISHMENT, PART 2, CHAPTER 1

Crime and Punishment

1866 ▪ TWO VOLUMES ▪ RUSSIA

FYODOR DOSTOEVSKY (1821–1881)

True to its title, *Crime and Punishment* is about a crime – the murder of two women in the Russian tzarist capital, St Petersburg, and the events that follow, including the murderer's eventual confession and punishment. The murderer is Rodion Raskolnikov, a young man from a genteel but impoverished family. A law student until recently, he cannot afford to continue his studies and now lives in dire poverty, so he resolves to kill a rich pawnbroker, a widow named Alyona Ivanovna, for her money. When her half-sister, the good-hearted Lizaveta, arrives shortly after the murder, he feels "obliged" to kill her too.

Raskolnikov is a character of contradictions – cruel, arrogant, and wilful, and yet capable of compassion and tenderness. He justifies his crime on "rational" grounds, stating that his life is more valuable than that of a grasping pawnbroker. He even compares himself to Napoleon, who in his eyes "transcends" conventional morality. He convinces himself that the old woman's money should be his, because he will use it to better ends, but after the murders, he fails to take it. Instead, having brutally axed two women to death, he falls into deep despair, which ultimately leads to his change of heart and redemption.

The novel is written in the third person, mostly from Raskolnikov's point of view, but it includes a host of other characters, including Raskolnikov's doting mother and sister,

▲ **HAYMARKET** Crowds throng St Petersburg's Haymarket in this painting by Alexander Bruloffo. In *Crime and Punishment*, many of Raskolnikov's feverish wanderings take him through the Haymarket, which is dominated by the baroque Cathedral of the Dormition of the Holy Virgin. The pillared guard house, in which Dostoevsky himself was detained in 1874, stands on the left.

his loyal friend Razumikhin, the shrewd police investigator Porfiry Petrovich, the corrupt landowner Svidrigailov, and Sonya, the daughter of an alcoholic. Sonya forms a counterbalance to Raskolnikov – her saintliness is undimmed by the fact that she works as a prostitute to provide for her stepmother and young half-siblings. Raskolnikov falls in love with her, and she becomes the means of his redemption.

In context

◀ **EXECUTION** This pamphlet illustration shows French murderer Pierre François Lacenaire and his associate, Victor Avril, being led to the guillotine in 1836. They had killed a transvestite bank clerk and his mother. At trial, an unrepentant Lacenaire tried to justify the crime as an act of social cleansing. The case intrigued Dostoevsky, and inspired the character of Raskolnikov.

◀ **ANNA DOSTOEVSKAYA** This photograph taken in 1878 captures the intense gaze of Dostoevsky's second wife, Anna. His first wife, Maria, had died in 1864. He and Anna met when she came to work for him as a stenographer while he was writing *Crime and Punishment*. She helped him to bring order to his life, including curbing his chronic gambling addiction.

NOTES AND DOODLES The doodles in Dostoevsky's notebooks are mostly of people's faces, details of Gothic church architecture (the neo-Gothic style was popular at the time), and leaves. Although the faces are not labelled, people have speculated about who they may represent. The doodles clearly helped Dostoevsky to visualize and form his characters.

This may be a sketch of Porfiry, the detective, who investigates Raskolnikov's crimes

" You see, I wanted to become a Napoleon, that's why I killed... Well, is it clear now? **"**

CRIME AND PUNISHMENT, PART 5, CHAPTER 4

Extreme as it is, *Crime and Punishment* draws on Dostoevsky's personal experiences, notably of some of the hardships that Raskolnikov faces in the novel. When he was a young man, his involvement with a left-wing circle in St Petersburg had led to his arrest, solitary confinement, mock execution, and eight years' exile in Siberia, including four years of hard labour. The experience of the labour camp – being shackled and pushed to the limits of human endurance, and living cheek by jowl with men from very different backgrounds to his own – changed him profoundly. He was also diagnosed with epilepsy while in Siberia. After reading and rereading the Gospels of the Bible, he underwent a religious conversion. When he returned to St Petersburg in 1859, he no longer aligned himself with the French-influenced socialism of his youth, and instead espoused a deeply Russian and Orthodox Christian way of life.

Crime and Punishment was the first great novel of Dostoevsky's later years. It appeared in monthly instalments in 1866, in the journal *Russky Vestnik (Russian Herald)*, at the same time that Tolstoy's *War and Peace* was being published in the magazine. Both novels received acclaim, and both would come to be regarded as great works of 19th-century literature. Arguably, however, *Crime and Punishment* had a greater literary impact. By closely following the tortuous workings of Raskolnikov's tormented mind, Dostoevsky opened up a whole new territory for the novel. The power of the book lies in its

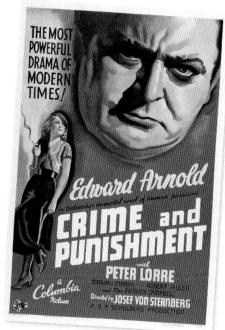

◀ **HOLLYWOOD ADAPTATION**
This poster advertises the 1935 Columbia Pictures adaptation of *Crime and Punishment*. Still widely regarded as the most compelling screen version of the novel, the film was directed by Josef von Sternberg, and starred Peter Lorre as Raskolnikov and Marian Marsh as Sonya.

depiction of what Dostoevsky once described as "the dark sides of the human soul that art does not like to approach". This, *Crime and Punishment* explores in depth. The list of the book's admirers starts with Dostoevsky's contemporary, Tolstoy, and continues with leading figures of 20th-century literature, including Hermann Hesse, James Joyce, Franz Kafka, Ernest Hemingway, and Albert Camus.

" Sonya glanced at him quickly. After her first passionate and tormented sympathy for the unhappy man, the horrible idea of the murder struck her again. In the changed tone of his words she suddenly could hear the murderer. She looked at him in amazement. As yet she knew nothing of why, or how, or for what it had been. Now all these questions flared up at once in her consciousness. And again she did not believe it: 'He, he a murderer? Is it really possible?' **"**

CRIME AND PUNISHMENT, PART 5, CHAPTER 4

DOSTOEVSKY'S OTHER WORKS

The young Dostoevsky first won literary fame with a novella, *Poor Folk*, published in 1846, but his best work dates from the 1860s and '70s. *Notes from the Dead House* (1862), his fictionalized account of his exile in Siberia, was followed by the novella *Notes from Underground* (1864). Then came the four great novels that underpin his reputation: *Crime and Punishment*, *The Idiot* (1868–69), *The Devils* (1871–72), and *The Brothers Karamazov* (1879–80), which was completed shortly before his death in 1881. Dostoevsky was also a prolific journalist, and edited two short-lived journals, *Time* and *Epoch*, with his brother Mikhail, in the 1860s, and *A Writer's Diary* in the 1870s.

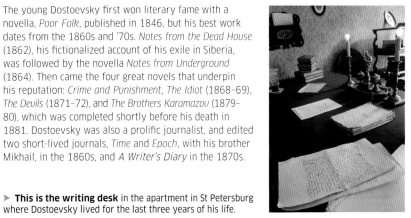

▶ **This is the writing desk** in the apartment in St Petersburg where Dostoevsky lived for the last three years of his life.

Directory: 1800–1870

INDIANA

GEORGE SAND, 1832

A romance published by French author Amantine-Aurore-Lucie Dupin (1804–76) under the masculine pseudonym George Sand, *Indiana* is recognized as a groundbreaking work in its assertion of a woman's right to independence. Written at a time when Sand had deserted her own husband to live a free life in Paris, the novel tells of a woman, Indiana, who makes a similar gesture of liberation, only to be rejected by Raymon, the callous libertine with whom she has fallen passionately in love.

At her lowest point of despair, she forms a suicide pact with her inexpressive English cousin, Ralph, who secretly loves her. Travelling to the French island of Réunion, in the Indian Ocean, they prepare to plunge to their deaths in a waterfall. With an unexpected ending, *Indiana* secured Sand's reputation, both as a novelist and as a cultural personality. The

book made an enduring statement of opposition to Black enslavement in the French colonies, and its impassioned tirades against France's patriarchal divorce laws were highly influential.

▼ DEAD SOULS

NIKOLAI GOGOL, 1842

Dead Souls is the masterpiece of Ukrainian-born Russian writer Nikolai Gogol (1809–52). The antihero of the novel, Chichikov, sets out to make his fortune by buying serfs ("souls") who have died, but have not yet been erased from the official register, and so can be exploited even after death. This corrupt money-making scheme takes him on a journey around Russia in which he encounters grotesque individuals brought vividly to life by Gogol's gift for verbal caricature.

When the book was first published, to great acclaim, it was naturally seen as an attack on the bureaucratic hell of Russia's Tsarist state and the

self-satisfied vulgarity of its landowning class, but Gogol's aim went far beyond social satire. He wanted to portray human life as a banal inferno, its "dead souls" threatened by the absurd and the surreal. Gogol worked on a sequel to *Dead Souls* for 10 years, but he destroyed the manuscript and then died by suicide at the age of 42, after starving himself.

THE COUNT OF MONTE CRISTO

ALEXANDRE DUMAS, 1844–45

The story of a man who is wrongfully imprisoned and escapes to wreak vengeance upon his persecutors, *The Count of Monte Cristo* is a popular Romantic historical novel. Written by French author Alexandre Dumas (1802–70), it is set in the period of monarchy in France that followed the fall of the Napoleonic Empire.

The sailor Edmond Dantès is the innocent victim of an intrigue that leads to his being incarcerated in the formidable Chateau d'If for 14 years. After a dramatic escape, Dantès transforms himself into the fabulously wealthy Count of Monte Cristo, and hunts down his enemies, now ensconced among the corrupt Parisian elite.

The plot twists are extravagant, featuring kidnaps and poisonings, hidden identities and unexpected revelations. Dumas gives the reader an entertaining cast of bandits, bankers, treacherous schemers, and alluring beauties. The book made his reputation as one of the most successful writers of his time, and its story has retained its power to grip the imagination.

VANITY FAIR

WILLIAM MAKEPEACE THACKERAY, 1847

Vanity Fair, subtitled "A Novel Without a Hero", is set in England's Regency period. English author William Makepeace Thackeray (1811–63)

introduces his story ironically, as a puppet show, and its puppeteer-narrator comments drily on the action as it unfolds. The book is filled with sharply drawn comic figures, but the star turn is the unscrupulous, amusing Becky Sharp, an orphan bent on making her way in society. Her clear-eyed cynicism and self-interested pragmatism contrast with the insipid virtue of her friend Amelia, whose passive naivety can lead only to victimhood in a world of exploitative men.

The perfectly handled plot draws readers irresistibly to identify with the characters and their fates, via historical set pieces that include a visit to the Vauxhall Pleasure Gardens and the Battle of Waterloo. Although love ultimately triumphs, and vice is seen to be punished, the book's moral universe is never so simple, and the corrupt society that it depicts is wholly convincing.

THE SCARLET LETTER

NATHANIEL HAWTHORNE, 1850

A dark, psychological drama of sin and redemption, *The Scarlet Letter* is played out in the repressive Puritan society of 17th-century Massachusetts. American author Nathaniel Hawthorne (1804–64), called his book "a Romance", to distinguish its blend of the real and the fantastic from the realism of novels. The protagonist, Hester Prynne, bears a child out of wedlock, but refuses to reveal who the father is. She is isolated from the community and forced to wear a letter A, for "Adultery", as the mark of her sin.

The book follows Hester's inner growth, and her encounters with the two men in her life – her estranged husband, Chillingworth, and the church minister Dimmesdale, who is the father of her child. At the climax of the story, when the tormented Dimmesdale finally admits his guilt, events verge on the supernatural. The character of Hester dominates the book – an epitome of spiritual strength drawn from adversity.

Chichikov, the antihero of *Dead Souls*, prepares for a day of scheming.

UNCLE TOM'S CABIN

HARRIET BEECHER STOWE, 1852

Few novels divide opinion as much as *Uncle Tom's Cabin*. Written by American anti-slavery campaigner Harriet Beecher Stowe (1811–96), it became the bestselling fictional work of the entire 19th century, but critics have denounced both its melodramatic narrative and its allegedly patronizing depiction of Black people.

Appearing at a time when the continuation of Black enslavement was the leading issue in American politics, *Uncle Tom's Cabin* sought to marshal Christian sentiment in favour of abolition. The saintly, enslaved Tom is a Christian who refuses to renounce his faith while undergoing martyrdom at the hands of brutal enslaver Simon Legree.

The religious theme might now seem heavy-handed, and the scene in which the angelic white girl Eva has a deathbed vision of heaven does not appeal to readers today, but the book's account of the realities of slavery, including sexual exploitation, is powerful and convincing. Its depiction of "kindly" slave-owners and their inevitable moral corruption adds a layer of subtlety to a necessarily stark moral picture.

NORTH AND SOUTH

ELIZABETH GASKELL, 1854–55

English novelist Elizabeth Gaskell (1810–65) took as her subject the new society that was being shaped by the Industrial Revolution in Victorian England. In *North and South*, she transports high-minded young Margaret Hale from the gentility of rural southern England to the northern mill town of Milton (a fictionalized Manchester). Appalled by the ugly factories and the poverty of the slums, Margaret engages with the workers in their struggle for better conditions. This brings her into conflict with the mill-owner John Thornton, a self-made man with rough manners.

The plot follows their love story, as, through numerous vicissitudes, they learn to respect each other and develop a lasting attachment. Gaskell's account of the workers' strike action is convincing, and her authentic

Cosette, a street urchin who is saved by Jean Valjean in *Les Misérables*

representation of northern patterns of speech adds freshness to the dialogue. Despite some plot contrivances designed to force the leading characters to recognize each other's virtues, it is both a psychologically convincing romance and a complex picture of social division.

THE WOMAN IN WHITE

WILKIE COLLINS, 1859

The Woman in White established the Victorian genre of the "sensation novel", from which the modern "thriller" was born. English author Wilkie Collins (1824–89) found mystery and terror in ordinary settings, such as a smart Surrey estate or a North London villa.

Young drawing teacher Walter Hartright, playing detective, confronts a mystery of swapped identities and illegitimate births. From Walter's first hallucinogenic moonlit encounter with the white-clad, distressed Anne Catherick, the reader is led into a spine-chilling world peopled by such memorable grotesques as the evil Sir Percival Glyde and the frighteningly charming Count Fosco. They conspire to defraud the beautiful, vulnerable Laura Fairlie of her inheritance, while she is defended by her resourceful half-sister, Marian Halcombe.

The narrative viewpoint changes cleverly from chapter to chapter as different characters present their version of events, like witnesses in a court of law. This narrative ingenuity has helped the novel to survive as a literary classic.

FATHERS AND SONS

IVAN TURGENEV, 1862

The masterpiece of Russian writer Ivan Turgenev (1818–83), *Fathers and Sons* was a novel written out of intense engagement with the problems of Russian society. Shortly before the abolition of serfdom, two young men, Arkady and Bazarov, equipped with advanced ideas, return from the city to their landowning families. A yawning generation gap separates them from their tradition-bound parents. Bazarov, the dominant personality of the two, is a medical student and self-proclaimed nihilist. A disturbed personality fuelled by anger and despair, he advocates a cynical materialism and absolute rejection of established society.

Set against the young men's radicalism, Turgenev presents a deftly drawn cast of rural characters and a lyrical evocation of the Russian countryside, suggesting complexities beyond the understanding of either man. Bazarov's cynicism is challenged by the experience of falling in love, while Arkady escapes his friend's influence and is reconciled to his society. Ultimately, the nature of Bazarov's death leaves all moral and political issues unresolved in a novel of exquisite subtlety.

◀ LES MISÉRABLES

VICTOR HUGO, 1862

The French Romantic poet, dramatist, and novelist Victor Hugo (1802–85) was endowed with the most Herculean energy. He wrote his massive novel *Les Misérables* while living on the Channel Islands as a political exile from Second-Empire France.

Set in the period between the fall of Napoleon in 1815 and the Paris uprising of 1832, it centres on the story of convict Jean Valjean, who struggles for redemption, and his pursuit by the obsessive police inspector Javert. The plot unfolds against a background of the sufferings and defiance of the Parisian poor.

About a third of the book consists of digressions, in which Hugo explores topics ranging from the Battle of Waterloo to the histories of convents and sewers. However, the book's ramshackle structure, daunting length, and improbable plot did not prevent it from being a runaway success when first published, the force of Hugo's creative energy trampling over all critical defences. A huge work of colossal ambition, *Les Misérables* has earned its status as a literary classic.

3

1870–1920

▼ **MULTIPLE VOLUMES** *Middlemarch* was originally published in eight "Books" (see below) over the course of a year, from December 1871 to December 1872. Each Book had its own title, and was itself the length of a short novel. Eliot adopted this form of publication partly to maximize sales, by allowing people to buy it in instalments, but also to let readers experience the complex narrative over a period of time.

> " One morning, some weeks after her arrival at Lowick, Dorothea – but why always Dorothea? Was her point of view the only possible one with regard to this marriage? I protest against all our interest, all our effort at understanding being given to the young skins that look blooming in spite of trouble; for these too will get faded, and will know the older and more eating griefs which we are helping to neglect.
>
> In spite of the blinking eyes and white moles objectionable to Celia, and the want of muscular curve which was morally painful to Sir James, Mr. Casaubon had an intense consciousness within him, and was spiritually a-hungered like the rest of us. He had done nothing exceptional in marrying – nothing but what society sanctions, and considers an occasion for wreaths and bouquets. "

***MIDDLEMARCH*, CHAPTER 29**

Middlemarch

1871-72 ▪ EIGHT VOLUMES ▪ UK

GEORGE ELIOT (1818-1880)

George Eliot's most complex novel is "A Study of Provincial Life", as its subtitle proclaims. It braids together the different, but connected, stories of many characters, to give a rich understanding of how a whole society, centred on the town of Middlemarch, functions. Minutely anatomizing its many characters' marriages, family quarrels, and professional fortunes, it shows how they cope with social and economic changes. (The novel is particularly astute about how characters manage to make or lose money.)

Eliot's two leading characters, Dorothea and Lydgate, are both idealists. Dorothea wants to use the money she has inherited to do good. Having rejected the marriage proposal of Sir James Chettam, a local squire, she is drawn to Edward Casaubon, whom she believes to be a man "whose work would reconcile complete knowledge with devoted piety". Alas! Casaubon is neither so brilliant nor so saintly. During the months after their marriage, Dorothea realizes that his supposed masterwork, "A Key to All Mythologies", is not only insignificant, it will never be completed. Lydgate, on the other hand, is a young doctor who arrives in Middlemarch with ideas about using the latest medical knowledge to improve the lives of its inhabitants.

THE **OMNISCIENT NARRATOR**

The narrator is always present in *Middlemarch*, sometimes speaking directly to the reader in the first person. Although she is often ironical, her voice seems to be that of George Eliot herself, reflecting sympathetically on the complexities of human psychology, as demonstrated by her characters. To give us a picture of a whole community, *Middlemarch* interweaves different stories and moves between different points of view. A famous example of this is the passage (quoted opposite) in which, while exploring Dorothea's feelings about her still-recent marriage, Eliot suddenly interrupts herself to ask: "Was her point of view the only possible one with regard to this marriage?" In *Middlemarch*, every character has their own "intense consciousness". Eliot seems to understand human nature well enough to know how the world looks through the eyes of each different character.

In order to put his ideas into practice, he has to enter into an uneasy alliance with the powerful local banker, Bulstrode. He is also compromised by love, and finds himself marrying the beautiful but spoilt Rosamond Vincy, whose material expectations he cannot meet. "Poor Lydgate! or shall I say, Poor Rosamond! Each lived in a world of which the other knew nothing." Eliot says this even as the two are falling in love with each other.

These are private dramas, intimately explored by Eliot, yet they take place under the eyes of neighbours and relations, in a novel in which no character can quite escape the opinions and the gossip that circulate in Middlemarch.

In context

◄ **VIEW OF COVENTRY**
Mary Ann Evans (Eliot's real name) was born in Warwickshire and went to schools in Nuneaton and Coventry. Later, she lived in Coventry, shown here in a contemporary painting, where she found a circle of progressive, intellectual friends. The society of *Middlemarch* is based on the Midlands world in which she grew up.

▲ **ARRIVAL OF THE RAILWAY** Although written and published at the beginning of the 1870s, *Middlemarch* is set some 40 years earlier. Late in the novel we hear that "one form of business which was beginning to breed just then was the construction of railways". Some of the characters are fearful of it, and hostile.

Chapter I.

5

Each chapter of the novel opens with an epigraph, or literary quotation

"Since I can do no good because a woman,
Reach constantly at something that is near it."

The Maid's Tragedy: Beaumont & Fletcher

Miss Brooke had that kind of beauty which seems to be thrown into relief by poor dress. Her hand & wrist were so finely formed that she could wear sleeves not less bare of style than those in which the Blessed Virgin appeared to Italian painters, & her profile as well as her stature & bearing seemed to gain the more dignity from her plain garments, which by the side of provincial fashion gave her the impressiveness of a fine quotation from the Bible, or from one of our elder poets, in a paragraph of today's newspaper. She was usually spoken of as being remarkably clever, but with the addition that her sister Celia had more common sense. Nevertheless, Celia wore scarcely more trimmings; Nor Miss Brooke's plain dressing was due to mixed conditions in most of which her sister shared. The pride of being ladies had something to do with it: the Brooke connexions though not exactly aristocratic, were unquestionably "good": if you inquired backward for a generation or two you would not find any yard-measuring or parcel-tying forefathers; nothing lower than an admiral or a clergyman; & there was even an ancestor discernible as a Puritan gentleman who served under Cromwell, but had afterwards conformed, & had managed to come out of all political troubles as the proprietor of a respectable family estate. Young women of such birth, living in a quiet country town,

& it was only to close observers that her dress differed from her sister's, & had a shade of coquetry in its arrangements

Eliot adds subtle details about the differences between Dorothea and her sister Celia

▶ **MANUSCRIPT** This page is from one of the four notebooks in which Eliot wrote her final draft of *Middlemarch*. There are few alterations, because she based it on an earlier story, *Miss Brooke*, the manuscript of which is lost. She combined this with an entirely separate fragment, also lost, of a work about a provincial town to make *Middlemarch*.

❝ Miss Brooke had that kind of beauty which seems to be thrown into relief by poor dress. Her hand and wrist were so finely formed that she could wear sleeves not less bare of style than those in which the Blessed Virgin appeared to Italian painters; and her profile as well as her stature and bearing seemed to gain the more dignity from her plain garments, which by the side of provincial fashion gave her the impressiveness of a fine quotation from the Bible… She was usually spoken of as being remarkably clever, but with the addition that her sister Celia had more common-sense. ❞

KEY CHARACTERS

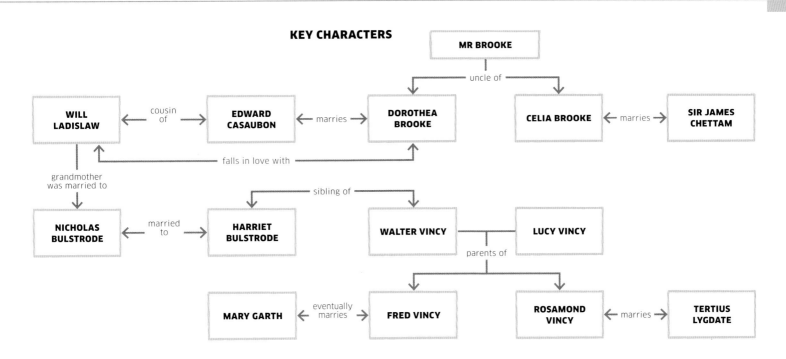

By the time she wrote *Middlemarch*, Eliot was in her fifties and a famous woman of letters. She had been a translator, reviewer, and essayist before she published her first novel, *Adam Bede*, when she was 39. The book was a success, and she published four more novels before writing *Middlemarch*. She challenged Victorian conventions by living openly with a married man, George Henry Lewes, a fellow writer and a great support in her own literary career. Despite this, she had become widely admired as an intellectual and a moral guide, as well as a novelist.

Middlemarch carries the influence of Eliot's intellectual interests. Characters discuss the role of women in society, while the narrator sometimes comments satirically on male expectations of women. Different kinds of religious belief (and unbelief) come into conflict in ways that shape the fortunes of various characters. Eliot herself rejected religious belief, but as a novelist remained fascinated by its social importance. The novel also has a complex plot. This involves the unearthing of actions hidden in the past, revealing that respectability can cloak larceny and conspiracy. It brings blackmail and worse into the sometimes complacent world of Middlemarch. The odiously self-righteous banker Bulstrode will get his comeuppance, and yet, just at the moment when he is revealed to be a hypocrite, Eliot makes him a surprising object of sympathy. It is typical of this most humane of novels.

POLITICS

The novel opens at the end of the 1820s, as debates about the reform of Britain's corrupt political system are becoming widespread. These arguments reverberate through the provincial community of Middlemarch. It is characteristic of Eliot that her focus on the influence of contemporary politics on her characters is, in part, comic. For example, Dorothea's uncle, Mr Brooke, develops an enthusiasm for political change, and decides to stand as a reforming candidate for parliament. However, his campaign ends in failure, when his empty-headedness is exposed at the town hustings, in a scene that is both funny and painful.

◀ **DOROTHEA AND CASAUBON** In the first Book of *Middlemarch*, Dorothea becomes engaged to the dry scholar and clergyman Edward Casaubon, portrayed here in a 1994 BBC adaptation. She is 19 and he is in his forties. Although others are appalled at the match, Eliot is careful to show how Dorothea and Casaubon are led by their own deluded ideals to believe that they are made for each other.

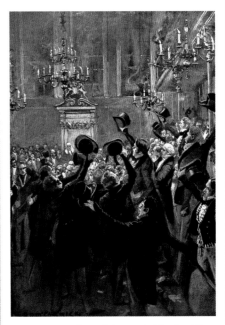

▲ **The 1832 Reform Act** extended the franchise and gave parliamentary seats to cities.

Anna Karenina

1878 ▪ THREE VOLUMES ▪ RUSSIA

LEO TOLSTOY (1828-1910)

When the Nobel Prize-winning American novelist William Faulkner was once asked what he considered to be the greatest novel ever written, he unhesitatingly replied, "*Anna Karenina*". He has never been alone in that judgment - even though its author, Leo Tolstoy, once repudiated his masterpiece, along with its predecessor, *War and Peace*. However, in the early 1870s, before he renounced his earlier habits and achievements to embrace radical religious abstinence instead, Tolstoy was toying with a novel about a "social woman", whose infidelity and resulting fall from grace would be viewed sympathetically, and not judgmentally. Around the same time, he heard that a despairing woman, jilted by her lover, had thrown herself beneath a moving train at the station near Tolstoy's country estate, Yasnaya Polyana, 322 km (200 miles) south of Moscow. The fusion of these two themes would eventually grow into *Anna Karenina*.

The new novel was not set in the past, as *War and Peace* had been, but in the contemporary world of the Russian aristocracy in the years 1873-78 - a world that Tolstoy knew well. The nobility was larger in Russia than in most other European countries, and since every child of a count or prince inherited a title, the nobility was overflowing with princes and princesses, counts and countesses. It was a world of palaces and balls, of boxes at the opera and horse races - and of country estates near Moscow and St Petersburg, where people went for the summer. This is the backdrop against which the intertwining stories of *Anna Karenina*'s eight books and multiple chapters take place. The narrative is delivered with Tolstoy's Olympian-like omniscience, which also allows the novelist to probe deep into the human heart. The overall theme is similarly grand in scale - nothing less than the quest for a happy marriage and for what constitutes a meaningful life.

▲ **KITTY AND LEVIN** Anna and Vronsky are not the only couple that Tolstoy created so memorably in this novel. They are always being compared to Kitty and Levin, shown here in the early pages, skating together in Moscow. Tolstoy loved to skate, finding it the perfect metaphor for a graceful relationship between a man and a woman: not without its risks, but at its best, approaching balletic perfection.

▶ **ANNA IN THE CINEMA**
Many great actresses have interpreted Anna Karenina, including Greta Garbo, Vivian Leigh, Claire Bloom, Jacqueline Bisset, Sophie Marceau, and Keira Knightley. Here, she is played by Tatyana Samoilova in the 1967 Russian adaptation of the book.

> ❝ Happy families are all alike; every unhappy family is unhappy in its own way. ❞
>
> **ANNA KARENINA, PART 1, CHAPTER 1**

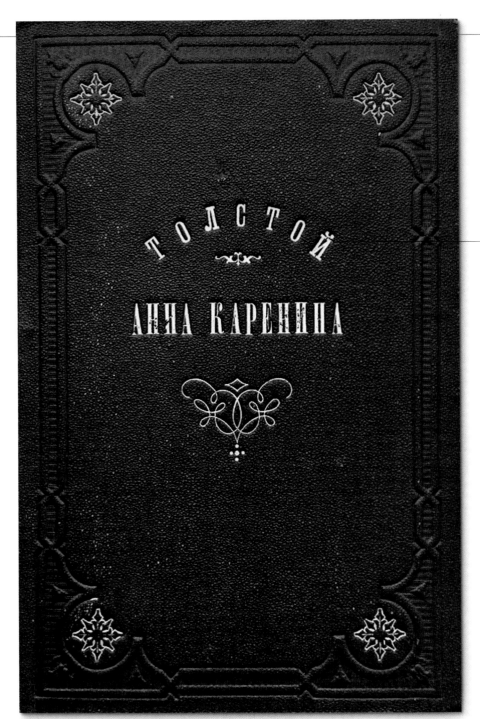

◄ **FIRST EDITION** Like most Russian novels at this time, *Anna Karenina* first appeared in instalments. It was written between 1875 and 1877, and was first published in book form in early 1878. It was so enthusiastically received that one St Petersburg bookshop sold 500 copies of it in a single day.

By 1878, Tolstoy was so famous that only his surname appeared on the cover of the first edition

> " Two maids who were walking along the platform turned their heads round to look at her... The stationmaster, as he walked past, asked her if she was continuing her journey. The boy selling kvass could not take his eyes off her. 'Oh, God, where should I go?' she thought, as she walked further and further down the platform. At the end she stopped. Some ladies and children meeting a gentleman in spectacles, and laughing and talking loudly, fell silent and turned their eyes on her as she came level with them. She quickened her pace and walked away from them to the edge of the platform. A goods train was approaching... "

ANNA KARENINA, PART 7, CHAPTER 31

REFORM IN RUSSIA

The Oblonskys were not the only family thrown into confusion in Russia during the 1860s and '70s. Alexander II became Tsar in 1856, and instituted a series of long-overdue political reforms. He famously freed the serfs, but also eased the once-stifling censorship, which led to the founding of new journals, museums, and cultural institutions. The 1860s became a golden age for Russian literature. It was the decade when Turgenev's *Fathers and Sons* (1862), Dostoevsky's *Crime and Punishment* (1866), and Tolstoy's *War and Peace* (1865–69) were all published. Alexander II also promoted industrialization, and an extensive national railway system soon crossed the entire land. Inevitably, tensions arose between supporters of the old ways and the new. Radicals opposed reactionaries, free-thinkers spurned the church, and the "woman question" challenged the old patriarchal system. All this ferment is mirrored in *Anna Karenina*.

► **Tsar Alexander II** is shown here, reading the Emancipation of the Serfs Act in 1861. This freed a third of the Russian population.

KEY CHARACTERS

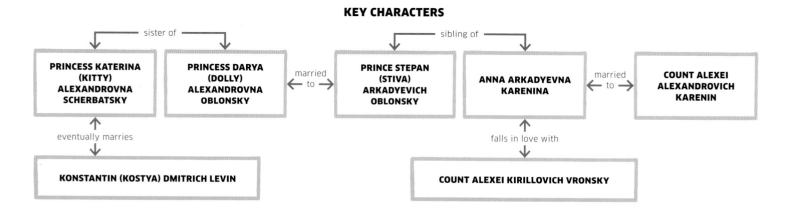

sister of

| PRINCESS KATERINA (KITTY) ALEXANDROVNA SCHERBATSKY | PRINCESS DARYA (DOLLY) ALEXANDROVNA OBLONSKY | married to | PRINCE STEPAN (STIVA) ARKADYEVICH OBLONSKY | ANNA ARKADYEVNA KARENINA | married to | COUNT ALEXEI ALEXANDROVICH KARENIN |

sibling of

eventually marries

KONSTANTIN (KOSTYA) DMITRICH LEVIN

falls in love with

COUNT ALEXEI KIRILLOVICH VRONSKY

Two story lines intertwine through the book and meet in a third one. The first is the story of the beautiful, charming, and warm-hearted Anna Arkadyevna Karenina, married too young to the much older Count Alexei Alexandrovich Karenin. Now in her late twenties, she has a son and she is trapped in a loveless union. Hungry for love and admiration, she is excited by the attentions of an infatuated young cavalry officer, Count Alexei Kirillovich Vronsky. Though she initially resists him, Anna eventually enters into a passionate affair. However, the impossible relationship will lead to tragedy for her.

The second story line follows the courtship and marriage of Konstantin "Kostya" Dmitrich Levin and Princess Katerina "Kitty" Alexandrovna Scherbatsky. Their union, set mostly in a lyrically described Russian countryside, is not perfect, but is perhaps as warm and abiding as fallible human beings can hope for. These two story lines connect through the tale of the flawed marriage between Anna's brother, Prince Stepan "Stiva" Arkadyevich Oblonsky – an affectionate but unfaithful husband – and Kitty's sister, Princess Darya "Dolly" Alexandrovna Oblonsky.

And the quest for what constitutes a meaningful life? It, too, is largely played out in the countryside, where the philosophical Levin struggles with bouts of existential despair – a battle that mirrored Tolstoy's own doubts when writing the novel. This quest concludes on a resigned but affirmative note – one that ends the book. The focus on contrasting marriages, the Karenins' failed one and the Levins' happy one, lay behind one of Tolstoy's early titles for the novel, *Two Marriages*, but he realized that Anna's was the heart of the story. Indeed, the reader remembers Anna as Vronsky recalls his first sight of her: beautiful, alluring, and loving. It is a memory that lingers long after her suffering has ended.

In context

▲ **RUSSIAN ORTHODOX CHURCH** Moscow's St Basil's Cathedral typifies the splendour of the Russian Orthodox Church, which in the 1870s still wielded jurisdiction over any case of divorce in the land. Divorce was not illegal, but it was difficult to obtain without stigma. This is why Anna's husband will not grant her wish for a divorce, although she is anxious to procure one.

▲ **ST PETERSBURG TO MOSCOW EXPRESS** Throughout the novel, many characters shuttle between Moscow and the Russian capital, St Petersburg, on the country's new railway system. Tolstoy, however, detested trains, and in *Anna Karenina*, trains and railway stations are associated with runaway passion, adultery, and death. Ironically, in 1910, Tolstoy himself died in a railway station.

▲ **LETTER FROM TOLSTOY TO N.N. STRAKHOV** Three years after first considering a story about a society woman, Tolstoy discovered a story fragment beginning with "The guests were gathering at the dacha", in a volume of Pushkin, Russia's most beloved writer. As he told his friend, N.N. Strakhov, in a letter dated 25 March 1873 (see above), Tolstoy promptly sat down and outlined the novel that became *Anna Karenina*.

❝ Involuntarily, unexpectedly, without knowing myself why or what would come of it, I thought up characters and events, began to continue it, then, of course, altered it, and suddenly it came together so neatly and nicely that there emerged a novel, which I have today finished in rough, a very lively, ardent, and finished novel, with which I am very pleased and which will be ready, if God grants me health, in two weeks. ❞

LETTER FROM TOLSTOY TO N.N. STRAKHOV, 25 MARCH 1873

WAR AND PEACE

Leo Tolstoy's first big success, the massive *War and Peace*, first published in its entirety in 1869, made him Russia's most famous (and best paid) author, and the book is still regarded by many as the most sweeping historical novel ever to have been written. Set against the backdrop of the Napoleonic Wars, with vivid descriptions of the battles of Austerlitz and Borodino, *War and Peace* dramatizes the impact of the war on four aristocratic Russian families over a period of eight years.

Featuring a cast of thousands, and told from a truly Olympian viewpoint, the principal characters are the sparkling Natasha, the philosophic Pierre, and the brave but doomed Prince Andrei. The book's climax is Napoleon's 1812 invasion of Russia, the burning of Moscow, and the French army's ill-fated retreat. The story is interleaved with Tolstoy's succinct reflections on the nature of history. It is a titanic reading experience.

▲ *War and Peace* is a 1,400-page work of fiction, but Tolstoy considered *Anna Karenina*, which he wrote later, to be his "first real novel".

The Portrait of a Lady

1881 ▪ 520 PAGES ▪ US

HENRY JAMES (1843–1916)

The Portrait of a Lady was a pivotal work in the career of the American novelist Henry James. When he started to write it, James was a popular author of novels and stories about expatriate Americans in Europe. *The Portrait* took his writing to new levels of subtlety and depth, both in terms of his descriptive language and his understanding of human consciousness and perception.

The book is about Isabel Archer, a wealthy young American woman who begins the story full of hope and independence of spirit, only to have her ambition and optimism crushed by the stifling values that she encounters abroad. She rejects two suitors, Lord Warburton and Caspar Goodwood, but accepts the proposal of Gilbert Osmond. However, this relationship turns out to be a disaster for her, mainly due to the scheming of Osmond himself, but also due to that of Madame Merle, whose machinations lie at the heart of the tale. These relationships, and Isabel's friendships with her sickly cousin, Ralph Touchett, for whom she feels great tenderness, and Madame Merle's daughter, Pansy, are meticulously described.

James's skilful use of point of view helps the reader to penetrate his character's thoughts and emotions, and this is perhaps the most important aspect of the book. His analysis

> What shall we call our 'self'? Where does it begin? Where does it end? It overflows into everything that belongs to us – and then it flows back again. I know a large part of myself is in the clothes I choose to wear. I've a great respect for things! One's self – for other people – is one's expression of one's self; and one's house, one's furniture, one's garments, the books one reads, the company one keeps – these things are all expressive.

THE PORTRAIT OF A LADY, CHAPTER 19

of Isabel's character and the values of the people around her also give him the chance to question social norms, notably the roles of women. By setting the book in Europe, particularly in England and Italy, James highlights the privileged social standing of these Americans, who have enough money and free time to enjoy extended periods abroad. He also shows, however, that money does not help Isabel to escape the suffocating society in which she finds herself. She inherits a fortune, but instead of giving her freedom, it simply makes her life more complicated. Henry James shows that being able to understand people's characters and motivations is far more important than gaining wealth or social status – and the insights that he provides help the reader to do just that.

In context

▶ **AMERICANS ABROAD** Several of Henry James's early novels, such as *The Europeans* and *Roderick Hudson*, are set in Europe, and James himself spent extended periods in France, Italy, and England. *The Portrait of a Lady* is set mainly in Rome, and James lived in Florence and Venice while writing it. The European setting of the novel gave James the opportunity to place his characters in a self-contained community far away from their families and the society to which they were accustomed. They establish new social networks, but these have shallow foundations.

> ❝ You wished a while ago to see my idea of an interesting woman. There it is! ❞

THE PORTRAIT OF A LADY, CHAPTER 2

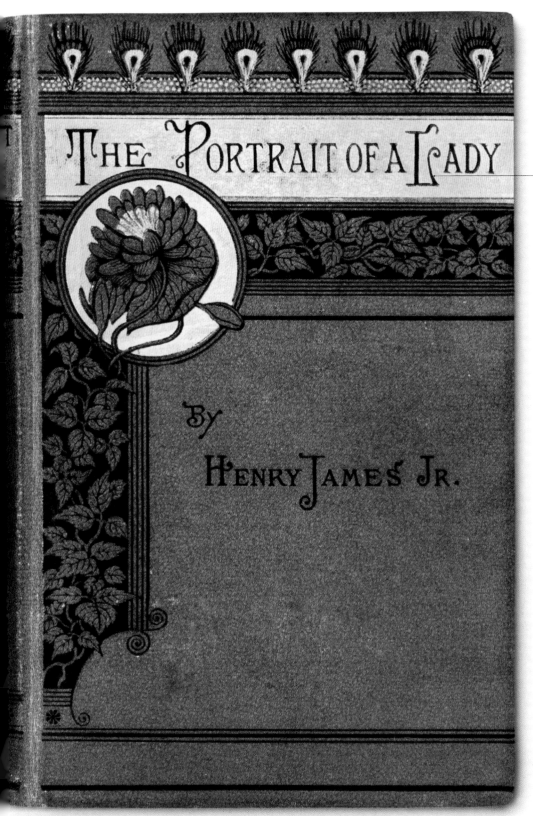

◄ **FIRST EDITION** *The Portrait of a Lady* first appeared in instalments in 1880–81 in *The Atlantic Monthly* and *Macmillan's Magazine*, before this first book edition came out in 1881. It was published in the US by Houghton, Mifflin, and Company, and a UK edition soon followed, published by Macmillan. The US cover was very much of its time, featuring dark green cloth, golden ornamentation, floral and leaf motifs, and decorative typography.

The book cover was influenced by the Aesthetic Movement, which encouraged "art for art's sake"

POINT OF VIEW

The Portrait of a Lady is narrated in the third person, and the narrator's tone sometimes suggests an emotional distance from his characters. However, the novel is also often narrated from Isabel's point of view, shaped by her feelings and beliefs. The reader gains a particularly close and compelling insight into Isabel's mind two-thirds of the way through the book, in Chapter 42, when she spends all night pondering the state of her life and relationships. James was a pioneer of intense focus on a character's point of view, and this style of writing was to have a huge influence on writers throughout the 20th century.

▲ **Nicole Kidman** as Isabel Archer in the film *The Portrait of a Lady* (1996).

▲ **FIRST EDITION** *Huckleberry Finn* was a controversial book when it was first published in 1884, and remains so today. Many early commentators attacked its earthy humour and everyday language, regarding it as improper for young readers; more recently, critics have pointed out that Twain's characterization of Jim draws on harmful racial stereotypes. However, its publication has also been celebrated as a watershed moment in American literature. Ernest Hemingway later wrote that "All modern American literature comes from one book by Mark Twain called *Huckleberry Finn*."

Adventures of Huckleberry Finn

1884 ■ 366 PAGES ■ US

MARK TWAIN (1835-1910)

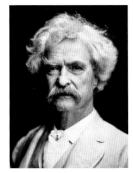

Mark Twain's novel of the Mississippi River tells the story of a boy, aged 13 or 14, and his adventures with a fugitive from slavery named Jim. Huck Finn had played a minor role in Twain's earlier work *The Adventures of Tom Sawyer* (1876), but in this book, he narrates his experiences in his own, unique voice. Speaking directly to the reader in a colloquial, everyday language full of humour and youthful insights, Huck guides us through his frustrations with domesticated life and schooling in a small Missouri township in the 1830s. He is wary about the return of his abusive and drunken father, and decides to escape by journeying down the Mississippi on a raft. On the way, he meets Jim, a local African American who has fled slavery because he fears that he will be sold further south.

As the pair move down the Mississippi, Huck's narration captures the tranquil aspects of the journey, including the discussions he has with Jim on the nature of language, society, family, and morality. Occasionally they touch shore and become entangled in small-town escapades, such as a feud between two families, the Shepherdsons and Grangerfords, and a violent encounter between two men, the drunken Boggs and Colonel Sherburn. These exchanges introduce us to a diverse cast of characters, and facets of Mississippi culture that Twain experienced as a child. These enable Twain to examine the political, social, economic, and cultural world of the American South in the early 19th century. At first, Huck fears that he will go to hell for helping Jim to escape from slavery, but he finally decides to embrace damnation rather than betray his friend. Twain later explained that *Adventures of Huckleberry Finn* was a novel in which "a sound heart and a deformed conscience come into collision and conscience suffers defeat".

TWAIN'S OTHER WORKS

Although best known for writing children's books, including *The Adventures of Tom Sawyer* (1876) and *The Prince and the Pauper* (1881), Mark Twain was also an influential journalist and essayist. His travel books, such as *A Tramp Abroad* (1880), gave him a reputation as an American traveller with a flair for irony. He also explored inequalities in American society and politics, in works such as *The Gilded Age* (1873) and *Pudd'nhead Wilson* (1894), and later wrote anti-Imperialist articles denouncing the US takeover of Cuba and the Philippines after the Spanish-American War of 1898.

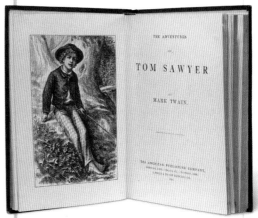

▲ **The title page** of the first edition of *The Adventures of Tom Sawyer* (1816)

◄ **LIFE ON THE MISSISSIPPI**
The young Samuel Clemens (later known as Mark Twain) worked as a steamboat pilot on the Mississippi, taking his pen name from a phrase used by captains when measuring the depth of the water. In *Life on the Mississippi* (1883), he looked back with great affection on the characters and culture of the river, linking this experience to his own destiny as a storyteller. This lithograph, produced by Currier and Ives in 1850, shows paddle steamers racing on the river.

Deception and lying about identity are persistent themes in *Huckleberry Finn*. They are brought to the fore when the raft is effectively highjacked by two Mississippi con men who go by the names of the Duke and the King, claiming – not very convincingly – to be descended from European royalty. Actors and tricksters, they rehearse for hastily assembled performances of Shakespeare's plays, relying on the ignorant excitability of their riverside audiences and their own outrageous acting to cheat people out of their money. Ultimately exposed as fraudsters, the Duke and the King kidnap Jim and sell him into captivity on a riverside farm, which happens to belong to relatives of Tom Sawyer – an event that sets the stage for the later part of the novel.

In the final chapters of the book, Tom Sawyer appears once again, and he and Huck hatch a variety of schemes to free Jim before he can be returned to his enslaver, all of which playfully draw upon European Romantic fiction, from the works of Walter Scott to Alexandre Dumas. Tom's keen interest in solving mysteries comes to influence the plot of the novel and the focus shifts from the earlier expansive treatment of the river journey to the style that Twain had used previously in *The Adventures of Tom Sawyer*. Stylistically, however, Huck's language remains the defining feature of the book, especially as it is combined with the symbolism of the Black man and the white boy travelling together, outlined against the majesty of the Mississippi, during a period when slavery and racial bigotry seemed to predominate.

In the final passages of the novel, Huck remains untamed, claiming that he will "light out for the Territory ahead of the rest" to escape the clutches of those who want to school and civilize him. A true free spirit, he heads west for more adventures, and to take his place in the history of American literature.

▲ **HUCK AND JIM** The relationship between Huck and Jim, depicted here by E.W. Kemble, is one of the abiding images of the novel. Their friendship deepens on their journey down the Mississippi. As the shadow of slavery haunts Jim, so that of an abusive father pursues Huck. Jim becomes a surrogate father to Huck while Huck shields Jim from his captors.

> ❝ We said **there warn't no home like a raft,** after all. **Other places** do seem **so cramped up...** ❞

ADVENTURES OF HUCKLEBERRY FINN, **CHAPTER 18**

ABOLITION OF SLAVERY

Slavery was the most divisive issue in the 19th-century US, and debates about its continuation led to the American Civil War in 1861. Twain set the novel in the 1830s, a time when slavery was integral to the economy and culture of the southern states. The Civil War of 1861–65 led to the Emancipation Proclamation of 1863, issued by President Abraham Lincoln. Although it freed Black people from bondage, and later amendments to the US constitution sought to enshrine the political and civil rights of African Americans, racism was still widespread: it re-emerged in other forms, such as racial segregation, during the 19th century. Twain therefore had one eye on the past and one on the present when treating the issue of race.

Jim remains a controversial character, and his depiction is inextricably linked to the legacy of slavery in the US. The novel argues for his freedom and humanity; at the same time, however, it draws on contemporary racial stereotypes that modern readers may find offensive.

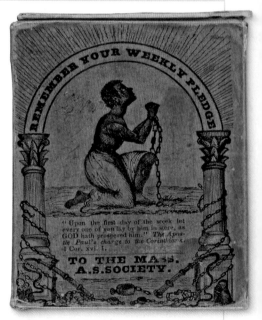

▲ **A collection box** of the Massachusetts Anti-Slavery Society illustrates the plight of enslaved Black people in the early 19th century.

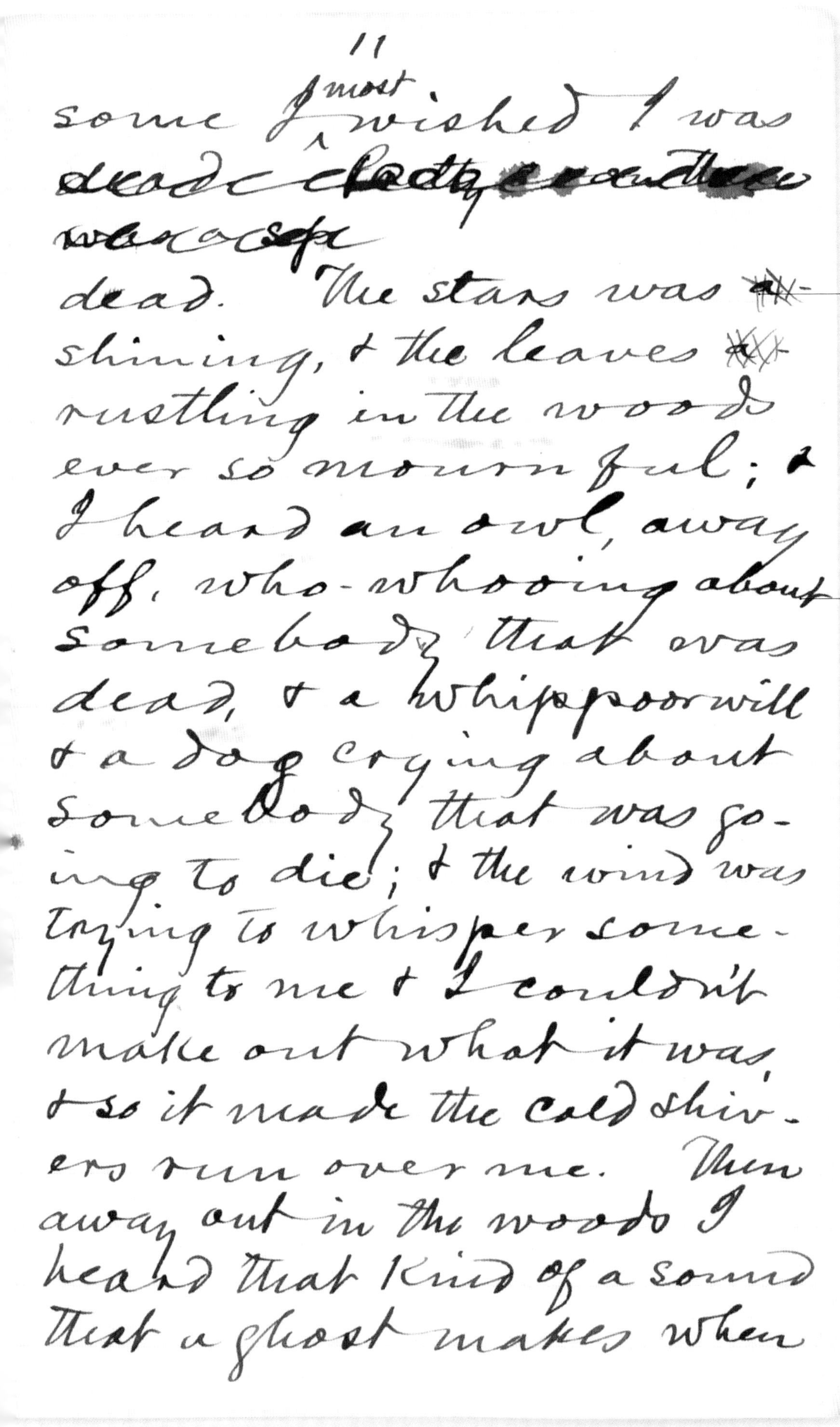

11

some I ^most^ wished I was
dead ~~clothy~~
~~was~~
dead. The stars was ~~all~~
shining, & the leaves ~~xxx~~
rustling in the woods
ever so mournful; &
I heard an owl, away
off, who-whooing about
somebody that was
dead, & a whippoorwill
& a dog crying about
somebody that was go-
ing to die; & the wind was
trying to whisper some-
thing to me & I couldn't
make out what it was,
& so it made the cold shivers run over me. Then
away out in the woods I
heard that kind of a sound
that a ghost makes when

◄ **MANUSCRIPT** Twain wrote *Huckleberry Finn* in several stages, often leaving it aside, uncertain how to finish it. He finally completed it in 1883. This part of the text contains an early passage that describes Huck's awareness of nature and the sounds outside his window. It conveys his sensory perception in the authentic language of a child who is acutely receptive to the outside world.

Twain made multiple adjustments to the colloquial language that defines Huck's narrative voice

The text was handwritten by Twain in ink on notepaper

" Then I set down in a chair by the window and tried to think of something cheerful, but it warn't no use. I felt so lonesome I most wished I was dead. The stars were shining, and the leaves rustled in the woods ever so mournful; and I heard an owl, away off, who-whooing about somebody that was dead, and a whippowill and a dog crying about somebody that was going to die; and the wind was trying to whisper something to me, and I couldn't make out what it was, and so it made the cold shivers run over me. "

ADVENTURES OF HUCKLEBERRY FINN, CHAPTER 1

Germinal

1885 ▪ 591 PAGES ▪ FRANCE

ÉMILE ZOLA (1840-1902)

Germinal is one of the most famous and overtly political of Zola's novels, the 13th in his 20-volume series of stories about the Rougon-Macquart family. It tells the tale of a young migrant worker, Étienne Lantier, who arrives at the bleak coal-mining town of Montsou in northern France, looking for employment. A hot-headed but hardworking socialist, he finds work in the pit, where he befriends the Russian anarchist Souvarine, and falls in love with fellow-miner Catherine, who is romantically entangled with the jealous and abusive Chaval. As his training progresses, readers gain a comprehensive view of the gruelling conditions inside the mines, as well as the poverty-stricken existence of those whose livelihoods depend on them. Eventually, pushed to the limit, and with Étienne as their leader, the miners go on strike. This leads to a violent stand-off with the police and the army, just as it had in real life, at Anzin, while Zola was planning the novel. At the climax of the tale, Étienne, Catherine, and Chaval are trapped in the pit after Souvarine sabotages the entrance – and we realize that not all of them will survive.

As always, Zola researched his subject thoroughly. He visited the strikers at Anzin, and, posing as an official from the Chamber of Deputies, was given a tour of the site. He made good use of these observations in *Germinal*. The minutiae of the mining

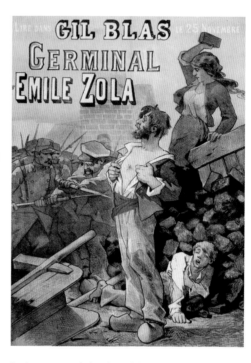

industry and the hardships suffered by the colliers and their families are described with realistic precision. Alongside this, Zola employs an ominous form of symbolism, portraying the pits as monsters that chew up and swallow the men labouring there. One pit "lay lower and squatter, deep in its den, crouching like a vicious beast of prey, snorting louder and longer, as if choking on its painful digestion of human flesh".

➤ **IN THE MINES**
Germinal won acclaim for its accurate portrayal of working life in the pit. Under dangerous, bulging timbers, the miners had to stretch out on their sides, picking away at the coalface, as shown in this engraving. At meal breaks, they gulped their food down, anxious to get back to work so that they could meet their quota of filled tubs.

> ❝ The mine never rested, day and night human insects were digging out the rock... ❞
>
> **GERMINAL, PART 1, CHAPTER 6**

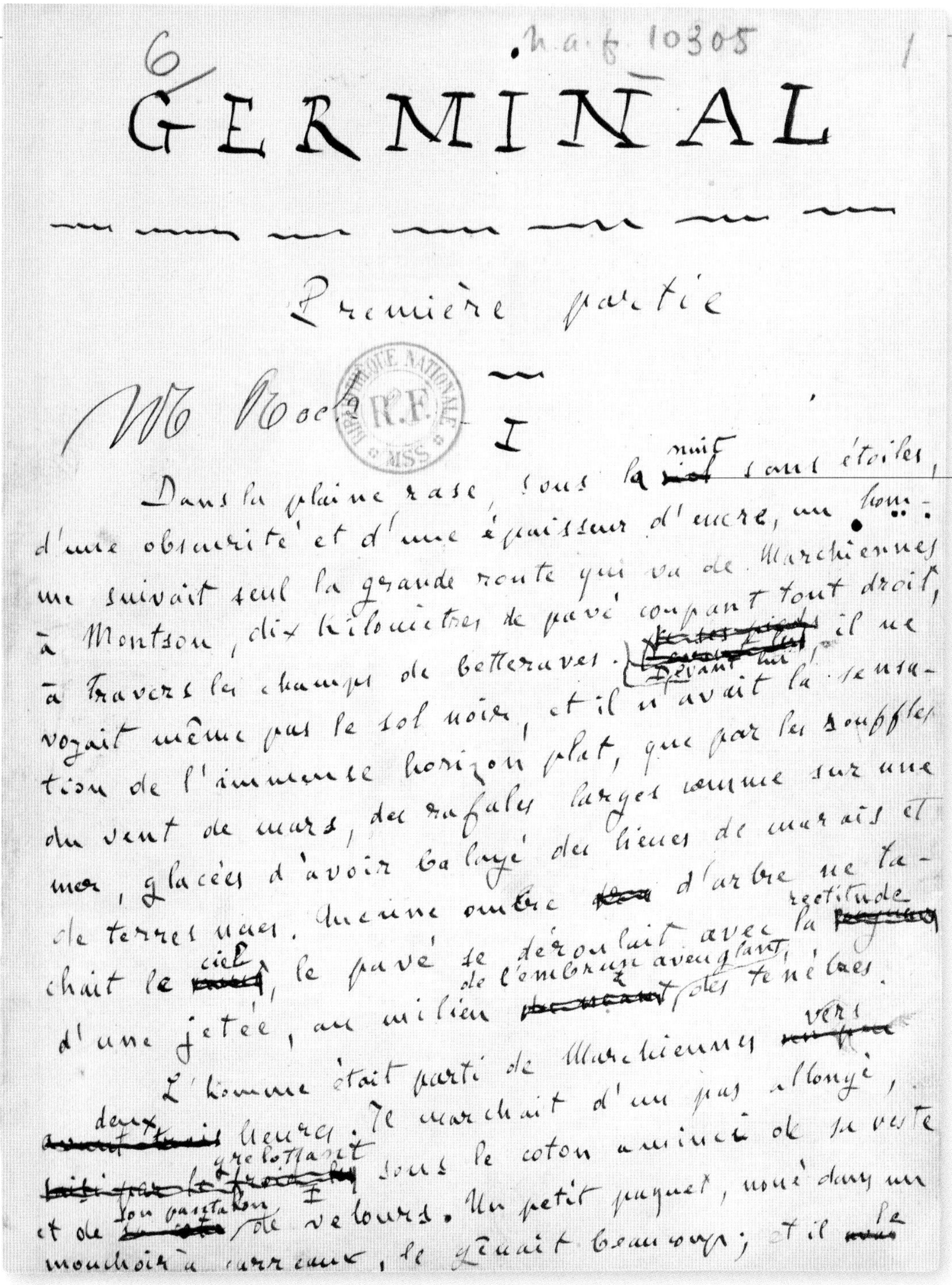

GERMINAL

n.a.f. 10305   1

Première partie

[handwritten manuscript text of Germinal, Part 1, Chapter 1 in French]

◀ **MANUSCRIPT** This is the first page of Zola's handwritten draft of the novel, which is housed at the Bibliothèque Nationale in Paris. A note on the back of the page records that it was begun on 2 April 1884. The original proofs for the serialized version in *Gil Blas* have also survived and these are held in the New York Public Library. They contain many handwritten corrections by Zola.

There are many revisions in the manuscript, as Zola was still working on the novel when the serial began to appear

> " On a pitch-black, starless night, a solitary man was trudging along the main road from Marchiennes to Montsou, ten kilometres of cobblestones running straight as a die across the bare plain between fields of beet. He could not even make out the black ground in front of him, and it was only the feel of the March wind blowing in great gusts like a storm at sea, but icy cold from sweeping over miles of marshes and bare earth, that gave him a sensation of limitless, flat horizons. "

GERMINAL, PART 1, CHAPTER 1

THE **COAL STRIKES**

Zola drew inspiration from real events for some of the most dramatic incidents in his book. In 1869, around the time that *Germinal* was set, there were two major coal strikes in France. These took place at Aubin and La Ricamarie, and both resulted in soldiers opening fire on the miners. Initially, the Aubin dispute centred around two unpopular officials, Imbert and Tissot. As things became more heated, the strikers burned down a warehouse and threatened to drown the chief engineer, Tissot. Soldiers moved in and opened fire, killing 14 civilians, including two women and a boy. The killings became a national scandal. Napoleon III donated money to the relatives of the dead and injured, but many miners were either fired or sent to trial, and their grievances were largely ignored.

> **A military patrol** passes close to groups of miners and steelworkers during the Decazeville strike of 1886.

> # " Blow the candle out, I don't need to see what my thoughts look like. "

GERMINAL, PART 1, CHAPTER 2

Germinal was far more than a political tract. It was a key novel in *Les Rougon-Macquart*, Zola's monumental study of life under Napoleon III. The inspiration for this idea came from Honoré de Balzac's *La Comédie Humaine*, a huge collection of interlinked novels about French society earlier in the century (see p.51).

Zola's theories about naturalism meant that each of his characters had a complex backstory. Born into the Macquart side of the family, Étienne Lantier first appears as a child in *L'Assommoir*, which is mainly about his mother's life of poverty and alcoholism. He is a young man when he arrives at Montsou, at the start of *Germinal*. He had been working as a railway mechanic, but lost his job after striking a superior. Intelligent, idealistic, and hard-working, he gradually rises through the ranks in the mines to become the miners' leader.

Zola's self-imposed restrictions in *Les Rougon-Macquart* had mixed benefits. As the series appeared after Napoleon's fall from power, they were effectively historical novels. This did allow Zola to escape the censorship that Napoleon's regime

➤ **ROUGON-MACQUART FAMILY TREE** The central project of Zola's career was a huge cycle of novels focusing on the lives of a single family, during the period of the Second Empire (1852–70). Zola used these books to illustrate his naturalist theories. He drew up several family trees, but this one is the most elaborate. It dates from 1892 and was published in *Le Docteur Pascal*, the last novel in the series.

would have imposed, but it also led to anachronisms. Zola was anxious to present a balanced view of the issues at stake in *Germinal*, but some of the industrial abuses described in his narrative had in fact been rectified after 1870.

There are some heartrending moments in the novel, but Zola's view was upbeat. He chose "Germinal" as his title, because it was one of the months in the short-lived Revolutionary calendar introduced during the Revolution. Originating from the Latin *germen*, meaning a sprout or bud, this was a Spring month. Whatever the outcome of the strike, Zola seemed to imply, there was an unstoppable force moving beneath the earth. It was germinating, growing, and would one day burst into bloom.

▲ **NAPOLEON III** A nephew of Napoleon Bonaparte, Napoleon III ruled France from 1848 to 1870. He was an unpopular leader – Zola loathed him – and he lost his throne after defeat in the Franco-Prussian War, spending his final years in exile in England. He was long gone by the time *Germinal* was written, but Zola set the novel in the final years of his reign.

NATURALISM

Zola was the prime exponent of naturalism in France. Essentially, this was an extension of realism (see p.49), where authors treated their subjects with an unsentimental sense of scientific detachment. Zola claimed: "I apply to living bodies the analytical method that surgeons apply to corpses." He also explored the effects of heredity, psychology, and the social environment. Zola took his ideas from contemporary medical and genetic studies, expounding his theories in controversial essays, such as "Naturalism in the Theatre" and "The Experimental Novel".

Throughout the Rougon-Macquart series, Zola's characters have to battle against the flaws that they have inherited. He explained: "I have chosen people completely dominated by their nerves and blood, without free will, drawn into each action of their lives by the inexorable laws of their physical nature… [they] are human animals, nothing more."

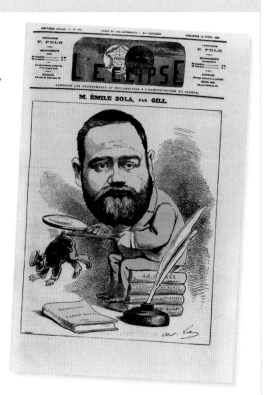

➤ **André Gill's caricature** satirizes how Zola treats his characters, holding them up and examining them with a magnifying glass.

The bottom right branch of the family tree relates to *Germinal*. Étienne Lantier was the son of the alcoholic, Gervaise Macquart

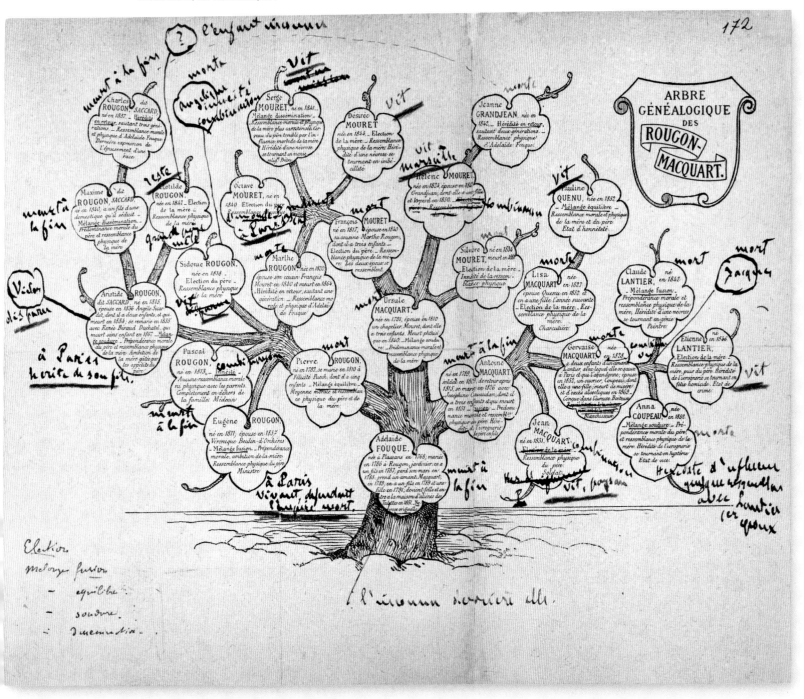

Deep down underfoot the picks were still obstinately hammering away. All his comrades were there, he could hear them following his every step... The April sun was now well up in the sky, shedding its glorious warming rays on the teeming earth... Everywhere seeds were swelling and lengthening, cracking open the plain in their upward thrust for warmth and light. The sap was rising in abundance with whispering voices, the germs of life were opening with a kiss. On and on, ever more insistently, his comrades were tapping, tapping, as though they too were rising through the ground. On this youthful morning, in the fiery rays of the sun, the whole country was alive with this sound. Men were springing up, a black avenging host was slowly germinating in the furrows, thrusting upwards for the harvests of future ages. And very soon their germination would crack the earth asunder.

GERMINAL, PART 7, CHAPTER 6

Fortunata and Jacinta

1886-87 ■ FOUR VOLUMES ■ SPAIN

BENITO PÉREZ GALDÓS (1843–1920)

Canary Island-born Benito Pérez Galdós gave his novel *Fortunata and Jacinta* the subtitle "Two Stories of Married Women". These women, one poor and one rich, inhabit radically different worlds, yet their lives become entangled because they are attached to the same man, Juanito. Fortunata is a beautiful young woman from a working-class background who falls pregnant while in a relationship with the wealthy Juanito. He ends the affair to marry his cousin, Jacinta, who tries, unsuccessfully, to have a baby. Fortunata also marries, but she and Juanito renew their relationship intermittently. In Galdós's Madrid, where the novel is set, people from all social strata are inescapably connected.

Madrid, Galdós's adopted home, was his great love and the source of much material for his panoramic explorations of human individuality, passion, and longing, of which *Fortunata and Jacinta* is often considered the greatest. Humorously and compassionately, the narrative weaves together the stories of the two women's lives. The narrator is like a member of the novel's cast, introducing and describing its many characters as he might acquaintances.

> A noise in the hall snapped her out of her trance-like state. When she turned around she had a shock: it was Jacinta peering in from the door to see who was there. Holding her hand was a little girl dressed stylishly but simply... '... we'll wait for awhile,' she said in an almost imperceptible voice, sitting down in one of the straw chairs. Fortunata didn't know what to do. She didn't have the courage to leave so she sat on the sofa. At almost the same moment she felt her chair wobble and moved to the sofa. The two were together, skirt to skirt.

FORTUNATA AND JACINTA: TWO STORIES OF MARRIED WOMEN, VOLUME 3, CHAPTER 6

Galdós greatly admired Charles Dickens, and translated *The Pickwick Papers* into Spanish in 1868. Unlike Dickens, Galdós created psychologically rounded characters, yet what he shared with the English author was political radicalism, and this, together with his literary success, made him enemies. Galdós's nomination for the Nobel Prize for Literature between 1912 and 1916 was sabotaged by objections from within Spain. Yet when he died, Galdós was a revered national figure, his novels regarded as true heirs of Cervantes's *Don Quixote*.

In context

◄ **STREET LIFE** A 19th-century painting depicts the flow of people, carriages, and horseback riders on the Calle de Alcalá, one of Madrid's main thoroughfares. Galdós arrived in Madrid aged 19 from his native Canary Islands, and its complex society would become the enlivening inspiration for his greatest works.

► **REAL CHARACTER** Wealthy Juanito embraces his lover, the poor Fortunata, in a 1970 film adaptation of the novel, starring Máximo Valverde and Emma Penella. Juanito's fickle, cavalier behaviour contrasts with the strength of character displayed by both Fortunata and Juanito's wife, Jacinta.

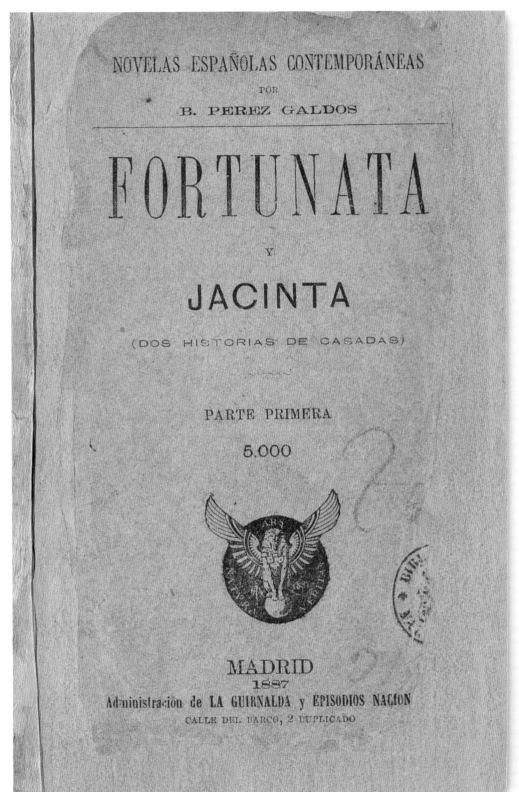

NOVELAS ESPAÑOLAS CONTEMPORÁNEAS

POR

B. PEREZ GALDOS

FORTUNATA

Y

JACINTA

(DOS HISTORIAS DE CASADAS)

PARTE PRIMERA

5.000

MADRID
1887
Administración de LA GUIRNALDA y EPISODIOS NACION
CALLE DEL BARCO, 2 DUPLICADO

◀ **FIRST EDITION TITLE PAGE** The title page of *Fortunata and Jacinta* claims its place in Galdós's *Novelas españolas contemporáneas* (*Contemporary Spanish Novels*). Inspired by Honoré de Balzac's *Comédie humaine*, these chronicles of Spanish life firmly associate Galdós with Madrid, just as his heroes Balzac and Charles Dickens have become associated with Paris and London respectively.

GALDÓS'S LITERARY CAREER

Galdós was a prolific writer, producing more than 100 works of fiction in a career of nearly 50 years, as well as stage plays and journalism. He originally moved to Madrid to study law, then switched to journalism. After having success with a historical novel, he wrote a sequence of short, carefully researched novels known as the *Episodios nacionales* (*National Episodes*), tracking Spanish history from 1805. In 1876 he published *Doña Perfecta*, regarded as his first mature work as a novelist. The 1880s and 1890s brought his finest achievement, as he turned to contemporary society in the 22 novels of his *Novelas españolas contemporáneas* (*Contemporary Spanish Novels*), notably *Fortunata and Jacinta*. In the late 1890s, he wrote another 26 of the profitable *Episodios*. Galdós's later years were affected by blindness.

▲ **Benito Pérez Galdós** is seen here at his desk, writing one of his *Episodios nacionales*.

> ❝ Why is it that we want what we don't have, and when we get it, we scorn it? ❞

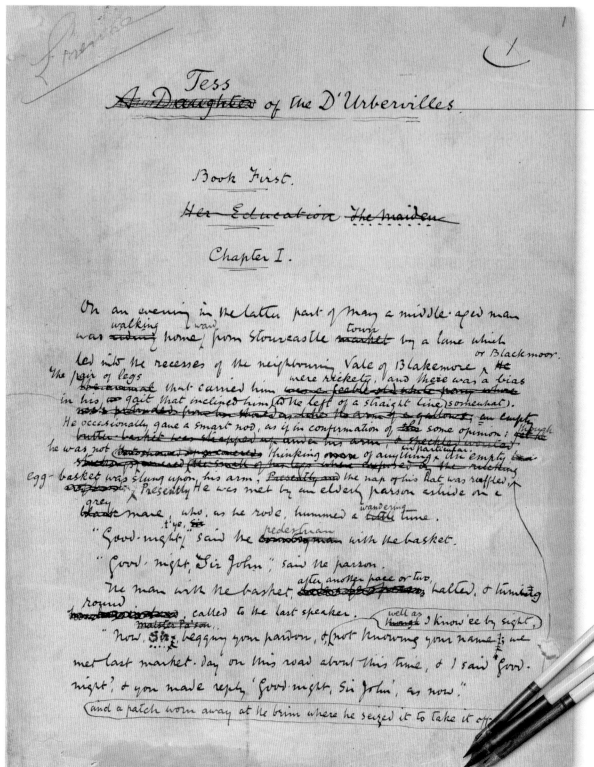

Hardy changed the book's title to include the name of the heroine, sharpening the focus on her

▼ **HARDY'S PENS** Like most 19th-century writers, Hardy used steel-nibbed pens, which had to be dipped into an inkwell before writing. He adopted the habit of inscribing his pens with the names of the books that he wrote with them. Several of them are kept at his birthplace at Brockhampton, in Dorset, which is now open to visitors.

▲ **MANUSCRIPT** Hardy's manuscript shows the author making careful changes as he goes along. Some of the alterations strengthen the descriptions by adding more detail; others include alterations of the dialogue to make it clear that a character is speaking with a West Country accent. He also changed the title of this section of the book to "The Maiden", to stress the following section, which is titled "Maiden No More".

66

She was a fine and handsome girl – not handsomer than some others, possibly – but her mobile peony mouth and large innocent eyes added eloquence to colour and shape. She wore a red ribbon in her hair, and was the only one of the white company who could boast of such a pronounced adornment. As she looked round Durbeyfield was seen moving along the road in a chaise… singing in a slow recitative – 'I've-got-a-gr't-family-vault-at-Kingsbere – and-knighted-forefathers-in-lead-coffins- there.'

99

TESS OF THE D'URBERVILLES, CHAPTER 2

Tess of the d'Urbervilles

1891 ■ THREE VOLUMES ■ UK

THOMAS HARDY (1840-1928)

Tess of the d'Urbervilles was highly controversial when it was first published. Its heroine, Tess Durbeyfield, is the daughter of a small-time "haggler", who sells local produce. The Durbeyfields' existence is economically precarious, and after the family's horse is killed in an accident for which Tess feels responsible, she agrees to visit Mrs d'Urberville, a rich widow to whom Tess's parents believe (wrongly) they are related. Her rakish son, Alec, takes a fancy to Tess and gets her a job on his mother's estate. He sets out to overcome her resistance to him. Eventually, on a night-time journey through an ancient woodland, he takes advantage of her vulnerability and either rapes or seduces her: Hardy carefully leaves it ambiguous as to which it is.

The bulk of the novel narrates the consequences of this. Tess has a baby, "Sorrow", who dies. Then she becomes a milkmaid in a different part of Wessex, and meets Angel Clare, a clergyman's son who wishes to become a farmer. The two fall in love, but Tess will not be able to escape the shadow of her past. Although Angel confesses that he has once had a sexual relationship, he is appalled to discover, after they marry, that Tess is not the virgin that he expected, and he abandons her. Hardy's defiant subtitle to the novel, "A Pure Woman, Faithfully Presented", made it clear that Tess is the guiltless victim of sexual hypocrisy.

Tess was a pivotal novel for Hardy. The son of a builder, he had trained as an architect when he was young, but his wife, Emma, a vicar's daughter, encouraged him to write. He published his first novel in 1871; 13 more novels and many short stories followed over the next 20 years. Although some critics deplored *Tess* for its attack on conventional sexual morality, the novel was a great success with readers in both Britain and America.

TESS DURBEYFIELD

Tess is a "country girl", but is better educated than her family. Hardy tells us that "she spoke two languages": the local dialect at home, and "ordinary English abroad and to persons of quality". However, she has an uncertain place in the world. Angel considers her to be a "child of nature", but that is his misguided ideal. She is innocent of her effect on men, alluring both Alec and Angel without any intention of doing so, but according to the moral standards of her time, she becomes a fallen woman. Hardy intended his Victorian readers to reject this stereotype, although many refused to do so. As is clear to modern readers, it is the conduct of the male characters in the novel that is troubling.

▲ **Nastassja Kinski** as Tess Durbeyfield in *Tess*, the 1979 film adaptation of the book

In context

▶ **RURAL SETTING** Hardy lived in Dorset, in England's West Country, for most of his life. He used the area, which he called "Wessex", as the setting for his novels. Many of the places in his Wessex are based on real locations, but Hardy changed their names: Beaminster becomes Emminster, for example, and Bournemouth becomes Sandbourne. In Wessex, most people face a hard life working on the land, and many speak in a West Country dialect.

KEY CHARACTERS

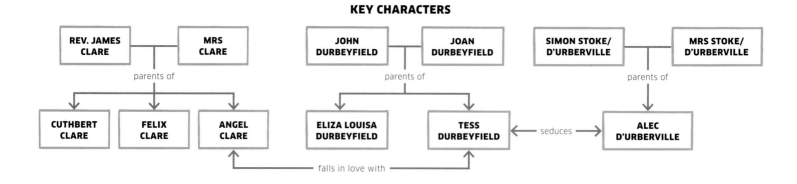

| REV. JAMES CLARE | MRS CLARE | | JOHN DURBEYFIELD | JOAN DURBEYFIELD | | SIMON STOKE/ D'URBERVILLE | MRS STOKE/ D'URBERVILLE |

parents of — *parents of* — *parents of*

| CUTHBERT CLARE | FELIX CLARE | ANGEL CLARE | | ELIZA LOUISA DURBEYFIELD | TESS DURBEYFIELD | ← seduces → | ALEC D'URBERVILLE |

falls in love with

With *Tess of the d'Urbervilles*, Hardy succeeded in writing a tragedy whose protagonist came from a humble background and was the victim of ordinary Victorian double standards. His outlook in the novel often seems bleak. Accident and ill luck conspire to doom Tess. In one crucial episode, Angel does not see a letter that Tess has written to him because she pushes it under the carpet by mistake when leaving it under his door. One of the most painful aspects of Tess's tragedy is that it is as much the fault of the high-minded Angel, who loves her, as of the callous libertine, Alec, who assumes that women of a lower social class are available to him.

Hardy is attentive to the ways in which class shapes, and sometimes twists, his characters' aspirations. Tess's drunken father deludes himself with the idea that he is related to an aristocratic family. Alec d'Urberville's family, whose real name is "Stoke", are nouveaux riches who have renamed themselves. Angel's father and two brothers are clergymen – members of the educated middle class – who cannot see Tess as a suitable wife. Angel believes he is enlightened, but is influenced by their assumptions. The plot is also subtly shaped by economic forces. Most importantly, after Angel has left Tess, Alec pursues her and uses the fact that her family is impoverished to pressure her into becoming his mistress. He has the power to save them from absolute destitution. Angel returns from an unprosperous farming venture in Brazil, finally realizing that he has wronged Tess, but he is too late. After Tess avenges herself on Alec, she and Angel have a short time together again before "justice" catches up with her in an extraordinary climax at Stonehenge.

Hardy recognized that he had created an uncommon heroine in Tess, and was in the habit of speaking of her as if she were a real person. He sympathizes with her, and allows the reader to understand her peculiar blend of innocence and intelligence. He also sees her from the outside, through others' eyes, a creature of the natural world through which she moves.

CRITICAL **RECEPTION**

Today, many people consider *Tess of the d'Urbervilles* to be Hardy's greatest novel and value its frank portrayal of a wronged woman confronting prejudice and misogyny. When the book came out, however, the reaction was far more mixed. Some writers praised the power of the writing, and one periodical, *The Atlantic Monthly*, said it was Hardy's best novel yet, but many Victorian critics were unable to accept the book's frank portrayal of sexuality, even though it was very restrained by modern standards.

They also objected to the author's sympathetic portrayal of a woman who, according to the moral conventions of the times, had committed a sin that should be condemned. One critic maintained that Hardy had "told an unpleasant story in an unpleasant way". Another described the novel as "a clumsy sordid tale of boorish brutality and lust". This kind of response, and the even more negative critical reaction to his later novel, *Jude the Obscure*, made Hardy give up writing novels and turn to poetry instead.

▲ **Hardy (above left)** sits with his friend, the poet Edmund Gosse, to whom he wrote (see right), describing in some detail the critics' reactions to *Tess of the d'Urbervilles*.

► **THE BOOK'S CLIMAX**
Near the end of the novel, Tess and Angel Clare arrive at the prehistoric stone circle of Stonehenge. Angel says that the monument or temple is "older than the d'Urbervilles", whose ancient lineage has brought so much trouble to them. Tess, who is exhausted, lies down on a large, flat stone, which both she and Angel believe to be the altar of the temple. In placing her here, Hardy suggests that Tess has become a sacrificial victim.

> 'It is Stonehenge!' said Clare. 'The heathen temple, you mean?' 'Yes. Older than the centuries; older than the d'Urbervilles! Well, what shall we do, darling? We may find shelter further on.' But Tess, really tired by this time, flung herself upon an oblong slab that lay close at hand, and was sheltered from the wind by a pillar. Owing to the action of the sun during the preceding day the stone was warm and dry, in comforting contrast to the rough and chill grass around, which had damped her skirts and shoes. 'I don't want to go any further, Angel,' she said, stretching out her hand for his. 'Can't we bide here?'… One of my mother's people was a shepherd hereabouts, now I think of it. And you used to say at Talbothays that I was a heathen. So now I am at home.'

TESS OF THE D'URBERVILLES, CHAPTER 58

MANUSCRIPT The first manuscript page of *Buddenbrooks* is dated October 1897. Mann was 22 at the time, and had already achieved some acclaim with short stories and novellas. By 1897, he was in Italy with his brother, gathering material for the new work. "I am making preparations for a novel, a big novel", he wrote to a friend. The provisional title for this novel, which became *Buddenbrooks*, was *Downhill*.

FIRST EDITION Mann finished *Buddenbrooks* in July 1900, and his Berlin publisher, Samuel Fisher, brought it out in two volumes just over a year later. At six marks per volume, the novel was comparatively expensive, and initial sales were modest. People in Lübeck were outraged, as they claimed to recognize themselves and resented the picture painted of their city.

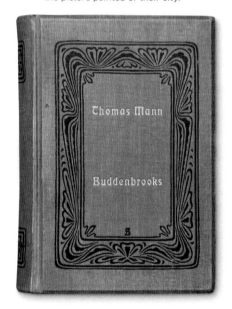

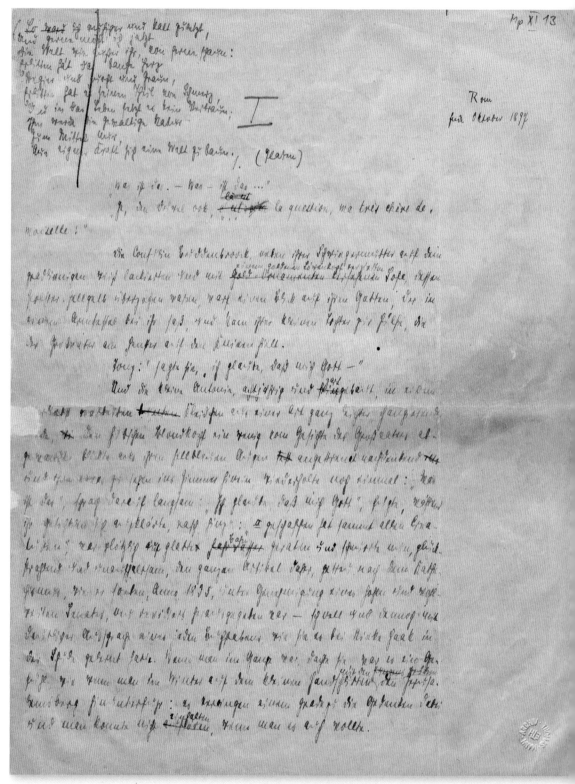

> Once more she repeated 'What comes next?' and went on slowly: "'I believe that God'–' and then, her face brightening, briskly finished the sentence: "'created me, together with all living creatures.'" She was in smooth waters now, and rattled away, beaming with joy through the whole Article, reproducing it word for word through the Catechism... When you were once fairly started, she thought, it was very like going down 'Mount Jerusalem' with your brothers in the little sled: you had no time to think, and you couldn't stop even if you wanted to.

BUDDENBROOKS, PART 1, CHAPTER 1

Buddenbrooks

1901 ■ TWO VOLUMES ■ GERMANY

THOMAS MANN (1875–1955)

The subtitle of Thomas Mann's first novel is "The Decline of a Family". Based closely on Mann's own family history, the novel tells the story of four generations of the Buddenbrooks, who, like Mann's forebears, are wealthy grain merchants in the German Baltic port of Lübeck. The novel starts at the peak of their commercial success: the current head, old Johann, with his son and partner, young Johann, have just confirmed their high social standing by buying one of the city's grandest townhouses from a former merchant dynasty that is now defunct. In the opening chapters, the Buddenbrook family and friends are celebrating at a housewarming dinner, with confident, burgher opulence.

Yet this prosperity is precarious. After his father's death, young Johann takes over. He has business acumen, energy, and the authority of his predecessors, but he dies suddenly. Foreboding gathers around his children, including Thomas, the eldest, who becomes head of the firm. Elegant and artistic, he marries an Amsterdam heiress from outside the usual local circles, who has a passion for music. Initially, it seems that

THE CITY OF LÜBECK

Although never mentioned by name in *Buddenbrooks*, Lübeck is the novel's setting, identifiable by real landmarks, such as Mengstrasse. The city where Mann grew up retains the imprint of its medieval heyday, when it was one of northern Europe's busiest trade centres, chief port of the Baltic, and the principal city of the Hanseatic League. This league, named from the German *hanse*, meaning "guild", was a confederation of more than 100 Baltic and North Sea trading communities. From 1226, Lübeck was a "free city" of the Holy Roman Empire and, apart from two years of French Napoleonic rule from 1811–13, it remained free for 700 years, with its own laws, constitution, and senate. Trade was its lifeblood, controlled by a handful of families, including the real-life Manns and the fictional Buddenbrooks in the 19th century. From 1871, it became an autonomous state within the German Empire.

Thomas will successfully combine tradition and adaptation, commercial hard-headedness and cultural sophistication. His election onto the city's Senate is a recognition of his status, but is followed by some bad business decisions and his own growing apathy. He looks as immaculate and successful as ever, but he has lost his belief in the family's values and his knack for commercial innovation. He dies suddenly and prematurely. His heir is his sickly son, Hanno, who shares his mother's passion for music, but no interest in the family business.

In context

▲ **MEDIEVAL GLORY** Walter Moras's late 19th-century painting of Lübeck from across the River Trave captures the city's charm. The spire of St Peter's Church rises behind the quayside buildings, and the Holsten Gate is visible through the trees. These scenes, which Mann knew as a child, became the setting of his novel.

◄ **PHILOSOPHICAL INFLUENCE**
In 1899, while writing *Buddenbrooks*, Mann read works by the philosopher Arthur Schopenhauer (see left). His philosophical concept of the blind, instinctive "will-to-live" impressed Mann, and influenced his writing. In the novel, Thomas reads Schopenhauer's work, and it helps to prepare him for death.

Influenced by the philosophers Friedrich Nietzsche and Arthur Schopenhauer, Mann's depiction of this family's decline is distinctive. The world changed hugely in the decades covered by the novel, with developments such as the railways, the growth of industry, political upheavals, and the emergence of the German Empire. Yet Mann's focus is inward, spiritual, and psychological. He plots the family's fragmentation, the clashes between the ideals of different family members, and the Buddenbrooks' loss of belief in social and moral values that once seemed self-evident to them. Mann also drew inspiration from the composer Richard Wagner, adapting his *leitmotif* – a musical phrase linked to a particular character or place – for literary use. In *Buddenbrooks*, it takes the form of descriptive tags attached to characters whenever they appear, signalling their preoccupations or fates.

As *Buddenbrooks* is the story of a family, there is no central main character. The family's decline is most vividly captured in the life of the outwardly impeccable, but inwardly anguished, Thomas Buddenbrook. The legacy of that decline, and its

◄ **SMOKING STYLE** This lacquered Russian cigarette case belonged to Mann and is on display in the Buddenbrooks House Museum in Lübeck. In the novel, the elegant Thomas Buddenbrook, with his perfectly waxed moustache, often smokes Russian cigarettes and is described as owning a case like this.

victim, is Thomas's son, Hanno, whose story dominates the final part of the novel. The one person present throughout the novel is Thomas's sister, Antonie, who is pressured by her father to reject the man she loves. Disappointed in both of her subsequent marriages, Antonie shows a seemingly boundless resilience in the face of suffering.

Mann was 26 when *Buddenbrooks* was published. It was slow to take off, but when success came, it was immense. He wrote several other works, becoming the foremost German novelist of the early 20th century, but *Buddenbrooks*, his first novel, established his reputation and, for all its bleakness, remains for many his best-loved creation.

▲ **CHILDHOOD HOME** The rococo facade of the former Mann family home looks out onto Lübeck's Mengstrasse. Now a museum, the house was originally built in 1758 and was the model for Mann's Buddenbrook mansion. Severely damaged in World War II, it was restored in the 1950s.

> ❝ Death was... the opening of doors – it put right again a lamentable mischance. ❞

BUDDENBROOKS, **PART 10, CHAPTER 5**

MANN'S OTHER WORKS

Inevitably, the events of 20th-century history marked Mann's career. After *Buddenbrooks*, his principal works before World War I were *Royal Highness* (1909) and the novella *Death in Venice* (1912). Then, in 1918, he published a political treatise, *Reflections of an Unpolitical Man*, which argued for an authoritarian government rather than a democratic one – a view that he later repudiated. *The Magic Mountain* was published in 1924, and in 1929, Mann was awarded the Nobel Prize for Literature. When the Nazis came to power, Mann and his Jewish wife settled in Switzerland, then moved to the US. His major novel of the postwar years was *Doctor Faustus* (1947). In 1952, he and his wife returned to Switzerland.

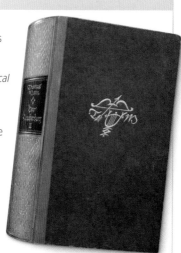

▶ **This first edition** of Mann's lengthy novel *The Magic Mountain* is one of two volumes.

◄ **SINGLE-VOLUME BESTSELLER** The publication of this single-volume edition of *Buddenbrooks* in 1903 gave the novel new impetus. Sales of the original two-volume edition, although lacklustre at first, had escalated by the summer of 1902. As a result, Mann's publisher, Samuel Fischer, decided to bring it out in one volume, for half the price of the earlier one. By the end of 1903, more than 10,000 copies had been sold.

❝ He had looked forward for a whole week to this evening with a joy which absorbed his entire existence... And then the dream became reality. It came over him with all its enchantment and consecration, all its secret revelations and tremors, its sudden inner emotion, its extravagant, unquenchable intoxication. It was true that the music of the overture was rather too much for the cheap violins in the orchestra; and the fat conceited-looking Lohengrin with straw-coloured hair came in rather hind side foremost in his little boat... But the sweet, exalted splendour of the music had borne him away upon its wings. ❞

BUDDENBROOKS, PART 11, CHAPTER 2

Sons and Lovers

1913 ▪ 517 PAGES ▪ UK

D.H. LAWRENCE (1885-1930)

British writer D.H. Lawrence published his third novel, *Sons and Lovers*, in 1913, and it proved to be his breakthrough work. Set in a poor mining community in the English Midlands, it explores the lives of its characters with unusual frankness, and accurately captures the local dialect. The novel focuses on Paul Morel and his relationships with his mother and two other women – the inexperienced, spiritual Miriam, and the married, more worldly Clara. Paul, who was modelled on Lawrence himself, is a sensitive young man who has grown up feeling at odds with his environment. Lawrence graphically describes his self-consciousness, his shame about his father's illiteracy, his sexual awakening, and his ambition to do well. He also details Paul's realization that he seems to be unable to love anyone except his mother, who, disappointed with her husband, has spent years loving her sons instead.

In vibrant, direct prose, Lawrence paints one of the most authentic pictures of the lives of the industrial working-class of the time. This was particularly interesting when so many of Lawrence's best-known contemporaries, such as Virginia Woolf and E.M. Forster, set their books mainly among the upper classes. The novel describes the miners' poor housing and the "ash-grey coal pits", but also the recreation and fellowship that the workers found both in the mine and in the pub.

Although *Sons and Lovers* received favourable reviews, Lawrence's reputation has since become contentious. Critics have questioned his male-oriented attitude towards his female characters – encouraging readers to see Miriam in a positive light, for example, because she submits to Paul. Others have pointed out, however, that the novel also reveals Paul's faults, and that it is this honesty that makes the book stand out.

> " Lads learn nothing nowadays, but how to recite poetry and play the fiddle. "
>
> **SONS AND LOVERS**, CHAPTER 5

In context

▲ **A MINING COMMUNITY** *Sons and Lovers* is set in a Nottinghamshire mining village similar to the one in which Lawrence grew up. The book depicts miners working in punishing conditions that leave many of them injured or crippled with lung disease. The landscape is also scarred by spoil heaps, creating a pervasive ugliness that alienates Paul, the novel's protagonist.

◄ **THE LAWRENCE FAMILY** The author is shown here (third from the right) with his parents and four siblings. His father was a miner who could barely read or write, whereas his mother had been a teacher and, unlike her husband, encouraged her son's interest in books. His parents' differing outlooks caused marital tensions that Lawrence drew upon when he was writing *Sons and Lovers*.

From BILLING & SONS, LTD., GUILDFORD.

MARKED PROOF

Which please return to Publisher.

Date *Feb 21/13*

177   SONS AND LOVERS

too flagrantly give herself away before the other girls. She invariably waited for him at dinner-time for him to embrace her before she went. He felt as if she were helpless, almost ~~like his shadow~~, and it irritated him.

a burden to him

"But what do you always want to be kissing and embracing for?" he said. "Surely there's a time for everything."

She looked up at him, and the hate came into her eyes.

"*Do* I always want to be kissing you?" she said.

"Always, even if I come to ask you about the work. I don't want anything to do with love when I'm at work. Work's work——"

"And what is love?" she asked. "Has it to have special hours?"

"Yes; out of work hours."

"And you'll regulate it according to Mr. Jordan's closing time?"

"Yes; and according to the freedom from business of any sort."

"It's only to exist in spare time?"

"That's all, and not always then—not the kissing sort of love."

"And that's all you think of it?"

"It's quite enough."

"I'm glad you think so."

And she was cold to him for some time—she hated him; and while she was cold and contemptuous, he was uneasy till she had forgiven him again. But when they started afresh they were not any nearer.

In the spring they went together to the seaside. They had rooms at a little cottage near Theddlethorpe, and lived as man and wife. Mrs. Radford sometimes went with them.

It was known in Nottingham that Paul Morel and Mrs. Dawes were going together, but as nothing was very obvious, and Clara was always a solitary person, it did not make much difference.

and he seemed so simple and innocent,

He loved the Lincolnshire coast, and she loved the sea. In the early morning they often went out together to bathe. The grey of the dawn, the far, desolate reaches of the fenland smitten with winter, the sea-meadows rank with herbage, were stark enough to rejoice his soul. As they stepped on to the highroad from their plank bridge, and looked round at the endless monotony of levels, the land a little darker than the sky, the sea sounding small beyond the sandhills, his heart filled strong with the sweeping relentlessness of life. She loved him then. He was solitary and strong, and his eyes had a beautiful light.

They shuddered with cold; then he raced her down the road to the green turf bridge. She could run well. Her colour soon came, her throat was bare, her eyes shone. He loved her for being so luxuriously heavy, and yet so quick. Himself was light, ~~and seemed to fly along~~; she went with a beautiful rush. They grew warm, and walked hand in hand.

A flush came into the sky, the wan moon, half-way down the west, sank into insignificance. On the shadowy land things began to take life, plants with great leaves became

◀ **MARKED UP PROOFS** Lawrence originally called his novel *Paul Morel*, after the central character, but changed it to reflect the book's broader themes. He wrote four drafts, before finally submitting the final manuscript to his publisher, Edward Garnett. Although Lawrence said he was pleased with the result, Garnett cut about one tenth of the text, removing some of the sexual references and deleting passages that had fleshed out characters such as Miriam and Mrs Morel.

Lawrence's final comments on the proofs are dated 21 February 1913

OEDIPUS COMPLEX

In *Sons and Lovers*, Mrs Morel becomes very close to her sons. She encourages them in their studies and smothers them with affection, but she also alienates each of them in turn. Paul describes his relationship with his mother in almost sexual terms, saying: "I'll never marry while I've got you", and accepting her "long, fervent kiss". The psychoanalyst Sigmund Freud referred to such closeness as an "Oedipus complex", after the Greek myth in which a man unknowingly kills his father and marries his mother. Whether he knew about this or not, Lawrence based Paul's relationship with his mother on his own experience.

▲ **This illustration by Sheila Robinson** shows a couple that might easily be Paul and his mother.

> ❝ He loved the Lincolnshire coast, and she loved the sea. In the early morning they often went out together to bathe… As they stepped on to the highroad from their plank bridge, and looked round at the endless monotony of levels, the land a little darker than the sky, the sea sounding small beyond the sandhills, his heart filled strong with the sweeping relentlessness of life. She loved him then. He was solitary and strong, and his eyes had a beautiful light. ❞

SONS AND LOVERS, CHAPTER 13

> **TITLE PAGE** This copy of the first edition of *The Way by Swann's* is inscribed by Proust to his American friend Walter Van Rensselaer Berry. The inscription extends over three pages, and in it, Proust remarks that: "the wisest, most poetic, and best people are not those who put all their poetry, goodness, and knowledge into their work, but those who, with a skilful and prodigal hand, also put a little into their lives".

The inscription was made in July 1916, not long after Proust and Berry first met

▲ **FIRST EDITION** Appearing in November 1913, the first edition of *The Way by Swann's* was launched by Parisian publisher Bernard Grasset with a meagre print run of 1,750 copies. Mystified by the book's unusual style and content, several other publishers had rejected Proust's manuscript, and Grasset only accepted it on the condition that the author paid all of its costs.

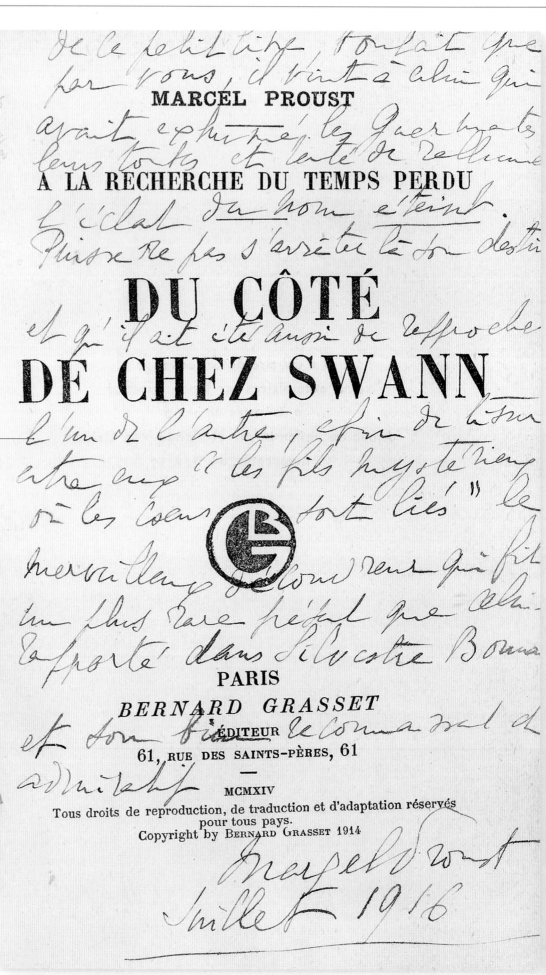

MARCEL PROUST

A LA RECHERCHE DU TEMPS PERDU

DU CÔTÉ
DE CHEZ SWANN

PARIS
BERNARD GRASSET
ÉDITEUR
61, RUE DES SAINTS-PÈRES, 61
—
MCMXIV
Tous droits de reproduction, de traduction et d'adaptation réservés pour tous pays.
Copyright by BERNARD GRASSET 1914

The Way by Swann's

1913 ▪ 523 PAGES ▪ FRANCE

MARCEL PROUST (1871–1922)

The Way by Swann's (also known as *Swann's Way*) is the first volume of the novel sequence *In Search of Lost Time*, the masterpiece of Marcel Proust. An aesthete of Jewish heritage, Proust led a public life of apparent idleness in smart Parisian society, while privately dedicating himself to creating his monumental work of fiction. The book is renowned for its elaborate prose style, with complex serpentine sentences giving full rein to the author's gift for sustained metaphor and meditations on memory, time, art, and love. However, Proust can also be wittily aphoristic, and wickedly funny in his shrewish depiction of the neuroses, snobbery, and hypocrisy of his vast cast of characters.

Proust's work takes the form of a fictional memoir, in which the first-person narrator, who resembles Proust, reflects on episodes from his past life. In the first part of *The Way by Swann's*, the narrator evokes his childhood holidays in rural Combray. Refracted through the child's imagination, bourgeois family life, small-town society, a village church, and the local countryside are saturated with magical beauty and emotional drama. In a poignant episode, the child is sent to bed early on a summer evening, an apparently trivial event that Proust transforms into an exploration of love, loss, and death.

INVOLUNTARY MEMORY

"Involuntary memory" is a term that Proust used to describe the detailed evocation of the past, in all its sensuous complexity, as a result of a precise stimulus in the present. In *The Way by Swann's*, this "Proustian moment" occurs when the narrator tastes a madeleine cake dipped in tea, taking him straight back to his childhood holidays in Combray, when his aunt used to treat him to a madeleine on Sundays. Central to the structure of Proust's work, involuntary memory is attributed redemptive power, making it possible to bring back the past.

▶ **Madeleine cakes dunked in tea** trigger the narrator's memories of Combray.

The child's inquisitive eye probes the peculiarities of human behaviour, as manifested by his hypochondriac, bedridden Aunt Léonie and her peasant servant, Françoise. His burgeoning erotic imagination is stimulated by spying on lesbian lovers in a country cottage, and by encountering Charles Swann's precocious daughter, Gilberte. Swann himself is a mysterious figure, the object of much ignorant speculation by the narrator's family. The family passes by his property near Combray on one of their regular walks, which they call "the way by Swann's". Their other walk takes them past the chateau of the noble Guermantes family, which the child's imagination endows with the glamour of an idealized French history.

In context

▲ **INSPIRATION FOR PROUST'S COMBRAY** The small rural town of Illiers, near Chartres, was the main model for Combray in *The Way by Swann's*. Its roofline is dominated by the rustic church of Saint-Jacques, celebrated as Saint-Hilaire in the novel. The town was renamed Illiers-Combray in 1971.

◀ **HOLIDAY HOME** When Proust was a child, his Parisian parents often took him for country holidays in Illiers, where they stayed with his aunt and uncle. Transformed by Proust's imagination, the house where they stayed became "Aunt Léonie's house", which is evoked in exquisite detail in *The Way by Swann's*. The house is now open to the public as the Marcel Proust Museum.

In the second section of the novel, Swann and the Guermantes reappear, but seen from a wholly different perspective. The text shifts into a third-person narrative to deliver Swann's backstory, following his obsessively jealous involvement with the elusive courtesan Odette. Entitled "Swann in Love", this section is virtually a self-contained novel in its own right. Swann leads us into two contrasting Parisian social circles: that of the Verdurins, who pretend to value the arts, but are secretly obsessed with social status; and that of the Duchesse de Guermantes, at the apex of the Parisian social world, who is equally preoccupied with the minutiae of rank, but possesses far superior manners and style. The text sparkles with wit, especially in the dialogue between Swann and the Duchesse. Swann's unhappy passion is dissected at length, with minute analyses of the paradoxes of love, regarded by Proust as the futile pursuit of an unknowable figment of the lover's imagination. The resolution of the affair is unexpected and profoundly cynical.

The final section of *The Way by Swann's* is like a brilliant afterthought, carrying the memoirs forward to the narrator's adolescence in Paris and his early love for Gilberte. It stresses the inevitable disillusionment resulting from the collision of imagination with reality, which happens often and painfully in youth. Although *The Way by Swann's* puzzled many of its early readers, it soon achieved the status of a classic of world literature. The overarching theme of Proust's work is the triumph of memory and literature over the erasures of time, and it achieves this magnificently.

IN SEARCH OF LOST TIME

Proust originally intended *The Way by Swann's* to be the first part of a three-volume sequence of novels, *In Search of Lost Time*. This shorter version of the sequence was near completion when the outbreak of World War I in 1914 interrupted publication. During the war, Proust embarked on a radical expansion of the work. The second volume, *In the Shadow of Young Girls in Flower*, appeared in 1919 to great acclaim. *The Guermantes Way* and *Sodom and Gomorrah* followed before the novelist's death in 1922. Three more volumes were published posthumously, although Proust would not have considered them finished texts. The complete sequence comprises some 1.27 million words.

▶ **After *The Way by Swann's*,** the rest of Proust's novel sequence was published by Gallimard between 1919 and 1927.

5   10

[Handwritten manuscript page in French with numerous crossings-out and revisions]

▲ **THE REAL SWANN** Proust's acquaintance Charles Haas, an elegant Jewish socialite, was acknowledged by the novelist as "the departure point for my character Swann". A member of the exclusive Jockey Club, Haas described himself as "the only Jew ever to be accepted by Parisian society without being immensely rich".

◀ **DRAFT MANUSCRIPT** Proust wrote the first draft of *The Way by Swann's* by hand, in lined notebooks, working mostly at night, in his apartment on the Boulevard Haussmann in Paris. The notebooks show the endless second thoughts, excisions, and additions that were essential to his writing method. Major revisions continued at proof stage: Proust told a friend, "I've written a whole new book on the proofs."

◀ **INSPIRING COUNTESS** Comtesse Élisabeth Greffhule was the prime inspiration for Proust's beautiful and cuttingly witty Duchesse de Guermantes. Like the Duchesse, she was a prominent figure in Parisian society, and unhappily married to a husband who was both violent and unfaithful. She surrounded herself with a coterie of close friends, who included notable artists as well as socialites.

> ❝ But at the very instant when the mouthful of tea mixed with cake crumbs touched my palate, I quivered, attentive to the extraordinary thing that was happening in me. A delicious pleasure had invaded me, isolated me, without my having any notion as to its cause. It had immediately made the vicissitudes of life unimportant to me, its disasters innocuous, its brevity illusory, acting in the same way that love acts, by filling me with a precious essence: or rather this essence was not in me, it was me. I had ceased to feel I was mediocre, contingent, mortal. ❞

***THE WAY BY SWANN'S*, PART 1: "COMBRAY"**

Directory: 1870-1920

THE RED ROOM

AUGUST STRINDBERG, 1879

Better known internationally for his plays, August Strindberg (1849–1912) first came to public attention in his native Sweden with his debut novel *The Red Room*. Subtitled "Scenes of Literary and Artistic Life", it follows the experiences of Arvid Falk, a youthful idealist who resigns from the civil service in disgust at the all-pervasive corruption of officialdom. He then enters Stockholm's bohemian underworld in search of humanity and social justice. Falk's naïve eye provides the perspective for a sweeping satire of Swedish society, stretching from parliament and business to the theatre and radical politics. In writers and artists, he finds only cynicism and strategies for personal gain. Working-class radicalism proves equally disillusioning, and the temptations of sexual liberation fail to overcome his ingrained puritanism.

Heavily influenced by the foreign examples of Dickens and Zola, Strindberg achieved an aggressive realism previously unknown in Swedish literature. *The Red Room* is often credited with founding modern Scandinavian fiction.

AGAINST NATURE (À REBOURS)

JORIS-KARL HUYSMANS, 1884

Against Nature was written by Huysmans (1848–1907), a French novelist in revolt against the tasteless materialism of his times. His antihero, Duc Jean des Esseintes, is a degenerate aristocrat who withdraws from a life of debauchery to the isolation of a country house, where he devotes himself to cultivating exquisite sensations and pursuing refined ecstasies. Menaced by boredom and self-disgust, he contrives elaborate novelties to gratify his senses – including a meal of exclusively black foods served on black plates, and a "mouth organ" that squirts different liqueurs into his mouth, depending on which notes are played. Inevitably, such absurdities fail to satisfy, and much of the novel is a comedy of frustration.

Huysmans uses arcane vocabulary and an elaborate style to evoke Des Esseintes' sensuous but despairingly private universe. Although it is devoid of plot, the novel holds readers by its rich invention. Huysmans' poseur found many imitators in literature and in life, launching the Decadent movement of the late 19th century.

BEL-AMI

GUY DE MAUPASSANT, 1885

Bel-Ami (meaning "Good Friend") is the story of a handsome and unscrupulous young journalist, Georges Duroy, pursuing women and fortune in fin-de-siècle Paris. French author Guy de Maupassant (1850–93) paints a world in which greed, lies, lust, and betrayal are universal principles of behaviour. Writing with the amoral detachment of a naturalist, he puts such gusto into his portrayal of the boulevards, cafés, salons, and boudoirs, that a riotous enjoyment of life prevails over distaste at human baseness.

From one seduction to another, Duroy progresses inexorably to the top of his profession and of the social pile. The married women who adore him, and act as his accomplices, fulfil none of the hackneyed expectations of "fallen women", being neither passively exploited nor punished for their vice. Duroy achieves his final ascent by seducing his boss's daughter, forcing the boss to accept him as his son-in-law and the heir to his fortune. The triumph of the scoundrel caps an enjoyably cynical view of French society.

HUNGER

KNUT HAMSUN, 1890

Norwegian author Knut Hamsun (1859–1952) planned his breakthrough novel, *Hunger*, when he was a poor, aspiring writer on the streets of Kristiania (Oslo). The first-person narrator evokes the experience of vagrancy and destitution with powerful immediacy. Using interior monologue, Hamsun builds an often complex and fragmentary text that interweaves fantasies and mysterious encounters, accounts of petty crimes, and gestures of self-abasement. Shifts of tense and fractured grammar convey his disturbed relationship with the world. His behaviour lacks any clear logic – he often refuses food or money although he is desperate, and his stream of consciousness veers into delirium. Yet he is an acute self-observer, cataloguing his psychological states and his delusions of grandeur.

In creating a character at odds with God and society, Hamsun owed much to the work of Dostoevsky, but his stylistic originality presaged 20th-century modernism. The success of *Hunger* ensured that Hamsun never experienced poverty again, but in later life he was disgraced by his association with Nazism.

THE PICTURE OF DORIAN GRAY

OSCAR WILDE, 1890

In his only novel, *The Picture of Dorian Gray*, Irish author Oscar Wilde (1854–1900) fused the Gothic horror genre with fin-de-siècle decadence. The eponymous antihero, a beautiful young man, makes a wish that his portrait should age rather than himself. He soon realizes that his wish is

A page from the manuscript of Natsume Sōseki's *The Gate*

coming true. As he allows himself to be corrupted by a life of unbridled sensual pleasure, his physical self remains young and beautiful. Meanwhile, his ageing and spiritual ugliness are transferred to the picture.

Dorian's crimes become ever more extreme, evolving from the betrayal of love to outright murder. The final plot twist is satisfyingly neat. Wilde's witty and light writing style should ensure that no-one treats his macabre fairy story too solemnly. Still, he felt compelled to defend himself against accusations of immorality, stating in his preface to the 1891 edition: "There is no such thing as a moral or an immoral book. Books are well written or badly written. That is all."

EFFI BRIEST

THEODOR FONTANE, 1896

The German author of *Effi Briest*, Theodor Fontane (1819–98), was an acute critic of social attitudes in Germany and their frustrating impact on women. Based on a real-life event, the novel tells of a young woman who is pushed by her family into marrying a man twice her age for reasons of social status. Consigned to a lonely existence in a Baltic port, and neglected by her husband, Effi has a brief, meaningless affair with a predatory married man. She then withdraws into the dutiful role of a wife and mother. Years later, her husband discovers evidence of the affair and divorces her. Shunned by all, she descends into isolation and nervous depression.

Fontane narrates this sad tale in a level, ironic tone that undercuts any possibility of melodrama. None of the characters can see that the tragedy is caused by the narrowness of conventional attitudes. Only the toughest of readers will resist tears at the terrible fate of an innocent woman.

DRACULA

BRAM STOKER, 1897

The most famous of all vampire tales, *Dracula* was the work of Irish author Bram Stoker (1847–1912). The lurid story is told chiefly in the form of diaries and letters written by the principal characters. A naïve Englishman, Jonathan Harker, travels to Count Dracula's castle in Transylvania, where he narrowly escapes vampiric predation. The action then shifts to England. Arriving by ship at the port of Whitby, Dracula begins stalking women, who are transformed into vampires by his bite. Led by a vampire hunter, Professor Van Helsing, Harker and his friends mount an ultimately successful attack on the count.

Dracula took the Gothic horror tradition to new extremes. It features, for example, a man who eats vermin, and a graveyard scene in which an undead corpse is disinterred and beheaded. However, excesses that could have been laughable achieve true horror through the seriousness with which they are played. The sexual implications of the vampire's bite render the plot particularly disturbing, and have ensured the story's enduring hold on the popular imagination.

THE SECRET AGENT

JOSEPH CONRAD, 1907

Polish-born British novelist Joseph Conrad (1857–1924) made his reputation with stories set in the backwaters of empire. However, with *The Secret Agent*, he turned his sardonic eye on the heart of darkness in London, the imperial metropolis.

Adolf Verloc, a member of an ineffectual circle of left-wing would-be revolutionaries, is paid by a foreign power to carry out an absurd anarchist outrage. Verloc's sordid social environment amid the gloom of London's back streets is powerfully evoked. A potential terrorist suicide bomber, the Professor, introduces a note of genuine nihilistic menace. Conrad's narrative plays subtly with time shifts to draw out the ironies of the failed outrage, a fiasco that only results in the death of Verloc's vulnerable brother-in-law, who has been tricked into taking part.

The novel's dark melodrama, culminating in murder and suicide, did not appeal to Conrad's public, and the book flopped on first publication. It is now admired as a complex take on the themes of revolutionary politics, terrorism, and the baleful influence of the modern city.

Willa Cather, the author of a series of novels about the Great Plains

◀ THE GATE

NATSUME SŌSEKI, 1910

The Gate is a sad, contemplative novel about a childless Japanese couple, Sosuke and Oyoni, living in Tokyo. Japanese author Natsume Sōseki (1867–1916) draws the reader into their quiet, isolated domesticity, in which unspoken loyalty to each other compensates for their lack of friends and their alienation from their families. We gradually learn how their lives have been blighted by past events, which spread poison into the present.

Sosuke is pressured by his family to pay for the education of his younger brother, which he cannot afford to do. Devoted to avoiding confrontation, he fails to challenge the obligation, although he knows it is unfair. Seeking an answer to the problems that are paralysing his life, he enters a Zen Buddhist retreat, but he cannot accept the solution that Zen offers – he cannot pass through the metaphorical "gate" of the book's title. The tale offers its characters no redemption, and has no happy ending – only the appeal of human solidarity in the passive acceptance of fate.

▲ MY ÁNTONIA

WILLA CATHER, 1918

My Ántonia is the third of a series of novels by American author Willa Cather (1873–1947), and is set in the Nebraskan prairies of the American West. The story is told by Jim Burden, a middle-aged lawyer, looking back on his rural childhood on the Great Plains.

His loosely structured reminiscences centre on his fascination with Ántonia Shimerda, the daughter of Bohemian immigrants, whose free-spirited presence as a neighbour dominated his early life. Ben and Ántonia share the hardships, dangers, and freedoms of the frontier environment. Ántonia undergoes many harsh tribulations, including her father's suicide and an attempted rape, but her lust for life is undaunted.

Cather excels at lyrically evoking the awe-inspiring natural beauty of the plains. Her descriptions of the many diverse characters in the tough farming environment give full human value to the settler experience. She largely avoids sentimentality, and the memorable figure of Ántonia, a strong woman bearing a great burden in life, dominates the book, as it should.

4

1920—1950

- The Age of Innocence
- Ulysses
- The Good Soldier Švejk
- The Great Gatsby
- The Trial
- The Sun Also Rises
- To the Lighthouse
- Berlin Alexanderplatz
- The Sound and the Fury
- The Man Without Qualities
- Journey to the End of the Night
- Their Eyes Were Watching God
- The Grapes of Wrath
- The Outsider
- Snow Country
- Nineteen Eighty-Four

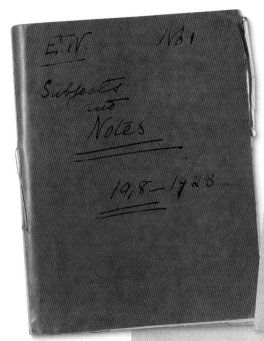

◄ **NOTEBOOK** Wharton planned
her novels carefully before she
began to write. This notebook,
entitled "Subjects and Notes
1918–1923", contains a page
on which she drafts what will
happen in Book 1 of *The Age of
Innocence*. The title of the novel is
written over a crossed-out earlier
heading that says "Old New York".

5

► **MANUSCRIPT**
Edith Wharton worked
hard on her writing,
revising her drafts. This
page from Chapter 34
shows fluent handwriting,
suggesting that it was
written at speed, together
with many corrections. It
describes Archer at the end
of the book. Although he is
respectable and popular, he
feels that he has missed the
prize in "the lottery of life".

The Age of Innocence

1920 ▪ 365 PAGES ▪ US

EDITH WHARTON (1862-1937)

American author Edith Wharton published *The Age of Innocence* in 1920, when she was in her 50s and at the height of her powers as a novelist. The book is set 50 years earlier, during the time when Wharton was growing up in New York in a rich family. It was a period of prosperity in the US known as the Gilded Age. The novel is set among the upper classes, whose values it describes and criticizes through its three central characters: Newland Archer, a rich, young lawyer; May Welland, Archer's seemingly naïve but secretly perceptive fiancée and later wife; and Countess Ellen Olenska, May's cousin, who has fled her Polish husband and returned from Europe at the start of the book.

At first, Archer simply accepts the materialistic values of Gilded-Age New York, particularly that the display of wealth and success is important; that women should be subservient to men; and that separated women such as Ellen should keep away from "polite" society. However, when he falls in love with Ellen, having already committed himself to May, he begins to question those values – just as Ellen has done on returning from her exile in Europe to renew acquaintance with her American relations.

> ❝ He had been, in short, what people were beginning to call 'a good citizen'. In New York, for many years past, every new movement, philanthropic, municipal or artistic, had taken account of his opinion and wanted his name. People said: 'Ask Archer' when there was a question of starting the first school for crippled children, reorganizing the Museum of Art... inaugurating the new Library, or getting up a new society of chamber music. His days were full and they were filled decently. He supposed it was all a man ought to ask. ❞
>
> **THE AGE OF INNOCENCE, CHAPTER 34**

Wharton portrayed the complex and strained relationships between her characters in subtle and compelling prose. Her literary style was influenced by the work of her friend, Henry James. She chose a setting in which women are constrained in what they can say: feelings must be conveyed by suggestion. The moment when Ellen touches Archer lightly on the knee with her fan, for example ("it thrilled him like a caress"), is highly charged. Wharton powerfully imparted strong emotions and moral dilemmas, using them to build a gripping story and winning *The Age of Innocence* lasting acclaim.

▲ **GILDED-AGE NEW YORK** In the late 19th century, glamorous dresses and horse-drawn carriages were the outward signs of success among New York's elite. Wharton, who was born near Madison Park (depicted here), questions the values of the rich, and shows how they often hide dishonesty. May Welland, the heroine of *The Age of Innocence*, inherits a fortune, but it only brings her trouble.

THE **PULITZER PRIZE**

The Pulitzer Prize for the Novel was established in 1917, and quickly became one of the most prestigious literary awards. The prize, one of several honouring achievements in the arts, was funded from the will of American newspaper publisher Joseph Pulitzer, and was to be awarded annually to an outstanding novel.

Pulitzer's will stipulated that the prize should be awarded to the book that best presented "the wholesome atmosphere of American life". As many of Wharton's characters question and break social taboos, this stipulation seemed to exclude her from ever winning the prize. However, the committee that set it up changed the text of the conditions from "wholesome atmosphere" to "whole atmosphere". *The Age of Innocence* impressed the judges, and the book won the prize in 1921. Edith Wharton was the first woman novelist to win a Pulitzer.

Ulysses

1922 ▪ 730 PAGES ▪ IRELAND

JAMES JOYCE (1882-1941)

It is often said that James Joyce's *Ulysses* stretches the novel form to its limits. Inventive in its use of language and thick with quotations and allusions, it is a literary compendium as well as a story. Joyce first conceived it as a short story in the style of his collection *Dubliners* (1914), but expanded the idea of following a character as he moved around Dublin. The resulting book is both an experimental recreation of everyday experience, and an imaginative recreation of the city that Joyce knew before he left Ireland in 1904.

Set on 16 June 1904, *Ulysses* is composed of 18 "episodes" (a term that Joyce preferred to chapters). In the first of these, we meet Stephen Dedalus, an alter ego of Joyce, who had already appeared in *A Portrait of the Artist as a Young Man* (1916), Joyce's novel of personal, social, and artistic development in an Ireland dominated by both the British Empire and the Catholic Church. At the beginning of *Ulysses*, Stephen is working as a teacher, and is engaged in personal and literary rivalry with friends and colleagues. He spends a great deal of time pondering the death of his mother, as well as the complexities of Irish history and culture.

> Mr Leopold Bloom ate with relish the inner organs of beasts and fowls. He liked thick giblet soup, nutty gizzards, a stuffed roast heart, liverslices fried with crustcrumbs, fried hencods' roes. Most of all he liked grilled mutton kidneys which gave to his palate a fine tang of faintly scented urine. Kidneys were in his mind as he moved about the kitchen softly, righting her breakfast things on the humpy tray. Gelid light and air were in the kitchen but out of doors gentle summer morning everywhere. Made him feel a bit peckish.

ULYSSES, "CALYPSO" EPISODE

Joyce's style inhabits the thoughts of his characters, challenging the reader to work out their logic. At times, narrative takes the form of "interior monologue". In the opening episodes, he gives the reader intimate access to Stephen's thoughts, memories, and feelings. When Stephen walks along the beach of Sandymount Strand, for example, ruminating about nature, being, and eternity, there is no narrator present to clarify what is a recollection, what is a fact, or what is simply a flight of Stephen's imagination.

In context

◄ **DUBLIN** In *Ulysses*, Joyce records a day in the life of Ireland's capital city at a time when the country was still a part of the UK. He takes the reader into Dublin's institutions, homes, and pubs to offer an unparalleled portrait of Edwardian Ireland and its people.

► **NORA BARNACLE** Joyce first stepped out with the Galway-born Nora Barnacle in Dublin on 16 June 1904, the date on which *Ulysses* is set. A chambermaid at Finn's Hotel near Trinity College, Nora influenced some of Joyce's finest work, such as his short story "The Dead". She later eloped with Joyce, and supported him throughout his life.

Mr Leopold Bloom ate with relish the inner organs of beasts and fowls. He liked thick giblet soup, nutty gizzards, a stuffed roast heart, liverslices fried with crustcrumbs, fried cods' roes. Most of all he liked grilled mutton kidneys which gave to his palate a fine tang of faintly scented urine.

Kidneys were in his mind as he moved about the kitchen softly, righting her breakfast things on the humpy tray. Gelid light and air were in the kitchen but out of doors gentle summer morning everywhere. Made him feel a bit peckish.

The coals were reddening.

Another slice of bread and butter: three, four: right. He didn't like her plate full. Right. He turned from the tray, lifted the kettle off the hob and set it sideways on the fire. It sat there, dull and squat, its spout stuck out. The cat walked stiffly round a leg of the table with tail on high.

— Mkgnao!

— O, there you are, Mr Bloom said, turning from the fire.

The cat mewed in answer and stalked again stiffly round a leg of the table, mewing. Mr Bloom watched curiously, kindly the little black form. Clean to see: the gloss of her sleek hide, the white button under the butt of her tail, the green flashing eyes. He bent down to her, his hands on his knees.

— Milk for the pussens, he said.

— Mrkgnao! the cat cried.

They call them stupid. They understand what we say better than we understand them. She understands all she wants to. Vindictive too. Cruel. Her nature. Curious mice never squeal. Seem to like it.

— Afraid of the chickens she is, he said mockingly. Afraid of the chookchooks. I never saw such a stupid pussens as the pussens.

— Mrkrgnao! the cat said loudly.

She blinked up out of her avid shameclosing eyes, mewing plaintively and long, showing him her milkwhite teeth. He watched the dark eyeslits narrowing with greed till her eyes were green stones. Then he went to the dresser, poured milk on a saucer and set it for her.

▲ **BREAKFAST AT HOME** In this part of the manuscript, Leopold Bloom has breakfast at his home in 7 Eccles Street before attending a funeral, while his wife Molly lies in bed upstairs waiting for her lover to arrive. Joyce introduces us to Bloom through his habits and reflections before we accompany him on his walk through Dublin.

THE ODYSSEY

The structure of *Ulysses* is derived from Homer's epic poem *The Odyssey*, in which the resourceful Odysseus, known as Ulysses in Latin, spends 10 years attempting to return home to his wife Penelope after the Trojan War. Many of the characters in the novel are modern stand-ins for Homeric figures. Also, although the episodes of *Ulysses* are not titled or numbered, they are often known by their Homeric counterparts, such as "Hades" and "Sirens".

In a celebrated episode of the book, set at lunchtime in a Dublin pub, Bloom meets a figure known as the Citizen – a xenophobic nationalist given to antisemitic statements and a blinkered view of politics and culture. He embodies the monstrous, one-eyed Cyclops that features in *The Odyssey*.

▲ **An ancient Greek vase** depicting Odysseus lashed to a mast, resisting the sirens' calls

▼ **LEOPOLD BLOOM** This is a sketch that Joyce made of Leopold Bloom. A middle-aged Dubliner of Jewish descent, Bloom makes a living selling advertising space for newspapers. Joyce based him on several real-life people and gives us unrivalled access to his thoughts and desires. We also learn about his background – his father died by suicide, and he has a living daughter called Milly, and a son named Rudy, who died in infancy.

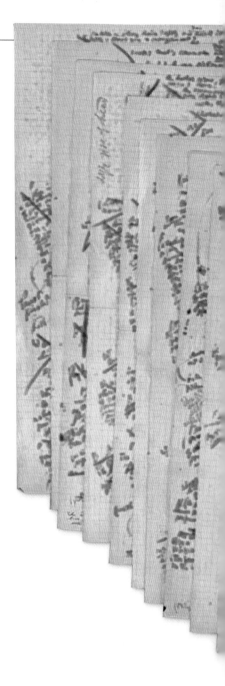

> ❝ Ineluctable modality of the visible... Signatures of all things I am here to read... ❞

ULYSSES, "PROTEUS" EPISODE

The main focus of Ulysses is the character of Leopold Bloom, a Jewish Dubliner, whose private life, memories, and perceptions give Joyce the opportunity to explore myriad aspects of Irish politics, identity, and popular culture. Following Bloom throughout the day as he wanders around the city, *Ulysses* introduces a wealth of Dublin characters via the eyes, ears, and mind of Bloom. We get all his uncensored thoughts: everything that goes through his mind finds its way into the novel. His amblings have specific parallels with Homer's *Odyssey*. After attending a funeral, Bloom goes to a chemist's, drinks in Barney Kiernan's pub, fantasizes while standing on Sandymount Strand, and encounters several other people, before finally meeting Stephen and inviting him back, in a fatherly way, to spend the rest of the night at his home.

These events may be unremarkable, but each episode is narrated with its own ingenious use of form, whether playful or challenging. The "Oxen of the Sun" episode in the maternity ward of Holles Street hospital tackles the theme of fertility in a succession of different styles, parodying the language and tone of each major period of English literature. Similarly, in the "Circe" episode, Bloom hallucinates in a brothel in a late-night sequence that captures the essence of suppressed desire and hidden fantasies.

The humorous, masculine conversation of Stephen and Bloom, much taken up with politics and reflections on literary and paternal authority, gives way to exhaustion at the end of the day. After the two men part, the final pages of the novel introduce one of its best-known episodes, in which Molly Bloom thinks in a flowing "stream of consciousness" that captures the energy and scope of her memories, emotions, and thoughts. Lying in bed early the next morning and musing about herself and the world, she pulls the novel back from its darker reaches to an illuminating celebration of everyday experience, the human body, and the possibilities of language in her final, joyful affirmation: "Yes."

◀ **FIRST EDITION** *Ulysses* was first published as a complete edition in Paris by Shakespeare and Company. This legendary bookshop and (in this one instance) publisher was run by Sylvia Beach, an American expatriate who offered Joyce unstinting support. Published in a run of 1,000 copies, the book was considered scandalous, and so quickly became a contraband article.

▶ **OBSCENITY TRIAL** *Ulysses* was successfully published in Europe by Sylvia Beach (seen right with Joyce), but the editors of *The Little Review* in the US had already been prosecuted for obscenity for serializing it. The novel was not cleared for publication until 1932 in the US, and until 1936 in the UK.

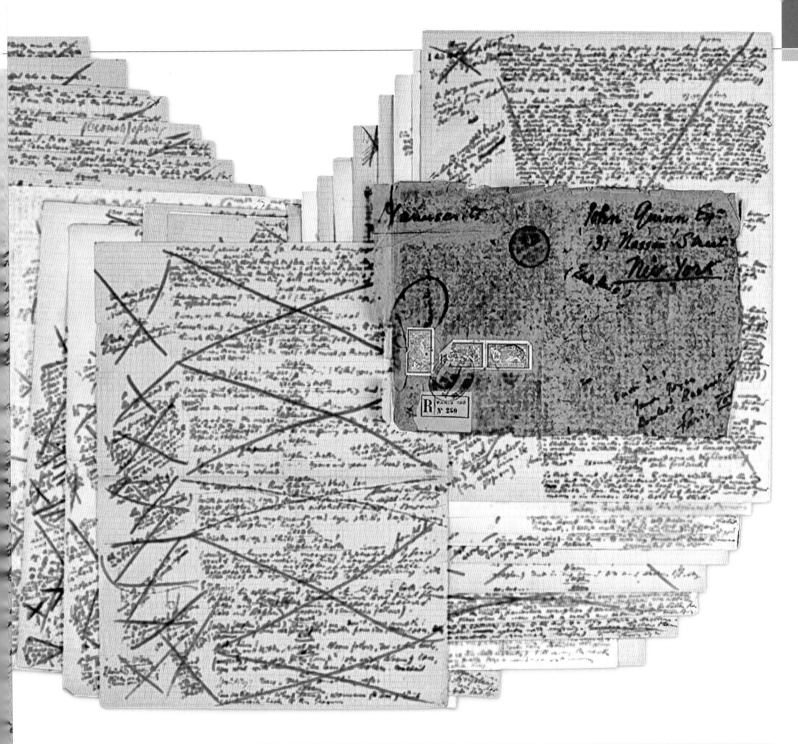

▲ **MANUSCRIPT PAGES** This newly discovered 27-page manuscript of the "Circe" episode of *Ulysses* has copious notes and corrections. Committed to literary style, like Flaubert before him, Joyce laboured over every word and phrase of *Ulysses*. One day, after producing only two sentences, he is said to have observed: "I have the words already. What I am seeking is the perfect order of words in the sentence." His manuscripts give us a glimpse of his commitment to fine-tuning his use of language.

MODERNISM IN LITERATURE

Ulysses is among the great modernist works of literature. Modernism was one of the dominant movements in the arts in Western Europe and the US from the early to mid-20th century. In literature, as in the other arts, it was characterized by experimentation in an attempt to find new and more truthful forms of representation. Early modernist writers reacted in part to the horrors of World War I and the ensuing sense of disillusionment, and replaced traditional realist narratives with fragmented ones written from several different points of view, or as an interior stream of consciousness. They did this in an attempt to create a new form of psychological realism or "truth". Joyce employs this method in *Ulysses*, shaping the world as Bloom experiences it. T.S. Eliot was an admirer of *Ulysses*, and his modernist poem *The Waste Land* (1922) is similarly fragmented in structure, perhaps to convey Eliot's views about the world around him.

▶ **The poet T.S. Eliot** wrote *The Waste Land*, one of the finest examples of modernist poetry.

▶ **MANUSCRIPT** One of Fitzgerald's early titles for *The Great Gatsby* was *Among Ash-Heaps and Millionaires*, which refers to a grim industrial area that lies between Long Island and New York. When he takes us through this desolate place in Chapter 3, Fitzgerald memorably combines images of sterility and death with those of burgeoning life.

▲ **MESMERIC EYES**
The cover of the first edition of *The Great Gatsby* was designed by Spanish painter and graphic designer Francis Cugat. Inspired by the striking image of eyes and the Art-Deco design of the early sketches for the cover, Fitzgerald emphasized certain visual and stylistic elements in the text. These gave Gatsby's tale an added sense of fatalism.

(Number this page 1.)

3 exempl.

Chapter III

About half way between West Egg and New York the motor-road joins the railroad and runs beside it for a quarter of a mile so as to skirt a desolate wasted area of land. It is a valley of ashes — a fantastic farm where ashes grow like wheat into ridges and hills and grotesque gardens, where ashes take the forms of houses and chimneys and rising smoke and finally, with a transcendent effort, of ash-gray men who move dimly and already crumbling through the powdery air. Occasionally a line of grey cars crawls along an invisible track, gives out a ghastly creak and comes to rest, and immediately grey men swarm up with leaden spades and stir up an impenetrable cloud which screens their obscure purposes from your profane regard.

But above the grey land and above the spasms of bleak dust which drift endlessly over it, you perceive, after a moment, the eyes of Dr. T. J. Eckleburg. The eyes of Dr. T. J. Eckleburg are blue and gigantic — their retinas alone are one yard high. They look out of no face but, instead, from a pair of enormous yellow spectacles which pass over a non-existent nose. Evidently some wild wag of an oculist set them there to fatten his practice in the borough of Flushing and then sank down himself into eternal blindness or forgot them and moved away. But his eyes brood on, dimmed a little by many painless days under sun and rain, but wakeful and aware in a spot where every other aspect of life reeks of death.

The Great Gatsby

1925 ▪ 218 PAGES ▪ US

F. SCOTT FITZGERALD (1896-1940)

The Great Gatsby explores the life of one of the most elusive characters in the history of the American novel. The narrator, Nick Carraway, arrives in the Long Island village of West Egg and enters the world of the enigmatic Jay Gatsby, a millionaire socialite who seems to have realized all of his worldly desires. However, Gatsby keeps gazing at the green light of the dock by a house across the bay, consumed by the memory of his past. This past reappears in the figure of Daisy Buchanan, Gatsby's former lover and a cousin of Nick's, she is now married to the tough former college football hero Tom Buchanan.

Nick's exploration of Gatsby's life unveils a world of domestic jealousy, violence, deception, lies, and murder. Following the characters through a number of crises, Fitzgerald explores the defeated hopes and lingering aspirations of people from a cross-section of American society, some pursuing the American dream, and others living an American nightmare, either by accident or design.

In Nick, Fitzgerald creates a classic "unreliable narrator". His relationship with Gatsby and his understanding of what Gatsby represents are not entirely clear – even to himself. Is he attempting to reveal or conceal key aspects of the story?

▲ **ART-DECO GLAMOUR** *The Great Gatsby* takes place during the Jazz Age of the 1920s, as seen in the 1974 film version of the book. The 1920s was a time when liberated young women became known as "flappers". They rebelled against the conventions of how women were supposed to behave, cropping their hair and wearing short (knee-high) skirts.

Is he Gatsby's prosecutor or defender? And does Gatsby stand for profoundly true or essentially false values? The novel alternates between descriptive passages that capture a world of privilege and fabulous parties in the 1920s, vivid dialogue, and passages of lyrical prose. Gatsby's belief that he can revive the past sets the stage for the end of the novel, which captures a mournful sense of resignation: "So we beat on, boats against the current, borne back ceaselessly into the past".

> " But above the grey land and the spasms of bleak dust which drift endlessly over it, you perceive, after a moment, the eyes of Doctor T. J. Eckleburg. The eyes of Doctor T. J. Eckleburg are blue and gigantic – their retinas are one yard high. They look out of no face but, instead, from a pair of enormous yellow spectacles which pass over a non-existent nose. Evidently some wild wag of an oculist set them there to fatten his practice in the borough of Queens, and then sank down himself into eternal blindness or forgot them and moved away. But his eyes… brood on over the solemn dumping ground. "

**THE GREAT GATSBY,
CHAPTER 3**

THE **ROARING TWENTIES**

In the aftermath of World War I, the US and Europe enjoyed a period of growth and progress that became known as the Roaring Twenties. It was in many ways a backlash against the trauma of the war years, and those who could, lived to the full. The expatriate American community in Paris included novelists such as F. Scott Fitzgerald and Ernest Hemingway, and the dancer Josephine Baker. The rise of cinema ushered in the Golden Age of Hollywood, whose stars shaped attitudes towards masculine and feminine style.

In the US, 1920–33 also saw the era of Prohibition, when it was made illegal to produce or sell alcohol, and a network of crime syndicates controlled its distribution. This murky underworld forms a backdrop to *The Great Gatsby*'s tale of identity, crime, truth, and lies.

▶ **In 1927, Josephine Baker** became the first Black woman to star in a major motion picture.

The Trial

1925 ■ 412 PAGES ■ CZECHOSLOVAKIA

FRANZ KAFKA (1883-1924)

Although the German-speaking Czech writer Franz Kafka published very little in his lifetime, he is now considered one of the most influential novelists of the 20th century, largely because of his masterpiece, *The Trial*. The book tells the story of a man referred to simply as Joseph K., a senior cashier in a bank, who is arrested one day by an authority to which he has no access, and for a reason that is not explained. During his arrest, he is told to wait for instructions, and then to report at the court on a specific day. However, the harder he tries to carry out his accusers' instructions – and to find out why he has been arrested – the more trouble he finds himself in. The tension increases as K.'s difficulties escalate.

The book's narrative is told in the third person, but as seen through K.'s eyes. It describes a series of episodes, each of which makes his situation harder to understand: he finds two men being whipped in a storeroom at the bank where he works; he hires a lawyer who turns out to be incompetent; he encounters a priest who tells him a story that is meant to explain his predicament, but does not. These events lead to a conclusion that is just as

hard to understand – and shocking. The world of *The Trial*, a baffling, labyrinthine place, in which even institutions such as the law fail to provide any answers, forces readers to reexamine their own world, as well as Joseph K.'s. The story seems pertinent not just to the Austro-Hungarian bureaucracy of Kafka's time, but also, prophetically, to the totalitarian regimes of Germany, Italy, and the Soviet Union. It has even inspired the word "Kafkaesque", meaning inexplicable and nightmarish, that now exists in many languages.

> " Someone must have been telling lies about Joseph K., for without having done anything wrong he was arrested one fine morning... At once there was a knock at the door and a man entered whom he had never seen before in the house. He was slim and yet well knit, he wore a closely fitting black suit, which was furnished with all sorts of pleats, pockets, buckles, and buttons, as well as a belt, like a tourist's outfit, and in consequence looked eminently practical, though one could not quite tell what actual purpose it served. 'Who are you?' asked K., half raising himself in bed. "
>
> **THE TRIAL, CHAPTER 1**

In context

◄ **PRAGUE** Kafka was born in the city of Prague, where his novel is also set. As an educated Jew of the Austro-Hungarian Empire, he lived in the Jewish quarter, and spoke and wrote German. He knew the city well, and its winding, narrow streets are likely to have inspired the labyrinthine world of *The Trial*.

► **KAFKA AND FELICE BAUER** One of Kafka's closest relationships was with his long-term girlfriend Felice Bauer. They spent a lot of time living apart, and so much of their relationship was conducted through letters. Kafka's side of their correspondence has survived, and many of his letters convey his anxiety about not being able to express himself precisely.

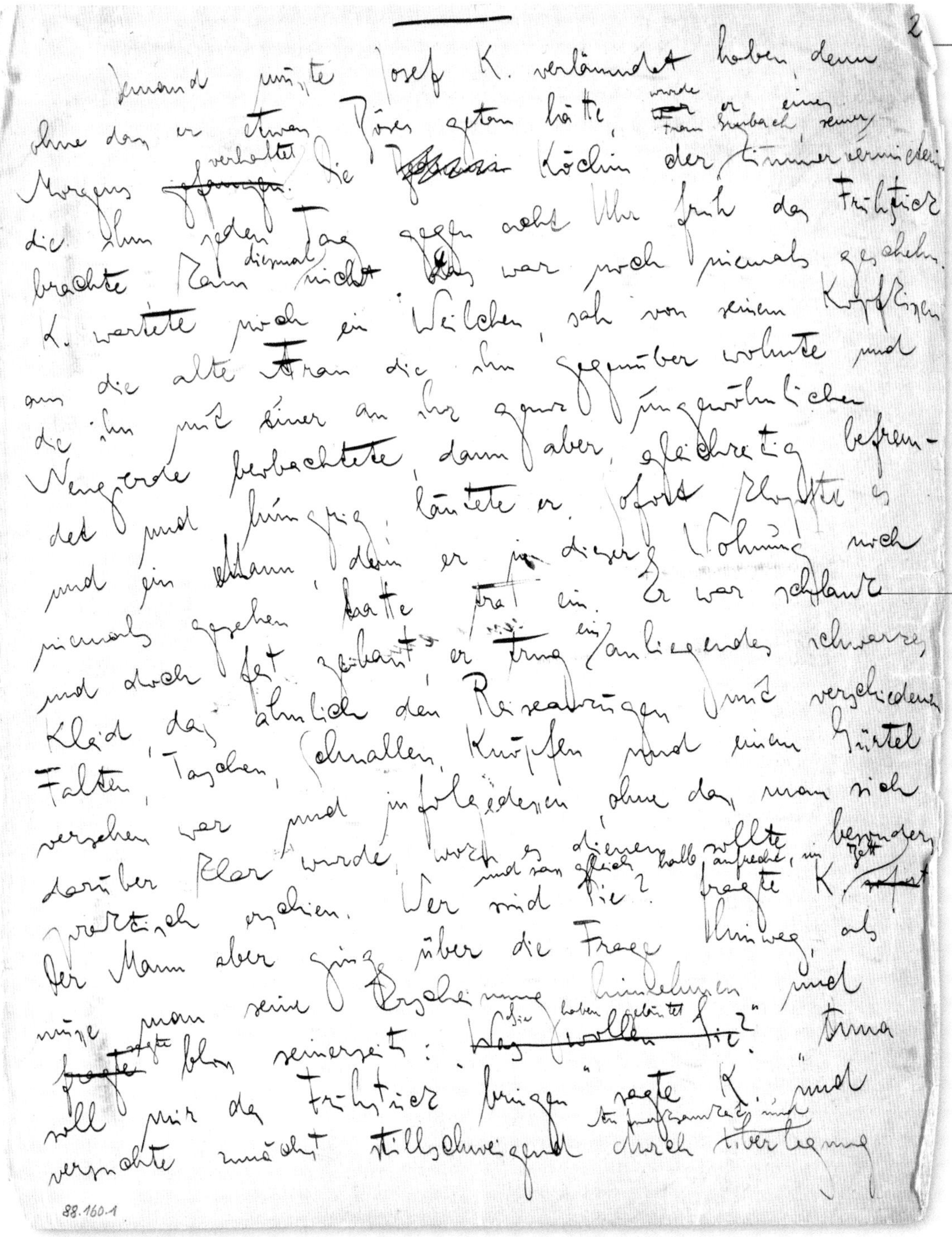

◄ **FIRST PAGE OF MANUSCRIPT**
The uncertainties in *The Trial* start at the very beginning of the novel: "Someone must have been telling lies about Josef K..." This opening statement introduces a narrator who is not sure of the facts. Even in reality, Kafka did not finish the book, but left it as a pile of chapters that had to be sorted out and put in order.

Kafka wrote Joseph K.'s ambiguous story in strong, decisive handwriting

> "Do you think you'll bring this fine case of yours to a speedier end by wrangling with us, your warders?"
>
> ***THE TRIAL*, CHAPTER 1**

AN **INEXPLICABLE WORLD**

In the world of *The Trial*, it seems impossible for people to understand what is happening to them, or for them to change anything for the better. Without an overarching religion or philosophy, or even a set of laws, nothing can explain the events that take place. Nor can Joseph K. appeal to any kind of logic to make sense of his predicament. This state of meaninglessness is often described as "the absurd", and long after Kafka's death, late-20th-century writers such as Albert Camus developed the philosophy of absurdism to describe the impossibility of understanding life in a world in which there is no God. Kafka seems to have anticipated this outlook several decades before it became widespread.

► **Jaroslav Rona's memorial to Kafka**, in Prague, shows the author riding the shoulders of an empty but animated suit.

▶ **FIRST EDITION** Shortly before he died, Kafka told Max Brod to destroy his unpublished literary works, including his three novels. Brod disobeyed, and steadily worked to bring them to publication. *The Trial* was published in Germany, a year after Kafka's death, by Verlag die Schmiede, a company that specialized in avant-garde literature. The cover is in a bold graphic style influenced by the Bauhaus, the radical school of art and design in Germany.

> Please don't ask me for names, take my warning to heart instead, and don't be so unyielding in future, you can't put up a resistance against this Court, you must admit your fault. Make your confession at the first chance you get. Until you do that, there's no possibility of getting out of their clutches, none at all. Yet even then you won't manage it without help from outside, but you needn't worry about that, I'll see to it myself.

THE TRIAL, CHAPTER 6

> ## It is not necessary to accept everything as true, one must only accept it as necessary.

THE TRIAL, CHAPTER 9

The Trial is a very oppressive book, because none of the authority figures in it, such as K.'s judges or his lawyer Herr Huld, offers him any kind of useful advice or any explanation for his arrest. Personal relationships cannot help him either: most of the characters in the novel seem to use sex as a means to gain power over their partners. Leni, Herr Huld's nurse, for example, tempts K. into having a sexual encounter with her, but she only finds him attractive because he is under arrest.

In Kafka's time, one place that a lost soul might have found help would have been in a Roman Catholic church. However, when K. meets a clergyman by chance during a visit to Prague Cathedral, the priest tells him a fable that is clearly meant to shine light on his own situation. This fable, a short story called *Before the Law* that Kafka had written before *The Trial*, tells of a man who wants to gain access to "the law", and is told that he has to wait by a gate until he is admitted. Neither he nor anyone else ever goes through the gate, and at the end the gatekeeper closes it for good, saying: "No one else could ever be admitted here, since this gate was made only for you".

KAFKA'S OTHER WORKS

Franz Kafka wrote two other novels, both of which were published after his death. His first, *America*, was partly based on the lives of some of his relatives who had emigrated to the US. It is lighter in tone and more humorous than Kafka's other books. The other novel, *The Castle*, is similar to *The Trial*: it is about another man named K. who is locked in a long battle with bureaucracy. Kafka also wrote several novellas and short stories, some of which were published before he died. Perhaps his most famous novella is *The Metamorphosis*, about Gregor Samsa, a young man who wakes up one day and finds that he has turned into a gigantic, monstrous insect. The story is an example of magical realism, although it was written long before that concept was ever defined.

▲ **The front cover** of a 1916 edition of Kafka's story *The Metamorphosis* (1915)

Although the priest recounts this fable to explain K.'s troubles, it tells K. nothing, other than that he has little or no hope of ever having his questions answered.

The book's conclusion is utterly bleak, but Kafka's close friend Max Brod, who edited it for publication after the author's death, claimed that Kafka found his novel amusing, and often laughed when he read it aloud to friends. Many of Kafka's readers have also found dark comedy in the novel's deadly anatomy of the ways in which institutional authorities, however incompetent, mislead and bewilder the individual.

▲ **PROPHETIC TEXT** Many people who have lived under totalitarian governments have felt that *The Trial* was written for them. This was especially true in the communist countries of eastern and central Europe, including Kafka's native Czechoslovakia. Under such regimes, people were persecuted arbitrarily, and had little access to proper legal representation.

▲ **IN THE COURTROOM** A film of *The Trial*, directed by Orson Welles (who also plays the lawyer) and starring Anthony Perkins as Joseph K., was made in 1962. It was praised for its use of unusual camera angles and lighting to enhance K.'s sense of alienation, particularly in the menacing courtroom.

THE SUN ALSO RISES

ERNEST HEMINGWAY

Author of

"IN OUR TIME" and "THE TORRENTS OF SPRING"

CLEON

> " The taxi went up the hill, passed the lighted square, then on into the dark, still climbing, then leveled out onto a dark street behind St. Etienne du Mont, went smoothly down the asphalt… then turned onto the cobbles of the Rue Mouffetard. There were lighted bars and late open shops on each side of the street. We were sitting apart and we jolted close together going down the old street. Brett's hat was off. Her head was back. I saw her face in the lights from the open shops, then it was dark, then I saw her face clearly as we came out on the Avenue des Gobelins. "

**THE SUN ALSO RISES,
CHAPTER 4**

◄ **FIRST EDITION** The dust jacket of the first edition of *The Sun Also Rises* was designed by Cleonike Damianakes, an American artist who also produced covers for Hemingway's *A Farewell to Arms* and F. Scott Fitzgerald's *All the Sad Young Men*. The illustration, which was meant to appeal to contemporary female readers, hints at a classical and tragic dimension to the work, but is somewhat at odds with the novel's bracing modern style.

The Sun Also Rises

1926 ■ 228 PAGES ■ US

ERNEST HEMINGWAY (1899–1961)

Set largely in Paris after World War I, *The Sun Also Rises*, Hemingway's first novel, tells the story of a love affair between an American war veteran, who bears the physical and emotional scars of combat, and a sophisticated English divorcée. In its depiction of a vibrant postwar Paris, Hemingway replicated the pattern of his own life as a writer in the city in the 1920s, and based the characters on people that he knew. Frequenting the bars and cafés of the Latin Quarter, former soldier Jake Barnes meets Brett Ashley, a free-spirited socialite with whom he cannot forge a sexual or emotional connection. The novel takes them and a motley group of expatriates seeking a carefree life to Spain.

Heading to Pamplona for a bullfighting festival, the novel explores the fleeting friendships and lasting rivalries of its characters in a bare, precise style interspersed with exchanges of combative dialogue. Following romantic misunderstandings in Pamplona, the antagonistic group of characters disperses, leaving the passions and intensity of Spain to go their own way and return to Paris. When Jake and Brett meet for the final time and acknowledge that they have no future together, the sun sets on their doomed love affair.

HEMINGWAY'S OTHER WORKS

Hemingway mastered several literary forms, including the short story, which particularly suited his restrained writing style. He continued to explore Spanish culture in *Death in the Afternoon* (1932) and *For Whom the Bell Tolls* (1940), which takes place during the Spanish Civil War. The influential novels *A Farewell to Arms* (1929) and *To Have and Have Not* (1937) were later made into films. *The Old Man and The Sea* (1952), a novella and perhaps his most famous work, is about what Hemingway described as "the good and true" and describes the final outing of a fisherman off the coast of Cuba.

▶ **A Farewell to Arms**, with a cover illustration by Cleonike Damianakes

The Sun Also Rises was highly influential. The impact of the novel was a result of its style more than its content: Hemingway's minimalist, declarative prose avoids effusive description and reflection and was greatly influenced by the direct style of writing that he had learnt as a journalist. This form of writing eventually became standard in fiction, but it was groundbreaking at the time.

In context

◀ **BULLFIGHTING** When *The Sun Also Rises* was published in the UK, it was given the title *Fiesta*. Spanish culture offers an antidote to the modern world in the novel. Hemingway admired the *corrida*, or bullfighting, especially the legendary Spanish bullfighter, Cayetano Ordóñez, who was the model for Pedro Romero. In *Death in the Afternoon*, Hemingway later explored his fascination with Spanish bullfighting in depth.

▲ **HEMINGWAY AND EUROPE** Hemingway came to Europe as a member of the American Red Cross during World War I, and worked as a journalist before devoting himself to writing. In Paris he was a regular at the Café du Dôme, as were many other intellectuals.

To the Lighthouse

1927 ▪ 310 PAGES ▪ UK

VIRGINIA WOOLF (1882-1941)

To the Lighthouse is one of the pioneering works of modernist literature. Although experimental in form, its subject matter is the ordinary life of a family very much like the one in which Woolf grew up. It is about the Ramsays (a couple and their eight children) and two holidays that they take – one shortly before World War I and another 10 years later – at their summer home on the Isle of Skye, Scotland. Various friends and acquaintances visit the family while they are on holiday, including Claude Tansley, a university pupil of Mr Ramsay's who is an aspiring philosopher; Lily Briscoe, a young artist who paints during her stay; and William Bankes, a shy botanist, who Mrs Ramsay vainly hopes might marry Lily. The novel begins with plans to visit a lighthouse off the island's coast, Mr Ramsay's certainty that the weather will prevent this, and his young son James's unspoken resentment at his father's domineering nature.

The novel's treatment of time is unusual. The first and last of its three parts, "The Window" and "The Lighthouse", each cover the events of a single day. The short central part, "Time Passes", covers some 10 years between these two days. Even more innovative is Woolf's narrative method. She moves deftly between the minds of her characters, describing the apparently insignificant events of two ordinary days from different viewpoints, which often switch rapidly, sometimes even mid-sentence. Fragments of dialogue are separated by stretches of reflection and memory.

Woolf initially intended to call the novel an "Elegy". In between the first part, which ends with a dinner party presided over by Mrs Ramsay, and the last, where the visit to the lighthouse finally takes place, we hear from an omniscient narrator of many changes, and of the deaths of several of the characters that we have met earlier. As we see the housekeeper bringing the house back from decay, we hear of the deaths, first, of Mrs Ramsay, then of her daughter Prue, in childbirth, then of her son Andrew, killed by shellfire in France.

In context

▲ **GODREVY LIGHTHOUSE** In her youth, Woolf spent many holidays at Talland House, in St Ives, Cornwall. Godrevy Lighthouse, which her family visited, can be seen from the house across St Ives Bay. Although her novel is set on Skye, this view, across a broad stretch of sea to the lighthouse, is thought to have inspired the journey at the end of the book.

▲ **FATHER AND DAUGHTER** This photograph shows Virginia Woolf with her father, Sir Leslie Stephen. A historian and literary critic, he directed her reading from early on and encouraged her to write. Mr Ramsay was inspired by him, just as Mrs Ramsay was based on Woolf's mother, who died when Virginia was a teenager.

◄ **FIRST EDITION** Virginia Woolf and her husband Leonard founded a publishing company, the Hogarth Press, which brought out books by Virginia and many other writers. Vanessa Bell, Virginia's sister, a prominent artist, designed many of the dust jackets. The stylized image of the lighthouse, with its spreading light and swirling waves, is typical of Bell's work. Her strong, graphic style was unlike anything else at the time and made Hogarth Press books instantly recognizable.

" Had there been an axe handy, a poker, or any weapon that would have gashed a hole in his father's breast and killed him, there and then, James would have seized it. Such were the extremes of emotion that Mr Ramsay excited in his children's breasts by his mere presence; standing, as now, lean as a knife, narrow as the blade of one, grinning sarcastically, not only with the pleasure of disillusioning his son and casting ridicule upon his wife, who was ten thousand times better in every way than he was (James thought), but also with some secret conceit at his own accuracy of judgement. "

TO THE LIGHTHOUSE, PART 1, SECTION 1

" So that is marriage, Lily thought, a man and a woman looking at a girl throwing a ball. "

TO THE LIGHTHOUSE, PART 1, SECTION 13

Although *To the Lighthouse* includes loss and bereavement, its structure also provides a sense of fulfilment. By the end of the novel, some of the Ramsays have grown closer – the children's resentment of their father seems to have dissolved. Meanwhile Lily Briscoe, whose perceptions are central to the third part of the novel, has developed as an artist. The novel ends with her completing a painting that once seemed impossible and a resonant final sentence that appears to identify her art with Woolf's own imaginative project: "Yes, she thought, laying down her brush in extreme fatigue, I have had my vision."

One striking feature of the novel is the attention that it gives the perceptions of women, often contrasted with the expectations of men. Lily Briscoe's artistic ambitions are set against the views of the dour young intellectual, Tansley, who voices the opinion that women are inevitably inferior as writers and artists. Mrs Ramsay, meanwhile, has accepted the self-effacing role of wife and mother, but, in the first part, she is at the centre of the reader's attention. We follow her thoughts as she sees, with uncanny understanding, her husband's self-doubts. She tends him as much as her children, and all the novel's minor characters rely, sometimes comically, on her reassuring influence.

Just as Mr Ramsay, the famous but darkly self-doubting intellectual, was based on Woolf's own father, for Mrs Ramsay Woolf drew on memories of her mother, who had died when she was 13. Her sister Vanessa wrote that the portrait of her was "more like her to me than anything I could ever have

▲ **BLOOMSBURY GROUP** The Woolfs and several other artists, intellectuals, and writers such as Lytton Strachey, met frequently to discuss art, philosophy, and literature. They became known as the Bloomsbury Group, after the area of London where Virginia and her siblings had a house. United by their interest in innovative art, they helped to shape Virginia's approach to writing.

conceived possible". Yet Woolf's novel goes far beyond family biography. Her picture of a privileged, slightly shabby middle-class family a century ago is also a poignant description of the ways in which everyday impressions can ignite deep emotions or reawaken buried memories in anyone. Woolf achieves this with an often poetic narrative prose, where sentences sometimes unspool in long digressive sequences, and where patterns of repetition are more important than any sense of plot.

◄ **THE GARDEN AT MONK'S HOUSE** The Woolfs bought a Sussex cottage, depicted here by Virginia's sister Vanessa, as a country home in 1919. It was not far from Charleston, the old farmhouse where Vanessa lived. Virginia liked the tranquillity of the garden, and had a wooden building there that she used as a study. It was here that she wrote many of her books, including *To the Lighthouse*.

> “ The great revelation had never come... Instead there were little daily miracles... ”

TO THE LIGHTHOUSE, PART 3, SECTION 3

> " She could have wept. It was bad, it was bad, it was infinitely bad! She could have done it differently of course; the colour could have been thinned and faded; the shapes etherealized... But then she did not see it like that. She saw the colour burning on a framework of steel; the light of a butterfly's wing lying upon the arches of a cathedral. Of all that only a few random marks scrawled upon the canvas remained. And it would never be seen; never be hung even, and there was Mr Tansley whispering in her ear, 'Women can't paint, women can't write...' "

TO THE LIGHTHOUSE, PART 1, SECTION 9

◀ **MANUSCRIPT** This page of Woolf's original manuscript contains a passage in which Lily Briscoe looks at her painting and remembers something that Claude Tansley had said: that women make poor artists. The novel shows how false this view is, and demonstrates how damaging it can be to women such as Lily who are unsure about their work. Woolf herself suffered similar uncertainties, and Lily represents her in some ways.

WOOLF'S OTHER WORKS

Virginia Woolf wrote seven novels, six of which were in the modernist idiom. She developed the "free indirect" style, in which aspects of third- and first-person narratives are combined to express multiple perspectives.

Her novels include *Jacob's Room*, in which the hero is absent; *Orlando*, which narrates a life that spans several centuries; *Mrs Dalloway*, a narrative with multiple viewpoints, which takes place in a single day; and *The Waves*, her most poetic work, which explores many issues, including the effects of school bullying. Her essay *A Room of One's Own* discusses the difficulties that women faced when trying to become writers in Woolf's time.

▲ *A Room of One's Own* (1929) is an essay about the role of women in society.

> " The subject of this book is the life of the former cement worker and haulier Franz Biberkopf in Berlin. As our story begins, he has just been released from prison, where he did time for some stupid stuff; now he is back in Berlin, determined to go straight. To begin with, he succeeds. But then, though doing all right for himself financially, he gets involved in a set-to with an unpredictable external agency that looks an awful lot like fate. Three times that force attacks him and disrupts his scheme... And finally it hits him with monstrous and extreme violence. "

BERLIN ALEXANDERPLATZ, PREFACE

A gang of thieves moves stolen goods into a car while one of them stands guard

▶ **FIRST EDITION** *Berlin Alexanderplatz* was published by Fischer Verlag in 1929. The first edition had a hand-drawn, hand-lettered dust jacket that was designed by Georg Salter, who went on to become an acclaimed book-cover designer both in Germany and the US. Its combination of words and images offers an intriguing invitation to a tale of alienation, thieving, murder, and appalling misfortune.

Alfred Döblin

BERLIN ALEXANDERPLATZ

DIE GESCHICHTE VOM FRANZ BIBERKOPF

S. Fischer Verlag

Von einem einfachen MANN wird hier erzählt, der in BERLIN am ALEXANDERPLATZ als Strassenhändler steht. Der MANN hat vor anständig zu sein, da stellt ihm das Leben hinterlistig ein Bein. Er wird betrogen, er wird in Verbrechen reingezogen, BRAUT auf rohe Weise zuletzt wird ihm seine genommen und auf umgebracht. Ganz aus ist es mit dem MANN FRANZ BIBERKOPF. Am Schluss aber erhält er eine sehr klare Belehrung: MAN FÄNGT NICHT SEIN LEBEN MIT GUTEN WORTEN UND VORSÄTZEN AN MIT ERKENNEN UND VERSTEHEN FÄNGT MAN ES AN UND MIT DEM RICHTIGEN NEBENMANN. Ramponiert steht er ALEXANDERPLATZ, zuletzt wieder an das Leben hat ihn mächtig angefasst.

Berlin Alexanderplatz

1929 ▪ 528 PAGES ▪ GERMANY

ALFRED DÖBLIN (1878–1957)

Alfred Döblin was both a doctor and a leading literary figure in 1920s Berlin, who set out to anatomize the social and moral chaos of the Weimar Republic (1919–33), the unstable period of German history between the collapse of Imperial Germany, defeated in World War I, and the rise of Hitler. He probed deeply beneath the life of the city, and discovered not just a malady that was unique to Germany, but a universal human one. He presented his diagnosis of the underlying problem in his most famous book, *Berlin Alexanderplatz*.

The novel is set in Berlin's working-class neighbourhoods, many of them clustered around the Alexanderplatz, a crowded square that in 1928 – the year in which the novel is largely set – was unusually chaotic because of building works, making for an apt symbol of urban confusion. Most of the characters in the book are hoodlums, thieves, or sex workers. Franz Biberkopf, the often unheroic protagonist, is defeated by circumstance and his own shortcomings, and endures an appalling fate.

The genius of this book lies in the way in which the story is told. A torrent of words streams across the pages – sometimes detached and objective, sweeping up bits of mythology, folktale, Biblical quotations, newspaper headlines, weather reports, and statistics in its wake – creating a verbal pastiche of astonishing narrative power.

The book became very popular very quickly and has been adapted into films on numerous occasions. The appeal is obvious. Urban life is the universal malady, economic circumstances the prison, and the varied tempo of the marching throngs in the final pages – "left right left right left" – can still be heard clashing today.

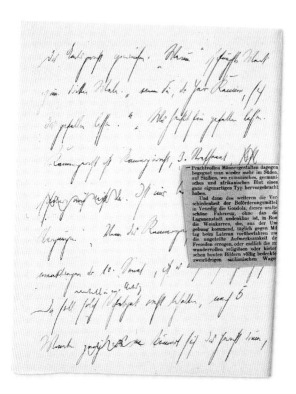

▲ **MANUSCRIPT** A newspaper clipping adorns a page of Döblin's manuscript of *Berlin Alexanderplatz*. The novel is littered with excerpts from newspapers, influenced by the montage technique that was popular in the Dada art movement of the time.

In context

▲ **THE ALEXANDERPLATZ** The statue of Berolina, the personification of Berlin, towers over the Alexanderplatz. In the mid-1920s, when this photograph was taken, it was the busiest spot in the city. Major avenues, tramlines, and railways converged at a plaza ringed by hotels, restaurants, and department stores.

◀ **WEIMAR CULTURE** This central panel of Otto Dix's 1928 triptych *Metropolis* captures the decadence and sexual permissiveness of Weimar Germany's cabaret culture. Despite the prevailing economic and social chaos, the period also boasted brilliant achievements in German art, music, philosophy, cinema, and literature.

The Sound and the Fury

1929 ▪ 326 PAGES ▪ US

WILLIAM FAULKNER (1897–1962)

A work in which Faulkner experiments with form, *The Sound and the Fury* describes the moral disintegration of an old Southern family. At its heart is Candace "Caddy" Compson, an enigmatic character who was Faulkner's own favourite, although she hardly has a voice in the novel. Caddy is the only Compson child willing to embrace life without regret. She is compassionate, but also sensual, and the story pivots on the differing reactions of her three brothers to what her father describes as "a piece of natural human folly" – her loss of virginity to a passing stranger.

In a piece of narrative brilliance, her brother Benjy, whose intellectual disability traps him in an innocent world without words, is given the first interior monologue. Quentin's very different voice reveals a former idealist driven to despair and the brink of suicide by his beloved sister's lapse. Meanwhile, Jason's thoughts disclose an angry and repulsive person who projects all of his repressed fury onto Caddy's illegitimate daughter. Rising above this emotional chaos, Faulkner adds a fourth perspective. This is the omniscient view of one of his most memorable creations, Dilsey, the African American cook, and the only character strong, generous, and faithful enough to achieve a measure of objectivity. Caddy herself, despite being Faulkner's "darling", and the central figure of a story that spans decades, never gets to speak. We only ever see her through the eyes of others.

With *The Sound and the Fury*, Faulkner greatly advanced the stream-of-consciousness literary technique, which gives the reader direct access to the narrators' trains of thought. The novel was also one of the major parts of his Yoknapatawpha Cycle of tales, all of which take place in a fictional county in Mississippi. Together, these stories are Faulkner's allegory of the South, and his testimony to the resilience of the human heart.

▶ **MANUSCRIPT** Faulkner wrote his early manuscripts in blue or black ink, and usually on Fidelity Onion Skin paper, legal size. This sheet opens the second part of the novel, with Quentin's stream of memory. Faulkner extensively reworked this material, as can be seen by comparing the opening lines of this manuscript page with those of the final published work (see extract, opposite).

▲ **FIRST EDITION** *The Sound and the Fury* was published in the US by Jonathan Cape and Harrison Smith. When asked about the uncredited cover illustration, Faulkner said that he knew nothing about it, but he supposed that it depicted the struggle between the powers of darkness and light.

◀ **FAULKNER'S DESK** In his office at Rowan Oak, his house in Oxford, Mississippi, Faulkner worked at a small desk that his mother gave him. He wrote quickly in longhand, and typed up the text while he could still decipher his own handwriting. If the weather was good, he would take both the table and typewriter outside to work.

> When the shadow of the sash appeared on the curtains it was between seven and eight oclock and then I was in time again, hearing the watch. It was Grandfather's and when Father gave it to me he said I give you the mausoleum of all hope and desire; it's rather excruciatingly apt that you will use it to gain the reducto absurdum of all human experience which can fit your individual needs no better than it fitted his or his father's.

***THE SOUND AND THE FURY*, "JUNE SECOND, 1910"**

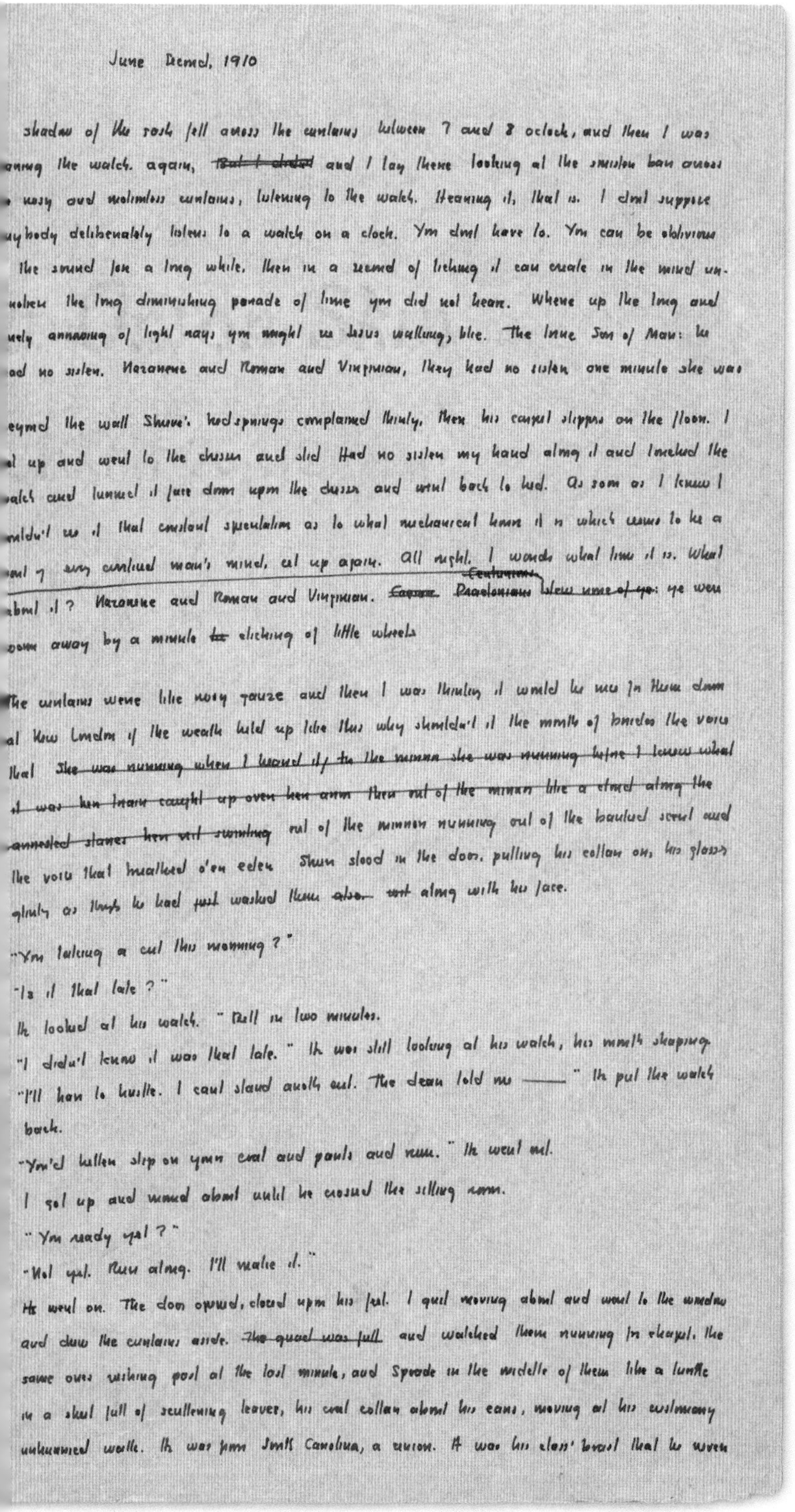

June Second, 1910

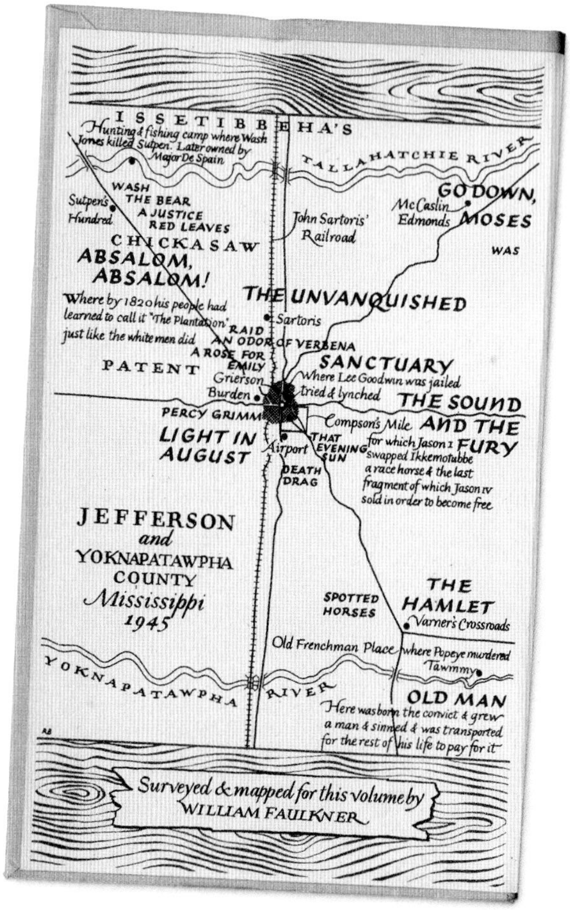

▲ **YOKNAPATAWPHA COUNTY** This map of the fictional Yoknapatawpha County, Mississippi, "surveyed and drawn" by Faulkner himself, is the setting for the author's Yoknapatawpha Cycle of stories. Taken together, these tales form a complete portrait of the American South.

FOUR-PERSPECTIVE NARRATIVE

Stream-of-consciousness narratives can be difficult to follow. Readers must play detective, staying alert to every clue that might surface in the jumbled torrent of a character's thoughts, feelings, observations, and memories. Multiple streams are even more demanding, and in *The Sound and the Fury* there are three: Benjy's is childlike and impressionistic; Quentin's is educated but suicidal; and Jason's is bitter, angry, and contemptuous. The three monologues are very different, and Faulkner experiments with typography and punctuation to convey his narrators' changing states of mind. As Quentin nears his end, for example, his "I" becomes an "i" to convey his diminishing sense of self. By bringing his readers so close to his characters, Faulkner tells his multidimensional story in a way that would not have been possible using traditional literary techniques.

The Man Without Qualities

1930-43 ▪ THREE VOLUMES ▪ AUSTRIA

ROBERT MUSIL (1880-1942)

Trained as an engineer, a behavioural psychologist, and a philosopher, Robert Musil was a man of so many talents that when he wanted answers to his existential questions, he chose to explore them in the form of a novel. The result was a book of huge intellectual scope that has become known as "the philosopher's novel", but that the author never managed to finish.

Essayistic in style, with an omniscient narrator, *The Man Without Qualities* is set in Vienna, the capital of an Austro-Hungarian Empire (called "Kakania" here) soon to be destroyed in World War I. Ulrich, its protagonist, is a philosophically inclined, wealthy young man "without qualities" – he passively observes and experiences the world around him – and he saunters among friends and acquaintances, ranging from the hostess of an intellectual salon to a murderer.

These characters have their prejudices and illicit love affairs, and much of the narrative is a satirical portrait of Viennese society, but it allows Musil to examine every aspect of modern philosophy, science, and technology. An incomparable prose stylist, he knits these threads together into a constant interplay of commentary and action, in which each idea is reflected in an

◄ **EMPEROR FRANZ JOSEPH** Dressed in blue, white-haired Emperor Franz Joseph receives guests at a court ball in the Hofburg, or royal palace, in Vienna. Crowned at the age of 18, in 1848, he had become such a symbol of the Austro-Hungarian Empire that a subplot in the novel features preparations to celebrate his 70th year on the throne in 1918. However, the Emperor dies two years short of this anniversary.

image, character, or circumstance. Writers and critics hailed *The Man Without Qualities* as a masterpiece. In German-speaking countries, Musil is ranked in the top tier of novelists, alongside Franz Kafka, Thomas Mann, and Hermann Hesse; elsewhere, his influence has been compared to that of James Joyce and Marcel Proust. For this novel is a moral allegory, an attempt to find the truly human life in the materialistic modern world, science and technology having destroyed so many of the old values and certainties. And rarely has this quest been envisioned with greater range, depth, and sheer imaginative audacity.

◄ **VIENNA** "City of Dreams!" a madman in the novel exclaims when Vienna (seen here in 1873) is mentioned. The circular Ringstrasse encloses St Stephen's Cathedral and the Hofburg, beyond which are the River Danube and the Vienna Woods. On the eve of World War I, the city was about to lose its imperial status for ever.

► **MANUSCRIPT** Although Musil was a polished stylist, a glance at his manuscript shows what a daunting task it must have been to publish his writings in book form. He also left hundreds of pages of "Posthumous Papers", which included additional notes, sketches, and alternate drafts. Sadly, the material that he left behind in Vienna when he fled the Nazis has been lost.

> " Ulrich inquired out of politeness how the Parallel Campaign had fared in his absence. 'Well, because of that hullabaloo in the street outside my house that afternoon, which you observed, we've set up a Commission to Ascertain the Desires of the Concerned Sections of the Population in Reference to Administrative Reform', Count Leinsdorf told him. 'The Prime Minister himself asked us to take this off his shoulders for the time being, because as a patriotic enterprise we enjoy, so to speak, the public's confidence.' "

THE MAN WITHOUT QUALITIES, VOLUME 2, CHAPTER 20

MUSIL AND FREUD

Robert Musil was not the only great thinker in early 20th-century Vienna – Sigmund Freud, the father of psychoanalysis, strolled the same streets. However, Freud's theory of the unconscious mind is one of the few ideas that Musil does not explore in *The Man Without Qualities*. With his background in experimental psychology, he was certainly familiar with the tenets of psychoanalysis, but he concluded that it was all a sham, a pseudo-science, or a substitute religion. Indeed, he saw it as the province of the "soul-improvement expert", who relieves one neurosis only to replace it (for a fee) with another. For the philosophically nimble Musil, it was also too conceptual, and concepts, he believed, always become dogmas. It is also possible that he did not want to help a rival – Freud was becoming famous, while Musil was not.

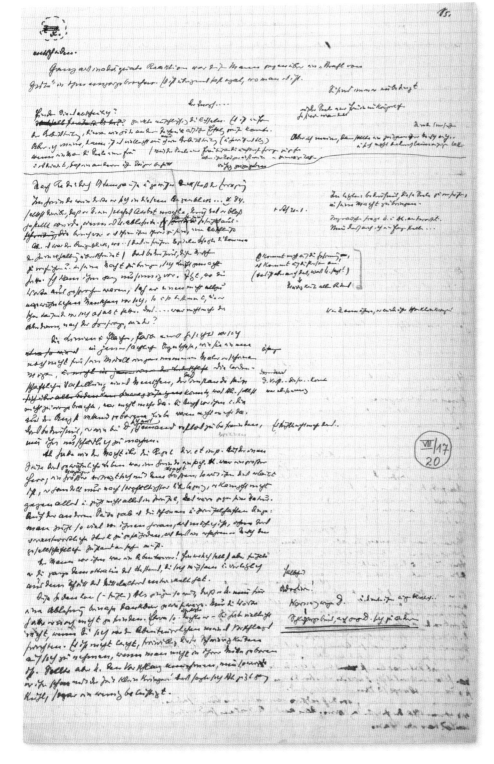

▲ **Sigmund Freud** lived and worked in an apartment in the heart of Vienna.

▲ **PUBLICATION HISTORY** *The Man Without Qualities* has had a long and convoluted publication history. Despite having laboured for nearly a decade on the book, Musil felt that he was pushed to publish the first volume prematurely in 1930. A second appeared three years later, and only after his death, in 1942, did his wife assemble a third and final one. Much of his manuscript was still left unpublished.

► **FIRST EDITION** When it was first published in 1932, *Journey to the End of the Night* received significant praise, and Céline was immediately recognized as a major new writer. The book was awarded the Prix Renaudot, although it missed out on the prestigious Prix Goncourt in the same year. However, in the divisive political climate of the 1930s, readers and critics wondered whether Bardamu's was the voice of the dispossessed or of the alienated political right.

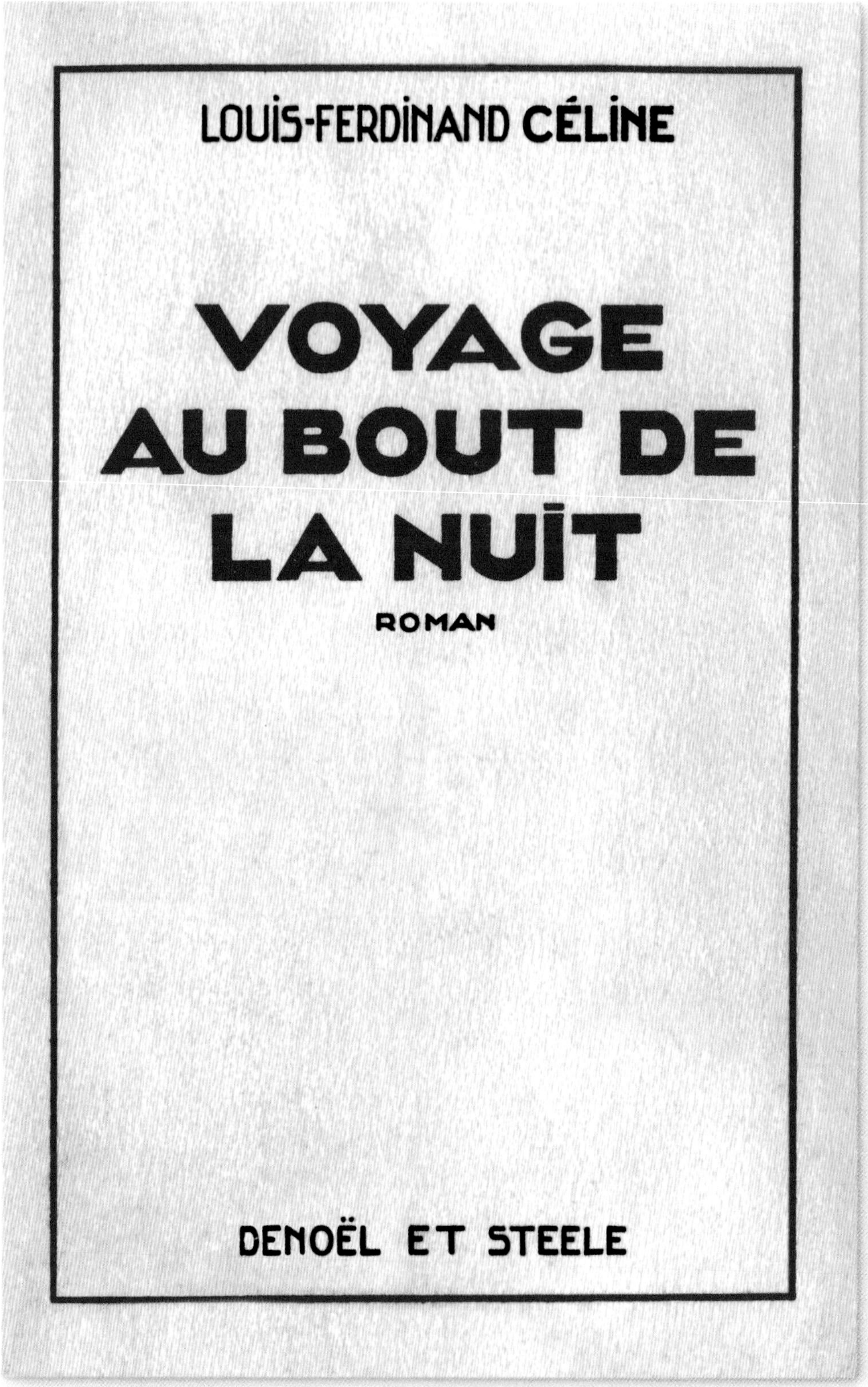

> The loneliness in Africa had been pretty rough, but my isolation in this American anthill was even more crushing. I'd always worried about being practically empty, about having no serious reason for living. And now, confronted with the facts, I was sure of my individual nullity… I seem to have disintegrated, I felt very close to nonexistence. I discovered that with no one to speak to me of familiar things, there was nothing to stop me from sinking into irresistible boredom, a terrifying, sickly sweet torpor. Nauseating… Philosophizing is simply one way of being afraid, a cowardly pretence that doesn't get you anywhere.

JOURNEY TO THE END OF THE NIGHT, CHAPTER 17

LOUIS-FERDINAND CÉLINE

VOYAGE AU BOUT DE LA NUIT

ROMAN

DENOËL ET STEELE

> As we grow older, we no longer know whom to awaken, the living or the dead.

JOURNEY TO THE END OF THE NIGHT, CHAPTER 13

Journey to the End of the Night

1932 ■ 623 PAGES ■ FRANCE

LOUIS-FERDINAND CÉLINE (1894–1961)

One of the most explosive works of the 1930s in France, *Voyage au bout de la nuit (Journey to the End of the Night)* was the debut novel of Louis-Ferdinand Destouches, who used the pen name Céline. Written in a strikingly frank style, the first-person narrative recounts the tale of Ferdinand Bardamu, a young Frenchman who enlists in the French army in World War I. He travels to the outposts of the French colonies in Africa, finds himself in the US pursuing an American woman named Lola, becomes a doctor in Paris, and then travels around France in the 1920s. In the midst of these comings and goings around the world, Bardamu occasionally encounters an enigmatic figure named Robinson, who becomes something of a shadowy counterpart to the narrator throughout the novel.

The defining feature of *Journey to the End of the Night* is its sceptical and cynical attitude towards almost every human belief. Throughout the book, a misanthropic yet self-critical voice comments on human behaviour and the forces shaping the modern world. Despite these weighty reflections, Bardamu is a witty and often riotously funny observer of human failings and delusions. Much of the novel draws on Céline's own experiences. His training as a doctor, for example, made him delight in dwelling on the human body and its functions in often crude language. Céline's unyielding desire to provoke and even outrage is evident in both the content and style of the novel. This desire shaped many of his later writings, especially his notorious antisemitic books of the 1930s.

CÉLINE'S STYLE OF WRITING

Journey to the End of the Night represents a watershed moment in modern French literature because of its bold and immediate literary style. Given to sometimes extreme statements that dwell on the darkness of human nature, the novel has tremendous energy. What appear to be spontaneous sentences were in fact the result of Céline's painstaking process of revision as he tried to forge an authentic voice of his own. His style of writing creates the impression that we are hearing things that have not been said before or that no one has dared to say explicitly. In his later works, Céline adopted an elliptical style of breaking off after every few words with three dots, capturing his unceasing effort to convey his unstable impressions of the world.

In context

◀ **WORLD WAR I** Céline describes his time on the Western Front with especially grim relish, presenting his participation in the war as an act of absurd and unthinking submission to nationalist ideology. This forms a marked contrast to the official portrayal of the war, as depicted in this contemporary poster by Lucien Jonas.

▲ **FORD FACTORY, DETROIT, 1917** In the American section of the novel, Bardamu works in Detroit after experiencing the alienating environment of New York. Céline explores many aspects of the emerging industrial world, often viewing events with a European's anxiety about America's rise to global prominence.

Their Eyes Were Watching God

1937 ▪ 286 PAGES ▪ US

ZORA NEALE HURSTON (1891-1960)

Folklorist and anthropologist Zora Neale Hurston grew up in Eatonville, Florida, one of the first towns in the US to be established solely by African Americans, and the setting for *Their Eyes Were Watching God*. The novel follows the life and romantic adventures of a Black woman named Janie Crawford. Janie's journey through three different marriages is described in poetic language, with her thoughts and feelings at the centre of the story, something that had seldom occurred for a Black female character in English literature before. Hurston uses a third-person narrator, who invites the reader to consider issues such as the impact of slavery on Black lives in 20th-century America, different attitudes to change within a Black community, and the challenges of female emancipation.

Hurston's belief in the importance of Black people's voices strongly influenced her writing. *Their Eyes* is written in the vernacular, authentically replicating Southern Black dialects in a way that had rarely been attempted. Some Black writers and critics disapproved of this, while non-Black readers struggled with the colloquial language. For these reasons, and because Hurston prioritized Black women's lives, the

▲ **MALE DOMINANCE AND FEMALE EMPOWERMENT** Volatile, even violent relationships are key to Hurston's novel, as depicted in this scene from Darnell Martin's 2005 film adaptation. Hurston explores the idea that although women may want independence, they still feel pressure to follow traditional gender roles and seek male protection.

novel was roundly dismissed and Hurston fell into obscurity. It was not until universities began to offer African American studies in the 1970s that the importance of her work was finally understood. While *Their Eyes* focuses on Black stories, the novel is universal in examining topics such as family trauma, gender roles, sexuality, race, and the conflict between romance and practicality.

THE **HARLEM RENAISSANCE**

Zora Neale Hurston was a key figure in the Harlem Renaissance, a cultural movement that began in New York City in the 1920s and '30s. In the city's Harlem neighbourhood, Black creativity in the arts, such as dance, music, and literature, blossomed and was accepted. People who had been enslaved or oppressed in the US moved to New York for freedom and the chance to fully be themselves. The Harlem Renaissance did not just influence Black people, but people from all backgrounds, as they began to recognize the contributions of a hitherto disrespected group. Key artists whose work was influenced by their historical and cultural backgrounds include the musicians Louis Armstrong and Gladys Bentley, and writers such as Langston Hughes, Nella Larsen, and W.E.B. DuBois.

▶ **The vibrancy** of Harlem's art is expressed in Louis Delsarte's 2005 mosaic *Spirit of Harlem*.

Ships at a ~~distance have every man's wish on board.~~

(~~made a raft of memories and rowed out to the ~~)

Women forget all those things they don't want to remember, and remember everything they don't want to forget. Then they act and do things accordingly. So the beginning of this was a woman, and she had come back from burying the dead. Not the dead of sick and ailing with friends at the pillow and the feet. She had come back from the sodden and bloated; the sudden dead, their eyes flung wide open in judgment.

The people all saw her come because it was sundown. The sun was gone, but he had left his foot-prints in the sky. It was the time for sitting on porches beside the road. It was the time to hear things and talk. These sitters had been tongueless, earless, eyeless conveniences all day long. Mules and other brutes had occupied their skins. But the sun and the bossman were gone. The skins felt human and powerful. Lords of sounds and lesser things. They passed nations through their mouths. They sat in judgment.

Seeing her as she was made them remember the envy they had stored up from other times. So they chewed up the ~~back~~ parts of their minds and swallowed with relish. They made burning statements with questions, and killing tools out of laughs. It was mass-cruelty. Words walking without masters; talking altogether like a song.

"What she doin' coming back here in dem overhalls? can't she find no dress to put on? -- Where's dat blue satin dress she left here in? -- Where all dat money her husband took died and left her? -- Whut dat old forty year old 'oman doin' wid her hair swingin' down her back lak some young gal? -- Where she left dat young lad of a boy she went off from here wid? -- Thought she was going to marry? -- Where he left her? -- What he done wid all her money? -- Betcha he off wid some gal so young she ain't even got no hairs -- Why she don't stay in her class? --"

When she got to where they were she turned her face on the bander log and spoke. They scrambled a noisy "good evenin'" and left their mouths setting open and their ears full of hope. Her speech was pleasant enough, but she kept walking straight on to her gate. The porch couldn't talk for looking.

The men noticed her firm buttocks like she had grape-fruits in her hip pockets; the great rope of black hair swingin' to her waist and unraveling in the wind like a plume; then her pugnacious breasts trying to bore holes in her shirt. They were saving with the mind what they lost with the eyes. The women took the faded shirt and muddy overalls and laid them away for remembrance.

But nobody moved, nobody spoke, nobody even thought to swallow spit until after her gate slammed behind her.

THEIR EYES
WERE WATCHING GOD
A NOVEL

ZORA N. HURSTON

◄ **MANUSCRIPT** This page is from the first chapter of the handwritten draft of *Their Eyes*. It deftly showcases Hurston's mastery of evocative language, as well as her acute portrayal of small-town Black communities. Hurston's use of the vernacular to convey the Southern dialect was one of the main reasons why the novel initially failed, and why it later became a cornerstone of Black literature.

▲ **FIRST EDITION** *Their Eyes* was first published in 1937, but after a poor reception it went out of print for nearly 30 years. Rediscovered in the 1970s by the novelist Alice Walker, it was reprinted and quickly sold out. The novel is now considered a classic of the genre and is hailed for its portrayal of Black culture.

❝ Seeing the woman as she was made them remember the envy they had stored up from other times. So they chewed up the back parts of their minds and swallowed with relish. They made burning statements with questions, and killing tools out of laughs. It was mass cruelty. A mood come alive. Words walking without masters; walking altogether like harmony in a song. 'What she doin coming back here in dem overhalls? Can't she find no dress to put on? – Where's dat blue satin dress she left here in? – Where all dat money her husband took and died and left her?' ❞

THEIR EYES WERE WATCHING GOD, CHAPTER 1

▶ **MANUSCRIPT** Steinbeck famously wrote the manuscript for *The Grapes of Wrath* in a 100-day frenzy of creativity during the summer of 1938. Despite the furious speed at which it was written, Steinbeck's text, a page of which is shown here, is extremely neat, with few corrections or rewrites. Steinbeck's notes to himself are scattered throughout. Towards the end, his writing becomes progressively smaller and lacks punctuation, reflecting the urgency of his need to conclude the work.

▲ **FIRST EDITION** The cover of the first edition of *The Grapes of Wrath* was designed by Elmer Hader, a children's book illustrator who Steinbeck felt would capture the directness of his writing. The Nobel Prize Committee acknowledged the author's style when it awarded him the Nobel Prize in Literature in 1962. It praised Steinbeck's "realistic and imaginative writings, combining as they do sympathetic humour and keen social perception".

> " 66 is the path of a people in flight, refugees from dust and shrinking land, from the thunder, of tractors and shrinking ownership, from the desert's slow northward invasion, from the twisting winds that howl up out of Texas, from the floods that bring no richness to the land and steal what little richness is there. From all of these the people are in flight, and they come into 66 from the tributary side roads, from the wagon tracks and the rutted country roads. 66 is the mother road, the road of flight. "

THE GRAPES OF WRATH, CHAPTER 12

The Grapes of Wrath

1939 ■ 464 PAGES ■ US

JOHN STEINBECK (1902-1968)

In the American Midwest of the 1930s, the economic slump of the Great Depression was compounded by the dust bowl – an environmental disaster when devastating dust clouds, caused by soil erosion from poor farming practices, swept across the land. Families driven from their farms by poverty seemed part of an apocalyptic vision of banishment and loss. It was in this harsh and unforgiving environment that John Steinbeck set his story of the hardworking Joad family – *The Grapes of Wrath*. The book follows the fortunes of Tom Joad, who has recently been released from prison in Oklahoma. Violating the terms of his parole, he rejoins his family of tenant farmers and sets off with them on the road to California and the uncertain promise of better times ahead. What they encounter instead is exploitation and rejection as they labour in the Californian fruit fields.

With a large cast of vibrant characters, including farmers, workers, preachers, and expectant mothers, *The Grapes of Wrath* focuses on the resilience of ordinary people faced with ruthless capitalists and agricultural corporations. Steinbeck alternates between broadbrush scenes of people on the move in the 1930s, describing the landscape and their way of life, and episodes about the hardships of the Joad family. He captures the upheaval and dispossession brought about by the Great Depression in general, but he also details the treatment of the Joads and their response to exploitation, criminally low pay, and the supposed improvements put in place by the US government. It is a world of conflict that Tom eventually has to flee after his friend, the former preacher and union organizer Jim Casy, is murdered. Before departing, however, Tom assures his mother that his spirit will endure, and that his voice will resonate in fights for justice and equality.

Steinbeck had trouble coming up with a title for the book, which was eventually suggested by his wife. It is taken from the patriotic song *The Battle Hymn of the Republic*, by the abolitionist writer Julia Ward Howe. It refers to the biblical Book of Revelation, and the anger of a people long oppressed: "Mine eyes have seen the glory of the coming of the Lord. He is trampling out the vintage where the grapes of wrath are stored."

▲ **THE GREAT DEPRESSION** *The Grapes of Wrath* grew from a series of articles that John Steinbeck wrote about migrant workers, which appeared in the *San Francisco News* in 1936. They were illustrated with photographs such as the one above, by Dorothea Lange.

STEINBECK'S OTHER WORKS

John Steinbeck's work focuses on the lives of the marginalized and the dispossessed in 1930s America. *The Grapes of Wrath* is his most famous book, but he also wrote the monumental *East of Eden* (1952), and various shorter novels, such as *Of Mice and Men* (1937) and *Cannery Row* (1945). Throughout his career, he also addressed political and cultural matters in his journalism and essays, discussing subjects such as the Ford Model T motor car, the musician Woody Guthrie, and the photographer Robert Capa.

In his later years, Steinbeck completed a celebrated journey around America with his dog, Charley, which he wrote up as *Travels with Charley* (1962). His final book was a collection of essays on American affairs called *America and the Americans* (1966), which rounded off a lifetime of literary engagement with his country.

▶ **Of Mice and Men** was first published by Covici-Friede in 1937.

OF MICE AND MEN

A Novel by JOHN STEINBECK
AUTHOR OF 'TORTILLA FLAT'

The Outsider

1942 ▪ 159 PAGES ▪ FRANCE

ALBERT CAMUS (1913-1960)

The book that made French philosopher Albert Camus famous, *The Outsider* tells the story of the last days of a French Algerian named Meursault. At the beginning of the book, Meursault finds out that his mother has died, but instead of grieving, he simply carries on with his daily routine, and starts a relationship with a colleague named Marie. He then has an altercation with an Arab whose name we don't know - the brother of his neighbour Raymond's mistress. Meursault kills the Arab after the latter stabs Raymond and threatens Meursault himself. These events take place in the first half of the book; in the second half, we follow Meursault as he is arrested and tried for murder.

Although the novel is narrated in the first person, we do not get close to Meursault, who is emotionally detached from the world. He expresses no grief when his mother dies, and seems indifferent to his girlfriend Marie, whom he admits that he does not love. However, Camus balances Meursault's coldness by capturing his intense physical responses to the world, such as the joy he takes in Marie's body, and in swimming in the sea. His physicality is heightened by Camus' descriptions of Meursault's surroundings, especially the extreme heat and blinding sunlight. These reduce Meursault to a stunned daze, so much so that it seems entirely credible when he says that he killed his victim because of the sun. This distorted view of reality reflects Camus' philosophy that it is precisely because life is meaningless that we give it meaning, however absurd that meaning is.

At the trial, the prosecutor uses Meursault's lack of grief at his mother's death as evidence of his cold-bloodedness, meriting a death sentence. Meursault refuses to lie about his feelings, even to save himself, and angrily rejects a chaplain's attempts to console him with thoughts of the afterlife. Camus makes readers question commonly approved human responses and wonder whether anyone can ever escape the absurdity of the human condition.

In context

▲ **FRENCH ALGERIA** Camus was born into a poor family in Algeria, at a time when the country was a French colony. Camus loved Algeria, but felt unwelcome when he returned there after he had moved to Paris. This sense of alienation shaped his philosophy, and became the theme of *The Outsider*.

▲ **THE ANTIHERO** A protagonist who lacks traditional heroic qualities, such as nobility and selflessness, is known as an antihero. It is difficult to like the emotionally detached Meursault - played by Marcello Mastroianni (see above) in the 1967 film of the book - but we admire his rigid honesty. In this sense, he is a classic antihero.

" Then everything began to reel before my eyes, a fiery gust came from the sea, while the sky cracked in two, from end to end, and a great sheet of flame poured down through the rift. Every nerve in my body was a steel spring, and my grip closed on the revolver. The trigger gave, and the smooth underbelly of the butt jogged my palm. And so, with that crisp, whip-crack sound, it all began. I shook off my sweat and the clinging veil of light. I knew I'd shattered the balance of the day, the spacious calm of the beach on which I'd been happy. "

THE OUTSIDER, PART 1, CHAPTER 6

◀ **FIRST EDITION** *The Outsider* was originally published in Gallimard's prestigious *Collection Blanche* (White Collection) series. The book's French title, *L'Étranger*, has been translated in various ways. The UK editions are titled *The Outsider* and US editions *The Stranger*.

ALBERT CAMUS

L'ÉTRANGER

ROMAN

nrf

GALLIMARD

THE **ABSURD**

In his essay *The Myth of Sisyphus* (1942), Camus outlined his philosophy of the absurd. This addresses the paradox of humanity's search for meaning in an apparently meaningless universe, a search that Camus thought hopeless. He described this paradox in terms of the ancient Greek story of Sisyphus, who had to roll a huge boulder up a steep slope. The boulder always rolled back down to the bottom, and Sisyphus had to roll it back up again, for eternity.

Camus' philosophy of the absurd lies behind several of his books, including *The Outsider* and *The Plague* (1947). The latter is the more optimistic of the two, but its heroes are unable to prevent a plague: they combat it by caring for those who are infected by it.

▲ **Sisyphus** struggles with his absurd and endless task in this painting by Titian.

Snow Country

1948 ■ ONE VOLUME ■ JAPAN

YASUNARI KAWABATA (1899-1972)

A melancholy and beautiful tale of love and loss, *Snow Country* is set in a hot-spring and ski resort in the Japanese Alps of Honshu, though these are never named as such in the novel. It is the story of the intense and anguished relationship that develops between Shimamura, a rich Tokyo writer and dilettante, and Komako, a young geisha from the resort. They meet when Shimamura, who is married and has a family in Tokyo, visits the resort. Over the course of several visits, the bond between him and Komako becomes more complex, as she falls in love with him and he, in his cooler way, becomes increasingly attached to her. Their relationship breaches the accepted boundaries of the client–geisha "contract", and it gradually starts to attract the attention of others in the resort.

Told in the third person, the novel closely follows the viewpoint of Shimamura, but rarely focuses on him. Naturally a detached observer of life, Shimamura acts almost like a camera for the novel, registering the frequently shifting moods and responses of Komako. Other key characters include a young woman, Yoko, and a young man, Yukio, the son of a music teacher in the resort. Shimamura becomes aware of the complicated

triangular relationship between this pair and Komako. Both women have been, or are currently, involved with the young man, who is dying of an incurable disease, and both are helping to support him.

Loneliness, loss, and death are common themes throughout Kawabata's work. Orphaned at a young age, he first made his mark as a writer with the short story "Izu Dancer", which was published in 1927. At the time, he was a leader of the so-called neo-sensualist movement, which drew on both avant-garde French influences and Japanese literary and dramatic traditions. Kawabata's work is lyrical, characterized by striking images and unusual juxtapositions, and the transitions between episodes are both abrupt and enigmatic. *Snow Country* was the novel that established his reputation, especially when it was published as an English translation in 1956. Kawabata was awarded the Nobel Prize in Literature in 1968, becoming the first Japanese writer to win the prize.

▶ **ALPINE RESORT** Snow-covered peaks surround Yuzawa, the "snow country" resort of the novel. When Kawabata was writing, this remote mountain setting was only accessible via a recently built railway tunnel, and its sense of isolation is an essential feature of the story. Komako's and Shimamura's tortured encounters take place in a zone that feels cut off from the normalities of everyday life.

◀ **MOUNTAIN GEISHA** A geisha named Matsuei stares into the camera with unusual forthrightness, revealing a personality that may have intrigued Kawabata when he visited Yuzawa where she worked in the 1930s. She is said to have inspired the character of Komako. Required to entertain weekend visitors, hot-spring (*onsen*) geishas such as Matsuei had dubious reputations compared with their city counterparts.

> "Shimamura, relaxed and warm, was gazing into Komako's face. A feeling of intense physical nearness came over him. The high, thin nose was usually a little lonely, a little sad, but today, with the healthy, vital flush on her cheeks, it was rather whispering: I am here too. The smooth lips seemed to reflect back a dancing light even when they were drawn into a tight bud; and when for a moment they were stretched wide, as the singing demanded, they were quick to contract again into that engaging little bud... She wore no powder, and the polish of the city geisha had over it a layer of mountain colour. Her skin, suggesting the newness of a freshly peeled onion or perhaps a lily bulb, was flushed faintly, even to the throat."

SNOW COUNTRY, PART 1

> "As he caught his footing, his head fell back, and the Milky Way flowed down inside him with a roar."

SNOW COUNTRY, PART 2

◀ NOBEL PRIZE
Kawabata received the Nobel Prize in Literature from the King of Sweden in 1968. He became the first Japanese writer to receive the prize, and the second Asian to do so, after the Indian writer Rabindranath Tagore. Four years later, in 1972, Kawabata was found dead by his own hand. There was no note or explanation of why he had taken his life.

PLOT DEVELOPMENT

Snow Country was refined by Kawabata over the course of more than a decade before it reached its final form. He started work on it in 1934, and built the story up gradually, adding sections when he felt inspired to do so. These sections were first published singly in magazines, and then brought together in one volume in 1937. Kawabata was not satisfied with the ending, however, and carried on experimenting with different concluding episodes, which again he published in magazines. These reworks were the basis of the new last chapter, and were incorporated when the expanded form of the novel was published in 1948. This version was later translated into English and other languages.

Kawabata's mastery of narrative was singled out by the Nobel Committee as one of the main reasons for him being awarded the Nobel Prize in Literature. It cited his narrative style as expressing "the essence of the Japanese mind", an assessment based on his three novels *Snow Country*, *Thousand Cranes* (1952), and *The Old Capital* (1962).

Nineteen Eighty-Four

1949 ■ 228 PAGES ■ UK

GEORGE ORWELL (1903-1950)

One of the most widely read and translated books of the 20th century, *Nineteen Eighty-Four* is a dystopian novel, depicting a nightmarish society that proclaims itself to be a utopian ideal. Although Orwell was a longstanding socialist, he was radically disillusioned about communism. By the time he wrote the novel, near the end of his life, he saw the Soviet Union as a totalitarian tyranny. In the future world of his novel, therefore, Britain (now "Airstrip One") is part of the one-party super-state of Oceania. It is perpetually at war with the world's two other states, Eurasia and Eastasia, and uses lies, surveillance, and censorship to impose its will upon its people.

The book's hero, Winston Smith, works for the Ministry of Truth, the propaganda agency of the regime's leader, Big Brother. Disillusioned by his work, which involves rewriting the historical record to suit the purposes of "The Party", he starts keeping a diary of his "thoughtcrimes". He begins an affair with a young woman, Julia, who shares his hatred of the state. They are betrayed by people who they think are fellow dissidents, but who are really members of the "Thought Police". Eventually, interrogation and torture push Winston to betray all he holds dear.

Nineteen Eighty-Four is written in the third person, but primarily from Winston's point of view. Orwell's language is plain and direct, but he coined several striking expressions – "Big Brother" (the dictator bolstered by a cult of personality),

◀ **FALSE ARITHMETIC**
This propaganda poster with the formula "2 + 2 = 5" was produced when Soviet leader Josef Stalin announced that the current five-year economic plan would be completed in four years. The total, "5", was said to include "the enthusiasm of the workers". Orwell adopted it as a slogan in his novel, to show how citizens of a totalitarian state could be made to believe anything.

"Room 101" (the torture chamber), "doublethink", and "thoughtcrime" were all invented by him and are still used today. Although they describe types of oppression that already existed around the world, his use of them in the novel made many more people aware of the dangers of totalitarianism. Ultimately, his book is a warning about how governments can use technology to brainwash and coerce their citizens, and shows what can happen if the idea that the individual exists to serve the state, rather than vice versa, is taken to its extreme.

SOCIALISM AND COMMUNISM

Orwell had a long interest in politics and particularly how socialism might lead to a better future. In his long essay *The Lion and the Unicorn*, he described a democratic socialism that would be fairer and more beneficial than the totalitarian communism of Soviet Russia. However, in *Animal Farm*, the novella he wrote before *Nineteen Eighty-Four*, he further attacked Soviet communism. Written as a fable, the book describes a farm in which the animals stage a socialist revolution, which sours when the pigs take over, become dictators, and cover up their cruelty with lies and deceptions. The action roughly parallels the history of the Soviet Union, from idealistic revolution to cruel dictatorship.

▶ **This still from the animated film** of *Animal Farm* (1954) shows the pigs celebrating their rise to power.

▶ **TYPESCRIPT**
This revised typescript shows how, despite his terminal illness, Orwell still had the energy to make meticulous corrections. These begin with the very first sentence, in which radios rather than clocks were originally "striking thirteen". Orwell completely rewrote the following paragraphs, and removed a conversation so that he could introduce Winston more quickly.

> The hallway smelt of boiled cabbage and old rag mats. At one end of it a coloured poster, too large for indoor display, had been tacked to the wall. It depicted simply an enormous face, more than a metre wide: the face of a man of about forty-five, with a heavy black moustache and ruggedly handsome features. Winston made for the stairs.
>
> It was no use trying the lift. Even at the best of times it was seldom working… On each landing, opposite the lift-shaft, the poster with the enormous face gazed from the wall. It was one of those pictures which are so contrived that the eyes follow you about when you move. BIG BROTHER IS WATCHING YOU, the caption beneath it ran.

NINETEEN EIGHTY-FOUR, CHAPTER 1

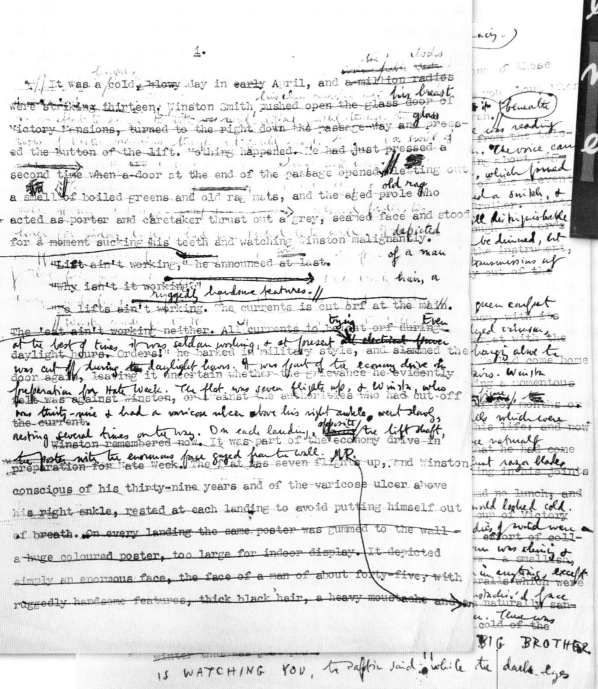

▲ **FIRST EDITION**
Nineteen Eighty-Four was first published by Secker & Warburg, in the UK, 35 years before the date mentioned in its title. The book's original title was *The Last Man in Europe*, but both Orwell and his editor, Frederic Warburg, agreed that *Nineteen Eighty-Four* was catchier.

The book's publishers followed Orwell's decision to use capital letters for the main totalitarian slogans

Directory: 1920-1950

▼ CHÉRI

COLETTE, 1920

Written by one of France's best-loved writers, Sidonie-Gabrielle Colette (1873–1954), *Chéri* is a novel about the tragedy of ageing. The characters belong to the wealthy, hedonistic Parisian elite. Approaching 50, Léa de Lonval is engaged in an affair with a man half her age – the beautiful but useless Fred Peloux, universally known as Chéri. Although their relationship has lasted for years, neither partner treats it seriously.

Chéri allows his mother to arrange for him to marry a young heiress, and the marriage is, predictably, a disaster. Meeting after a long separation, Léa and Chéri are forced to admit their need for each other, but the book has no happy ending. Léa knows that she has become too old, and that Chéri will inevitably desert her. Colette's prose is rich and sensuous, her ear for dialogue pitch perfect, and her perception of the psychology of love honed by a lifetime of amorous adventures.

WE

YEVGENY ZAMYATIN, 1921

Written shortly after the Russian Revolution, *We* is one of the first works of 20th-century dystopian science fiction. Russian author Yevgeny Zamyatin (1884–1937) used the book to criticize the dictatorial leanings of his country's communist regime, and as a result, *We* became the first novel banned in the Soviet Union.

Set in One State, a regimented, total-surveillance society in which people wear uniforms and are referred to by numbers, the book purports to be the diary of an engineer, D-503. Working on a spaceship that is designed to attack other worlds, D-503 accepts the State's theory that a good society can only be created by abolishing all kinds of personal freedom. Nevertheless, he illegally impregnates his state-assigned sexual partner, and becomes involved with a woman who is linked to a rebellious underground movement, actions for which he pays dearly. Despite its pessimistic conclusion, the book implies that humans will always rebel against totalitarianism.

THE CONFESSIONS OF ZENO

ITALO SVEVO, 1923

Set in the Adriatic city of Trieste, *The Confessions of Zeno* is a black comedy of neurosis and serial failure. Italian writer Italo Svevo (1861–1928) presents it as the autobiography of Zeno Cosini, a psychiatric patient who is undergoing psychoanalysis. Zeno is a man devoid of willpower, whose repeated efforts at giving up smoking always lead to "one last cigarette". His life is a series of disasters, but a strain of pure absurdity dogs every aspect of his existence, which undermines the seriousness of everything that he experiences. He finally concludes that he cannot be cured by psychoanalysis, because life itself is a sickness.

The Confessions of Zeno is written in a plain, unliterary style that put off Italian critics until Svevo's friend, James Joyce, drew attention to its exceptional merits. The novel is now accepted as possibly the funniest major work of literary modernism.

STEPPENWOLF

HERMANN HESSE, 1927

The novel that later became the favourite reading of the 1960s counterculture, *Steppenwolf* was written by German-Swiss author Hermann Hesse (1877–1962). The text is purportedly a manuscript abandoned by its main protagonist, Harry Haller – the "steppe wolf" of the title. Haller is an alienated, middle-aged man living an aimless, isolated existence. A stranger he encounters in the street hands him a "Treatise on the Steppenwolf", which seems to address him personally, describing a man who has two natures: a degrading, animal nature and a higher, spiritual one. Haller is eventually drawn into an underworld of drugs, jazz, and free love, where a saxophonist, Pablo, leads him to the Magic Theatre, which is filled with Haller's fantasies.

Hesse intended Haller's journey of self-exploration to be poised between the pull of madness and suicide and the "timeless world of faith". He regretted that, written by a 50-year-old author about a 50-year-old character, it would probably be read, and misunderstood, by the young.

▶ BRAVE NEW WORLD

ALDOUS HUXLEY, 1932

The "brave new world" of this novel by British intellectual Aldous Huxley (1894–1963) is a World State in which pain, grief, and conflict have been abolished. Universal happiness is induced by various means, including consuming the drug "soma". The pursuit of pleasure, including sex, is encouraged as a source of mindless contentment (all babies are bred in test tubes). Society is strictly stratified, but it is stable because all citizens are perfectly adapted to their social roles. This placid hedonism is challenged by a natural-born "noble savage" who has escaped conditioning and grown up reading Shakespeare. His masochistic rejection of pain-free conformism is doomed, however, to fail.

Brave New World is often interpreted as a dystopian fiction satirizing the idea of chemically induced happiness, but Huxley's ironic tone also suggests that clinging to the noble suffering of Shakespearean tragedy is an irrational sickness of the Western mind.

Colette, photographed wearing a man's suit, 1906–09

BEWARE OF PITY

STEFAN ZWEIG, 1939

An anguished psychological drama, *Beware of Pity* is the only full-length novel published by Austrian writer Stefan Zweig (1881-1942). The story is narrated by the guilt-ridden Anton Hofmiller, who is looking back on his youth as a junior officer in the Austrian army on the brink of World War I. Visiting a Hungarian landowning family, the young Hofmiller unwittingly humiliates a partially paralysed young woman, Edith Kekesfalva, by asking her to dance. In an attempt to compensate for this error, he lavishes attention upon Edith, who mistakes his pity for attraction and falls passionately in love with him. Hofmiller finds himself trapped in a deepening emotional entanglement, torn between a growing affection for Edith and his desire to escape. As the war approaches, he solves his dilemma, but with tragic results.

Sustaining tension throughout this slow-moving drama, Zweig achieves an almost unbearable level of emotional identification with his tormented protagonists.

THE BIG SLEEP

RAYMOND CHANDLER, 1939

English-born American writer Raymond Chandler (1888-1959) was one of the founders of a new school of crime fiction in the 1930s, one characterized by sharp, cynical dialogue and brutal action.

The Big Sleep introduces Philip Marlowe, a chivalrous but disillusioned private detective who is engaged in a solitary fight against corruption in Los Angeles. The plot is unfathomably complex, and as Marlowe explores the involvement of a rich man's daughters in an underworld of sleaze and crime, corpses litter the scene. The detective is given no backstory, and no life beyond the case he is investigating. He is a hero for our time – fallible, bruised, and world-weary. He rejects the advances of seductive women, and unravels the novel's mystery through no rational process.

The book's enduring appeal lies in its inimitable prose style, which is a virtuoso mix of baroque metaphors and wise-cracking repartee – and in the sinister atmosphere of corruption against which Marlowe stands out, like a battered knight in tarnished armour.

THE HEART IS A LONELY HUNTER

CARSON McCULLERS, 1940

American writer Carson McCullers (1917-67) was 23 when she achieved instant fame with her first novel, *The Heart is a Lonely Hunter*. The poignant story is set in a mill town in Georgia, the Deep South environment in which McCullers herself was raised.

The narrative viewpoint shifts around a group of characters at odds with themselves and society. An adolescent girl undergoes sexual awakening, but her musical ambitions are blighted by family circumstances. A café owner adapts to the death of his wife. The experiences of an embittered Black doctor and an alcoholic socialist raise political issues, but even for these committed individuals the core problem is loneliness. All of the characters are drawn to a deaf man, John Singer, in whose unresponsive company each finds an illusion of sympathy. Singer himself is attached to a fellow deaf man, who ignores him, but provides his only reason to live. The book's potent sadness lies in its depiction of an aching, but doomed, need for communication.

CRY, THE BELOVED COUNTRY

ALAN PATON, 1948

Written by white South African liberal Alan Paton (1903-88) at the beginning of the apartheid era, *Cry, The Beloved Country* is an eloquent appeal for human solidarity to combat racial hatred and social disintegration.

Zulu pastor Stephen Kumalo travels from his rural village to Johannesburg to aid relatives who have moved to the city. He finds his son Absalom in prison, charged with the murder of a young white man who was working for racial integration. Over the course of the novel, the pastor observes not only the degradation of Black Africans under oppressive white domination in the crime-ridden city, but also the fracturing of tribal ties in his beloved rural community. A gleam of hope is offered by a guarded friendship that grows between the pastor and the father of the murdered white man. The novel achieves epic stature in its lyrical evocation of a loved landscape and of faith being affirmed in the face of suffering.

Aldous Huxley, pictured in 1931, the year he wrote *Brave New World*

THE MOON AND THE BONFIRES

CESARE PAVESE, 1949

The last novel by Italian author Cesare Pavese (1908-50), *The Moon and the Bonfires* tells the tale of a man returning to a village in Piedmont after 20 years in the US. Born an orphan, and a rootless outsider all his life, he is searching for a home he has never had. Through conversations with a childhood friend, he learns of terrible events that occurred in the village during the period of fascism and partisan resistance, while he was away making his fortune in California. He also confronts the unchanging aspects of rural life – the poverty, the superstition, and brutality that continue to blight the villagers' lives. It is only in the weather and landscape that he finds the beneficial sense of continuity that he is seeking.

The narrative structure of the book is subtle, constantly shifting between present and past, observation and childhood memory. The melancholy of the main protagonist's isolation and alienation were those of Pavese himself. The author died by suicide shortly after completing the novel.

5
1950—1980

The Catcher in the Rye

1951 ▪ 272 PAGES ▪ US

J.D. SALINGER (1919-2010)

The Catcher in the Rye is Salinger's only major novel. It was an immediate bestseller when it came out, and its popularity has never waned. Over the years, it has sold more than 65 million copies and has been translated into 30 languages. Ironically, it has always appealed primarily to the young, even though Salinger intended it for adults. This is entirely due to the warped charisma of its young narrator, Holden Caulfield. An angst-ridden 16-year-old from an affluent background, he has just been told that he is being expelled from his private boarding school. He decides to leave in the middle of the night, and to spend the weekend in New York before returning home to face his parents.

The narrative then follows Holden on a chaotic odyssey as he drifts through cheap hotels and seedy bars. He drinks, chain-smokes, and talks to everyone he meets, although much of what he says is fantasy. "I'm the most terrific liar," he proudly admits. Increasingly, it becomes apparent that Holden feels disconnected from his surroundings: the adult world around him seems to be full of "phonies".

Critics have searched the text for parallels with Salinger's own life. There are a few, perhaps, but the main influence on its tone of disillusion was probably World War II. Salinger first

> " Anyway, I keep picturing all these little kids playing some game in this big field of rye and all. Thousands of little kids, and nobody's around – nobody big, I mean – except me. And I'm standing on the edge of some crazy cliff. What I have to do, I have to catch everybody if they start to go over the cliff – I mean if they're running and they don't look where they're going. I have to come out from somewhere and catch them. That's all I'd do all day. I'd just be the catcher in the rye and all. I know it's crazy, but that's the only thing I'd really like to be. I know it's crazy. "

THE CATCHER IN THE RYE, CHAPTER 22

wrote about Holden in 1941, and continued to add to his story throughout the war. He had the draft with him when he landed at Utah Beach, and eyewitnesses remembered him typing away under a table on one occasion, when his unit was under heavy fire. Towards the end of the war, Salinger was hospitalized with battle fatigue, which inevitably affected his writing. However, it is a mark of his genius that he was able to channel his depression not through war memoirs, but through the troubled outlook of an adolescent at odds with the world.

In context

◀ **FIFTH AVENUE** New York lies at the heart of the novel. Holden grew up there, his parents still live there, and it is where he spends his wayward weekend. The novel is set in the festive season, when Fifth Avenue is full of families shopping, Salvation Army girls, and "all those scraggy-looking Santa Clauses".

▶ **HOLDEN CAULFIELD** The Catcher in the Rye evolved over a number of years. Holden made an early appearance in a short story called I'm Crazy, which was published in Collier's magazine in December 1945. This included a couple of episodes that were reused in the novel.

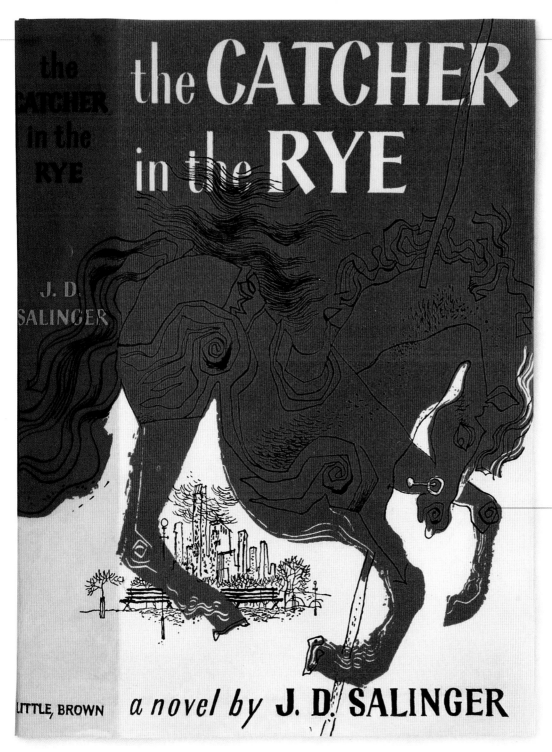

the CATCHER in the RYE

J. D. SALINGER

LITTLE, BROWN   a novel by J. D. SALINGER

◄ **FIRST EDITION** The first edition of *The Catcher in the Rye* was published on 16 July 1951, by Little, Brown and Company, priced at $3. The novel was a Book-of-the-Month Club selection, which doubtless helped to boost its phenomenal early sales. Within a fortnight, the book had been reprinted five times, and it remained on the bestseller lists for 30 weeks. The first paperback edition, published by Signet, came out in March 1953.

The attractive dust jacket was designed by Salinger's friend, Michael Mitchell. The horse is a reference to a carousel that Holden visits with his sister Phoebe

SALINGER'S **WARTIME EXPERIENCES**

Salinger's wartime traumas shaped the tone and character of *The Catcher in the Rye* and its hero. Salinger was drafted into the army in 1942, and served as a sergeant in the 12th Infantry Regiment. He took part in the Normandy landings on D-Day, and in the fighting that followed, more than half of his regiment was wiped out. Salinger was also involved in the Battle of the Bulge, and the brutal conflict in Hürtgen Forest against retreating German soldiers. For part of the war, he worked in counter-intelligence (the so-called "Ritchie Boys"), rooting out collaborators and interrogating prisoners, but his unit also entered the concentration camp at Dachau. As he later told his daughter: "You could live a lifetime and never really get the smell of burning flesh out of your nose".

▶ **American troops**, packed onto a landing craft, approach Utah Beach, on the Normandy coast, on 6 June 1944.

Invisible Man

1952 ▪ 581 PAGES ▪ US

RALPH ELLISON (1914–1994)

Named after the great 19th-century American writer Ralph Waldo Emerson, Ellison was a prolific writer of erudite, greatly admired essays, but he is best known for the one novel that he published during his lifetime, the acclaimed social satire *Invisible Man*. It is narrated in the first person by an eloquent and educated young Black man, who leaves the American South in the 1930s for New York City. There he becomes an orator for "the Brotherhood", a group resembling the Communist Party, before the group's rancorous disputes disillusion him.

Ellison does not write in a realistic or naturalistic manner, but prefers satire and symbolism. In crisp, sharp prose he gives us a modern *Pilgrim's Progress*, an allegory of an absurd world. It is a tale of one outrageous calamity after another, all of which the reader can see approaching, but the narrator cannot. And the narrator remains anonymous – for to give him a name would mean removing his cloak of invisibility.

The named characters who populate this narrative hall of mirrors include Tod Clifton ("Tod" is German for death), whose violent end at the hands of the police helps to spark a major riot in Ellison's imagined Harlem; Ras the Exhorter, who preaches a parody of Black nationalism, namely, complete separation from white people, preferably in Africa; and the mysterious Rinehart, apparently a confidence man, who is known only by his disguises. The "may not see myself as others see me not" quality of the story's symbolism is so well drawn that it earned Ellison the 1953 National Book Award, the highest literary accolade in the US.

▶ **FIRST EDITION** The dust jacket for the first edition of *Invisible Man* was one of the final works of the American artist E. McKnight Kauffer. Published by Random House, the book was the only novel on which Ellison ever saw his name. He spent more than four decades working sporadically on a second one, but died before finishing it. An edited version of the book was published in 1999 as *Juneteenth*.

INVISIBLE MAN

A NOVEL

BY RALPH ELLISON

A RANDOM HOUSE BOOK

INVISIBLE MAN

by Ralph Ellison

PROLOGUE

I am an invisible man. No, I am not a spook like such as those who haunted Edgar Allan Poe; nor one of your Hollywood movie ectoplasms. I am a man of substance, of flesh and bone, fiber and liquids -- I might even be said to possess a mind. I am invisible, you see, simply because people refuse to see recognize me. I am not complaining, nor am I protesting either. It is sometimes advantageous to be unseen, although it is most often rather wearing on the nerves. Then too, you're constantly being bumped against by those of poor vision. Or again, you often doubt if you really exist. You wonder whether you aren't simply a phantom in other people's minds. Say, a figure in a nightmare which the sleeper tries with all his strength to destroy. It's when you feel like this that, out of resentment, you begin to bump people back. And, let me confess, you feel that way most of the time. You ache with the need to convince yourself that you do exist in the real world, that you're a part of all the sound and anguish, and you strike out with your fists, you curse and swear to make them recognize you. And, it's alas, seldom successful.

Once night I accidentally bumped into a man, in the dark, and perhaps because of the near darkness he saw me and called me an insulting name. I sprang at him, seizing his coat lapels and demanded that he apologize. He was a tall blond man, and as my face came close to his he looked insolently out of his blue eyes and cursed me, his breath hot in my face as he struggled. And I pulled his chin down sharp upon the crown of my head, butting him as I had seen the West Indians do, and I felt his flesh tear and the blood

" I am an invisible man. No, I am not a spook like those who haunted Edgar Allan Poe; nor am I one of your Hollywood-movie ectoplasms. I am a man of substance, of flesh and bone, fiber and liquids – and I might even be said to possess a mind. I am invisible, understand, simply because people refuse to see me. Like the bodiless heads you see sometimes in circus sideshows, it is as though I have been surrounded by mirrors of hard, distorting glass. When they approach me they see only my surroundings, themselves, or figments of their imagination – indeed, everything and anything except me. *"*

INVISIBLE MAN, "PROLOGUE"

HARLEM RACE RIOTS

The dramatic action of *Invisible Man* climaxes with a race riot in Harlem, which is modelled on a real riot of 19–20 March 1935, about a year before Ellison arrived in New York. It led to widespread destruction, mainly targeting shops and stores owned by white people. Black retailers, like those in the novel, displayed the sign "Colored-owned" on their doors and windows, and largely escaped vandalism. The real-life riot ended with three dead, 100 injured, and 125 people arrested, but the fictional one is far bloodier. Rumours that the 1936 event was incited by communists also found their analogue in the novel, in which the violence serves the purposes of the shadowy Brotherhood.

▶ **Race riots** in Harlem in 1964 recalled previous protests in 1935 and 1943.

◀ **TYPESET PROOFS** These are the opening pages of *Invisible Man* as they appeared near the end of the proofing process. The extract from the published text (see above left) shows the changes that Ellison had yet to make to the first paragraph, including sharpening the imagery of mirrors, reflections, and distortions.

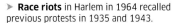

✓   2.

gush out, and I yelled, "Apologize! Apologize!" But he continued to curse and struggle, and I butted him again and again until he went down heavily, on his knees, profusely bleeding. I kicked him repeatedly, in a frenzy because he still uttered insults though his lips were frothy with blood. Oh yes, I kicked him! And in my outrage I got out my knife and prepared to slit his throat, right there beneath the lamplight in the deserted street, holding him in the collar with one hand, and opening the knife with my teeth -- when it occurred to me that the man had not <u>seen</u> me, actually; that he, as far as he knew, was in the midst of a walking nightmare! And I stopped the blade, slicing the air as I pushed him away, letting him fall back to the street. I stared at him hard as the lights of a car stabbed through the darkness. He lay there, moaning on the asphalt; a man almost killed by a phantom. It unnerved me. I was both disgusted and ashamed. I was like a drunken man myself, wavering about on weakened legs. Then I was amused: Something in this man's thick head had sprung out and beaten him within an inch of his life. I began to laugh at this crazy discovery. ~~Wonder~~ would he have awakened at the point of death, would Death himself have freed him for wakeful living? But I didn't linger. I ran away into the dark, laughing so hard I feared I might rupture myself. The next day I saw his picture in the <u>Daily News</u>, beneath a caption stating that he had been "mugged." Poor fool, poor blind fool, I thought with sincere compassion, mugged by an invisible man!

Most of the time (although I do not choose as I once did to deny the violence of my days by ignoring it) I am not so overtly violent. I remember that I am invisible and walk softly so as not

Ellison's edits appear to have been precise and exacting

▲ **BOOKER T. WASHINGTON** The "Lifting of the Veil of Ignorance" statue that stands on the campus of Tuskegee Institute in Alabama recurs symbolically throughout the first part of *Invisible Man*. The narrator finds this depiction of the historically Black school's most famous president both inspiring and troubling, as Washington had called for a gradual approach to ending segregation.

Go Tell it on the Mountain

1953 ■ 303 PAGES ■ US

JAMES BALDWIN (1924–1987)

Aged just 14 years old, James Baldwin began sketching out the autobiographical story that would become his most famous novel, *Go Tell it on the Mountain*. This coming-of-age narrative describes the passage of a young man, John Grimes, from a state of innocence to one of experience during the course of his 14th birthday – a Saturday in March 1935. Set in Harlem, New York, the novel focuses on an austere Pentecostal Church – the Temple of the Fire Baptized – where John's stepfather, Gabriel Grimes, is a deacon.

Within that 24-hour framework lies another series of intertwined stories, which collectively form the saga of Black America's painful rise from slavery into another form of oppression: second-class citizenship in a white-dominated society. The stories are told as flashbacks in the memories of Gabriel Grimes, his sister, and his wife, during an all-night prayer vigil in the Temple. Together they recall their struggles not just with their oppressors, but with their own passions, lusts, and feelings of guilt. Set during the Great Migration, when many Black Americans moved from the South to the cities of the North, these flashbacks compose a spiritual odyssey. The novel's many themes find their symbolic focus on the "threshing floor" before the altar, where John, the protagonist, undergoes a profound religious experience. Using richly allusive biblical imagery, the narrative merges John's spiritual longings with his sexual confusion and yearnings for independence.

Hailed as a masterpiece, *Go Tell it on the Mountain* was praised for its lyrical intensity and faultless ear for dialect. The novel propelled James Baldwin to the front rank of US authors, and remains a cornerstone of African American literature.

▲ **STOREFRONT CHURCHES** Harlem housed hundreds of "storefront" churches, such as the novel's Temple of the Fire Baptized. These made use of abandoned stores and even brownstone residences (shown here). Incongruously, this church was only a block away from "Swing Street", notorious for its jazz clubs and late-night lifestyle.

CULTURAL INFLUENCES

As James Baldwin developed as a writer, many cultural influences helped to mould his imagination and outlook. Foremost was the church in which he spontaneously preached as a teenager, as well as the Frederick Douglass Junior High School, where Baldwin was taught by the poet Countee Cullen, a revered figure of the Harlem Renaissance. By his early twenties, Baldwin had left Harlem and was living among the literati in Manhattan's Greenwich Village. There he met author Richard Wright, whose protest novel *Native Son* Baldwin would criticize for its stereotyped view of Black culture. In 1948, he moved to Paris, and wrote the first draft of his own original depiction of the Black experience in America – the novel that would become *Go Tell it on the Mountain*.

▶ **Celebrated African American** poet Countee Cullen was one of James Baldwin's early mentors.

> ❝ 'I'm ready,' John said. 'I'm coming. I'm on my way.' ❞
>
> ***GO TELL IT ON THE MOUNTAIN*, PART 3**

JAMES BALDWIN

> And he felt that this silence was God's judgment; that all creation had been stilled before the just and awful wrath of God, and waited now to see the sinner – he was the sinner – cut down and banished from the presence of the Lord. And he touched the tree, hardly knowing that he touched it, out of an impulse to be hidden; and then he cried, 'Oh Lord, have mercy! Oh, Lord, have mercy on me!' And he fell against the tree, sinking to the ground and clutching the roots of the tree. He had shouted into silence and only silence answered – and yet, when he cried, his cry had caused a ringing to the outermost limits of the earth.

GO TELL IT ON THE MOUNTAIN, PART 2, "GABRIEL'S PRAYER"

◀ **FIRST EDITION DUST JACKET**
Go Tell it on the Mountain was first published by Alfred A. Knopf in April 1953. The dust jacket shows the novel's principal characters, the Grimes family. Gabriel Grimes is flanked by his sister, Florence, and his wife, Elizabeth. The protagonist, John, stands next to Royal Grimes, Gabriel's true son. Royal, who later meets his death, is poignantly shown turned away from the family.

On the Road

1957 ■ 310 PAGES ■ US

JACK KEROUAC (1922-1969)

One of the most influential novels of the 20th century, *On the Road* was the defining text of the Beat Generation, and inspired many aspects of the 1960s counterculture. Kerouac liked to give the impression that he worked at great speed, pumped up on Benzedrine and coffee (he said the writing "went fast because the road is fast"). He did type out the draft on his celebrated *On the Road* "scroll" very quickly, but he had already written much of the material in his diaries of 1947-49, when the events in the novel took place. There was also a six-year gap from when he typed the scroll (1951) to the actual publication of the book (1957), as Kerouac struggled to find a publisher and was forced to make numerous revisions to his text.

Almost all of Kerouac's work is heavily autobiographical. The main characters in *On the Road* are thinly-veiled depictions of his fellow Beats. Dean Moriarty is Neal Cassady and Carlo Marx is Allen Ginsberg, Old Bull Lee is William S. Burroughs, and the narrator, Sal Paradise, is Kerouac himself. The book is chiefly a series of trips to visit these friends, and to revive their friendships. Cassady was a crucial catalyst for the novel. His long, rambling letters persuaded Kerouac to use the first-person narrative, composing his story as if it were a letter to a friend. His claim that writing should seem natural, like "a continuous chain of undisciplined thought", also inspired Kerouac's "spontaneous prose" style.

On the Road is partly a debauched odyssey and partly a quest for spiritual values in "tumbledown holy America". It celebrates the freedom and promise of the open road, even though the old two-lane roads were being replaced by the new Interstate Highway System, and, irony of ironies, Kerouac himself never held a driving licence.

In context

▲ **ROUTE 66** Dubbed the "Mother Road" by John Steinbeck, Route 66 was a two-lane highway that ran from Chicago to Los Angeles. It was used as an escape route by migrating farmers during the Dust Bowl crisis of the 1930s, and inspired the song *(Get Your Kicks on) Route 66* in 1948. It was still seen as a route to freedom and adventure in Kerouac's time; when describing "the beatest characters in the country", he included "the longhaired, brokendown hipsters straight off Route 66".

▲ **THE BEAT GENERATION** The term was coined by Kerouac in 1948. The Beats were a controversial circle of writers in the late 1940s, based mainly in San Francisco or New York. They rejected commercialism and middle-class conformity, and promoted spiritual self-discovery through a combination of Eastern mysticism, psychedelic drugs, jazz, and sexual liberation. Pictured here, from left to right, are: Hal Chase (an archaeologist), and writers Jack Kerouac, Allen Ginsberg, and William S. Burroughs.

> They rushed down the street together, digging everything in the early way they had, which later became so much sadder and perceptive and blank. But then they danced down the streets like dingledodies, and I shambled after as I've been doing all my life after people who interest me, because the only people for me are the mad ones, the ones who are mad to live, mad to talk, mad to be saved, desirous of everything at the same time, the ones who never yawn or say a commonplace thing, but burn, burn, burn like fabulous yellow Roman candles exploding like spiders across the stars...

ON THE ROAD, PART 1

▼ **SCROLL** Kerouac produced this famous typescript of his novel in a frenzied, three-week burst of activity in April 1951. The scroll is 36.5m (120ft) long, and consists of multiple sheets of tracing paper taped together. The text is very cramped, with tiny margins and no paragraph breaks. Tantalizingly, the end of the novel is missing, because it was "ate by Patchkee", a friend's cocker spaniel.

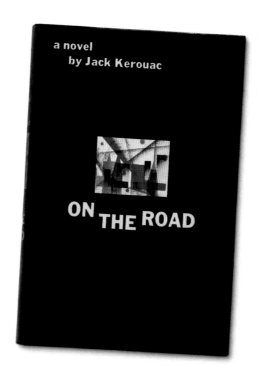

◄ **NEAL CASSADY**
The pivotal character of Dean Moriarty was modelled closely on Neal Cassady. Raised in Denver by an alcoholic father, he met Kerouac in New York in December 1946. Jack was fascinated by the young man's wildness and energy, and the pair became firm friends. When Cassady returned to Denver in the following year, his letters helped Kerouac to shape both the style and the content of *On the Road*.

a novel
by Jack Kerouac

ON THE ROAD

◄ **FIRST EDITION** *On the Road* was first published by The Viking Press Inc., in the US, in 1957. Some sections of the book had already appeared as short stories: *The Mexican Girl* in *The Paris Review*; *Jazz of the Beat Generation* in *New World Writing*; and *A Billowy Trip in the World* in *New Directions*.

The Leopard

1958 ▪ 330 PAGES ▪ ITALY

GIUSEPPE TOMASI DI LAMPEDUSA (1896-1957)

Il Gattopardo (*The Leopard*) is the only novel written by Count Giuseppe di Lampedusa; it is widely considered to be the greatest Italian novel of the 20th century. Set mainly in the 19th century, it tells the story of Don Fabrizio Corbera, Prince of Salina, a Sicilian aristocrat who finds himself out of time in a changing society: facing the ebbing of his own power and the destruction of traditions that he has always valued. Don Fabrizio is based on the author's own great-grandfather, and the rest of the book is drawn from Lampedusa's intimate knowledge of Sicily, its history, and the lives of its people.

One reason for the book's great success is the authenticity of its descriptions, but what makes it particularly powerful is its moving portrayal of a man facing the destruction of all that he holds most dear: his family's traditions, his children's futures, even his religious rituals. At times, his dog Bendicò seems to be the only thing that he can depend on.

Don Fabrizio is particularly attached to his nephew and ward, Tancredi, and hopes that he will marry his daughter, Concetta. However, although she loves him, Concetta accepts that it would be better for Tancredi to marry Angelica, the daughter of a local mayor who has become wealthy and powerful as a result of shady business dealings, and whom Don Fabrizio despises. The prince grows to like and admire Angelica, but his view of his nephew changes when Tancredi decides to support the revolutionary Giuseppe Garibaldi, who seems set on destroying Italy's noble families.

Don Fabrizio comes to recognize that it is his fate to have to try to reconcile these contradictory allegiances. Being a Sicilian, he decides, is about living in a harsh environment in which everything seems to decay and die. Indeed, the novel concludes with a chapter set 50 years later, describing the later lives of Concetta and two of her sisters. They are still living together in the family house, and are disposing of many of Don Fabrizio's possessions – including the stuffed pelt of his beloved dog, Bendicò.

◄ **COAT OF ARMS** The novel's title comes from the animal on the Lampedusa coat of arms. The creature is actually a serval, but it is often called a leopard because of its spots. It is also Don Fabrizio's symbol, representing his nobility and control over the peasant classes. He recognizes that the power of the leopards (the aristocrats) is waning.

◄ **SICILY** Over the centuries, Sicily has been fought for and ruled by many different peoples. The Greeks built Taormina's open-air theatre, depicted here by William J. Ferguson in 1876, and the Romans later reconstructed it. Then Byzantines came from the east, Spaniards came from the west, and Berbers came from the south. Don Fabrizio argues that frequent conquests have made the Sicilians a passive people, who find it difficult to take the initiative or to take part in movements that bring about political change.

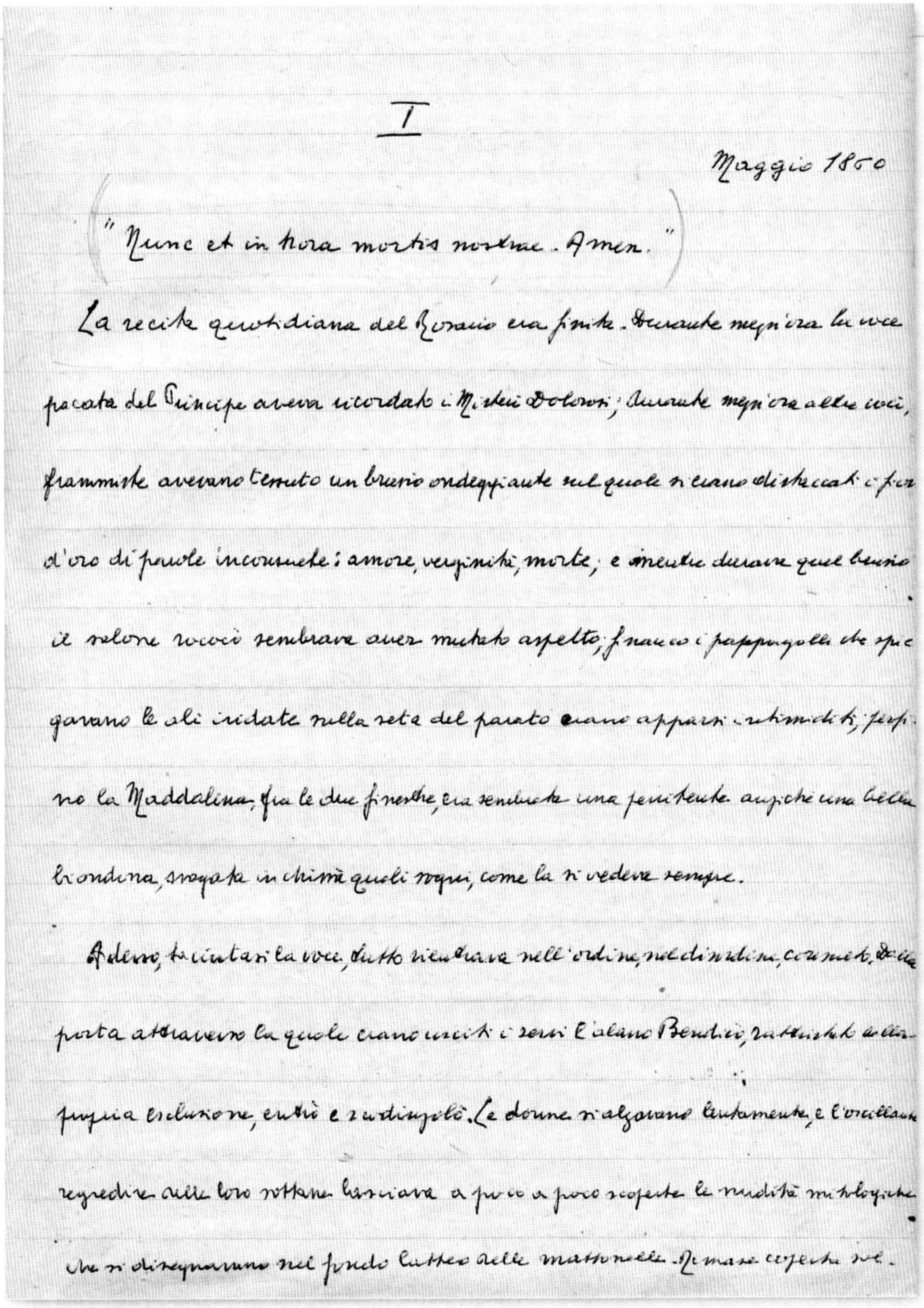

I

Maggio 1860

"Nunc et in hora mortis nostrae. Amen."

La recita quotidiana del Rosario era finita. Durante mezz'ora la voce pacata del Principe aveva ricordato i Misteri Dolorosi; durante mezz'ora altre voci, frammiste, avevano tessuto un brusio ondeggiante sul quale si erano distaccati i fiori d'oro di parole inconsuete: amore, verginità, morte; e mentre durava quel brusio il salone rococò sembrava aver mutato aspetto; financo i pappagalli che spiegavano le ali iridate sulla seta del parato erano apparsi intimiditi; perfino la Maddalena, fra le due finestre, era sembrata una penitente anziché una bella biondona, svagata in chissà quali sogni, come la si vedeva sempre.

Adesso, taciutasi la voce, tutto rientrava nell'ordine, nel disordine, consueto. Dalla porta attraverso la quale erano usciti i servi, l'alano Bendicò, rattristato dalla propria esclusione, entrò e scodinzolò. Le donne si alzavano lentamente, e l'oscillante regredire delle loro sottane lasciava a poco a poco scoperte le nudità mitologiche che si disegnavano sul fondo latteo delle mattonelle. Rimase coperta sol-

◀ **MANUSCRIPT** When Lampedusa had nearly finished *The Leopard*, some friends sent a typed copy of it to two Italian publishers, but both of them rejected it. After Lampedusa's death, another Italian writer, Giorgio Bassani, read the manuscript and realized at once how good it was. Bassani worked as an editor at the Italian publisher Feltrinelli, and persuaded them to publish it. Lampedusa's beautifully neat manuscript is now kept at his Sicilian home, Palazzo Lanza Tomasi, where visitors are able to see it.

> "The daily recital of the Rosary was over. For half an hour the steady voice of the Prince had recalled the Sorrowful and Glorious Mysteries; for half an hour other voices had interwoven a lilting hum from which, now and again, would chime some unlikely word; love, virginity, death; and during that hum the whole aspect of the rococo drawing-room seemed to change; even the parrots spreading iridescent wings over the silken walls appeared abashed; even the Magdalen between the two windows looked a penitent and not just a handsome blonde lost in some dubious daydream as she usually was."
>
> ***THE LEOPARD*, CHAPTER 1**

THE **RISORGIMENTO**

In the early 19th century, Italy was made up of kingdoms, duchies, and other states governed by local rulers, but under the overall control of first the French and then the Austrian Hapsburg empires. However, a nationalistic movement called the Risorgimento (rising again) swept across the country, aiming to unite it under a single government. After the revolution of 1848, Piedmont became the leading Italian power under King Victor Emmanuel. Then, in 1860, the revolutionary leader Giuseppe Garibaldi assembled an army (known as The Thousand or the Redshirts), conquered Sicily, and marched up the southern Italian mainland. However, the Piedmontese took over more of the north, and eventually defeated Garibaldi, making Victor Emmanuel ruler of a united Italy. In *The Leopard*, one of Don Fabrizio's dilemmas is whether or not to reject his feudal past by supporting the modern government.

▶ ***The Landing at Marsala***, by an unknown artist, portrays Garibaldi's army arriving in Sicily in 1860.

KEY CHARACTERS: THE SALINA AND SEDÀRA FAMILIES

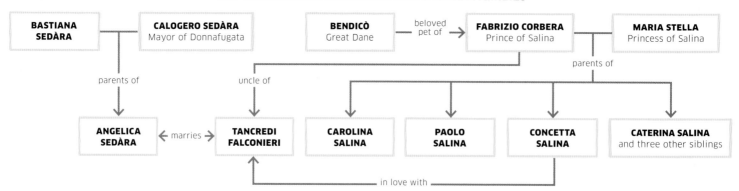

Among many things, *The Leopard* is a study of human longing. Many of the characters in the novel yearn for love and sexual fulfilment, but few of them find lasting happiness. Don Fabrizio himself has a distant relationship with his wife Maria Stella, whom he finds puritanical and lacking in sensuality; Concetta remains unfulfilled; the family priest Father Pirrone has to help a niece who is seduced by a relative. By arranging an advantageous marriage for his nephew and ward Tancredi, Don Fabrizio believes he is doing the right thing. However, although Tancredi and Angelica enjoy the physical side of their marriage, they do not love each other. Concetta, too, finds happiness impossible, since she loves Tancredi, and resents the fact that he seems to spurn her. She only discovers later in life that he did actually have feelings for her.

The novel is also about the political changes introduced by Italy's nationalist movement. Although it ushered in self-rule for Italy, some of the characters (especially Don Fabrizio) are sceptical of the Risorgimento. It seems that many of those who are fighting for change are only doing so to increase their personal wealth. In other words, the revolution is simply replacing one aristocracy with another – with self-made people such as Don Calogero, Angelica's upwardly mobile father.

Another theme of *The Leopard* is the long and gradual decline of Sicilian civilization. This preoccupies Don Fabrizio, who explains that for centuries the island has been fought over and ruled by outsiders, making it hard for Sicily to develop a vigorous culture of its own. The effort of surviving these onslaughts and changes has exhausted the Sicilians; Don Fabrizio's understanding of this, as well as the eloquence with which he expresses himself, dignifies his sense of loss. When he eventually dies, the family finally loses its last trace of distinction. By the end of the book, they have little prestige or wealth left – they are only held in esteem for their religious devotion, but even this is now open to question.

◄ **THE BALL** One of the turning-points in *The Leopard* is the scene of a grand ball at which Angelica impresses everyone with her beauty and poise. As portrayed in Luchino Visconti's 1963 film, it is also the scene in which Angelica and Tancredi, to Don Fabrizio's relief, appear to be genuinely in love. As Don Fabrizio dances with Angelica, he recalls his lost youth, when he and his wife danced together in the same room and were happy.

▲ **PALAZZO LANZA TOMASI** Named after Lampedusa's adopted son, Tomasi, who restored the building after World War II, this is the house in Palermo in which Lampedusa's great-grandfather lived and where many of the events of the novel take place. Part of it is now a museum, and contains Lampedusa's library, his manuscripts, and many family portraits.

Giuseppe Tomasi di Lampedusa

Il Gattopardo

Feltrinelli Editore

◀ **FIRST EDITION** When the novel was finally published posthumously, it had mixed reviews, partly because it managed to offend people on both extremes of the political spectrum. Those on the left objected to the way it questioned the reforms of the Risorgimento, while those on the right were angered by its portrayal of the demise of the aristocracy and the Catholic Church. Many readers, however, quickly recognized that it was a masterpiece.

THE **CATHOLIC CHURCH**

Life in Italy was dominated by the Catholic Church in the early 19th century. People worshipped regularly, priests were respected, and the church stressed the unbroken line linking the Pope to St Peter, and then back to Christ himself. In *The Leopard*, the Salinas worship in their own private chapel, which is full of holy relics, and begin each day with prayers. They have their own priest, Father Pirrone, who leads their worship and also serves as an adviser, even helping Don Fabrizio with his astronomical studies. The influence of the church is waning, however. For centuries it had been a major power, ruling the Papal States in northern Italy, but by 1871, these states had been unified with Italy, and only the Vatican City was still under the direct control of the Pope.

▲ **The Mother Church** in Palma di Montechiaro, Sicily, was built by the Lampedusa family in the 17th century, when they were lords of the town.

> ❝ Chevalley thought: 'This state of things won't last; our lively new modern administration will change it.' The Prince was depressed. 'All this shouldn't last; but it will, always; the human "always" of course, a century, two centuries... and after that it will be different, but worse. We were the Leopards and Lions; those who'll take our place will be little jackals, hyenas; and the whole lot of us, Leopards, jackals and sheep, we'll all go on thinking ourselves the salt of the earth.' They thanked each other and said goodbye. Chevalley hoisted himself up on the post-carriage, propped on four wheels the colour of vomit. The horse, all hunger and sores, began its long journey. ❞

THE LEOPARD, CHAPTER 4

▶ **FINDING A TITLE**
Achebe found the title for his novel in W.B. Yeats' poem "The Second Coming". Although the poem was written about Europe in the aftermath of World War I, the line "Things fall apart; the centre cannot hold" aptly describes the effect of colonialism on tribal societies. Originally published in the UK, the novel has since been translated into more than 50 languages.

Things Fall Apart

1958 ▪ 150 PAGES ▪ NIGERIA

CHINUA ACHEBE (1930-2013)

In *Things Fall Apart*, the most widely read modern African novel, Chinua Achebe created a story about the downfall of an Igbo tribe in Nigeria. Achebe consciously offered an alternative to the ways in which European literature depicted Africans. The first part of his novel gives a closely observed picture of the fictional Igbo village of Umuofia, with its inhabitants' rich culture, commerce, religious rituals, and social courtesies. Life revolves around the seasons as villagers plant, tend, and harvest crops of yams, and celebrate with palm wine feasts, wrestling, and storytelling. However, Achebe's story is also a tragedy, featuring a flawed hero and a plot that unveils the cataclysmic contact between traditional life and colonizers in the late 19th century.

Okonkwo is a legendary wrestler and warrior – an easily angered husband of three wives, and a proud owner of a large compound. His triumphs in conflicts with neighbouring tribes are brutal, and he is unflinching in performing sacrifices to appease the gods. However, his adherence to the old ways sets him apart from others of his tribe, who have begun to question their traditions even before the colonizers have arrived. Okonkwo the warrior is slow to understand that the real battles to be fought are for the hearts and minds of his people, who are first seduced by the songs and gifts of missionaries, and then subjugated by colonizers.

◄ **CLASH OF RELIGION**
This photograph, taken in 1920, shows two masked Igbo tribesman dressed as spirit guides standing on either side of a Christian convert, who is dressed as a missionary. In Achebe's novel, Okonkwo's eldest son, Nwoye, is one of many in the tribe who are drawn to Christianity by the "gay and rollicking tunes of evangelism".

In this groundbreaking novel, Achebe felt it was important to use the English language as a weapon in the struggle to tell his people's story. Christened Albert Chinualumogu, by parents who were converts to the Protestant Church, Achebe learned English at school, but spoke Igbo at home. "We lived at the crossroads of cultures," he recalled, and he later dropped the tribute to Victorian England in his name. His was the last generation of Africans to hear from their elders what life was like before Europeans arrived.

> ❝ And so nature was not interfered with in the middle of the rainy season. Sometimes it poured down in such thick sheets of water that earth and sky seemed merged in one grey wetness. It was then uncertain whether the low rumbling of Amadiora's thunder came from above or below. At such times, in each of the countless thatched huts of Umuofia, children sat around their mother's cooking fires telling stories, or with their father in his obi, warming themselves from a log fire, roasting and eating maize. It was a brief resting period between the exacting and arduous planting season and the equally exacting but light-hearted months of harvests. ❞

***THINGS FALL APART*, CHAPTER 4**

MODERN AFRICAN LITERATURE

Achebe is often described as the "father of modern African literature". He inspired writers such as Chimamanda Ngozi Adichie, whose debut novel, *Purple Hibiscus* (2003), tells the tale of a 15-year-old girl struggling with a Catholic upbringing in Nigeria. Her award-winning *Half of a Yellow Sun* (see pp.232-33) describes a family caught in the Biafran war of the 1960s. More recently, *The Hairdresser of Harare* (2010), by Tendai Huchu, sheds light on social struggles in postcolonial Zimbabwe, while Damon Galgut's Booker Prize-winning *The Promise* (2021) exposes white farmers' bigotry during apartheid. Also in 2021, Tanzanian-born Abdulrazak Gurnah was awarded the Nobel Prize for a series of works that examine the effects of colonialism on East Africa.

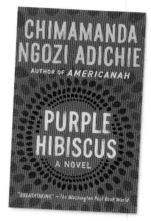

► ***Purple Hibiscus*,** by Chimamanda Ngozi Adichie, was first published by Algonquin Books.

The Tin Drum

1959 ▪ 576 PAGES ▪ WEST GERMANY

GÜNTER GRASS (1927-2015)

German writer Günter Grass had only published a collection of poems before he wrote his first novel, *The Tin Drum*. The book caused an instant stir, establishing him as one of Germany's most provocative writers. For many, it is one of the greatest German novels of the 20th century. It tells the story of Oskar Matzerath, who is born in Danzig, and lives through World War II and its aftermath, during which he contemplates Germany's past. It is told conversationally, in Oskar's own voice, though he often switches from first- to third-person narration.

Early on, Oskar informs us that he decided to stop growing at the age of 3 (to avoid becoming a grocer like his father). He can break glass by screaming and he beats his tin drum, a treasured possession given to him on his third birthday, as a loud protest against the world. Now in his late twenties, he keeps the drum close to him throughout the book, even during love affairs. After the war, he joins an acrobatic troupe, moves away from Danzig when it becomes part of communist Poland, then works in Germany as a tombstone carver, an artist's model, and a jazz musician. The book ends on an uncertain note. Oskar is about to be released from a mental

> " Granted: I am an inmate of a mental hospital; my keeper is watching me, he never lets me out of his sight; there's a peephole in the door, and my keeper's eye is the shade of brown that can never see through a blue-eyed type like me. So you see, my keeper can't be my enemy. I've come to be very fond of him; when he stops looking at me from behind the door and comes into the room, I tell him incidents from my life, so he can get to know me in spite of the peephole between us. "

THE TIN DRUM, BOOK 1, "THE WIDE SKIRT"

institution in which he has been wrongly detained for murder. He looks back over his life – the story that we have read – and wonders what he will embark upon next.

Oskar observes, and sometimes participates in, the history of 20th-century Germany. His story is inventive, irreverent, macabre, and funny, but he confronts issues such as the German nation's responsibility for Nazism at a time when the topic was rarely mentioned in Germany. Many praised Grass for his honesty, but the book courted controversy. This was revived years later, when Grass revealed that at the age of 17 he had been drafted into the SS for the last few months of the war.

In context

◄ **POLISH POST OFFICE**
At the beginning of World War II, the Nazis attacked the Free City of Danzig, firing on the Polish Post Office (shown here). Grass describes the episode in the novel, bringing real life and fiction together, and forcing readers to consider Germany's past.

◄ **EDELWEISS PIRATES**
During the war, Oskar joins a gang of criminal youths called the Dusters, and eventually becomes their leader. The group is similar to a gang that really existed in Danzig. The Edelweiss Pirates, as they were known (pictured here), rebelled against the Hitler Youth.

Grass produced this floridly written manuscript specially for this lithograph

▲ **LITHOGRAPH** Grass made this print by combining a hand-drawn image of Oskar with the book's opening words. It shows Grass's wit as well as his artistic skill. The text beneath the drummer's feet is Oskar's comment on the eccentric sculptures of his nurse, Bruno, but it also refers to Grass himself: "I wouldn't swear that he's an artist."

THE **UNRELIABLE NARRATOR**

Many novels have an unreliable narrator – a person whose version of events is not to be trusted for various reasons. The narrator might be immature or mentally unstable, or they might be distorting the truth to make people laugh. Alternatively, they might like to exaggerate, or have a vested interest in presenting a biased view of events.

Oskar is an unreliable narrator: he admits at the beginning of the book that he is in a mental hospital, and that many of the things he will say will seem improbable. For this reason, readers may doubt some of his most important statements. This has a powerful impact in *The Tin Drum*, because many Germans found it hard to admit the truth about their country's past, or about their own involvement in Nazism or World War II.

▶ **The 1979 film of *The Tin Drum*,** starring David Bennent, portrays Oskar, the narrator, as unreliable.

▶ **FIRST EDITION** A live oak, a feature of the landscape in Southern states, appears on the first edition of *To Kill a Mockingbird*. In the story, Scout and Jem find gifts from a mysterious benefactor (who turns out to be Boo Radley) in the knot hole of the tree. The novel won the Pulitzer Prize in 1961, a year after publication. Continuously in print, it still sells a million copies each year.

TO KILL A Mockingbird

A NOVEL BY

HARPER LEE

" And so a quiet, respectable, humble Negro who had the unmitigated temerity to 'feel sorry' for a white woman has had to put his word against two white people's... The witnesses... have presented themselves to you gentleman, to this court, in the cynical confidence that their testimony would not be doubted, confident that you would go along with them on the assumption – the evil assumption – that *all* Negros lie, that *all* Negros are basically immoral beings, that *all* Negro men are not to be trusted around our women, an assumption one associates with minds of their calibre. "

TO KILL A MOCKINGBIRD, CHAPTER 20

To Kill a Mockingbird

1960 ▪ 285 PAGES ▪ US

HARPER LEE (1926-2016)

Essentially a courtroom drama, *To Kill a Mockingbird* draws on Harper Lee's memories of her childhood in rural Alabama in the 1930s. In her fictional town of Maycomb, Southern resentment still lingers 70 years after the American Civil War. Black people scratch a living on white people's terms, but fear the consequences of the slightest transgression, and the deeply divided community is struggling to survive the Great Depression. The story is told by Scout, a spirited 9-year-old who lives with her older brother, Jem, their widowed lawyer father, Atticus Finch, and their Black helper, Calpurnia. All summer long, Scout and Jem play with their friend Dill and build fantasies about their mysterious, reclusive neighbour Boo Radley. Then an incident in a poor family's shack exposes simmering intolerance and violence: Tom Robinson, a Black man, is accused of raping Mayella Ewing, the 19-year-old daughter of the impoverished Bob Ewell.

The children's simple concepts of good and evil in people are undermined by how the community reacts when Atticus agrees to defend Tom Robinson. Scout and Jem watch their father tear into prejudices and present strong evidence of Tom's innocence, but what the jury finds hardest to understand is that a Black man might help a white woman because "he felt sorry for her".

▲ **THE TRIAL OF TOM ROBINSON** In a tense courtroom scene from the 1962 film based on Lee's novel, Atticus Finch (Gregory Peck) sits beside the defendant Tom Robinson (played by Brock Peters). After his Oscar-winning performance, Peck became fixed in the public's imagination as Atticus Finch – in 2003, his character was named the greatest movie hero of the 20th century.

Although Tom is convicted, Bob Ewell swears to take revenge on Atticus, but he is thwarted by Boo Radley, who saves Jem and Scout when they are attacked. Like Tom, Boo is an innocent, a mockingbird; Atticus says that it is a sin to kill a mockingbird because they never do harm, but only sing for our delight. Having a story of injustice suffered by a Black man narrated by a white child has made some uneasy, but Lee brilliantly created an innocent narrator, who sees adult cruelty and bigotry with fresh eyes.

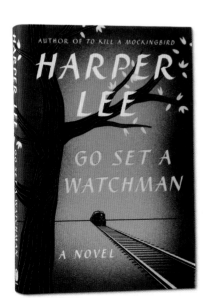

◀ **GO SET A WATCHMAN** After shying away from publicity for decades, Harper Lee produced a second novel at the age of 88. In *Go Set a Watchman*, published in 2015, she returns to Scout in her twenties, and portrays Atticus as a Ku Klux Klan sympathizer, to the wrath of many of her readers.

JIM CROW LAWS

Set in a small town in Alabama between 1933 and 1935, *To Kill a Mockingbird* mirrors Harper Lee's own childhood in a community with strict segregation. Jim Crow laws (a derogatory epithet coined from a minstrel routine) were passed after slavery was abolished, to segregate Black Americans in every area of social and commercial activity. Despite the 15th Amendment, which guarantees the vote of all citizens, Southern states introduced mandatory literacy tests and poll taxes to disenfranchise Black voters. These laws remained in force in most parts of the American South until they were overturned in the 1960s.

▲ **Drinking fountains** in Oklahoma in 1939 were designated for "colored" or "white" people.

Catch-22

1961 ▪ 453 PAGES ▪ US

JOSEPH HELLER (1923-1999)

Joseph Heller freely admitted that his World War II service in the US Army Air Corps, in which he flew 60 trouble-free missions as a bombardier, was far from appalling. Yet sometime during his wartime experiences the seed was planted that 16 years later burst upon the world as *Catch-22*, one of the most famous anti-war novels ever written.

Set in 1944, on an imaginary US air base on an island west of Italy, the book features the madcap antics of the men who fly B25s on bombing runs against the Germans, who are slowly withdrawing up the Italian peninsula. The novel is savagely funny, but its black humour masks despair at the futility of human endeavour, and the overwhelming influence of human folly. Its central character, Captain John Yossarian, is a classic antihero, a misfit who just wants "to live forever or at the least die trying to". He is pitted not against the Germans, who are barely glimpsed, but rather against anyone who can get him killed, especially his own superiors. The military hierarchy is depicted in the most grotesque and exaggerated forms that satire can devise. A simple mess officer, for example, runs a globe-spanning syndicate that not only includes the enemy, but also leads him to bomb his own comrades – cheerfully. Likewise, a lieutenant who only cares about parades is promoted to lieutenant general, and has a German surname, "Scheisskopf", which is unprintable in English. Military hierarchy (a metaphor for the world at large) has created an absurd, bureaucratic maze that thwarts every imaginable impulse and desire, as Heller describes with comic gusto. For all of the book's humour, however, its scenes of violent death are searingly realistic, and jolt the reader.

Catch-22 is satire of the highest order; it also appeared at the right time. A burgeoning 1960s counterculture provided receptive readers, who relished Heller's sly attacks on capitalism and, more widely, the hypocrisy of American culture. Sales soared during the anti-Vietnam War protests, ensuring the novel's continuing status as a subversive classic.

In context

▲ **INSPIRATION FROM AIR RAIDS** The B25 Mitchell medium-range bomber (seen here on a raid over Europe) is the warplane flown by the airmen in *Catch-22*. The harrowing experience of flying through barrages of anti-aircraft fire is vividly and repeatedly described in the novel, offsetting the prevailing black humour and satire.

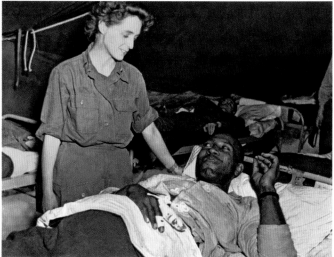

▲ **MILITARY HOSPITAL** A US Army nurse attends to a patient in a military hospital in France in 1944. *Catch-22* both opens and closes in a similar facility, where wounded and shell-shocked soldiers are given care. Ironically, in the novel, the hospital is a refuge where characters go to live instead of to die.

❝ There was only one catch and that was Catch-22, which specified that a concern for one's safety in the face of dangers that were real and immediate was the process of a rational mind. Orr was crazy and could be grounded. All he had to do was ask; and as soon as he did, he would no longer be crazy and would have to fly more missions... If he flew them he was crazy and didn't have to, but if he didn't want to he was sane and had to. Yossarian was moved very deeply by the absolute simplicity of this clause of Catch-22 and let out a respectful whistle. ❞

CATCH-22, CHAPTER 5

145   Φ

"You mean there's a catch?"

"Sure there's a catch," Doc Daneeka replied.

"What's the catch?"

"Catch-18," Doc Daneeka said. "Anyone who wants to get out of combat duty can't be too crazy."

There was only one catch and that was Catch-18, which reminded that a concern for one's own safety in the face of dangers that were real was the process of a rational mind and stipulated that a desire to be relieved from combat assignment was therefore always to be regarded as sufficient proof of the sanity of the individual making such request. Yossarian was moved by the absolute simplicity of this clause of Catch-18. Orr was crazy because he went right on flying combat missions when he didn't have to and could be grounded. All he had to do was ask to be grounded, and as soon as he did, he would be informed that he had just recovered his sanity and ordered back to fly more missions. Orr would be crazy to fly more missions and sane if he didn't, but if he was sane he had to fly them. If he flew them he was crazy and didn't have to, but the moment he said he didn't want to he would be judged sane again and sent back to fly the missions he had to be crazy to fly. Yossarian was moved very deeply and let out a soft, low, solemn whistle of profound respect.

"That's some catch, that Catch-18, he observed with sober rueful awe.

"It's the best there is," Doc Daneeka agreed.

"I'd like to see a copy sometime."

"I've got a copy lying around here somewhere," Doc Daneeka said. "I've never read it all the way through, but I'll let you borrow it if I find it, and you promise to give it back.

THE **ABSURDITY OF WAR**

In the topsy-turvy world of *Catch-22*, Yossarian always has his own unique perspective on events. When a psychiatrist diagnoses him as "crazy" – because of his morbid aversion to dying, his irrational resentment of possibly being killed on other people's orders, and his deep hatred of hypocrisy – Yossarian, who is mystified, reflects that those are signs of sanity. This makes him one of the few rational characters in a book in which the word "crazy" is found on practically every page.

War, in the world of this novel, amplifies the absurd meaninglessness of human life. However, individual human beings are still able to make moral choices, even when facing oblivion.

▲ **Yossarian** (right, played by Alan Arkin) sees "Doc" Daneeka (Jack Gilford) from a different perspective in the 1970 film of *Catch-22*.

◄ ▲ **TYPESCRIPT AND FIRST EDITION** Joseph Heller began writing *Catch-22* in 1953. It took him eight years to complete, due in part to his time-consuming day jobs at *Time*, *Look*, and *McCall's* magazines. This page of the typescript includes an early version of the famous definition of a "Catch-22" – today a byword for an absurd but inescapable dilemma. The extract above it is how the text appears in the finished novel.

One Day in the Life of Ivan Denisovich

1962 ■ 144 PAGES ■ RUSSIA

ALEKSANDR SOLZHENITSYN (1918–2008)

One Day in the Life of Ivan Denisovich, by Aleksandr Solzhenitsyn, is a short book that has had an enormous impact. Describing a single day in the life of a prisoner in a Soviet labour camp in the 1950s, it was the first account of prison life under Stalin's repressive regime to be published inside Russia. Rapidly translated into other languages, it brought the real consequences of Stalinist oppression to a global audience in a compelling narrative. The book helped Solzhenitsyn to win the Nobel Prize in Literature, but it also precipitated his arrest and expulsion from the Soviet Union.

Ivan Denisovich Shukhov is a peasant, who escaped German imprisonment in the 1940s but was subsequently branded a "spy". His day is described in a plain, spare style, often using the special slang of the prisoners (or "zeks"). Although unwell, Shukhov has to work on a building site in bitterly cold temperatures that make the mortar freeze. He and his fellow prisoners focus purely on survival – working hard to avoid punishment, and to earn extra food if they do well; saving part of their meagre rations for later, or to trade for favours; and maintaining good relations with their squad leader.

Shukhov is always on the lookout for objects that might come in useful – he finds a piece of steel, for example, which he hides away so that he can make it into a tool later. He also helps others, including a prisoner called Tsezar, who does office duties, and for whom he runs errands in return for food from Tsezar's food parcels. Survival strategies like these help Shukhov to overcome his illness and ease the fatigue of the relentless work, enabling him to get through the day. His day is therefore deemed a success – even though he is malnourished, has hardly any time to himself, and is only halfway through a 10-year sentence for a crime that he did not commit.

In context

▶ **JOSEF STALIN** The book is set in the time of Josef Stalin, who ruled the Soviet Union as a dictator for over 20 years, and was initially supported by the West because he helped defeat the Nazis in World War II. Stalin reigned with total ruthlessness, and used the country's system of prison camps to detain political opponents and dissidents.

▲ **THE LABOUR CAMP SYSTEM** The "gulag" was the Russian name for the system of forced labour camps that the Soviet regime used to detain criminals, including political prisoners. It already existed in Imperial Russia, but was hugely extended by the communists. Prisoners were often forced to do heavy labour on construction projects such as the White Sea–Baltic Canal (above).

А. СОЛЖЕНИЦЫН

ОДИН ДЕНЬ ИВАНА ДЕНИСОВИЧА

◀ **FIRST EDITION** When Solzhenitsyn sent his manuscript to the magazine *Novy Mir*, the editor submitted it to the Central Committee of the Communist Party to get permission to publish it. The committee members were so uncertain that they passed it to the Soviet leader Nikita Khrushchev, who approved it for publication. The magazine brought out the novella in 1962, and the work appeared in book form the following year (left). However, by the second half of the 1960s, libraries had begun to withdraw the book from circulation, and it was finally banned by the authorities in 1974.

> ❝ Why, you might wonder, should prisoners wear themselves out, working hard, ten years on end, in the camps? You'd think they'd say: No thank you, and that's that. We'll shuffle through the day till evening, and then the night is ours. But that didn't work. To outsmart you they thought up work-teams – but not teams like the ones in freedom, where every man is paid his separate wage. Everything was so arranged in the camp that the prisoners egged one another on. It was like this: either you got a bit extra or you all croaked. You're slacking you rat – d'you think I'm willing to go hungry just because of you? Put your guts into it, scum. ❞

ONE DAY IN THE LIFE OF IVAN DENISOVICH

> ❝ Here, lads, we live by the law of the taiga. But even here people manage to live. ❞

ONE DAY IN THE LIFE OF IVAN DENISOVICH

SOLZHENITSYN AND THE GULAG

In 1945, Solzhenitsyn, a maths teacher, was imprisoned for writing derogatory comments about Stalin, and for discussing the need for an alternative to the Soviet system with a friend. Much of his eight-year sentence was served in forced labour camps, including a camp for political prisoners in Kazakhstan, where he worked as a miner and bricklayer. These experiences informed not only *One Day in the Life of Ivan Denisovich* but also his three-volume, non-fiction account of the camps, *The Gulag Archipelago*, which he published in 1973. In this vast work, Solzhenitsyn drew on documentary sources, interviews, and his own experience to describe life in the camp, and to explain the legal and administrative system of the Soviet regime.

▶ **Solzhenitsyn in 1953,** at the end of his prison term in Kazakhstan

► **FIRST EDITION** *The Golden Notebook* was first published by Michael Joseph in 1962. The heavy line separating the title from the author's name references the bold black lines that Anna uses to end her notebooks. Each notebook deals with a specific aspect of her life, but she hopes one day to write a golden notebook that presents her entire life as a single, harmonious whole.

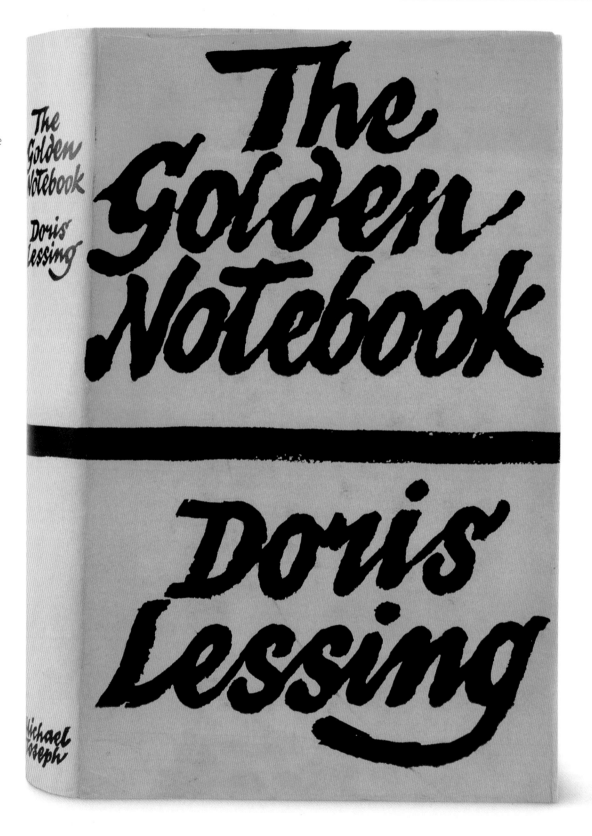

> " Stalin died today. Molly and I sat in the kitchen, upset. I kept saying, 'We are being inconsistent, we ought to be pleased. We've been saying for months he ought to be dead.' She said, 'Oh, I don't know, Anna, perhaps he never knew about all the terrible things that were happening.' Then she laughed and said, 'The real reason we're upset is that we're scared stiff. Better the evils we know... Sometimes I think we're moving into a new age of tyranny and terror, why not? Who's to stop it – us?' "

THE GOLDEN NOTEBOOK, "FREE WOMEN 1", "THE RED NOTEBOOK"

The Golden Notebook

1962 ▪ 567 PAGES ▪ UK

DORIS LESSING (1919–2013)

A "cocoon of madness" is how Doris Lessing described the world of her female characters in *The Golden Notebook*. They find their sexual desires and their political ideals sharply at odds; they have been moulded by a society that denies both of these to women. Some come close to schizophrenia, and one attempts suicide. Theirs is a tale of psychic dislocation, and it is told in a dislocating, multilevelled narrative. The upper narrative level is the ordinary, everyday one. Called "Free Women", it pivots around the friendship between Anna Wulf, a novelist with writer's block, and her friend Molly. The lower narrative levels are provided by the four notebooks that Anna keeps: a black one reserved for her thoughts about her years spent in the racially segregated British colony of Southern Rhodesia; a red one for her thoughts about communism, which she once espoused; a yellow one, which narrates the largely unhappy love life of her fictional alter-ego, Ella; and a blue one, which is a kind of diary.

Each notebook tells a disjointed tale that ends unfortunately for the narrator. Together, they mirror Anna's own increasingly chaotic mental state, and her need to compartmentalize the different aspects of her life. What she needs, and what she

◄ **COMMUNISM IN THE UK** Members of the Communist Party of Great Britain march through a London suburb in 1958. Financed by the Soviet Union, the party had few members, but it did influence trade unions and attracted left-wing intellectuals, including the fictional Anna Wulf.

begins, is a fifth notebook – a golden one, which will make sense of all the other notebooks, and so bring wholeness, integration, and understanding to her life.

Despite the exquisite storytelling of this multilayered novel, the initial reviews of *The Golden Notebook* were at best mixed and at worst downright hostile. Many readers, ignoring the book's innovative structure, thought its theme was the "sex war" between men and women, and it was hailed as a feminist bible by the burgeoning Women's Liberation movement of the 1960s. However, the novel has stood the test of time, and is now widely recognized as being the Nobel Prize-winning author's pivotal work, bridging the gap between her early realistic novels and her later "inner space" sagas and science-fiction epics.

▲ **1950s LONDON** Pedestrians, cycle deliverymen, vintage cars, and a profusion of signs and advertisements all throng Piccadilly Circus in 1957, the year in which the main story in *The Golden Notebook* is primarily set. Most of the action in this narrative takes place in two flats in Earl's Court, a London neighbourhood, but the bustling world outside symbolizes the mental chaos that swiftly engulfs Anna.

LESSING'S INNER SPACE FICTION

Anna's incipient schizophrenia towards the end of *The Golden Notebook* prefigures the subjective turn that Doris Lessing herself took in subsequent novels such as *Briefing for a Descent into Hell* (1971) and *The Memoirs of a Survivor* (1974). Characters in these tales explore the labyrinthine mazes of the mind, which Lessing called "inner space". Such journeys are mythic in scope, plunging beyond the personal unconscious into archetypal realms and even to the foundation of the universe itself. Lessing, who had exchanged her materialist Marxism for a mystical Sufism, capped her science fiction efforts in this direction with a series of five novels, published between 1979 and 1983, known collectively as the *Canopus in Argos* series.

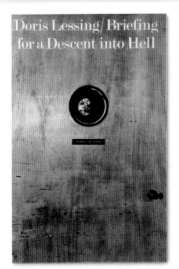

► **The first edition** of *Briefing for a Descent into Hell* (1971) explores inner space.

► **FIRST EDITION** Depicting the pain within the novel, the cover of the first edition of *A Personal Matter* shows a dream-like lionfish with a baby inside it. Like the truth that Bird has to face, the lionfish can kill a human being.

個人的な体験　大江健三郎

❝ 'I bet you haven't been comforted once since all this began. And that's not good, Bird. At a time like this you must be careful to have someone comfort you almost more than you need at least once. Otherwise you'll find yourself helpless when the time comes to summon up your courage and break away from chaos.' 'Courage?' Bird said without considering what Himiko might mean. 'When am I going to have to call on courage?' 'Oh you will Bird, lots of times from now on,' Himiko said carelessly, but with unsmiling authority in her voice. ❞

**A PERSONAL MATTER,
CHAPTER 7**

A Personal Matter

1964 ▪ 214 PAGES ▪ JAPAN

KENZABURŌ ŌE (b.1935)

After buying some road maps of Africa, in a half-hearted attempt to evade his responsibilities, the antihero of *A Personal Matter*, Bird, faces the worst sort of tragedy – his wife gives birth to a baby who is diagnosed with a brain hernia. Shame dawns on Bird as other people suggest denying the infant surgery, and even withdrawing care – then self-disgust, as he reflects on the fact that he is the father. Over the next few days, Bird spirals out of control. He drinks himself into a stupor, visits his mistress, vomits while teaching, and orders that the baby be fed sugar water rather than milk. He muses that its deformities may have been caused by nuclear fallout, or some unknown flaw in himself. Then Bird begins to recover. He admits to his employers that he was drunk in the classroom, and is fired. He then faces his new future – with no trips to Africa, but with a wife and a disabled child to look after. He rushes to donate blood for the infant's surgery, and both son and father emerge from the hospital, healed, but changed for ever.

Ōe's novel ingeniously makes the reader share the horror of Bird's situation. We are forced to make the matter "personal", and to explore our own reactions to disability. For Ōe, the subject was indeed personal – in 1963, his son Hikari was born severely disabled. In this brilliantly unsettling novel, published a year later, Ōe poured all of his darkest feelings into the character of Bird – a man who experiences an ugly form of insanity before he finally begins to accept his responsibilities.

Ōe himself describes his writing as a sort of grotesque realism – a way of confronting and highlighting the physical reality of the human body. The plight of his characters is seen comically as well as tragically. In *A Personal Matter*, the reader is constantly drawn back to Bird's initial trauma – to his shattered realization, after becoming the butt of doctors' jokes, that: "I'm the monster's father."

NUCLEAR LEGACY

Born in 1935, Kenzaburō Ōe sees the history of modern Japan in terms of nuclear catastrophes – the dead of Hiroshima and Nagasaki; the victims of the radiation from 1954's Bikini Atoll bomb tests; and failing nuclear power facilities, such as Fukushima.

Coming of age in the postwar period, Ōe has continually worked in the spirit of Japan's Three Non-Nuclear Principles (to neither manufacture, nor possess, nor import nuclear weapons) by protesting against nuclear power, which he calls a betrayal of Hiroshima's dead. "The Japanese should not be thinking of nuclear energy in terms of industrial productivity," Ōe writes. "They should not draw from the tragedy of Hiroshima a 'recipe' for growth."

▲ **The city of Nagasaki,** three months after it was levelled by a nuclear bomb

❝ The baby is abnormal; the doctor will explain. ❞

A PERSONAL MATTER, CHAPTER 2

◀ **ŌE WITH HIS WIFE AND SON** A brain hernia left Hikari Ōe (centre) severely disabled, but his parents' refusal to be ashamed of him (the norm in the 1960s) helped him to enjoy a rich and full life. Hikari began to play the piano at the age of 8, and at 13 he began composing to communicate what he felt. He has since sold more than one million albums.

One Hundred Years of Solitude

1967 ▪ 417 PAGES ▪ COLOMBIA

GABRIEL GARCÍA MÁRQUEZ (1927-2014)

Between the covers of Gabriel García Márquez's masterwork of magical realism (in which reality is a complex blend of ordinary and magical events that are described on equal terms) lies a complete world. *One Hundred Years of Solitude* centres on the remote Colombian village of Macondo, a cluster of 20 adobe houses, hemmed in between mountains and swamps, founded by the eccentric José Arcadio Buendía and his wife Úrsula Iguarán. Here, the world is "so recent that many things lacked names", and contact with other civilizations can only be made through the mystic Melquíades and a visiting band of gypsies, who intrigue the villagers with "inventions" such as ice and magnets. However, the outside world encroaches: the story spins through the pursuits of seven generations of the Buendía family and a cast of supporting characters who are either on the edge of insanity or from the wrong side of the grave. Macondo falls under plagues of insomnia, biblical storms, political conflicts, and the arrival of the railroad and an American-owned banana plantation.

The novel is set between the early 19th and early 20th centuries, in a version of García Márquez's childhood home, but its playful mix of allegory and history charts centuries of conquest and struggle in South America. Myth and magic are intricately entwined: clouds of yellow butterflies accompany a young mechanic, and one of many incestuous couplings in the book produces a baby with a pig's tail.

Throughout his career as a political journalist, García Márquez struggled to find a narrative voice for his novels until he realized "that reality is also the myths of common people". As a boy, he absorbed his grandfather's military tales alongside the fantastical explanations that his grandmother gave for everyday phenomena. Produced in a frenzy of inspiration, *One Hundred Years of Solitude* has sold more than 500 million copies, and is the most translated work in Spanish after *Don Quixote* (see pp.16–19).

THE **LATIN AMERICAN BOOM**

In the 1960s and '70s, a group of South American authors gained global recognition for their literary creativity. Dubbed the Latin American Boom, their wave of innovative books chimed perfectly with the culture of protest and rebellion that was prevalent at the time. South American writers such as Carlos Fuentes, Julio Cortázar, and Mario Vargas Llosa swept aside literary conventions to engage with the political struggles of Latin America in their experimental writing. Non-linear time, shifting perspectives, and magical realism – a technique considered by many to be the invention of South American literature – were hallmarks of the genre. García Márquez's novels became major works of the boom. In 1982, he was the second of three Latin American authors to win the Nobel Prize for Literature, between Miguel Angel Asturias in 1967 and Mario Vargas Llosa in 2010.

In context

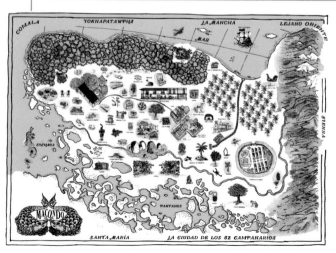

◀ **MAP OF MACONDO** This map shows the topography of Macondo, with its boulder-strewn river and scattered emblems from García Márquez's magical history. It was inspired by the geography of Aracataca, near Colombia's Caribbean coast: a village encircled by forest and swampland, where the author was raised by his grandparents, and where change was slow to arrive.

▲ **THE BANANA MASSACRE** A turning-point in the novel is the annihilation of 3,000 striking workers and their families on Macondo's banana plantation. The event is based on a real massacre of 1928, when the army opened fire on strikers from the Santa Marta banana estate near Ciénaga, Colombia.

Editorial Sudamericana **Gabriel García Márquez**

Cien años de soledad

▲ A LAND-WRECKED GALLEON The first edition of *One Hundred Years of Solitude*, published in May 1967 by Editorial Sudamericana, has a cover that draws from one of the novel's earliest flights of fancy. In search of a route to other civilizations, José Arcadio Buendía and his explorers fall asleep in a dense, enchanted wood. They wake to find that the wreck of a Spanish galleon has appeared, covered in barnacles and moss, and surrounded by ferns and palms.

❝ Many years later, as he faced the firing squad, Colonel Aureliano Buendía was to remember the distant afternoon when his father took him to discover ice. At that time, Macondo was a village of 20 houses, built on the bank of a river of clear water that ran along a bed of polished stones, which were white and enormous, like prehistoric eggs. The world was so recent that many things lacked names, and in order to indicate them it was necessary to point. ❞

ONE HUNDRED YEARS OF SOLITUDE

The author signs off with "Gabriel" and a flower to approve the first page

▲ TYPESCRIPT This typescript page, signed by García Márquez, includes the intriguing opening sentence of *One Hundred Years of Solitude* (see above). García Márquez has said that the line came to him as he drove his family to Mexico for a holiday. He turned back and shut himself away for 18 months to write the novel.

The Master and Margarita

1966-67 ■ AROUND 300 PAGES ■ RUSSIA

MIKHAIL BULGAKOV (1891-1940)

Written in Stalinist Russia during the 1920s and '30s, at a time when writers could be executed for criticizing the state, *The Master and Margarita* tells two stories about people who are silenced for speaking their minds. The first concerns a writer, known as the Master, who has committed himself to a lunatic asylum after burning his own novel when it was rejected by the authorities. The second concerns the execution of Jesus Christ by a regretful Pontius Pilate, who not only sympathizes with his prisoner, but agrees with his principal teachings. Indeed, the second tale is a summary of the Master's novel, which was rejected not only for having a pacifist message, but also for paying homage to the figure of Christ, whom the state has deemed fictional.

Both tales are recounted when a magician named Woland arrives in Moscow. He, it turns out, is the Devil in disguise; he has come to correct the idea that God, and therefore the Devil himself, does not exist. But this is not the Devil as we usually see him: Bulgakov's Devil shows up the corruption of the state's rulers and punishes the novel's main villains. He also takes pity on Margarita, the Master's partner, who, after learning to fly, rescues the writer from the asylum.

On its surface, *The Master and Margarita* is a story about love and redemption, but it is also a biting satire about censorship, the value of myth, and the folly of rewriting history. It takes aim at Russia's ruling elite, showing the contradiction between its petty selfishness and the official communist ideal. Given its incendiary nature, Bulgakov feared that his book was unpublishable and burnt the first manuscript. He rewrote it several times, but it was not published until the 1960s, at the behest of his widow, more than 20 years after his death.

◄ **OGPU BADGE** In 1925, Bulgakov fell foul of the OGPU, the Soviet secret police, who prohibited the publication of his novel *A Dog's Heart*. After that, Bulgakov doubted he had a future as a writer, and destroyed his manuscript of *The Master and Margarita*.

In context

◄ **THE FAUST LEGEND** Bulgakov was inspired by several versions of the German Faust story, in which the title character sells his soul to the Devil in return for hidden knowledge. He also drew on the opera *The Damnation of Faust*, by French composer Hector Berlioz, in which the heroine is called Marguerite. Faust's pact with the Devil is shown here in a painting by the 19th-century artist Eugène Delacroix.

► **KROKODIL** The magazine *Krokodil*, named after an animal that can bite while seeming to grin, was one publication in which Soviet writers could give vent to satire. They still had to be careful though, especially when dealing with politicians. They had to disguise their targets, or focus on bureaucrats who were responsible for administration rather than policy.

Вроде того, например, что эта сухонькая и набожная Анфиса, будто бы носила на своей иссохшей груди в замшевом мешочке двадцать пять крупных бриллиантов, принадлежащих Анне Францевне. Что, будто бы, в дровяном сарае на той же самой даче, куда спешно ездила Анна Францевна, обнаружились сами собой какие-то несметные сокровища в виде тех же бриллиантов, а также золотых денег царской чеканки... И прочее в этом роде. Ну, чего не знаем, за то не ручаемся. Как бы то ни было, квартира простояла пустой и запечатанной только неделю, а затем...

...сущенной рукой провел по бедру, чтобы определить, в брюках он или без брюк, но так и не определил. Наконец, видя, что он брошен и одинок, что некому ему помочь, решил подняться, каких бы нечеловеческих усилий это ни стоило.

Степа разлепил склеенные веки и увидел, что отражается в трюмо в виде человека с торчащими в разные стороны волосами, с опухшей, покрытою черной щетиной физиономией, с заплывшими глазами, в грязной сорочке с воротником и галстуком, в кальсонах и в носках.

Таким он увидел себя в трюмо, а рядом с зеркалом увидел неизвестного человека, одетого в черное и в черном берете.

Степа сел на кровать и, сколько мог, вытаращил налитые кровью глаза на неизвестного. Молчание нарушил этот неизвестный, произнеся низким тяжелым голосом и с иностранным акцентом следующие слова:

— Добрый день, симпатичнейший Степан Богданович!

Произошла пауза, после которой, сделав над собой страшнейшее усилие, Степа выговорил:

— Что вам угодно? — и сам поразился, не узнав своего голоса. Слово «что» он произнес дискантом, «вам» — басом, а «угодно» — у него вовсе не вышло.

Незнакомец дружелюбно усмехнулся, вынул большие золотые часы с алмазным треугольником на крышке, прозвонил одиннадцать раз и сказал:

— Одиннадцать. И ровно час, как я дожидаюсь вашего пробуждения, ибо вы назначили мне быть у вас в десять. Вот и я!

Степа нащупал на стуле рядом с кроватью брюки, шепнул:

— Извините... — надел их и хрипло спросил: — Скажите, пожалуйста, вашу фамилию.

Говорить ему было трудно. При каждом слове кто-то втыкал ему иголку в мозг, причиняя адскую боль.

— Как! Вы и фамилию мою забыли? — тут неизвестный улыбнулся.

— Простите... — прохрипел Степа, чувствуя, что похмелье дарит его новым симптомом: ему показалось, что пол возле кровати ушел куда-то и что сию минуту он головой вниз полетит к чертовой матери в преисподнюю.

50

Однажды в выходной день явился в квартиру милиционер, вызвал в переднюю второго жильца /фамилия которого утратилась/ и сказал, что того просят на минутку зайти в отделение милиции в чем-то расписаться. Жилец приказал Анфисе, преданной и давней домашней работнице Анны Францевны, сказать, в случае, если ему будут звонить, что он вернется через десять минут, и ушел вместе с корректным милиционером в белых перчатках. Но не вернулся он не только через десять минут, а вообще никогда не вернулся. Удивительнее всего то, что, очевидно, с ним вместе исчез и милиционер. Набожная, а откровенно сказать — суеверная Анфиса так напрямик и заявила очень расстроенной Анне Францевне, что это колдовство и что она прекрасно знает, кто утащил жильца и милиционера, только к ночи не хочет говорить.

Ну, а колдовству, как известно, стоит только начаться, а там уж его ничем не остановишь. Второй жилец исчез, помнится, в понедельник, а в среду как сквозь землю провалился Беломут, но — правда — при других обстоятельствах. Утром за ним заехала, как обычно, машина, чтобы отвезти его на службу, и отвезла, но назад никого не привезла и сама больше не вернулась. Горе и ужас мадам Беломут не поддаются описанию. Но, увы, и то и другое было непродолжительно. В ту же ночь, вернувшись с Анфисой с дачи, на которую Анна Францевна почему-то поехала, она не застала уже гражданки Беломут в квартире. Но этого мало: двери обеих комнат, которые занимали супруги Беломут, оказались запечатанными.

Два дня прошли кое-как. На третий день, страдавшая все это время бессонницей Анна Францевна, опять-таки спешно уехала на дачу... Нужно ли говорить, что она не вернулась!

Оставшаяся одна Анфиса, наплакавшись вволю, легла спать во втором часу ночи. Что с ней было дальше, неизвестно, но рассказывали жильцы других квартир, что будто бы в № 50-м всю ночь слышались какие-то стуки и будто бы с утра в окнах горел электрический свет. Утром выяснилось, что и Анфисы нет!

◄ **CENSORED PUBLICATION**
After burning his manuscript in 1930, Bulgakov rewrote it, and made further drafts. A heavily censored version was finally published in Russia in 1966-67, and the parts that were cut circulated as samizdat. Here, a reader has pasted samizdat typescript inserts into the censored publication, to create a version of the complete text.

This part of the censored text deals with a spate of disappearances that are clearly perpetrated by the police, but are attributed, tongue in cheek, to "sorcery"

▲ **MOSCOW MAGAZINE**
The Master and Margarita first appeared in Russia, heavily censored, in two issues of *Moskva* (*Moscow*) magazine: issue 11 for 1966 and issue 1 for 1967. A full version of the text was then smuggled out of the country and published in Paris, also in 1967.

> 'What is this novel about?' 'It is a novel about Pontius Pilate.' Here again the tongues of the candles swayed and leaped, the dishes on the table clattered, Woland burst into thunderous laughter, but neither frightened nor surprised anyone. Behemoth applauded for some reason. 'About what? About what? About whom?' said Woland, ceasing to laugh. 'And that - now? It's stupendous! Couldn't you have found some other subject? Let me see it.' Woland held out his hand, palm up. 'Unfortunately, I cannot do that,' replied the master, 'because I burned it in the stove.' 'Forgive me, but I don't believe you,' Woland replied, 'that cannot be: manuscripts don't burn.'

THE MASTER AND MARGARITA, CHAPTER 24

SAMIZDAT

Under the Soviet system, literature was censored, and writers were only allowed to express opinions that were compatible with the regime's communist ideology. Anyone who disobeyed had their work censored or banned, and risked being imprisoned or expelled from the writers' union and compelled to take another, often menial, job. However, writing that risked censorship was often circulated secretly and anonymously by authors who used typewriters and duplicating machines to produce copies of their work. These clandestine works were called samizdat, from the Russian words for "self" and "publication". People who produced them risked severe punishment, but the works were widely circulated nonetheless.

▲ **A collection of Russian samizdat writings,** including reels of photographic negatives of the texts

◄ **DRAFT TYPESCRIPT** In a 1984 interview for *The Paris Review*, Roth revealed that "Beginning a book is unpleasant… I often have to write a hundred pages or more before there's a paragraph that's alive". In this late draft of *Portnoy's Complaint*, Roth made handwritten amendments to what had, by that stage, become the opening passage of the novel.

So deeply imbedded was she in my consciousness that for the first few years of school I believed that each of my teachers was actually my mother in disguise. I would ~~run home from school~~ *rush for the door* when the last class was over, wondering ~~whether~~ *if* I could possibly make it home to our apartment before she had successfully managed her transformation. That she ~~was~~ *turned out to be* already back in the kitchen, *by the time I arrived* baking *the* cookies for ~~me to hold fresh and warm in my hands with my~~ my afternoon milk, did not cause me to doubt my fantasy; it only deepened my awe of her powers. It was always ~~an immense~~ *a* relief ~~to me~~ not to have caught her between identities, though I ~~did not~~ *never* seem able to ~~cease in~~ *stop making* the effort. I knew that my father and sister were innocent of my mother's real nature, and the burden of betrayal that I thought would fall to me if I ever came upon her unawares was more than I wanted to bear. I thought I might actually be done away with *in some way or other* if I were to catch sight of her flying in from school through the bedroom window, or causing herself to emerge limb from limb out of her invisible state and into her apron. I seemed ~~for s me reason to~~ *to* believe my mother to have the functions of a god and the ch*a*racteristics of a witch, and so of course when she asked me to tell her all about my day in school, I did so with the utmost scrupulosity. I did not pretend to understand *all* the ~~endless~~ implications of her ubiquitous-

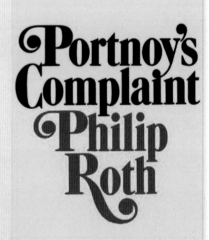

▲ **FIRST EDITION** *Portnoy's Complaint* was first published in 1969 with a distinctive, bright yellow cover. It has since been reprinted with different covers and in other languages. An unlicensed version with Roth's name misspelt was even found in Australia, where the book was banned for a time.

> " She was so deeply imbedded in my consciousness that for the first year of school I seem to have believed that each of my teachers was my mother in disguise. As soon as the last bell had sounded, I would rush off for home, wondering as I ran if I could possibly make it to our apartment before she had succeeded in transforming herself. Invariably she was already in the kitchen by the time I arrived, and setting out my milk and cookies. Instead of causing me to give up my delusions, however, the feat merely intensified my respect for her powers. "

PORTNOY'S COMPLAINT, CHAPTER 1

Portnoy's Complaint

1969 ■ 195 PAGES ■ US

PHILIP ROTH (1933–2018)

Jewish American writer Philip Roth shocked the world (and became a celebrity) when he published *Portnoy's Complaint* in 1969. Written as an unrestrained, scabrously comic, first-person monologue, delivered by a young Jewish man named Alexander Portnoy to his psychoanalyst, the novel follows Alex's obsessions: sexual desire, Jewishness, and his relationship with his mother. He believes she has controlled and repressed him, and feels that her presence permeates his life – he is obsessed with sex and unwilling to settle down with just one woman, perhaps because no one can, or should, replace his mother. The monologue includes many detailed and frank descriptions of Alex's masturbatory habits and his lustful views of women, leading a number of critics and readers to describe the book as obscene and even pornographic.

The novel explores antisemitism: the narrator is sensitive to the myriad ways in which the US, a Christian country, cannot recognize Christianity's roots in Judaism and readily allows dislike and suspicion of Jews. Yet Alex also resents many aspects of his own Jewish upbringing, especially the guilt it (and his mother) taught him: "I am marked like a road map from head to toe with my repressions."

While Alex's concerns are serious, much of the book is outrageously funny. Yet many readers were concerned that the novel promoted antisemitic stereotypes. Others were simply appalled by its sexual explicitness, and there were movements to challenge and even ban it. Roth, whose later books frequently explored similar territory to *Portnoy's Complaint*, is considered important for raising awareness about Jewish people and literature in the American consciousness – despite the controversy of his work.

JEWISH LITERATURE

For centuries, Jewish people have produced literature written in Hebrew, Yiddish, Ladino, English, and many other languages. Some texts are based on Jewish folktales and beliefs, while others explore what it means to be Jewish in different times and places. Renowned Jewish authors include Sholem Aleichem and Isaac Bashevis Singer, both of whom wrote in Yiddish; Hebrew-language novelists such as Amos Oz and David Grossman; and English-language writers such as Saul Bellow, Art Spiegelman, and Gertrude Stein. Of the 118 winners of the Nobel Prize for Literature, 16 have been Jewish writers, comprising 14 per cent of the total.

▲ **Canadian-American** author Saul Bellow was awarded the Nobel Prize for Literature in 1976.

In context

◄ **NEW YORK IN THE 1950s** After World War II, there was a population boom in both New York and its suburbs, including New Jersey, where *Portnoy's Complaint* is set. In New York and New Jersey, Jewish people tended to live in their own neighbourhoods where Yiddish was regularly spoken.

▶ **PSYCHOANALYSIS IN LITERATURE** Many authors applied Sigmund Freud's psychoanalytical beliefs to their works, by exploring a character's history or depicting them undergoing psychoanalysis, as in *Portnoy's Complaint*. Here, director Ernest Lehman shows Alex having therapy in his 1972 film of the novel.

History

1974 ▪ 352 PAGES ▪ ITALY

ELSA MORANTE (1912-1985)

Published in 1974 in Italian as *La Storia* (meaning both *History* and *The Story*), Elsa Morante's novel was later translated into English with the title *History: A Novel*. It opens in 1941 in Rome, when a teacher named Ida is brutally raped by a German soldier. Nine months later, she gives birth to a son, Useppe. With the baby and her elder son Nino, Ida must try to survive the war. Morante's narrative interleaves passages of impersonally related official history, from 1941 to 1947, with longer sections of Ida's more personal story. There are no famous historical figures in Ida's world, only the inhabitants of a poor urban community, facing the hardships and suffering endured by ordinary people during World War II.

Morante raises the question of what survival means: physical survival is no guarantee of happiness, or even sanity. Ida's Jewish heritage leaves her in mortal fear, and suffering from survivor's guilt. Meanwhile, Nino keeps leaving his family, joining first the Resistance and then a communist guerrilla group. When Rome is freed from Nazi occupation, its residents try to return to the lives that they had before, but the trauma runs deep, and no one can escape its hold. Nino refuses to return

◀ **PLIGHT OF THE ORDINARY**
In her novel, Morante aimed to show the plight of ordinary people whose stories do not appear in official histories of war. In this 1986 film directed by Luigi Comencini, Ida is shown clutching her son, the product of a brutal wartime assault, amidst the rubble of her devastated home.

to normal and dies smuggling guns, and Useppe, who suffers from epilepsy, has a fatal seizure. Unable to cope with her grief, Ida ends her life in an asylum after nine years of silence.

Half-Jewish herself, Morante became a writer in the 1930s, while living in Rome. When her husband, writer Alberto Moravia, was accused of anti-fascist activities in 1943, they fled to rural southern Italy. After liberation, she returned to Rome, to be faced with bombed homes and desperate people. In *History*, Morante drew on her own personal experience of the many faces of war and the devastation that it leaves behind.

◀ **NAZIS IN ROME** In July 1943, fascist Italian leader Benito Mussolini was overthrown, and Italy joined the Allies' cause. The Nazis invaded in September, taking over Rome for nine months. For the Roman people, Nazi occupation involved starvation, oppression, torture, and death. Rome's Jews were transported to Auschwitz two days after occupation began.

> " Man, by his very nature, tends to give himself an explanation of the world... "

HISTORY, "1946", SECTION 4

Elsa Morante
La Storia

Romanzo

EINAUDI

Uno scandalo che dura da diecimila anni.

▲ **FIRST EDITION** Morante insisted on publishing *History* in paperback, making it affordable to all. It sold more than 600,000 copies, leading to a national discussion about the nature of war and its effect on survivors. Yet some people were critical, including Pier Paolo Pasolini, Morante's friend, who wrote such a scathing review that she never spoke to him again.

> " A merrier baby than he had never been seen. Everything he glimpsed around him roused his interest and stirred him to joy. He looked with delight at the threads of rain outside the window, as if they were confetti and multicoloured streamers... You would have said, to tell the truth, from his laughter, from the constant brightening of his little face, that he didn't see things only in their usual aspects, but as multiple images of other things, varying to infinity. Otherwise, there was no explaining why the wretched, monotonous scene the house offered every day could afford him such diverse, inexhaustible amusement. "

HISTORY, "1942", SECTION 1

RESISTANCE MOVEMENT

La Resistenza was the Italian resistance group that fought first against Benito Mussolini's fascist government, and then, from 1943, against the occupying Nazi forces. In *History*, Ida's rebellious son Nino leaves school to become part of this movement. *La Resistenza* was an umbrella term for many smaller groups unable or unwilling to work together initially. The Nazi occupation ignited a coalition of anti-fascists, and in April 1945 these partisans led an uprising in Bologna that eventually spread throughout the north of Italy. Italians still celebrate 25 April as Liberation Day. By working together, *La Resistenza* helped to form a modern, united, and democratic Italy, rather than the city states of old. Yet this triumph brought great sacrifice: an estimated 75,000 partisans were killed, either in action or during reprisals, and another 20,000 were left permanently disabled.

▲ **In October 1944**, partisans entered the city of Cesena, recently freed from Nazi forces.

Directory: 1950-1980

▼ MEMOIRS OF HADRIAN

MARGUERITE YOURCENAR, 1951

The Belgian-born French novelist Marguerite Yourcenar (1903–87) had her greatest popular and critical success with a historical novel set in the golden age of the Roman Empire. *Memoirs of Hadrian* comprises letters purportedly written by the emperor, who ruled from 117–138CE.

Anticipating death, Hadrian tells his life story, presenting his meditations upon history, love, and power for the benefit of the future emperor, Marcus Aurelius. Yourcenar adopts a formal classical style that convincingly represents how a Roman emperor might have written. The historical facts of Hadrian's life are scrupulously researched and the ideas attributed to him accurately reflect the thinking of educated Romans – heavily influenced by Stoic philosophy.

As well as its historical interest, the novel has an emotional pull – narrated by a man at the end of his life, ruling an empire facing inevitable decline, it is infused with a luminous melancholy that resonates with modern readers.

LORD OF THE FLIES

WILLIAM GOLDING, 1954

A fable about human nature set on a desert island, *Lord of the Flies* was written by a British teacher, William Golding (1911–93). Basing the story on his observations of the behaviour of children at school, Golding describes a group of boys whose aircraft has crashed on the island during wartime. No adult survived the crash.

At first, they try to create an orderly democratic society, but this rapidly degenerates into brutal hierarchies of power. The lessons of civilized life are forgotten as a primitive tribalism releases suppressed impulses towards sadism and murder. The use of stock figures of the English public-school novel, such as the bespectacled fat boy, Piggy, effectively laces the exotic horror with ironic familiarity. In Golding's first version of the novel, never published, the savagery on the island was explicitly situated in a future nuclear war. This remains implicit in the novel. The boys are in effect reenacting the process by which their elders have come to destroy civilization in World War III.

THE TEMPLE OF THE GOLDEN PAVILION

YUKIO MISHIMA, 1956

Japanese author and political activist Yukio Mishima (1925–70) was devoted to preserving his country's national spirit and traditions, and hated seeing it influenced by the West. He based *The Temple of the Golden Pavilion* on a notorious real-life event: the burning of a Buddhist temple in Kyoto by a novice monk in 1950.

Tormented protagonist Mizoguchi grows up in the shadow of World War II. Unattractive and poor, with a crippling speech impediment, he develops an obsession with the Golden Pavilion as the symbol of a beauty that is cruelly lacking from his own existence. The novel follows his mental disintegration through lurid episodes of sadism and masochism, until his love for the Pavilion's beauty sours to a destructive hatred.

In its obsession with eroticism and death, Mishima's writing works with the grain of major Japanese cultural traditions, but Mizoguchi's tortured psychology sets the book firmly in the genre of 20th-century modernism.

DOCTOR ZHIVAGO

BORIS PASTERNAK, 1957

Celebrated as a lyrical poet before becoming a novelist, Boris Pasternak (1890–1960) was a Russian who grew up in a privileged family before the Bolshevik Revolution in 1917, and who never fitted easily into the ensuing Soviet era.

In his epic love story *Doctor Zhivago*, Pasternak depicts the vast sufferings that his country endured in political upheaval and civil war, but his focus is on individual, rather than collective, experience. Yuri Zhivago's doomed love for Lara is the axis around which the novel's complex cast of characters whirls. The enduring appeal of Pasternak's novel lies in its combination of panoramic historical sweep and intimate feeling. A series of love poems, ostensibly written by Zhivago, conclude the work.

Although the book was not an attack on communism, it was rejected for publication in the Soviet Union. Published in the West, it won Pasternak the Nobel Prize for Literature, to the fury of Soviet authorities. The novel remained banned in the Soviet Union.

THE PRIME OF MISS JEAN BRODIE

MURIEL SPARK, 1961

The most successful novel of Scottish author Muriel Spark (1918–2006), *The Prime of Miss Jean Brodie* is a wickedly unsentimental account of the influence of a charismatic, manipulative teacher on a select group of pupils, the "Brodie set", at a private girls' school in Edinburgh. Spark's audacious time shifts let us see the later consequences of these school-time dramas.

Miss Brodie is an astonishing fictional creation. An authoritarian dedicated to liberation, convinced of her own rightness in the eyes of God, and with a maxim for every occasion, her enthusiasms range from history of art to fascism. She attempts to guide the love lives of her pupils, while pursuing her own in an eccentric and largely ineffectual manner. Her pupils, reflecting critically from later on in their careers, make comments that

Marguerite Yourcenar, the first woman elected to the influential French Academy

darken our understanding of their childish actions and motivations. One member of the set finally betrays Brodie, leading to her downfall.

Creating her own imaginative world brimming with originality, Spark created an outrageous comedy with disturbing undertones.

▶ THE GARDEN OF THE FINZI-CONTINIS

GIORGIO BASSANI, 1962

Written by Jewish Italian author Giorgio Bassani (1916–2000), *The Garden of the Finzi-Continis* seeks to recreate a world destroyed by the Holocaust. Its unnamed narrator lives in the city of Ferrara in the 1930s. He becomes obsessed with a rich Jewish family whose garden acts as a sociable Eden: a place of innocence and joy, where Ferrara's Jewish community can find relief from the antisemitic policies of Italy's fascist government. Over endless games of tennis, the narrator falls in love with Micól, the daughter of the family. Both in love and politics, he eventually grows into the sad knowledge of adulthood.

Bassani's slender and understated narrative, delivered in a refined elaborate prose, evokes with aching nostalgia a society from the recent past that has been obliterated.

HOPSCOTCH

JULIO CORTÁZAR, 1963

The Argentinian author Julio Cortázar (1914–84) described his experimental book *Hopscotch* as a "counter-novel". The book has 155 chapters. The first 56 tell the story chronologically, but the author suggests an alternative "open-ended" path through the book, incorporating the other 99 chapters out of sequence. Or, the reader can play hopscotch with the text, skipping back and forth between chapters.

The novel's protagonist, Horatio Oliveira, lives a Bohemian life in Paris, experiencing love and listening to modern jazz. He is then deported to Buenos Aires, to work in a circus and a mental institution, where he undergoes a slow-motion breakdown. Surreal episodes alternate with discussions of art and philosophy.

The text is as disorienting as the novel's subject matter. Packed with obscure, learned vocabulary as well as slang expressions, Cortázar's writing distorts traditional grammar and veers into a free-flowing stream of consciousness. Like James Joyce, by whom he was influenced, Cortázar is a challenging writer, but one whose work is full of imaginative riches.

HERZOG

SAUL BELLOW, 1964

The protagonist of *Herzog* is often taken as the alter ego of the novel's American author, Saul Bellow (1915–2005). Like Bellow, Moses Herzog is a Jewish intellectual; both men are a similar age and have trouble with women. An acrimonious divorce from his second wife, who left Herzog for one of his friends, has left him prey to feelings of failure and paranoia. The novel follows Herzog through five days of manic restlessness.

Much of the text consists of mental letters that Herzog fires off to dead philosophers, world leaders, and ex-lovers, exploring major issues of Western civilization, as well as the complexities of his own personal life. Obsessed with his friend's betrayal, Herzog plans revenge, but violent fantasy peters out into farce. Resentment is defeated by self-mockery, allowing some kind of acceptance of life.

The slight plot supports a torrent of jokes and insights, verbal invention, and intellectual speculation, delivered in Bellow's scintillating prose, which mixes erudition with colloquial wit. The energy of the writing grips the reader through Herzog's clowning, self-pity, and dabbling in misogyny.

GRAVITY'S RAINBOW

THOMAS PYNCHON, 1973

Widely regarded as the masterpiece of American writer Thomas Pynchon (b.1937), *Gravity's Rainbow* is set in Europe at the end of World War II. Much of the action revolves around the German V2 rocket programme, but the novel is so complex, so absurd in its premises and so free in its digressions, that it cannot be reduced

Giorgio Bassani, seen here in 1942, was an Italian novelist, poet, and intellectual.

to a rational narrative. Pynchon draws on comic strips, urban myths, movies, conspiracy theories, physics, jazz, theology, drug lore, sexual fetishism, and the occult to create a text that is wildly funny, paranoid, and sometimes obscene. Through a mad world, his characters pursue the V2 rocket like a holy grail, although its significance, if any, is certainly not the point. Despite the opacity of the plot, the novel powerfully states its values: anti-corporate, anarchic, eco-friendly, and firmly on the side of the damned rather than the saved.

IF ON A WINTER'S NIGHT A TRAVELLER

ITALO CALVINO, 1979

Written by Italian postmodernist Italo Calvino (1923–85), *If on a Winter's Night a Traveller* is a playful fiction that takes the reader (or a reader)

as its protagonist. The book opens with a man (addressed as "you" in the text) reading a book called *If on a Winter's Night a Traveller* by Italo Calvino. His attempt to read fails because his copy of the book is spoiled, with missing and disordered pages. The search for an elusive authentic copy brings him into contact with a female reader called Ludmilla. Their quest and developing relationship provide the core narrative of the novel.

Inserted between those sections devoted to the readers are 10 first chapters of stories in a variety of genres, none of which is completed. Fun is had with inventions such as the fictional country of Cimmeria, as well as the imaginary detective writer Silas Flannery. Subtle and charming, the consistently amusing text can be taken as an elaborate reflection on authorial authenticity and the art of reading.

6

1980— PRESENT

Desert

1980 ▪ 410 PAGES ▪ FRANCE

J.M.G. LE CLÉZIO (b.1940)

Desert tells two stories, one set in Algeria in 1910–13, and the other in present-day France and Morocco. The earlier story describes the French invasion and colonization of North Africa. Set in the Saguia el-Hamra area of the Western Sahara, and seen through the eyes of a boy named Nour, it follows the Tuareg tribe as they are driven from their homelands and make a gruelling journey across the desert to safety. En route, Nour joins the religious leader Ma al-'Aïnine, who has proclaimed a holy war against the French, and they set off for the fortress town of Smara.

The second story tells the tale of the orphaned Lalla, a descendant of the Tuareg, who grows up in a shanty town on the Moroccan coast. Haunted by the Blue Man, a spectre that represents her tribal past, Lalla travels to France to escape from an arranged marriage, and faces a new kind of hostile environment – one in which she is an unwelcome immigrant. After working first as a prostitute, and then as a cleaner, Lalla is taken up by a photographer and becomes a famous fashion model, but she fails to settle in France, and returns to Morocco to find her childhood love – a mute shepherd called "the Hartani", by whom she becomes pregnant. Poignantly, Lalla gives birth to her child in the desert, while Nour fades from sight.

The novel's greatest achievement lies in its powerful, painterly descriptions of the desert, which is not so much the setting of the novel as its central focus. It takes on the character of a driving force that gives the protagonists the will to survive. The relationship between humans, animals, plants, and the earth that they inhabit is also a major source of inspiration in Le Clézio's later work, such as *The Flood* and *Terra Amata*. When he was awarded the Nobel Prize in Literature in 2008, the Swedish Academy praised him as an "ecologically engaged author".

> It was as if there were no names here, as if there were no words. The desert cleansed everything in its wind, wiped everything away. The men had the freedom of the open spaces in their eyes, their skin was like metal. Sunlight blazed everywhere. The ochre, yellow, grey, white sand, the fine sand shifted, showing the direction of the wind. It covered all traces, all bones. It repelled light, drove away water, life, far from a centre that no one could recognize. The men knew perfectly well that the desert wanted nothing to do with them: so they walked on without stopping...

DESERT, "SAGUIET AL-HAMRA, WINTER 1909–1910"

▲ **THE VAST SAHARA** The desert dominates the novel. In 1910, Nour travels the Sahara, fleeing the French army with his tribe as they search for refuge and enlightenment. "Out there, in the open desert, men can walk for days without passing a single house, seeing a well, for the desert is so vast that no one can know it all."

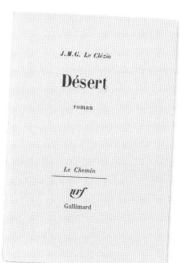

J.M.G. Le Clézio

Désert

roman

Le Chemin

nrf
Gallimard

▲ **FIRST FRENCH EDITION** *Desert* was published by Gallimard in 1980, and contributed to the author winning the Nobel Prize in Literature in 2008. The prize committee described Le Clézio as an "explorer of a humanity beyond and below the reigning civilization".

◄ **THE BLUE PEOPLE** The Tuaregs are Berbers and live in a huge area of the Sahara Desert. Traditionally nomadic, they follow herds of goats and sheep across North Africa. They are known as the "blue people" due to the indigo dye that they use in their clothes, which often stains their skin.

FIGHTING THE FRENCH

By the time that Nour is born, the French war on Algeria and Morocco has been raging for 75 years. In 1907, a new phase began as the result of pressure from Franco-Algerian settlers to take the land between Algeria and Senegal. Starting with skirmishes that forced the redrafting of the border between Algeria and Morocco, it ended with Morocco becoming a French protectorate, and being free in name only. The conflict forced the remaining Tuareg people to migrate, first to Smara, in present-day Western Sahara, and then further north, into Morocco, where Lalla is born in the novel. It is also in Smara that Nour meets Ma al-'Aïnine, a freedom fighter and Islamic scholar.

▲ **Soldiers of the French Foreign Legion** stand guard in Mestigmeur, Morocco, in 1910.

Midnight's Children

1981 ■ 446 PAGES ■ UK

SALMAN RUSHDIE (b.1947)

Even though his own life resembles that of his protagonist, Saleem, Salman Rushdie has always maintained that *Midnight's Children* is not autobiographical. Both their lives have spanned that of independent India, born at the stroke of midnight, 15 August 1947, when the new nation officially left the British Empire. Upon opening the novel, however, all superficial resemblances vanish as the reader is propelled into a world of marvellous stories, tales nested within tales, modelled on *The Thousand and One Nights*, which Rushdie read as a child. All are so saturated with the mythological universe of an India long entwined with the UK that, as the narrator, says, "Perhaps it would be fair to say that Europe repeats itself, in India, as farce".

Saleem is one of 1,001 Indian babies born as India became independent. "Midnight's children", they are all endowed with some miraculous power – Saleem can read other people's minds. As a Muslim, he grows up in India but spends his early adulthood in Pakistan – the two nations, once conjoined, were torn apart on religious lines during the Partition in 1947. His mock-heroic misadventures, and those of myriad relatives and acquaintances, are woven into a grimly realistic narrative of modern Indian history – its wars with Pakistan, the massacre of Muslims at the "Friday Mosque" in Delhi, and the country's succumbing to dictatorship in the mid-1970s. Thus, the life of one midnight's child mirrors the epic struggles of the new nation.

Rushdie's superb handling of a magical-realist narrative and his deft use of irony and satire made *Midnight's Children* a worldwide bestseller. It revolutionized the way in which Indian and Anglo-Indian writers understood their shared history, and launched the author's literary career to new heights.

INDIRA GANDHI

Indira Gandhi was the daughter of Jawaharlal Nehru, the first prime minister of independent India. After the death of her father, she became the most powerful person in the country, serving two terms as prime minister. She is called "The Widow" in *Midnight's Children*, and is depicted as a tyrant who illegally holds on to power. In the book, as in life, she institutes the crackdown known as "The Emergency" (1975–77), during which civil rights are stifled and many people disappear after being sent to prison. In 1984, the same year in which she sued Rushdie for a single defamatory sentence in the novel, she was assassinated by her own bodyguards.

▲ **Indira Gandhi** was the first female prime minister of India; her legacy remains controversial.

In context

◄ **THE PARTITION OF INDIA**
When Pakistan and India became separate countries in 1947, hundreds of thousands of people were killed in ethnic violence, and millions more were displaced. Here, a family flees a refugee camp near Delhi's Jama Musjid, or "Friday Mosque".

► **SCHEHERAZADE** The number 1,001 recurs throughout the book, and represents the night, magic, and alternative realities. It also references *The Thousand and One Nights*, a book in which Scheherazade (see right) has to tell the Persian King Shahryar a different story each night.

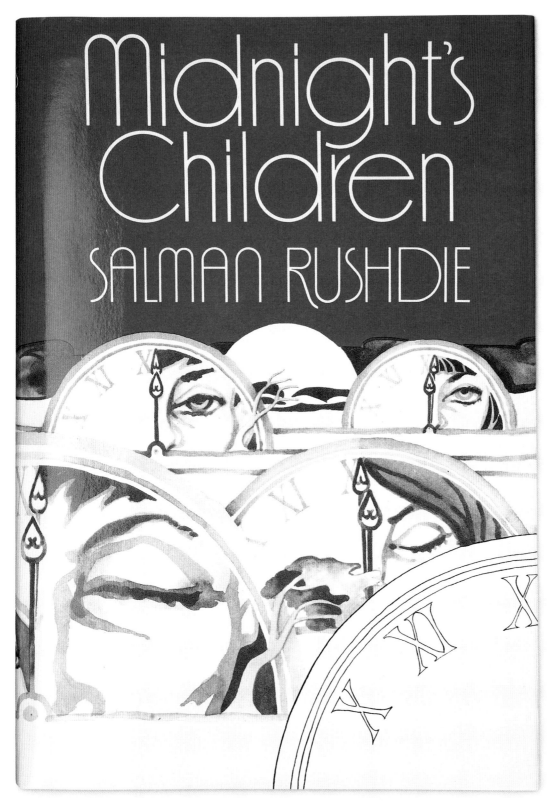

◄ **FIRST EDITION** *Midnight's Children* was first published by Jonathan Cape in 1981, and won not only the Booker Prize, but also two other Booker Prizes, in 1993 and 2008. Bill Botten's cover design features some of the "midnight's children", whose faces show the imprint of the time that they were born: midnight, 15 August 1947. The arrows recall the novel's opening paragraph, in which "Clock-hands joined palms in respectful greeting".

> Yes, they will trample me underfoot, the numbers marching one two three, four hundred million five hundred million six, reducing me to specks of voiceless dust, just as, all in good time, they will trample my son who is not my son, and his son who will not be his, and his who will not be his... until a thousand and one midnights have bestowed their terrible gifts and a thousand and one children have died, because it is the privilege and the curse of midnight's children to be both masters and victims of their times...

MIDNIGHT'S CHILDREN, "ABRACADABRA"

▶ **FIRST EDITION**
The House of the Spirits was originally published in Spanish and was named the Best Novel of the Year in Chile. It has since been translated into more than 20 languages, including English. Allende's debut novel received great critical acclaim, but it has caused outrage and controversy because of its sexually explicit and violent content.

The House of the Spirits

1982 ■ 496 PAGES ■ CHILE

ISABEL ALLENDE (b.1942)

La casa de los espíritus (*The House of the Spirits*) was Isabel Allende's first novel. Allende, who had worked as a journalist, began writing it as a letter to her grandfather. Using mostly third-person narration, it traces the lives of three generations of the Trueba family. Clara, who can see the future but cannot change it, marries her dead sister's former fiancé, Esteban Trueba, a tyrannical, conservative patriarch who exploits and abuses his workers. The couple have a daughter, Blanca, who falls in love with Pedro Tercero, a revolutionary socialist who is the son of Esteban's foreman. Blanca and Pedro Tercero's relationship puts them at odds with Esteban, but it also leads to the birth of Alba, his beloved granddaughter. In time, Alba suffers terrible punishments in revenge for her grandfather's past abuses. Instead of seeking vengeance in turn, she persuades Esteban to help her write their family's story, enabling both of them to let go of the past.

The House of the Spirits centres on women's written words: the novel opens with a young Clara writing in her diary, and closes with Alba writing her own tale. It is women's voices that explore the bonds between the female characters, and detail the violence, rape, and coercion that they endure. The novel is also a work of magical realism, a literary style with strong roots in Latin America: Allende wove fantastical elements – such as Clara's clairvoyance and, later, the appearance of her ghost – into the story, alongside more realistic events, such as a military coup and dictatorship similar to those that existed in Chile when she was writing the novel. The latter enabled Allende to show how each character's personal experience is entwined with politics and class struggle, and to lay bare the devastating impact that political events can have on individual people's lives.

> " The big house on the corner was sadder and older than I had remembered, and looked absurd, with its architectural eccentricities, its pretensions to French style, its façade covered with diseased ivy. The garden was a tangle of weeds and almost all the shutters were hanging from their hinges. As always, the gate was open. "
>
> **THE HOUSE OF THE SPIRITS**, EPILOGUE

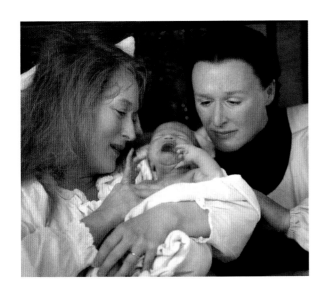

▲ **PURITY** This image from the 1993 film adaptation shows the bonds of sisterhood in Allende's story. Four of the women have names related to the word "white" in Spanish or Latin. This suggests purity (of body and mind) and clarity (of vision and feelings). It also emphasizes the bonds between the women.

THE **CHILEAN REVOLUTION**

In 1973, the president of Chile, Salvador Allende, was overthrown by a military coup led by General Augusto Pinochet. Salvador Allende is thought to have refused exile, and died by suicide. He had been a first cousin of Isabel Allende's father, and after the coup, her whole family was under threat. Isabel fled to Venezuela, where she lived for more than 12 years and wrote *The House of the Spirits*. The military coup took control of Chile's government and media, and had a devastating effect on the country. It became a dictatorship, dominated by violence and torture. After almost two decades of military control, Chile began to return to democracy in the 1990s.

▶ **President Salvador Allende** is captured on camera for the last time before dying in the palace after Pinochet's coup.

The Year of the Death of Ricardo Reis

1984 ▪ 415 PAGES ▪ PORTUGAL

JOSÉ SARAMAGO (1922-2010)

Portuguese Nobel laureate José Saramago was a writer with working-class roots and a strong commitment to the political left. He had reached the age of 60 before he won recognition as a writer, his novels being associated with the "magical realism" wave of the 1980s. *The Year of the Death of Ricardo Reis* seamlessly blends fantasy and historical fact. Saramago's basic idea was to portray Ricardo Reis, one of Portuguese poet Fernando Pessoa's fictional creations, as a real person who outlives his creator.

The novel opens with Reis returning to Portugal from Brazil after the poet's death. Reis visits Pessoa's grave, which triggers a series of encounters with the poet's sad, wandering ghost. Meeting haphazardly at the ghost's initiative, the dead creator and his living creation discuss death, love, and literature in dialogues that are both whimsical and profound. These fantasy episodes take place in the precisely described world of 1930s Lisbon. Civil war has just broken out in neighbouring Spain, and Portugal's right-wing regime is pursuing subversives. Reis comes under suspicion, and is interrogated by the police. He also witnesses grotesque scenes of religious hysteria, whipped up by the pro-Catholic authorities, and embarks on an affair with a chambermaid, Lydia, whom he treats with patronizing disdain.

Saramago is implicitly critical of the pessimism and elitism represented by Pessoa and Reis: they show contempt for the vulgarity and brutality of Portugal's Salazar regime, but are too fastidious to identify with the working-class people who seek to resist it. If the novel has a hero, it is Lydia, who shames Reis with her passionate response to oppression. However, both Pessoa and Reis are amusing, intelligent, and engaging figures, redeemed by their shared sense of the loneliness of existence and the need for companionship in the face of death. The fluid, multilayered text – by turns ironic, humorous, gentle, and satirical – above all mines a rich vein of melancholy.

In context

▲ **ATMOSPHERIC CITY** The novel is set in the Portuguese capital, Lisbon, in 1936, when the country was governed by the oppressive right-wing dictatorship of António de Oliveira Salazar. The atmosphere of the rain-soaked city is powerfully evoked as Reis wanders the streets, observing the decaying grandeur and pervading poverty.

▲ **NAVAL REVOLT** The historical event that provides the climax of the novel was a left-wing naval revolt against the Salazar dictatorship, staged in Lisbon in September 1936, which was crushed. Two warships seized by the mutinous sailors were crippled by shellfire in the Tagus estuary. Hundreds of sailors were arrested and sent to concentration camps.

▼ **TYPESCRIPT** Saramago wrote in long paragraphs and his dialogue does not have conventional punctuation, but the effect is entirely lucid and readable. Although the action is seen from the point of view of Ricardo Reis, there are frequent interruptions by the authorial voice, commenting with ironic humour on the attitudes and behaviour of his chief protagonist.

N4s/11   48

nada disso, que essas coisas, se ainda as há em Lisboa, oculta-as a terra movida por aterros ou causas naturais, aqui é somente uma pedra rec-
tangular, embutida e cravada num murete que dá para a Rua Nova do Carva-
lho, dizendo em letra de ornament ~~ornamentada letra~~ Clínica de Enfermedades de los Ojos y
Quirúrgicas, e mais sobriamente Fundada por A. Mascaró em 1870, as pe-
dras têm a vida longa, ~~quando nascem, quando morem~~, tantos anos passa-
ram sobre esta e hão-de passar, morreu Mascaró e desfez-se a clínica,
porventura algures descendentes do Fundador, ocupados em outros ofí-
cios, quem sabe se já esquecidos, ou ignorantes sempre, de que neste lugar
público a sua pedra de armas, não fossem as famílias o que
são, inconstantes, e esta viria aqui lembrar a memória do antepassado
curador de olhos e outras cirurgias, é bem verdade que não basta gravar
o nome numa pedra, a pedra fica, sim senhores, salvou-se, mas o nome, se
todos os dias o não ler, apaga-se, esquece, não está cá.
estas contradições enquanto se a Rua do Alecrim, pelas calhas dos
eléctricos ainda correm regueirinhos de água, o mundo não pode estar
quieto, é o vento que sopra, são as nuvens que voam, da chuva nem fale-
mos, tanta tem sido. Ricardo Reis pára diante da estátua de Eça de Quei-
rós, ou Queiroz, por cabal respeito da ortografia que o dono do nome
usou, ai como podem ser diferentes as maneiras de escrever, e o nome ainda é o menos, assombroso é falarem a mesma língua e serem um, Reis, o
utro, Eça, provavelmente a língua que escolhe os escritores, serve-se
eles para que exprimam uma parte do que ela é, quando as línguas tiverem
ito tudo, sempre quero ver como iremos entender-nos nós. Já as primeiras
ficuldades começam a aparecer, ou não serão ainda dificuldades, antes
madas diferentes e questionarias do sentido, sedimentos removidos, por exemplo, Sobre
nudez forte da verdade o manto diáfano da fantasia, parece clara a sen-
ça, clara fechada e conclusa, uma criança é capaz de ~~perceber~~ perceber e re-
tir no exame sem se enganar, mas essa mesma criança perceberia e repe-

> ❝ Ricardo Reis stops before a statue of Eça de Queirós, or Queiroz, out of respect for the orthography used by the writer of that name, so many different styles of writing, and the name is the least of it, what is surprising is that these two, one called Reis, the other Eça, should speak the same language. Perhaps it is the language that chooses the writers it needs, making use of them so that each might express a tiny part of what it is. Once language has said all it has to say and falls silent, I wonder how we will go on living. ❞

THE YEAR OF THE DEATH OF RICARDO REIS

The Handmaid's Tale

1985 ▪ 311 PAGES ▪ CANADA

MARGARET ATWOOD (b.1939)

In her 1985 novel *The Handmaid's Tale*, Canadian author Margaret Atwood imagines Massachusetts, New England, as part of Gilead, a "republic" founded after a coup by a despotic religious regime that restricts women to being home-makers and child-bearers. The coup, which happens in the late 20th century, overturns a society beset by social unrest, with a declining birth rate due in part to radioactive waste making many people infertile.

Chilling first-person, present-tense narration takes us into the life of Offred, a Handmaid who has been stripped of her identity and liberty. Dressed in red to denote the supposed immorality of her past, her only worth is her fertility. She is assigned to Gilead's Commanders to bear children for their infertile wives, and endures bizarre monthly ceremonies of emotionless sexual intercourse. In flashbacks, Offred (named literally "Of" her Commander, Fred) recalls her past life, in which she worked in a library, was married, and had a daughter. The family were captured and separated after attempting to flee to Canada.

In Gilead, whose laws are loosely based on Old Testament teachings, boys are prized and educated, and girls are raised to be illiterate and married off at 14. The law defines all women by their role, and dresses them accordingly: wives of Commanders wear pale blue; Aunts, who control the Handmaids, wear brown; housekeepers and cooks, called Marthas, wear green. Male Guardians enforce the law with violence, and spies, known as Eyes, constantly monitor behaviour. Insubordinate "unwomen" are sentenced to hard labour in the Colonies, and militants are hanged or ripped apart in grotesque, quasi-religious executions.

Atwood says that she based Gilead on 17th-century Puritan New England, which had a marked bias against women. She adds that there is nothing in her novel that has not existed somewhere in the world at some time, and that it might only take a period of social chaos for such attitudes to reassert themselves.

> " I'm sorry there is so much pain in this story. I'm sorry it's in fragments, like a body caught in crossfire or pulled apart by force. But there is nothing I can do to change it. I've tried to put some of the good things in as well. Flowers, for instance, because where would we be without them? Nevertheless it hurts me to tell it over, over again. Once was enough; wasn't once enough for me at the time? But I keep on going with this sad and hungry and sordid, this limping and mutilated story, because after all I want you to hear it, as I will hear yours too if I ever get the chance... "

THE HANDMAID'S TALE, CHAPTER 41

◄ **WALKING IN PAIRS**
Dressed in red and blinkered by their stiff, white veils, the Handmaids are allowed to go on daily walks to shop for supplies for the Marthas, who cook and clean. As depicted in this still from the 2017 Netflix adaptation, Offred and her assigned partner, Ofglen, synchronize their steps and keep their eyes lowered, but whisper to each other about an underground liberation movement.

MARGARET ATWOOD
THE HANDMAID'S TALE

ATWOOD'S DYSTOPIAN FICTION

Atwood's attraction to dystopian fiction began in adolescence, when she read George Orwell's *Nineteen Eighty-Four* and Aldous Huxley's *Brave New World*. Appropriately, she began her first dystopian novel, *The Handmaid's Tale*, in 1984. She returned to the genre in 2003 with *Oryx and Crake*, the first of a trilogy of novels concerning the unfolding of a plague-induced apocalypse. Likewise, in her surreal, darkly satirical novel *The Heart Goes Last* (2015), she imagines a community in which people must regularly swap their comfortable lives for time spent in prison. In 2019, Atwood became the co-winner of the Booker Prize for *The Testaments*, her sequel to *The Handmaid's Tale*.

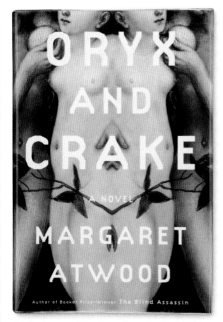

▲ The cover of the American edition of *Oryx and Crake*, which was published in 2003, is based on a Renaissance depiction of the Fall.

❝ I must forget about my secret name and all ways back. My name is Offred now... ❞

***THE HANDMAID'S TALE*, CHAPTER 41**

> **DRAFT PAGE** After writing four novels, Morrison gave up her day job as an editor to write *Beloved*. In a 1993 interview with *The Paris Review*, she revealed that she was more confident working in the morning. She wrote her first version of the story in pencil on a yellow legal pad, and continued to edit and add to the typed drafts that followed.

309
Beloved 13

I am Beloved and she is mine. Sethe is the one that picked flowers, yellow flowers in the place before the crouching. Took them away from their green leaves, *And put them on the quilt where I sleep now.* She was about to smile at me when the men without skin came and took us up into the sunlight with the dead and shoved them into the sea. Sethe went into the sea. She went there. They did not push her. She went there. She was getting ready to smile at me and when she saw the dead people pushed into the sea she went also and left me there with no face or hers. Sethe is the face I found and lost in the water under the bridge. When I went in, I saw her face coming to me and it was my face too. I wanted to join. I tried to join, but she went up into the pieces of light at the top of the water. I lost her again, but I found the house she whispered to me and there she was, smiling at last. It's good, but I cannot lose her again. All I want to know is why did she go in the water in the place where we crouched? Why did she do that when she was just about to smile at me? I wanted to join her in the sea but I could not move; I wanted to help her when she was picking the flowers, but the clouds of gunsmoke blinded me and I lost her. Three times I lost her: once with the flowers because of the noisy clouds of smoke; once when she went into the sea instead of smiling at me; once under the bridge when I went in to join her and she came toward me but did not smile. She whispered

▲ **FIRST EDITION** With a simple typographic cover for its first edition, *Beloved* was dedicated to the "Sixty Million and more" believed to have died on slave-carrying ships and in captivity. Globally acclaimed, it is now considered one of the most influential works of African American literature.

"
I AM BELOVED and she is mine. Sethe is the one that picked flowers, yellow flowers in the place before the crouching. Took them away from their green leaves. They are on the quilt now where we sleep. She was about to smile at me when the men without skin came and took us up into the sunlight with the dead and shoved them into the sea. Sethe went into the sea. She went there. They did not push her. She went there.
"

BELOVED, PART 2

Beloved

1987 ■ 275 PAGES ■ US

TONI MORRISON (b.1931)

The story begins in Bluestone Road, in the US city of Cincinnati, Ohio, where a formerly enslaved woman, Sethe, and her 18-year-old daughter, Denver, are haunted by a spiteful baby spirit called 124. It is 1873; in the aftermath of the American Civil War, slavery has been abolished, but freedom is a fragile thing reliant on sympathetic white folks, and undermined by segregation.

Toni Morrison's *Beloved* is both a ghost story and a socio-political novel that reclaims Black experience from the silences in history. Using interlocking time frames, it shows how the horrors of the past encroach on the present and threaten the future. Morrison's narrative slips between the present day and Sethe's early life enslaved on Sweet Home Farm, Kentucky, where a new farm manager known as "schoolteacher" and his nephews impose intolerable conditions on Sethe and five enslaved men.

Given the chance to flee to Ohio, she sends her two sons and baby girl on ahead to Cincinnati, where her freed mother-in-law, Baby Suggs, is waiting. Heavily pregnant, Sethe travels alone and gives birth to a second daughter, Denver, on the way.

Sethe and her children enjoy 28 days of "healing, ease, and real-talk" with Baby Suggs and the free Black community, until schoolteacher crosses state lines to reclaim the family under Fugitive Slave laws. Rather than return them to slavery, Sethe cuts the throat of her two year old and attempts to kill the others. The boys' injuries save them from being recaptured, and Sethe herself is spared the gallows by abolitionists.

The novel jumps forwards 18 years. Paul D., an escapee from Sweet Home Farm, finds Sethe free from jail and living alone with her surviving daughter, but haunted by the baby spirit. He drives off the first poltergeist, but then a mysterious 20-year-old woman arrives. Dressed in silk with unmarked shoes, she has no lines on her palms and feet. She calls herself Beloved.

In context

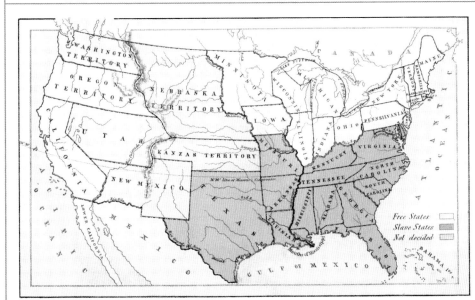

▲ **A DIVIDED NATION** An 1857 map shows the fragile Union just before the American Civil War. The 16 free states (white) include Ohio, where *Beloved* is largely set; the 15 slave states (red), include Kentucky, where Sethe was enslaved. Green-tinted territories are listed as undecided.

▶ **FUGITIVE SLAVE ACT 1850** In an effort to compel citizens to help capture enslaved people fleeing to free states, the Fugitive Slave Act imposed financial penalties and jail time for interference. Opposed in Northern states, it was repealed by Congress in 1864.

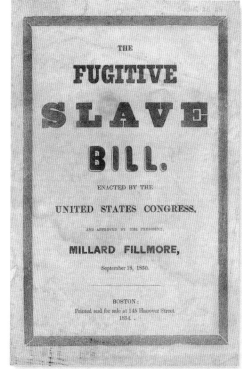

Sethe is slow to recognize that the violently selfish Beloved is a revenant: her murdered two year-old, grown into a woman and intent on clawing back the life and love that she was denied. When Denver is later asked if she believed that the destructive incomer was her sister, she says, "At times I think she was more." In her childish voice, Beloved references the cramped holds of slave ships, lost faces, and bodies tipped into the sea, and in doing so appears to embody the suffering of "the 60 million and more" victims of the slave trade.

Beloved is a landmark work that emerged from a flourishing of Black writing in the 1970s and 1980s, when authors such as Alex Haley, Maya Angelou, and Alice Walker sought new ways to explore race, identity, and the legacies of slavery. While it has the unexamined reality of Black history at its core, it avoids conventional realism, using forms of narrative that have their roots in African folklore and the mythology of Black Americans. The sometimes lyrical, sometimes anguished narration revolves around motherhood, sisterhood, tribal rites, Afro-Christian revivalism, and the presence of ghosts: Morrison asks the reader to engage with a retelling of history, based on a natural intimacy with the supernatural. Rather than offering a pastiche of Black speech, the text presents a lyrical, incantatory voice with repetitive interior monologues: "She's mine, Beloved. She's mine"; "I am Beloved and she is mine".

"Rememory" is Morrison's name for the kind of remembering that takes the previously enslaved back to the appalling places which are always waiting to reclaim them. Fragments of earlier events in Sethe and Paul D.'s lives surface and coalesce into a horrific account of conditions in the South. Robbed of normal family life, raped, beaten, and traded, these people saw their offspring being sold on, and believe that there is nothing left for them to own. Reclaiming self, a central theme in Morrison's work, is the true "beloved" to be sought out and nurtured. As Sethe, Denver, Paul D., and the Black community take their first steps, the reader is all too aware of the difficult road ahead.

▲ **MARGARET GARNER** *Beloved* was inspired by the real-life case of enslaved fugitive Margaret Garner, who in 1856 killed her baby daughter and injured her three children after she was recaptured in Cincinnati. Thomas Noble's 1867 painting depicts Garner confronting her pursuers with the carnage.

NOBEL LAUREATE

Toni Morrison is the author of 11 novels for adults, as well as children's books and essay collections. She was the first African American woman to win the Nobel Prize for Literature.

Originally Chloe Anthony Wofford, Morrison was born in Ohio in 1931. After earning two degrees she worked as an editor at Random House publishers in the 1960s, then started to write fiction. Her early novels, *The Bluest Eye* and *Sula*, were followed by *Song of Solomon*, which received the National Book Critics Circle Award in 1977. Her masterwork, *Beloved*, won the Pulitzer Prize in 1988. Globally recognized as a towering novelist of the Black experience, Morrison became a Nobel laureate in 1993 for works that were "characterized by visionary force and poetic import". In 2012, Morrison was awarded the US Presidential Medal of Freedom.

▶ **US President Barack Obama** presents the Presidential Medal of Freedom, the US's highest civilian honour, to Toni Morrison in May 2012.

> " And in **all those escapes** he could **not help being astonished** by the beauty of this land **that was not his.**

BELOVED, PART 3

NOW A MAJOR MOTION PICTURE STARRING
OPRAH WINFREY DANNY GLOVER

B E L O V E D
TONI MORRISON

'A magnificent achievement...an American masterpiece'
A. S. Byatt, *Guardian*

◄ **REALIZED ON SCREEN** Slender, sinister, and clothed entirely in black silk, the figure of Beloved is conjured from the novel's vague and enigmatic descriptions of her for the 1998 film directed by Jonathan Demme. Oprah Winfrey stars as Sethe and Danny Glover as Paul D., while Thandiwe Newton plays the revenant, Beloved. This striking image of her was repeated on the cover of a special film tie-in edition of the novel, published by Vintage in 1999.

❝ ... in this here place, we flesh; flesh that weeps, laughs; flesh that dances on bare feet in the grass. Love it. Love it hard. Yonder they do not love your flesh. They despise it. They don't love your eyes; they'd just as soon pick em out. No more do they love the skin on your back. Yonder they flay it. And O my people they do not love your hands. They only use, tie, bind, chop off and leave empty. Love your hands! Love them. Raise them up and kiss them. Touch others with them, pat them together, stroke them on your face 'cause they don't love that either. You got to love it, you! ❞

BELOVED, PART 1

▶ **MANUSCRIPT** This is the first page of the manuscript of *Red Sorghum*. The novel consists of five independent but related novellas: "Red Sorghum", "Sorghum Wine", "Dog Ways", "Sorghum Funeral", and "Strange Death". These were first published separately in various literary magazines in 1986, then as a collection the following year.

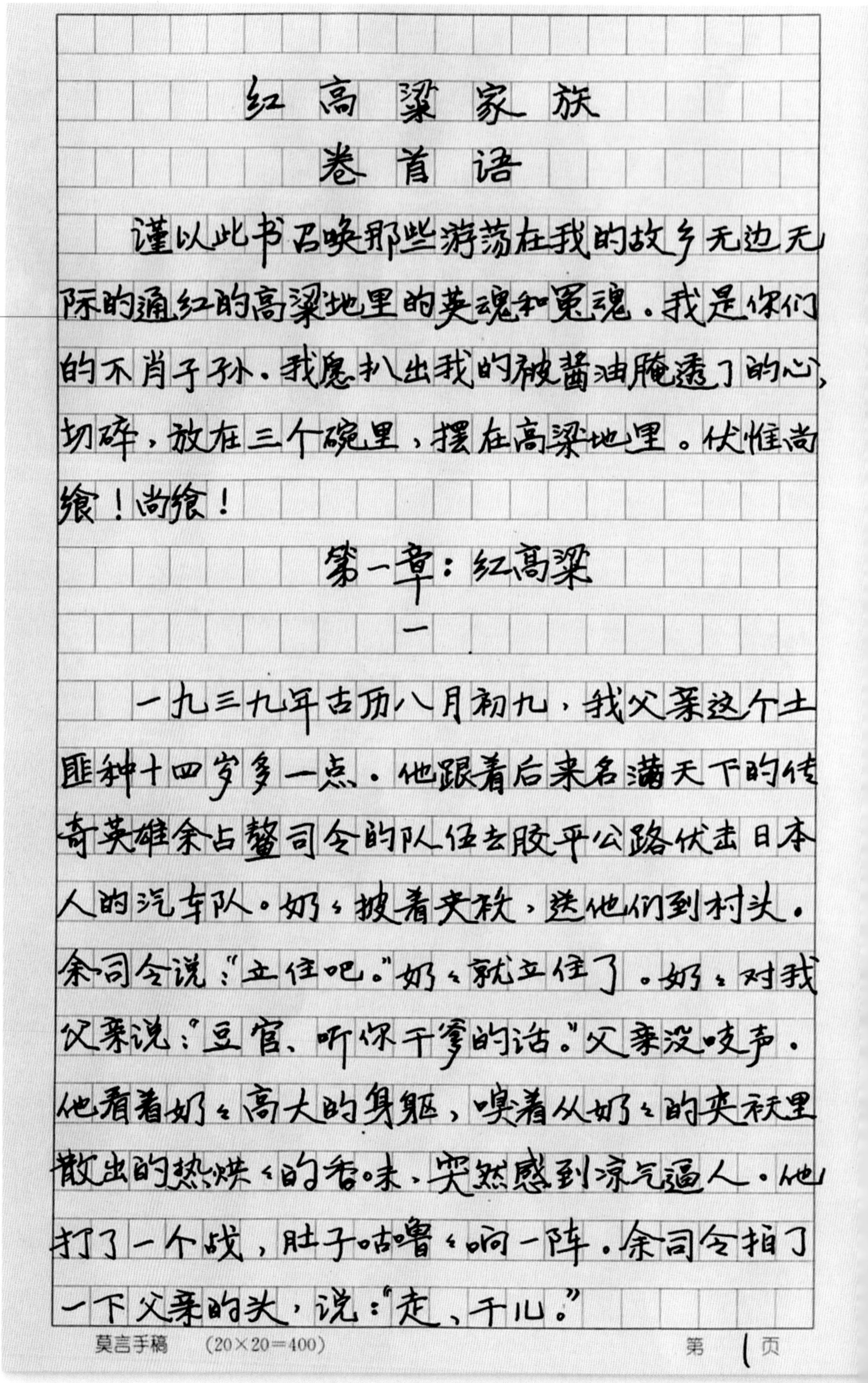

Here, Mo Yan poignantly dedicates his novel to "the heroic, aggrieved souls wandering the boundless bright-red sorghum fields of my hometown"

> Yu Zhan'ao removed his rain cape and tramped out a clearing in the sorghum, then spread his cape over the sorghum corpses. He lifted Grandma onto the cape. Her soul fluttered as she gazed at his bare torso. A light mist rose from the tips of the sorghum, and all around she could hear the sounds of growth. No wind, no waving motion, just the white-hot rays of moist sunlight crisscrossing through the open cracks between plants. The passion in Grandma's heart, built up over sixteen years, suddenly erupted.

RED SORGHUM, CHAPTER 8

红高粱家族
卷首语

谨以此书召唤那些游荡在我的故乡无边无际的通红的高粱地里的英魂和冤魂。我是你们的不肖子孙，我愿扒出我的被酱油腌透了的心，切碎，放在三个碗里，摆在高粱地里。伏惟尚飨！尚飨！

第一章：红高粱

一

一九三九年古历八月初九，我父亲这个土匪种十四岁多一点。他跟着后来名满天下的传奇英雄余占鳌司令的队伍去胶平公路伏击日本人的汽车队。奶奶披着夹袄，送他们到村头。余司令说："立住吧。"奶奶就立住了。奶奶对我父亲说："豆官，听你干爹的话。"父亲没吱声。他看着奶奶高大的身躯，嗅着从奶奶的夹袄里散出的热烘烘的香味，突然感到凉气逼人。他打了一个战，肚子咕噜咕噜响一阵。余司令拍了一下父亲的头，说："走，干儿。"

莫言手稿　(20×20＝400)　　　　第 1 页

Red Sorghum

1987 ▪ 854 PAGES ▪ CHINA

MO YAN (b.1955)

Guan Moye adopted the pen name Mo Yan, meaning "don't speak". Born into a peasant family, he left school aged 12 to work in the fields, in a factory, and then in an army library. His home town – a rural village in Gaomi, Shandong Province – became the setting for Mo Yan's most famous novel, *Red Sorghum*. Told in a series of flashbacks by an unnamed narrator, it follows the fortunes of three generations of one family in Gaomi during the Second Sino-Japanese War (1937–45). The fields of red sorghum (a grain crop) that grow in Gaomi form a dramatic backdrop to the events of the novel, linked to both life and death. They are where the narrator's grandparents, Yu Zhan'ao and Jiu'er, make passionate love after Yu has rescued Jiu'er from an unhappy marriage. They are also where Jiu'er is later shot by Japanese soldiers, while Yu and his village militia are hiding in preparation for an ambush on the invading Japanese.

Mo Yan uses the red sorghum as a symbol representing the junction between the past and future, desire and fantasy, history and memory. The sorghum is a source of both food and shelter, and yet its blood-red colour at harvest time is also a reminder of the violence of war and death.

◀ **FILM ADAPTATION**
In 1988, director Zhang Yimou's film based on *Red Sorghum* became an international success, winning the Golden Bear at the Berlin International Film Festival. It was the first time that an Asian film had won the award.

Red Sorghum is often described as a work of magical realism. Mo Yan's narrative is not chronological and sometimes has a dreamlike quality, as the narrator shifts from one person's viewpoint to another, blurring the boundaries between reality and fantasy. He blends a wild and surreal imagination with a strong sense of colour, depictions of eroticism and cruelty, and sympathy for his characters.

Although the official history of the Second Sino-Japanese War focuses on China's military success, *Red Sorghum* emphasizes the cruelty and brutality of war. Drawing on historical events experienced in his hometown in Gaomi, Mo Yan weaves into his story the heroic actions and spirit of ordinary Chinese people.

XUNGEN LITERATURE

The movement that became Xungen literature started in the People's Republic of China during the mid-1980s. It superseded "Scar Literature", a genre that had dwelt on the negative influence of the Cultural Revolution (1966–76) under Mao Zedong. Xungen (root-seeking) writers, on the other hand, were searching for the roots of Chinese literature, culture, and identity. They focused mainly on the peasant communities in the countryside. These, they thought, epitomized Chinese culture because they were uncorrupted by Western influence or political upheaval, and had therefore retained their humanity.

Xungen writers had a much broader view of literature than the earlier rural realists, and they incorporated different influences in their work. These included some aspects of Western culture – notably Latin-American magical realism – as well as ancient Chinese traditions. Notable writers of Xungen literature include Ah Cheng, Mo Yan, and Han Shaogong.

▶ **A painted section** from a 16th-century Chinese handscroll, entitled *Landscape*, encapsulates the pastoral idyll revered by Xungen writers.

A Heart So White

1992 ▪ 320 PAGES ▪ SPAIN

JAVIER MARÍAS (b.1951)

At the very core of Javier Marías's book *A Heart So White* lies a question. Why, 40 years ago, did Juan's Aunt Teresa – his mother's older sister, whom his father, Ranz, had been married to before he married Juan's mother – die by suicide? And why did she kill herself within days of returning from their honeymoon? Juan, who narrates the novel, is newly married to fellow interpreter Luisa. After they return from honeymoon, Juan finds out that his aunt's death was by suicide. This prompts him to question his father's past, about which Juan has been uneasy since his own wedding day, when his father advised him, cryptically, to make sure not to share any secrets with his wife.

This insidious suggestion gnaws away at Juan, who now questions whether in fact he got married for convenience or for love. As an interpreter, he is obsessed with words and gestures, and spends his life observing others – but when it comes to himself, not to mention his father, he shies away from the truth. Meanwhile, Luisa takes the initiative and gets Juan's father to talk. While Juan is away on business, she spends eight weeks befriending his father, and learns, among other things, that the first of his three wives died in Cuba, possibly in a fire. When Juan returns from his trip, she coaxes father and son to talk, and to come to terms with the past.

The book's title comes from Shakespeare's play *Macbeth*, in which Lady Macbeth accuses her husband of cowardice after he expresses regret for murdering the king. In Marías's hands, the question of courage becomes the central focus of the novel: do you really want to discover the truth about the things you do not know? After all his reflection and self-analysis, when Juan approaches the truth, it still manages to shock.

> 66 **Listening is the most dangerous thing of all, listening means... knowing what's going on...** 99
>
> **A HEART SO WHITE**

▲ **LADY MACBETH** "My hands are of your colour, but I shame to wear a heart so white", says Lady Macbeth to her husband, angered by his cowardice, when he shrinks from returning to the murder scene to implicate the guards in the king's murder. In *A Heart So White*, Juan also shrinks from what "I did not want to know but I have since come to know".

MARÍAS'S OTHER WORKS

A prolific author, Marías writes stories that appeal to both critics and the public alike. He has sold more than five million books worldwide, and has won numerous literary awards. Especially renowned are *Tomorrow in the Battle Think on Me* (1994) and *The Infatuations* (2011). In *Tomorrow in the Battle*, a man is picked up by a lonely married woman, who takes him home, but before they can make love she dies in his arms. In *The Infatuations*, a woman sits in her local café, observing a besotted couple day after day, until one day they disappear. Where have they gone? Marías's tales meditate on the darker side of human nature, dwelling not merely on murder or espionage, but on cowardice, obsession, and deceit.

▶ **The Infatuations** uses a couple's disappearance to explore ideas about love, grief, and truth.

◄ **FIRST EDITION** *A Heart So White* was first published in Spain, in 1992, and then in English in 1995. The book won the International Dublin Literary Award in 1997, which helped secure the author's reputation. Marías describes novel-writing as a process of composing a few key passages that need the whole architecture of a story to support them.

JAVIER MARÍAS

Corazón tan blanco

ANAGRAMA
Narrativas hispánicas

❝ I have a tendency to want to understand *everything*, everything that people say and everything I hear, even at a distance, even if it's one of the innumerable languages I don't know, even if it's in an indistinguishable murmur or imperceptible whisper, even if it would be better that I didn't understand and what's said is not intended for my ears or is said precisely so I won't hear it. Once the door of my bedroom was half-open, the murmur was distinguishable, the whisper perceptible and both were in a language that I knew perfectly, my own... ❞

A HEART SO WHITE

▶ **FIRST EDITION** Published in the original Japanese in three separate volumes from 1994–95, *The Wind-Up Bird Chronicle* brought Haruki Murakami international recognition. In 1995, it was named winner of the Yomiuri Prize for Literature. An English translation was published in 1997 by Jay Rubin. This edition, in which the original Japanese text was significantly cut and altered, is recognized as the official English translation.

▲ **THREE VOLUMES** Each of the three original volumes contains a musical reference: Volume 1 cites Rossini's overture "Book of the Thieving Magpie"; Volume 2, "Book of the Prophesying Bird", comes from Schumann's *Forest Scenes: The Prophet Bird*; Volume 3, "Book of the Bird-Catcher Man", refers to Mozart's opera *The Magic Flute*.

ねじまき鳥クロニクル

第2部 予言する鳥編

村上春樹

新潮社

❝ 'Hatred is like a long, dark shadow. In most cases, not even the person it falls upon knows where it comes from. It is like a two-edged sword. When you cut the other person, you cut yourself. The more violently you hack at the other person, the more violently you hack at yourself. It can often be fatal. But it is not easy to dispose of. Please be careful, Mr Okada. It is very dangerous. Once it has taken root in your heart, hatred is the most difficult thing in the world to eradicate... If you stay here, something bad is going to happen to you. I know it. I am sure of it.'... Creta Kano prophesied – in a small but penetrating voice, like the prophet bird that lived in the forest. ❞

THE WIND-UP BIRD CHRONICLE, BOOK 2, CHAPTER 14

The Wind-Up Bird Chronicle

1994–95 ▪ 607 PAGES ▪ JAPAN

HARUKI MURAKAMI (b.1951)

Set in modern-day Tokyo, Haruki Murakami's surreal novel *The Wind-Up Bird Chronicle* is narrated by Toru Okada, a young unemployed man with little ambition, who is drawn out of the quiet mundanity of his life into an unexpected voyage of self-discovery.

When Toru's cat disappears, he begins a vague and initially unsuccessful search, but soon his wife, Kumiko, disappears as well. Toru blames himself, and embarks on a bizarre and almost dreamlike journey on which he encounters unexpected people: a morbid girl, a malevolent politician, clairvoyant sisters, and a traumatized old soldier, in odd locations – an abandoned house, a deep well, a city corner. Heard periodically in the background throughout Toru's search is the cry of a wind-up bird as its spring is rewound. As each character shares their story, Toru realizes that they are all linked in some way, but ultimately, it is Toru's self-acceptance that saves him from the madness that is revealed in the real world.

With his characteristic use of magical realism, Murakami explores the concepts of alienation, loneliness, and identity, as Toru meanders through an increasingly unfamiliar world.

▲ **GINZA DISTRICT, TOKYO** Rebuilt in 1872 after a devastating fire, Ginza is now home to luxury stores and high-rises. It is the setting of much of the action in *The Wind-Up Bird Chronicle*. At one point, Toru and his neighbour stand in front of the famous Wakō building, looking out for bald men in the passing crowds on behalf of a wig company.

He listens to war veterans relate their horrific experiences of the Second Sino-Japanese War in Manchuria (1937–45), a war in which Murakami's own father served and suffered traumatic ordeals. By setting the action against a backdrop of modern Japan, Murakami reveals a culture grappling with the long-term effects of war and its subsequent economic recovery.

▲ **ALIENATION** The theme of alienation runs through the novel, notably in the character of Toru, who often seeks solitude. The people that he meets are all connected, but seem to exist in isolation. In Japan, there is a high suicide rate among white-collar workers, such as Toru, driven by exhaustion.

MURAKAMI'S OTHER WORKS

A prolific writer, Haruki Murakami is celebrated for his novels as well as his short stories and non-fiction. He originally ran a jazz bar with his wife, then began writing in his late 20s. He sent his first manuscript, *Hear the Wind Sing*, to a Japanese literary magazine in 1979, and won the Gunzo Prize for New Writers. Among his best-known novels are the coming-of-age story *Norwegian Wood* (1987), and *Kafka on the Shore* (2002). Murakami gained a new audience with his works of non-fiction, such as *What I Talk About When I Talk About Running*, an insight into his preparation for the New York Marathon, and *Underground*, about the aftermath of the 1995 Tokyo subway sarin attack. Murakami has a global following, but has been criticized in Japan for the strong influence of Western culture evident in his writing.

▶ **First published** in two volumes, *Norwegian Wood* takes its title from the name of a Beatles song.

The God of Small Things

1997 ▪ 339 PAGES ▪ INDIA

ARUNDHATI ROY (b.1961)

The God of Small Things was Arundhati Roy's first book. She had previously trained as an architect and had written screenplays. The huge international success of her novel, which draws on memories of her childhood in the village of Aymanam, has allowed her to follow a high-profile career as a political activist. The novel traces the lives of fraternal twins Rahel, a girl, and Estha, a boy, who grow up together and then live apart for more than 20 years. The narrative switches back and forth between the 1960s and 1990s. It is told from a third-person, omniscient point of view, but somewhat more from Rahel's perspective. We follow the twins' stories, and see how just a few hours or particular events can affect the course of people's lives.

Although it is essentially a family story, the book is also about Indian history and culture. One of the characters is a Dalit, or "untouchable", introducing the question of India's rigid caste system, and religious and racial discrimination in general. Another theme is misogyny, and Roy's activist, feminist perspective comes to the fore in the character of Ammu, the twins' divorced mother, who has a secret lover.

The God of Small Things explores topics often avoided in literature, such as sexual abuse, notably incest. Indeed, in India, some condemned the book for its explicit depictions of sex, and Roy was charged with obscenity in her home state of

▲ **CASTE SYSTEM** The age-old Indian caste system groups people by role or position, from the "lowest" Dalits to the "highest" Brahmins. As seen above, Dalits are often banned from places such as temples. It is very difficult for people to move beyond the caste into which they are born.

Kerala. It is not just the content of the book that is challenging. Roy's style engages with the British colonial inheritance by playing creatively with the patterns of "correct" English. She invents words and expressions, and her punctuation is unconventional. Her sometimes fragmented narration shows how memories resurface. *The God of Small Things* is a domestic story with a greater significance. Roy suggests through this novel that there are rules – whether about social status, gender, literary style, or anything else – in a given time and place, but that these rules can be challenged and broken.

◄ **KOTTAYAM, KERALA**
The village of Aymanam, which means "five forests", is in Kerala, in southwestern India. Criss-crossed by rivers and backwaters, it is one of the wettest areas of India and has a hot, tropical climate.

▶ **FIRST EDITION** *The God of Small Things* was first published in 1997, with a cover depicting lotus leaves and pink waterlilies. The book won the Booker Prize, despite some critics claiming that it was too confusing or too controversial.

The God *of* Small Things

ARUNDHATI ROY

❝ The Great Stories are the ones you have heard and want to hear again. The ones you can enter anywhere and inhabit comfortably. They don't deceive you with thrills and trick endings. They don't surprise you with the unforeseen. They are as familiar as the house you live in. Or the smell of your lover's skin. You know how they end, yet you listen as though you don't. In the way that although you know that one day you will die, you live as though you won't. In the Great Stories you know who lives, who dies, who finds love, who doesn't. And yet you want to know again. ❞

THE GOD OF SMALL THINGS, CHAPTER 12

INDIAN LITERATURE IN ENGLISH

Although there are several recognized languages in India, including Hindi, Tamil, and Telugu, many Indian writers choose to write in English, which was imported into the country when it was part of the British Empire. After nearly a century of British rule (from 1858 until 1947), India has been greatly influenced by British culture, and many Indian writers have learned English as their mother tongue, either at home or at school.

Although it is the language of their former colonizers, English is also an international language, and having their books published in it has helped many Indian writers to reach a wider audience. As well as Arundhati Roy, other authors of Indian descent who have written in English include Vikram Seth, V.S. Naipaul, Salman Rushdie, Anita Desai, Kiran Desai, and Aravind Adiga.

▲ **V.S. Naipaul,** a Trinidadian writer of Indian descent, won the Nobel Prize in Literature in 2001.

Atomised

1998 ▪ 392 PAGES ▪ FRANCE

MICHEL HOUELLEBECQ (b.1956)

Michel Houellebecq, the *enfant terrible* of contemporary French literature, is a bitter, despairing satirist who denounces every aspect of modern life. His novel *Atomised* (also published as *The Elementary Particles*, a direct translation of its French title *Les Particules élémentaires*) tells the story of two half-brothers, Bruno Clément and Michel Djerzinski, both of whom are emotionally crippled as a result of childhood neglect by their hippy mother. Bruno grows up to be a sex-obsessed loser: he manages to attain some kind of normality (his experiences of "liberated" sex are both depressing and hilarious), but his inner life is barren. Michel is a scientific genius, but also a loner, who briefly tries to attach himself to life by keeping a canary. Specializing in molecular biology, he researches a way to replace the human race with clones.

Houellebecq's use of language is direct and harsh, and often veers into vivid and offensive slang. He can be laugh-out-loud funny in the style of a transgressive stand-up. His characters are presented in bald, sociological terms, their experiences embedded in a precise chronology of developments in French culture and society from the 1960s to the 1990s. Houellebecq also places mini-lectures on molecular physics in the style of popular science alongside matter-of-fact, detailed descriptions of his characters' sexual exploits.

▲ **MICHEL DJERZINSKI** The scientist brother of sex-obsessed Bruno, Michel's existence is largely devoid of human connection. When Annabelle, a woman who adored him when they were children, writes to him in a moment of crisis, he is too wrapped up in intellectual concerns to reply.

Essentially a novel of ideas, *Atomised* is a full-frontal assault on the heartlessness of contemporary society, particularly the raw contest for status and power unleashed by liberal individualism. It claims that consumerism is a farce, and that the sexual revolution has merely opened up a new area of competition and destroyed any hope of finding love. It also points to an ideal future in which, thanks to Michel, a hapless humanity has been superseded by perfect clones.

A **MODERN *ENFANT TERRIBLE***

When it was published in 1998, *Atomised* caused a sensation far beyond literary circles because it broke so many taboos. Presenting himself as a plain speaker of the truth in a world immersed in evasions and lies, Houellebecq set out to offend, and he succeeded. The novel was accused of not only being reactionary, but of promoting sexism, racism, and paedophilia. However, this did not prevent Houellebecq from establishing himself as a cultural celebrity in France, and in 2010, he received a stamp of approval from the French cultural elite when his novel *The Map and the Territory* was awarded the prestigious Prix Goncourt. His writing is a venomous assault on what he sees as the dominant liberal-left values and attitudes of Western society and culture.

Michel Houellebecq
La carte et le territoire
roman

PRIX GONCOURT 2010

Flammarion

▶ **The prizewinning *The Map and the Territory*** features Houellebecq himself – as a character who is murdered.

❝ This book is principally the story of a man who lived out the greater part of his life in Western Europe, in the latter half of the twentieth century. Though alone for much of his life, he was nonetheless occasionally in touch with other men. He lived through an age that was miserable and troubled… Feelings such as love, tenderness and human fellowship had, for the most part, disappeared; the relationships between his contemporaries were at best indifferent and more often cruel. ❞

***ATOMISED*, PROLOGUE**

"

In my own terms,
I am being punished for what
happened between myself and
your daughter. I am sunk into a
state of disgrace from which it
will not be easy to lift myself. It is
not a punishment I have refused.
I do not murmur against it. On
the contrary, I am living it out
from day to day, trying to accept
disgrace as my state of being.
Is it enough for God, do you
think, that I live in disgrace
without term?

DISGRACE, CHAPTER 19

"

▼ **FIRST EDITION** A starving, stray
dog embodies the atmosphere of
Coetzee's *Disgrace*. The Nobel Prize-
winning novelist, linguist, essayist,
and translator describes his writing
process as an exploration of new forms
of storytelling. *Disgrace* is enhanced
by the irony of using the voice of
a white, middle-aged academic to
describe post-apartheid South Africa.

▲ **MANUSCRIPT** Coetzee started writing *Disgrace* four
years before it was published. He wrote his first drafts
in university exam books, revising extensively with a red
pen before transferring the text to a computer. This page
is part of a very early draft of what became Chapter 19.

A rewrite for the crossed-
through text appears at
the end of the section

Disgrace

1999 ▪ 220 PAGES ▪ SOUTH AFRICA

J.M. COETZEE (b.1940)

Published five years after the first free elections in South Africa, J.M. Coetzee's second Booker Prize-winning novel, *Disgrace*, was a stark counterpoint to the new nation's outpouring of "honeymoon" literature. Throughout this third-person, present-tense narrative, the new South Africa is viewed through the eyes of David Lurie, a middle-aged professor reduced to teaching "communications" to students who have no interest in the Romantic poetry that is the bedrock of his life's work. He embarks on an affair that borders on sexual assault with his student, Melanie; is brought before a tribunal; and, unrepentant and silent, is dismissed. The story then shifts from Cape Town to the "rural idyll" of the Eastern Cape, where Lurie joins his daughter Lucy on her smallholding and helps to dispatch neglected animals in a veterinary clinic. His anxiety about the changing order in the Black and white community appears to be confirmed when the farm is attacked and Lucy is raped.

Coetzee peoples his novel with characters whose commentary and dialogue reveal what Lurie is gradually recognizing in himself: he is a cipher for European values, with language skills that are

◀ **ROMANTIC HERO**
In his fifties and twice divorced, Lurie regards himself as a "servant of Eros" in his pursuit of women. A specialist in English Romantic poetry, he compares his affairs to those of Lord Byron, depicted here, and becomes immersed in writing an operetta about Teresa, one of Byron's lovers.

redundant in this changed world. Voices range from Melanie's religious father, protective and aspirational for his family, who tries to coax penitence from his daughter's abuser, to Petrus, the Black farmer rising from employee to landowner and becoming a protector of sorts. Through Lucy's silence after her assault, and her attempts to explain the practicalities and penances that are now necessary in South Africa, the reader, and perhaps Lurie, see the difficult path ahead and a glimmer of hope in the distance.

▲ **A CHANGING LANDSCAPE** As portrayed in the 2008 film adaptation, Lurie finds echoes of an idealized rural past in the Eastern Cape, where his daughter Lucy is a smallholder. However, after three Black youths attack the farm and rape Lucy, he struggles to come to terms with the new political order.

THE **END OF APARTHEID**

In 1948, the newly elected white, Afrikaner-led National Party introduced a system of apartheid ("separate development") for the Black, Indian, and mixed-race population of South Africa. Laws enforced discrimination in employment and education, prohibited interracial sex and marriage, and relocated millions of Black people to designated, bleak "tribal homelands".

The African National Congress responded by organizing an armed struggle against the South African government. After the country became isolated by trade and sport sanctions, negotiations with the ANC led to a change of government in 1994, when Nelson Mandela was elected president.

▲ **Black and white protestors** unite to demand an end to apartheid at a demonstration in the 1980s.

Austerlitz

2001 ▪ 416 PAGES ▪ GERMANY

W.G. SEBALD (1944-2001)

Austerlitz follows the journeys undertaken by Jacques Austerlitz, an architectural historian, in an attempt to recover the truth about his childhood experience as a refugee from Nazi persecution. As he searches for answers about his own life and the fate of his parents, the book deals with history, the Holocaust, memory, travel, architecture, childhood, photography, and the power of literature to heighten our engagement with the past. Before his untimely death in a car accident in 2001, Sebald had become known for works such as *The Emigrants* (1992), which explored the boundaries between fact and fiction, often in the context of the Jewish experience of European history.

As the book follows Austerlitz's investigations, relayed to the reader by an anonymous narrator who has become friends with Austerlitz, it examines history itself, suggesting that readers, like the novel's characters, must sift through it if they are to engage fully with the world. Austerlitz says that we have "appointments to keep in the past, in what has gone before and is for the most part extinguished, and must go there in search of places and people who have some connection with us".

After growing up in a foster family in Wales, the young Jacques Austerlitz slowly finds out about his earliest years in Prague, and starts to delve into his family history. As he travels across Europe, the past reveals itself in a disturbing light. The novel probes the darkness of his personal history using the metaphor of submerged depths, from the image of a drowned village in Wales that Austerlitz remembers from his youth to the many ways in which the past lies buried deep within ourselves and in collective archives. Apparently innocuous sites, such as railway stations, libraries, markets, and state buildings, all played their part in the past – a past that has long gone but that can still be retrieved. Austerlitz learns that surface appearances conceal the traumas of the past.

In context

▲ **THERESIENSTADT GHETTO** Austerlitz traces his mother's final whereabouts to the Theresienstadt Ghetto in Czechoslovakia, a site where the Nazis used to detain Jews before sending them to extermination camps. Images from the Nazi propaganda film *Theresienstadt* (1944) feature in Sebald's novel.

◀ **A BRUTAL PAST** Born in 1944, Sebald grew up in Germany when the country was focusing on rebuilding and forgetting rather than remembering the horrors of the Third Reich. Sebald was ashamed of this denial of the past, and wrote *Austerlitz* to revisit that period of German history.

> Such ideas infallibly come to me in places which have more of the past about them than the present. For instance, if I am walking through the city and look into one of those quiet courtyards where nothing has changed for decades, I feel, almost physically, the current of time slowing down in the gravitational field of oblivion. It seems to me then as if all the moments of our life occupy the same space, as if future events already existed and were only waiting for us to find our way to them at last.

AUSTERLITZ

◄ **FIRST EDITION** *Austerlitz* was first published in Germany in 2001. The cover features a picture that is supposedly the young Jacques Austerlitz, dressed as a cavalier. It is in fact a picture of one of Sebald's friends, who was an architectural historian, like Austerlitz. Having worked as a professor of literature and translation in the UK for most of his adult life, Sebald personally oversaw the English translation of the book, which appeared later the same year.

W.G. SEBALD
AUSTERLITZ
Hanser

KINDERTRANSPORT

In the months leading up to World War II, some 10,000 children were evacuated from Germany, Austria, Czechoslovakia, Poland, and elsewhere and brought to the UK in a rescue effort known as the *Kindertransport* (children's transport). Taken in by foster families, many of the children were given completely new identities and never saw their birth parents again. In *Austerlitz*, this experience is a repressed and traumatic memory that surfaces when Jacques Austerlitz visits certain places. At Liverpool Street Station, in London, for example, he experiences ghostly memories of his first arrival in England, and this inspires him to travel back to his homeland. In doing so, he hopes to find out what happened to his parents – and how they died.

▲ **Children queue** to board a *Kindertransport* train in Germany.

> " ... I now think, said Austerlitz, that time will not pass away, has not passed away, that I can turn back and... there I shall find everything as it once was... "

AUSTERLITZ

Jacques Austerlitz is mysteriously drawn to "places which have more of the past about them than the present". He is fascinated by military fortifications in particular, but also by labyrinthine city streets that have to be explored on foot if they are to yield up clues to the past. He constantly explores the subject of memory, both in architecture and various archives. Documents, photographs, and buildings provide a way back into the past. In exploring Europe, however, he is essentially delving back into himself, looking for evidence of the long-forgotten events that shaped his childhood. Even Austerlitz's name conjures up the past – it is not only linked to the celebrated Napoleonic battle of Austerlitz, but also evokes the name of Auschwitz.

For Austerlitz, this is no magical adventure, but a dangerous journey into unknown territory. Indeed, history is portrayed in the book as a kind of monster – a malevolent force that covers its tracks but leaves behind scattered traces of its atrocities. This deliberate covering up of the past is a central theme of the novel, and Austerlitz learns how easily it is done – not only by individuals, but by entire nations, when the past has become too painful or too shameful to remember. He still embarks on his journey, however, setting in motion a process that may one day lead to closure. The power of history informs the novel throughout. It can provide both solace and trauma, offering the possibility of either recovery or oblivion.

Several writers and artists informed the style and mood of *Austerlitz*. Sebald's late 20th-century world of historical obsession was influenced by the work of French writer Patrick Modiano, whose book *Dora Bruder* (1997) was based on documentation about the true case of a young Jewish girl who disappeared in Paris in 1941. He was also drawn to the work of French film-maker Alain Resnais, who directed the Holocaust documentary *Night and Fog* (1956). Resnais also directed *Last Year at Marienbad* (1961) and *All the Memory in the World* (1956), which have a dreamlike quality similar to that of *Austerlitz*. Sebald alludes to these films in the book; they share his fascination for exploring the past through architecture, and for understanding the ways in which history continues to cast its shadow over the present.

▲ **PALAIS DE JUSTICE** As an architectural historian, Jacques Austerlitz is interested in monumental buildings. In an early conversation with the narrator, he describes his visit to the massive Palais de Justice in Brussels, outlining its scale and its labyrinthine interior. It is one of several grand structures in which Austerlitz gets lost during his travels.

▲ **BIBLIOTHÈQUE NATIONALE DE FRANCE** Another important site of investigation in the novel is the Bibliothèque Nationale de France, in Paris. As Austerlitz does research in the archives here, he realizes the extent to which we are able to both preserve and obscure the past through selective cataloguing and classification.

◀ **TEXT AND IMAGES** A striking feature of *Austerlitz* is the way in which Sebald inserted photographs into the text. The significance of these images is not always obvious, but this first set of pictures compares two different ways of seeing in the dark: the night vision of nocturnal animals, and the vision of philosophers, "who seek to penetrate the darkness which surrounds us purely by means of looking and thinking".

er, durch dieses, weit über jede vernünftige Gründlichkeit hinausgehende Waschen entkommen zu können aus der falschen Welt, in die er gewissermaßen ohne sein eigenes Zutun geraten war. Von den in dem Nocturama behausten Tieren ist mir sonst nur in Erinnerung geblieben, daß etliche von ihnen auffallend große Augen hatten und jenen unverwandt

The eyes of two nocturnal animals are compared with those of the writer Peter Jan Trapp and the philosopher Ludwig Wittgenstein (below)

forschenden Blick, wie man ihn findet bei bestimmten Malern und Philosophen, die vermittels der rei-

nen Anschauung und des reinen Denkens versuchen, das Dunkel zu durchdringen, das uns umgibt. Im üb-

NARRATIVE STYLE

Austerlitz is related by an anonymous narrator, who meets Austerlitz over a period of 30 years (from 1967-97). This narrator listens to Austerlitz as he recounts the key moments of his journey into the past, so we actually hear the story in Austerlitz's own words.

The book sometimes reads like a novel, and at other times like a history book, a piece of travel writing, or a memoir. Sebald wanted to recreate the rhythms of earlier German prose writing in his own work, and so it often reads like a piece from a different era. He evokes the mood of the past in rich, sonorous sentences that often carry on for page after page, and adopts a meditative tone suited to the gravity of his subject. The book has no chapters or paragraph breaks, and this gives it a mesmeric quality, as if the text flows on continuously, without reference to time.

► **FIRST EDITION** *Snow* was written between April 1999 and December 2001, and was first published by İletişim in Istanbul in 2002. An English translation by Maureen Freely appeared in the UK and the US two years later. *Kar* is the Turkish word for snow, and it is echoed in the text, in both "Kars", the frontier town in which the novel is set, and "Ka", the name of the novel's protagonist.

ORHAN PAMUK

KAR

İletişim

" She talked about how, as children in Istanbul, she and [her sister] always wanted the snow to continue. The sight of snow made her think how beautiful and short life is and how, in spite of all their enmities, people have so very much in common; measured against eternity and the greatness of creation, the world in which they lived was narrow. That's why snow drew people together. It was as if snow cast a veil over hatreds, greed, and wrath and made everyone feel close to one another. They fell silent for a while... This walk with Kadife through the snow brought Ka as much anxiety as happiness. "

SNOW, CHAPTER 13

Snow

2002 ▪ 426 PAGES ▪ TURKEY

ORHAN PAMUK (b.1952)

Turkish novelist Orhan Pamuk was already an established, prizewinning author when he began work on *Snow*. Outwardly, the plot seems melodramatic: Ka, a Turkish poet and political exile, returns to his native district to report on upcoming elections and a rash of suicides among young girls in Kars, a fortress town on the borders of Turkey and Armenia. A blizzard traps him there for three days, during which he is embroiled in a military coup, is taken for an informer, negotiates with a suspected terrorist, and falls in love with the beautiful Ipek. The plot ends in a betrayal.

But the narrative is too deeply layered to be a melodrama. In those three days, Ka writes 19 poems, which are collected into a manuscript, called *Snow*. Or so we think, because as the novel progresses, it becomes apparent that the story is not being told by Ka, the "true poet", but by his friend, a "simple-hearted novelist" named, tellingly, Orhan, who is compiling it from Ka's extensive journals. Ka himself is dead, and his manuscript of poems is missing, probably stolen. Orhan becomes an increasingly unreliable narrator, jealous of Ipek's feelings for Ka. The snow, both beautiful and deadly, gives everything a fairy-tale feel. Its "deep mysteries" reveal underlying structures – the hexagonal shape of a snowflake is an analogy for human life, a map of the spiritual course that each human must follow.

Snow soon became a bestseller in Turkey, perhaps because it captured so well the historical tensions between the adherents of modern secular Turkey and its domestic opponents, the Islamic traditionalists and Kurdish separatists. After it was translated into English, Pamuk was acclaimed worldwide, winning a Nobel Prize in 2006.

ARMENIAN GENOCIDE

The "Armenian thing", as one character in *Snow* puts it, continues to stalk Turkey's troubled 20th-century history. In 1915–17, during World War I, around 1.5 million Armenians living in the eastern reaches of the Ottoman Empire were either executed, intentionally worked to death, or sent to perish in nearby deserts without food and water – all reportedly at the hands of the Turks in a deliberate attempt at ethnic cleansing. The very mention of it still inflames passions in both Turkey and Armenia today. In the novel, Ka is accused of reawakening "old accusations about the Armenian massacre that should have been buried long ago".

▲ **Armenian refugees**, shown here in 1918, found a haven in Old Jerusalem's Armenian Quarter.

In context

◄ **SACRED SPACE** For more than 1,000 years, the Holy Apostle's Church in Kars has been alternately Christian, Muslim, or abandoned, as the fortunes of what is now eastern Turkey have changed. Kars, the setting for *Snow*, was for a long time the Russian Empire's principal fortress town in the contested borderlands between Anatolia, Armenia, and the Caucasus Mountains.

▲ **HEADSCARVES** The debate about Turkish women wearing headscarves, evident in *Snow*, pivoted on their being forbidden in schools and colleges as a symbol of "political Islam". This deep rift between Westernized (secular) and traditional (devout) came to the fore in 2008, when Turkish women (above) protested about a proposal to renew the ban.

Never Let Me Go

2005 ▪ 282 PAGES ▪ UK

KAZUO ISHIGURO (b.1954)

All the best memories are of Hailsham, an apparently progressive boarding school with extensive grounds, a sports pavilion, and an ethos of creativity. Our narrator is Kathy H., a 31-year-old carer, whose recollections of her schooldays feel as poignant and as unremarkable as many others. However, in Kazuo Ishiguro's novel *Never Let Me Go*, this bucolic picture of England in the late 1990s conceals a darkly skewed vision of scientific progress. Kathy and her friends Ruth and Tommy are clones, reared to donate organs in early adulthood until they die, or "complete", and to serve as carers for each other after surgery. All they have is each other, and Kathy describes their short lives through spare, repetitive accounts of their games, conversations, hopes, fears, and triumphs in art and sport. The sinister side of Hailsham only surfaces in brief interludes. When a teacher, "Madame", watches Kathy cradling a pillow as she dances to her favourite song, for example, she is overwhelmed by empathy, but also by horror at what she and her fellow guardians are doing to the children.

As teenagers, during a brief spell of normal life before they are designated as either donors or carers, Kathy, Ruth, and Tommy take a trip to Cromer, in Norfolk. In their student days, Norfolk was regarded as a lost corner of England because their geography teacher had no pictures of it. In their later years, it becomes a site of longing – a place where lost things are found or restored, whether it be a lost tape recording of the song "Never Let Me Go", or the memory of a friend who has died after their final donation. Ishiguro makes no attempt to underpin his tale with authentic biotechnology. He has suggested that the cloning element of the story is simply a device to compress a lifespan and reveal the hope that we invest in love and relationships to help us make the best of the time we have.

ISHIGURO'S OTHER WORKS

Japanese-born Kazuo Ishiguro, one of the UK's most decorated authors, is celebrated for writing first-person stories by unreliable narrators. Living in England from the age of 5, the author set his first two novels *A Pale View of the Hills* (1982) and *Artist of the Floating World* (1986) in Japan. At the age of 35, his Booker Prize-winning *The Remains of the Day* (1989), narrated by a butler who works for a Nazi sympathizer, earned him worldwide recognition. He has since published a collection of short stories, and written five other novels, including *The Buried Giant* (2015), set in Britain in the Dark Ages, and *Klara and the Sun* (2021), which explores the theme of artificial intelligence. In 2017, Ishiguro won the Nobel Prize in Literature for the range and emotional force of his work.

▲ **The Remains of the Day** is a tale of duty and denial set in 1930s England.

◄ **FRIENDS ON THE BRINK** In an interlude of freedom in their teenage years, Ruth and Tommy start a relationship. Many years later, Tommy and Kathy form a deep attachment. In this scene from the 2010 film adaptation, Kathy (centre), now a carer, drives Tommy and Ruth, who is weak after her first donation, into the countryside. There they find a boat that has been stranded on land far from the sea. They sit by the vessel, which perfectly represents their interrupted lives.

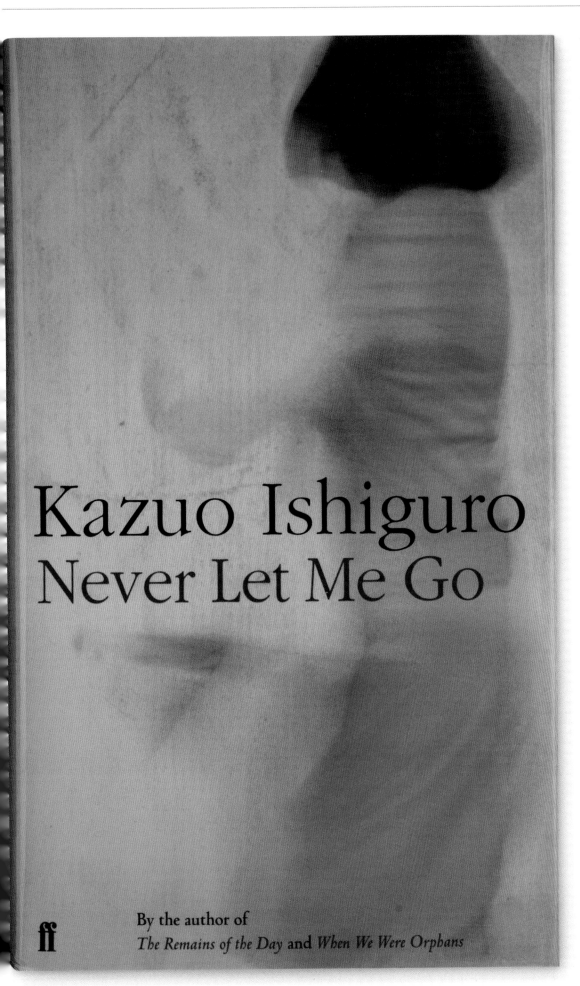

Kazuo Ishiguro
Never Let Me Go

By the author of
The Remains of the Day and *When We Were Orphans*

ff

◄ **FIRST EDITION** Ishiguro's Booker Prize-nominated sixth novel was named best novel of 2005 by *Time* magazine. Like most of his novels, *Never Let Me Go* took Ishiguro five years to write. Describing his writing process, he says that the first draft is always a mess that has little style or coherence. He then numbers the sections and moves them around to form the basis for a more careful second draft.

66   I was weeping for an altogether different reason. When I watched you dancing that day, I saw something else. I saw a new world coming rapidly. More scientific, efficient, yes. More cures for the old sicknesses. Very good. But a harsh, cruel world. And I saw a little girl, her eyes tightly closed, holding to her breast the old kind world, one that she knew in her heart could not remain, and she was holding it and pleading, never to let her go. That is what I saw. It wasn't really you, what you were doing, I know that. But I saw you and it broke my heart. And I've never forgotten. 99

NEVER LET ME GO, CHAPTER 22

▶ **FIRST UK EDITION** Adichie, a graduate of Johns Hopkins University in the US, was 29 years old when her second novel, *Half of a Yellow Sun*, was first published, but she was a 12-year-old Nigerian schoolgirl when she began to delve into newspaper cuttings and archives to find out more about the war that cast a shadow over her family. The novel received critical acclaim, and won Adichie the 2007 Orange Prize for Fiction.

❝ —————— They ran – Master, Olanna holding Baby, Ugwu, some guests – to the cassava patch beside the house and lay on their bellies. Ugwu looked up and saw the planes, gliding low beneath the blue sky like two birds of prey. They spurted hundreds of scattered bullets before dark balls rolled out from underneath, as if the planes were laying large eggs. The first explosion was so loud that Ugwu's ear popped and his body shivered alongside the vibrating ground. A woman from the opposite house tugged at Olanna's dress. 'Remove it! Remove that white dress! They will see it and target us!' ❞

**HALF OF A YELLOW SUN,
CHAPTER 18**

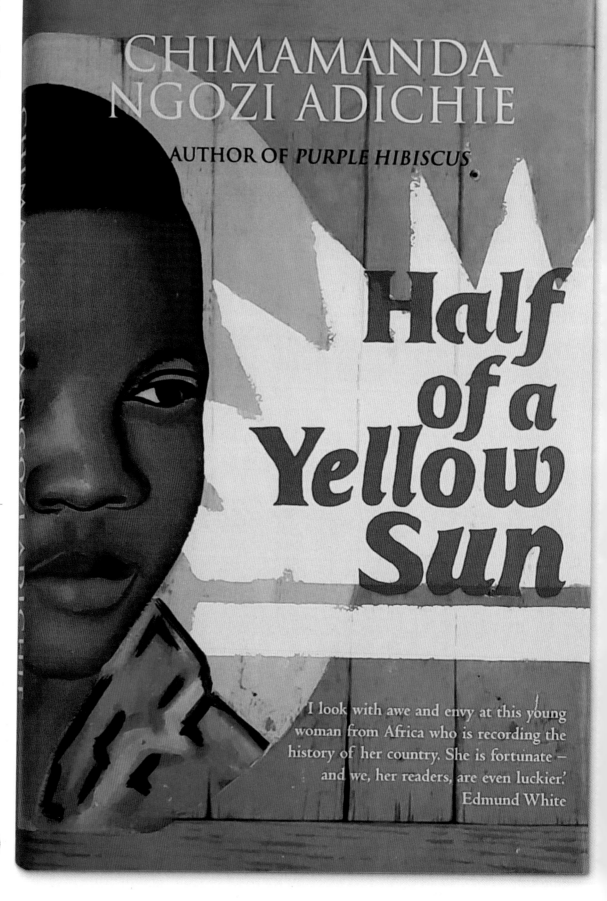

CHIMAMANDA
NGOZI ADICHIE

AUTHOR OF *PURPLE HIBISCUS*

Half of a Yellow Sun

'I look with awe and envy at this young woman from Africa who is recording the history of her country. She is fortunate – and we, her readers, are even luckier.'
Edmund White

Half of a Yellow Sun

2006 ▪ 400 PAGES ▪ NIGERIA

CHIMAMANDA NGOZI ADICHIE (b.1977)

Chimamanda Ngozi Adichie's *Half of a Yellow Sun* is based on the author's exhaustive research into the Nigerian Civil War (1967–70), which ended seven years before she was born. In an endnote Adichie says: "I wrote this novel because I wanted to write about love and war, and in particular because I grew up in the shadow of Biafra." Divided into four parts, the book begins in Nsukka, where 13-year-old Ugwu housekeeps for Professor Odenigbo and his beautiful mistress Olanna, the British-educated daughter of a wealthy chief. Ugwu watches and learns as Nsukka's intelligentsia argue about corruption and capitalism over drinks and dinners, while the houseboys cook rhubarb crumbles and lemon meringue pies.

Part 2, set a few years later, begins with the joyful declaration of a new Igbo republic called Biafra, and ends with Odenigbo, Ugwu, and Olanna, now with a child, fleeing invading Nigerian forces from the North. Dipping backwards, Part 3 focuses on the relationship between Odenigbo and Olanna, the arrival of Baby, and the affair that develops between Olanna's complicated sister Kainene and an English writer, Richard Churchill. In Part 4, the full force of the civil war hits home. Beloved family members and friends are slaughtered; wealth and privilege are swept away, and Olanna queues for meagre rations in inhuman conditions. Ugwu, Baby's gentle minder, takes part in killings and a rape after being recruited into the Biafran army. Between these compelling third-person narratives, a writer, unnamed until the end, describes how British colonizers pieced together different ethnic groups early in the 20th century to create a Nigeria that suited their own ends, and how global powers took sides in the civil war. The result, Adichie says, was this devastating moment in African history.

◄ **THE STRUGGLE TO SURVIVE** During the Nigerian Civil War, millions of Igbo people fled to insanitary refugee camps with pitiful food rations. After Nigeria blocked food and supplies, newspaper and television images of emaciated children in Biafran refugee camps prompted a global relief effort.

▲ **THE YELLOW SUN** The short-lived Biafran flag was a symbol of loss, hope, and future joy for the Igbo people in their struggle to form a new republic. Red signified the blood of the families that were massacred in the North, black signified mourning, and green signified prosperity. The half of a yellow sun, with 11 rays representing the 11 provinces of Biafra, stood for a glorious future.

THE **NIGERIAN CIVIL WAR**

The brutal conflict known as the Nigerian Civil War began in 1967, when the Igbo people of Eastern Nigeria seceded to form a new Republic of Biafra. Nigeria was in its first decade of independence from British colonial rule, but was still suffering from the political tensions that were created when it was pieced together by the British 50 years earlier.

Coups and counter-coups between the dominant ethnic groups – the Hausa-Fulani in the north, Yoruba in the southwest, and Igbo in the southeast – led to three years' fighting between Nigerians from the North and the new Biafrans. The 500,000 people who perished in combat and up to two million who died from starvation live long in the memory of the survivors.

▲ **Nigerian troops** enter Port Harcourt in 1968, after prolonged resistance from Biafran forces. The capture of the port denied Biafra access to the sea.

Gilead

2004 ■ 256 PAGES ■ US

MARILYNNE ROBINSON (b.1943)

The title of Marilynne Robinson's Pulitzer Prize-winning novel is the name of the small, fictional Iowa town in which the story is set. "Gilead" is also a place name in the Bible, meaning "hill of testimony". The novel is written in the form of a letter from lifelong Gilead resident Reverend John Ames to his 6-year-old son, Robby, to be read when Robby is older. It is composed in 1956, as the reverend, aged 76, anticipates the end of his life. *Gilead* is not only a meditative, deeply religious memoir, but also a passionate reckoning with the reverend's own life, exploring themes of spirituality and filial responsibility.

By contemplating ideas and invoking memories inherited from his father and grandfather, John Ames tells stories about Iowa that date back to the 1850s. Three generations of Ames men had been preachers at the same Congregationalist church. Ames's grandfather was a radical who gave sermons with a gun in his belt, and helped the abolitionist John Brown move people escaping enslavement through Iowa. Ames's father, who witnessed the violence of the American Civil War (1861–65), was a devoted pacifist, who believed that the need for radicalism passed with the supposed end to slavery in 1863.

➤ **THE GILEAD NOVELS** *Gilead* was followed by three companion novels: *Home* (2008), *Lila* (2014), and *Jack* (2020). Each novel takes a different minor character from *Gilead*, such as Ames's godson or Lila, his young wife, and explores their lives, told in the third person, but from each character's own point of view.

The novel focuses on the relationships between fathers and sons, as Ames contemplates dying while his own son is still a child. While he is writing the letter, Ames meets up again with his godson, Jack Boughton, the black sheep of Gilead, who has returned to the town to ask forgiveness for his past misdeeds, and permission to marry his Black sweetheart. At the climax of the novel, Ames's concern for what his congregation might find socially acceptable, and his habitual indecision, prevent him from being able to offer his godson comfort.

In *Gilead,* Robinson draws on the drama of father-son relationships to raise questions about the failure of white Americans to challenge racism. Although he is writing at the beginning of the American civil rights movement, Ames refuses to take sides with his pacifist father or abolitionist grandfather, thereby helping to erase the legacy of Iowa's radical past.

In context

▲ **INSPIRATION IN IOWA** The fictional town of Gilead is based on Tabor, Iowa, shown here in the 1950s. Founded by Congregationalist families in 1852, Tabor inspired Robinson with its abolitionist history: several residents had been conductors on the Underground Railroad, which helped fugitives from slavery to freedom. They also held abolitionist prayer meetings.

WHITE ABOLITIONISTS

A central tension in the novel lies between the active role of white preachers, such as Ames's grandfather, in the abolition of slavery (before and during the American Civil War), and the structural racism, violence, and white apathy that characterized the ensuing era of Reconstruction. Before the war, the US was split into slave states and free states, depending on the legal status of owning or trading people. The Fugitive Slave Act of 1850 stated that passage into a free state would not liberate an enslaved person. Ames recalls in *Gilead* how white abolitionists enabled enslaved people to rebel in states bordering Iowa, and helped escapees travel north, where most of the states were free.

➤ **Abolitionist leader** John Brown was executed for inciting a failed rebellion.

By "son" I mean another self, a more cherished self. That language isn't sufficient, but for the moment it is the best I can do.

John Ames Boughton is my son. If there is truth in anything I believe, that is true also. I fell to thinking about that passage in the Institutes where it says that the image of the God in anyone is reason enough to love him, and that the Lord stands ready to take our enemies' sins upon Himself. Not that I mean to call young Boughton my enemy, exactly. Calvin is simply making the most extreme case — a fortiori, how much more readily should I forgive transgressions which generally amounted to nothing more than annoyances, insofar as they affected me, he has grieved his father terribly and has been forgiven always, instantly. I believe most of that grief was just old Boughton's loneliness for the boy, who has been such a stranger to him. Now here is the point I wish to make because this is the thought that came to me as I was putting all this before the Lord. Existence is the essential thing and the holy thing. If the Lord chooses to make nothing of our transgressions then they are nothing. Or whatever reality they have is trivial and conditional beside the exquisite primary fact of existence. Of course the Lord would wipe them away just as I wipe dirt off your face, or

◄ **MANUSCRIPT** Although there was a 24-year gap between the publication of Robinson's first novel *Housekeeping* (1980) and *Gilead*, the author claims to have written the latter in just 18 months. She sent her editors handwritten drafts of text segment by segment, including the manuscript page seen here. Robinson also recalls that the character of John Ames came to her as a complete and forceful voice, during a Christmas period when she was stranded in a snowstorm.

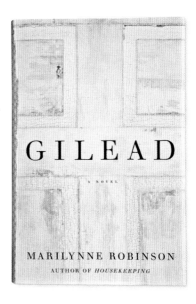

FIRST EDITION *Gilead* was first published in the US in 2004 by Farrar, Straus and Giroux to wide acclaim. Praised for its lyrical narrative and sensitive portrayal of the human condition, it was awarded the National Book Critics Circle Award in 2004, and the Pulitzer Prize for Fiction in 2005.

> John Ames Boughton is my son. If there is any truth at all in anything I believe, that is true also. By 'my son' I mean another self, a more cherished self. That language isn't sufficient, but for the moment it is the best I can do... It seems to me people tend to forget that we are to love our enemies, not to satisfy some standard of righteousness, but because God their Father loves them. I have probably preached on that a hundred times. Not that I mean to call young Boughton my enemy. That is more than I know.

▶ **FIRST EDITION** *A Death in the Family* was published as *Min Kamp 1* in Norway, its title deliberately recalling that of Adolph Hitler's infamous book *Mein Kampf* (*My Struggle*). The title reflects the series' concern with the difficulties of living, including the author's own struggle with writer's block. Norwegians bought the series in unprecedented numbers; some 500,000 copies had been sold by 2014, in a country of only five million people.

KARL OVE KNAUSGÅRD

MIN KAMP

ROMAN | FORLAGET OKTOBER

1

" … there was no longer any difference between what once had been my father and the table he was lying on, or the floor on which the table stood, or the wall socket beneath the window… For humans are merely one form among many, which the world produces over and over again, not only in everything that lives but also in everything that does not live, drawn in sand, stone, and water. And death, which I have always regarded as the greatest dimension of life, dark, compelling, was no more than a pipe that springs a leak… "

A DEATH IN THE FAMILY

A Death in the Family

2009 ■ 435 PAGES ■ NORWAY

KARL OVE KNAUSGÅRD (b.1968)

After suffering from writer's block for several years, Karl Ove Knausgård realized that there was "a threshold for writing about real people", and decided to use his family history as material for a series of books. The first instalment, *A Death in the Family*, caused an immediate sensation when it was published in Norway. The book focuses on the death of Knausgård's father, Kai-Åge, which left the family both devastated and relieved, because Kai-Åge was an alcoholic and a bully. Knausgård describes in exacting detail the squalor of the family home, where his father and grandmother lived in the years leading up to Kai-Åge's death, and even suggests that his grandmother was complicit in her eldest son's demise. The book is clearly autobiographical, and yet both the author and his publisher described it as fiction.

As a courtesy, Knausgård sent the manuscript of the book to members of his family before it was published. They received it badly, but he carried on nonetheless, and Norwegian journalists rushed to be the first to interview his "characters" for their reaction. Knausgård was particularly hurt when his uncle, Kai-Åge's brother, publicly accused him of lying about his father's death, prompting him to question whether he had gone too far with his fictionalization of reality. Relief came in the form of a letter from a doctor who had witnessed his father's death, and who even suggested that the author had understated what really happened.

Knausgård finished his series in 2018, but the controversy continues to simmer. First, his ex-wife narrated a podcast to talk about her reaction to the book, then his second (now ex-)wife wrote her own "revenge novel" about a female writer whose husband publishes a novel about their separation and divorce. Another Norwegian writer, Vigdis Hjorth, took up the torch, writing a novel that, it turned out, included verbatim quotes from family emails and other documents. As the demarcation between life and art continues to blur, so-called "autofiction" looks set to stay.

▲ **BERGEN** At the age of 19, Knausgård joined a prestigious writing academy in Bergen, Norway, where he was by far the youngest student. After graduating, he was disappointed with his work, and tried other careers before publishing his award-winning novel *Out of the World* at the age of 30.

AUTOFICTION

A Death in the Family belongs to a genre of writing known as autofiction. This moves beyond memoir into a realm in which the author not only acknowledges that memory can be faulty, but also reflects self-consciously on the writing process. It is different from faction, a genre exemplified by Truman Capote's *In Cold Blood*, which tells a true story as if it had been witnessed by an omniscient narrator. It is also different from autobiographical fiction, in which the author may draw from personal experience, but invents fictitious names for their characters. Other writers of autofiction include Marcel Proust, James Joyce, and Jack Kerouac.

◀ **TEENAGE YEARS**
As a student, Knausgård (right) channelled his creativity into rock music. He played the drums for his older brother Yngve's band, and then moved to a campus radio station during his Norwegian national service. As time went by, he realized that "music was the rope" that bound his memories together.

▲ **The *My Struggle* (*Min Kamp*) series** follows Knausgård's life over six books.

Wolf Hall

2009 ▪ 672 PAGES ▪ UK

HILARY MANTEL (b.1952)

Hailed as one of the great historical novels of the modern age, *Wolf Hall* is the first in a trilogy of books that follow the personal and political journey of Thomas Cromwell, one of the most influential figures of the 16th century. Cromwell was the son of a Putney blacksmith, born around 1485. From these humble beginnings, he rose to political prominence within the court of Henry VIII, becoming chief minister to the king and a key instigator of the English Reformation, when the Church of England separated from the Roman Catholic Church.

Wolf Hall opens dramatically as Cromwell, aged 15, is being beaten so viciously by his father that he leaves home. The story shifts forwards 27 years, to when Cromwell, now a lawyer, works in the service of Cardinal Wolsey, Lord High Chancellor to Henry VIII. The king is seeking an annulment of his marriage to Catherine of Aragon, and when Wolsey fails to deliver this, he falls out of favour. Cromwell helps Wolsey, but manages to gain the king's confidence for himself. Through his skilful

political manoeuvres, Cromwell engineers the king's divorce from Catherine and his subsequent marriage to Anne Boleyn, triggering the English Reformation and ushering England into Protestantism. Cromwell also secures his own position within the king's council, a move that gains him many enemies.

Mantel writes in the third person, yet entirely from Cromwell's perspective. The narrative is in the present tense, making well-known historical events seem as unpredictable as they once must have been. We follow Cromwell's ascent to power, inhabiting his inner world, haunted by family ghosts. With *Wolf Hall*, Mantel made Cromwell – vilified throughout history as a ruthless political operator – a thoroughly sympathetic protagonist. This meticulously researched fictionalization of his life won the Man Booker Prize, and in 2014 Mantel was made a DBE (Dame Commander of the Order of the British Empire) for services to literature.

◀ **FIRST EDITION** *Wolf Hall* was first published in 2009 and has since been translated into many other languages. The title comes from the family home of Jane Seymour (Henry VIII's third wife), which was named Wolfhall or Wulfhall. It also references the idea that people can behave fiendishly, like wolves, in the king's court.

In context

◀ **THE FIRST MEETING** Henry VIII and Anne Boleyn first met in 1526, depicted here in this 19th-century painting by Daniel Maclise. Anne refused to become Henry's mistress, and the pair were secretly married in 1532 and then officially in 1533. Henry later accused Anne of treason and had her executed in 1536.

▶ **THOMAS CROMWELL** This portrait of Thomas Cromwell by German-Swiss artist Holbein the Younger was painted in the early 1530s, when Cromwell was securing his political ascent to power. He made many enemies on the way, so this painting was intended to cement his position as the king's key advisor.

at that moment, that Arthur (God rest him) was only for now: that she would never be his wife, in any real sense: her body was reserved for him, the second son, upon whom she turned her beautiful grey eyes, and her compliant smile. She always loved me, the King would say. Seven years or so of diplomacy, if you can call it that, kept me from her side. But now I need fear no one. Rome has dispensed. The papers are in order. The alliances are set in place. I have married a virgin – since my poor brother did not touch her: I have married an alliance, her Spanish relatives: but, above all, I have married for love.

And now? Gone. Or as good as gone: half a lifetime waiting to be expunged, eased from the record.

'Ah, well,' the Cardinal says. 'You look gratified, Thomas?'

Why not? He likes a fight; the winners are not, at this stage, obvious. He knows another story about Katherine, a different story. Henry went to France to have a little war; he left Katherine as regent. Down came the Scots, and they were cut up at Flodden, by Surrey, later Duke of Norfolk: the Norfolk that was then, not the Norfolk that is now, that sinewy little twitcher constantly twitching towards his advantage. They cut off the head of the Scots king; and Katherine, that pink-and-white angel, proposed to send that head in a bag, cross-channel, by the first boat, to cheer up her husband in his camp. They dissuaded her; told it was, as a gesture, un-English. She sent, instead, a letter. And with it, the garments in which the Scottish king had died, his surcoat: which was stiffened, black and crackling with his pumped-out blood.

The fire dies, an ashy log subsiding ; the Cardinal, wrapped in his dreams, rises from his chair and personally kicks it. He stands looking down, twisting the rings on his fingers, lost in thought. He shakes himself and says, 'Long day. Go home. Don't dream of Yorkshiremen.'

Thomas Cromwell is now about forty years old. He is a man of strong build, not especially tall. Various expressions are available to his face, though only one is readable: an expression of stifled amusement. His dark hair is cropped and his small dark eyes, which are of very strong sight, light up in conversation: so the Spanish ambassador will tell us, quite soon. It is said he knows by heart the entire New Testament, in the Latin version of Erasmus. ~~Test him; you'll see.~~ And ~~therefore~~ as a servant of the Cardinal, he is apt - ready with a text if abbots flounder. Travel and the Cardinal ~~has~~ have softened his more bruising aspects. ~~Economical with effort, he'd rather talk you round than knock you down;~~ he speaks softly, likes poetry, will say it in Italian. He doesn't lie about where he comes from. ~~He works all hours, gets about the country at a pace that half-kills horses;~~ he never loses his temper. He will take a bet on anything. His friends say he has no nerves.

Except when he has special instructions

He is ✓ — ≠ —

▲ **PAGE PROOF** Mantel used a third-person, present-tense narrative to create the perspective of her protagonist. This marked-up page shows her detailed construction of Cromwell, referred to only as "He" to avoid jolting the reader out of his mindset. While adhering to historical fact, Mantel let her imagination fill in missing information about his character and life.

66 Thomas Cromwell is now a little over forty years old. He is a man of strong build, not tall. Various expressions are available to his face, and one is readable: an expression of stifled amusement... It is said he knows by heart the entire New Testament in Latin, and so as a servant of the cardinal is apt - ready with a text if abbots flounder. His speech is low and rapid, his manner assured; he is at home in courtroom or waterfront, bishop's palace or inn yard. He can draft a contract, train a falcon, draw a map, stop a street fight, furnish a house and fix a jury. 99

***WOLF HALL*, PART 1, SECTION 2**

THE *WOLF HALL* TRILOGY

Mantel originally intended *Wolf Hall* to be a stand-alone book, but soon realized that the scope of her story extended far beyond a single volume. *Wolf Hall* covers Cromwell's rise to power up to 1535. Its sequel, *Bring Up the Bodies* (2012) continues his story from when he is master secretary to the king's Privy Council, plotting to get rid of Anne Boleyn and help the king to marry Jane Seymour. Finally, *The Mirror and the Light* (2020) recounts the final four years of his climb to wealth and power, until in 1540 he abruptly loses the king's favour, and his head. Mantel's masterstroke was placing Cromwell at the heart of the story. In making a flawed hero of a figure who is often seen as a background villain, her *Wolf Hall* trilogy offers a new perspective on this period of Tudor history.

▲ **Epic in its scope**, the *Wolf Hall* trilogy was published over the course of more than a decade.

▶ **FIRST ITALIAN EDITION**
My Brilliant Friend was first published as *L'amica geniale*, in Italy, in 2011. At the time, it was criticized for both its style and content, although Italian reviews became more favourable once the series gained global attention. Feminist critics have suggested that the book was poorly received initially because of its realistic depictions of violence against women.

My Brilliant Friend

2011 ■ 385 PAGES ■ ITALY

ELENA FERRANTE

My Brilliant Friend begins the story of a 60-year friendship, tracing the ways in which two women grow and change over a lifetime. The "brilliant" friend of the title could be either Elena, known as Lenù, or Lila, known as Lina. They are both born and raised in the same poor neighbourhood in Naples, Italy, during the tumultuous postwar period of the 1950s. The city is still recovering from Nazi occupation, and crime levels are high. The girls meet in primary school, and discover that they have the same intellectual and creative interests. However, despite being a prodigy (she teaches herself to read and write), Lila is less privileged than Elena, who, due to her better education, is later able to move away from the area.

The fourth novel by the anonymous writer known as Elena Ferrante, *My Brilliant Friend* is the first volume of Ferrante's most famous work: the Neapolitan quartet. All four books cover the history of Elena and Lila's relationship, but this first novel begins in the present day, when Elena, now a famous writer and academic in her mid-sixties, hears that Lila has disappeared from their old neighbourhood. Startled by the news, but suspecting that Lila has left deliberately, Elena begins to write the story of their friendship. It is a task that she has previously avoided due to the intense rivalry between the two friends, both of whom have always had literary ambitions. Elena tells the tale of their childhood,

◄ **NAPLES IN THE 1950s**
During World War II, Naples was bombed more than 100 times. When the Nazis left in 1943, the city's entire port, as well as its gas, electricity, and water systems, had been destroyed. By the 1950s, its infrastructure had been repaired, but the black market was booming and crime was on the rise.

making it clear that her parents had always expected her to leave the neighbourhood, whereas Lila's parents thwarted her ambitions. The girls are as close as they are competitive, but their future lives will diverge. Lila stays behind in a vibrant but violent district that offers few opportunities for women, but the academic life that Elena now lives, while tranquil, has alienated her from the complex and colourful world of her childhood.

> ❝ I feel no nostalgia for our childhood: it was full of violence. Every sort of thing happened, at home and outside, every day, but I don't recall having ever thought that the life we had there was particularly bad. Life was like that, that's all, we grew up with the duty to make it difficult for others before they made it difficult for us. Of course, I would have liked the nice manners that the teacher and the priest preached, but I felt those ways were not suited to our neighbourhood. ❞
>
> **MY BRILLIANT FRIEND, "CHILDHOOD: THE STORY OF DON ACHILLE", CHAPTER 5**

THE **NEAPOLITAN NOVELS**

The Neapolitan Novels are one long story about the lives of Elena and Lila. The sequel to *My Brilliant Friend*, *The Story of a New Name* (2012), covers Elena's time at university and her marriage into a wealthy academic family. It also describes Lila's affair with their shared paramour, Nino, and her eventual pregnancy. *Those Who Leave and Those Who Stay* (2014) elaborates on the women's romantic and professional lives, as Nino leaves Lila and starts an affair with Elena. *The Story of the Lost Child* (2015) concludes the quartet. It tells how Elena becomes a successful writer and leaves her husband for Nino, while Lila's daughter disappears amid threats and intrigue involving the criminal Solara family.

▲ **Three sequels** to *My Brilliant Friend* complete the tale of Lila and Elena's lifelong friendship.

The Underground Railroad

2016 ■ 306 PAGES ■ US

COLSON WHITEHEAD (b.1969)

In his story of a teenage girl's escape from slavery via the Underground Railroad, Colson Whitehead creates a world that is both a searing reimagining of America's brutal history of slavery and an alternate reality. The Underground Railroad is really a network of overland escape routes, but in Whitehead's novel it is an underground train that travels beneath farms and houses on its way north towards the free states. Although Whitehead uses artistic licence in his portrayal of the railroad, there is nothing fanciful about this harrowing portrait of the horrors of 19th-century slavery.

When her sufferings as an enslaved worker on a Georgia plantation become overwhelming, 15-year-old Cora runs away with fellow escapee Caesar and they board the Underground Railroad, a train filled with passengers all intent on escaping the South. They travel from state to state looking for safety, and eventually arrive in South Carolina where enslaved people become government property and are treated as free. Their hope is shattered, however, when they realize that they are to be used in a medical experiment. Returning to the railroad, Cora heads north, but is forced into hiding. Throughout her journey she is relentlessly pursued by Ridgeway, a bounty hunter obsessed with bringing Cora back to face torture and death.

▲ **THE UNDERGROUND RAILROAD** Unlike the rail transport of the novel, the real Underground Railroad was a path to freedom via safe houses owned by abolitionists or formerly enslaved people. Escapees, such as those shown in this 1850 engraving, faced innumerable dangers in their quest to evade recapture.

Colson Whitehead draws on many historical events, such as the Tuskegee Syphilis Study, an experiment in which Black men were infected with syphilis, then left untreated in order to plot the disease's course. Other elements recall past atrocities such as ancient Rome's mass crucifixion of rebellious enslaved people, and the use of forced sterilizations in Nazi Germany. It is the chilling realization that these elements are based on real human behaviour that makes the novel so powerful.

▲ **EMANCIPATION** In 1863, President Lincoln signed the Emancipation Proclamation, liberating 3.5 million enslaved Black people. This print published in *Harper's Weekly* depicts the atrocities of slavery (left) as well as the promised spoils of freedom (centre and right).

SLAVERY LITERATURE

During the fight for abolition, texts describing the conditions endured by enslaved people – a genre known as slavery literature – became influential. The most famous work, *Uncle Tom's Cabin* by Harriet Beecher Stowe (see p.77), was fiction, but there were many popular works of narrative non-fiction that described the lives of formerly enslaved people. Of these, the works of Harriet Tubman, Harriet Jacobs, and Frederick Douglass are best known. Whitehead was strongly influenced by Harriet Jacobs's story: forced to hide in her grandmother's attic for seven years, Jacobs, like Whitehead's heroine Cora, could not stand up in the attic, and had to use light from small holes bored into the wall in order to read and sew.

▶ **Harriet Jacobs** published her autobiography, *Incidents in the Life of a Slave Girl*, in 1861.

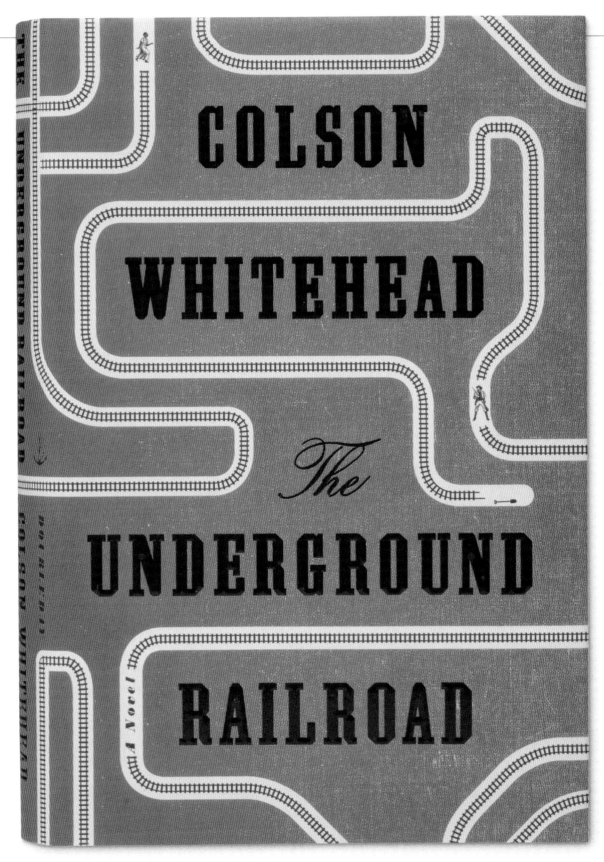

COLSON WHITEHEAD *The* **UNDERGROUND RAILROAD** *A Novel*

◄ **FIRST EDITION** Published to great critical acclaim in 2016, *The Underground Railroad* spent 37 weeks on the *New York Times* bestseller list, selling nearly one million copies. It was named winner of the 2016 National Book Award for Fiction, and also of the Pulitzer Prize for Fiction 2017. As a result of the novel's success, Whitehead found himself at the centre of a national conversation about the legacy of slavery, one which continues to reverberate today.

> Here's one delusion: that we can escape slavery. We can't. Its scars will never fade... Who told you the negro deserved a place of refuge? Who told you that you had that right? Every minute of your life's suffering has argued otherwise... And America, too, is a delusion, the grandest one of all. The white race believes – believes with all its heart – that it is their right to take the land. To kill Indians. Make war. Enslave their brothers. This nation shouldn't exist, if there is any justice in the world, for its foundations are murder, theft, and cruelty. Yet here we are.

THE UNDERGROUND RAILROAD, "INDIANA"

Directory: 1980-Present

THE LOVER

MARGUERITE DURAS, 1984

French author Marguerite Duras (1914–96) published this short, intense novel when she was 70 years old. Loosely autobiographical, it narrates the experiences of a 15-year-old French girl growing up in the colony of Indochina (now Vietnam) during the 1920s. Fatherless, and neglected by her mother, the girl begins an illicit affair with a wealthy Chinese man. Defying taboos of both age and ethnicity, their relationship is doomed to an unhappy conclusion.

Duras offers no moral judgement: it is the man who loves most and is hurt the most. She writes in the first person but, looking back from old age, often refers to her younger self as "she". The prose is sparse, plain, and yet sensual, evoking the young girl's keen sense of the beauty of Vietnam as well as the physicality of love. The narrative's chronology is disjointed, in convincing imitation of memory. A painful sense of loss gives the book's nostalgia a sharp edge.

THE UNBEARABLE LIGHTNESS OF BEING

MILAN KUNDERA, 1984

The most celebrated work of the Czech-born writer Milan Kundera (b.1929), *The Unbearable Lightness of Being* is a series of reflections on philosophy, politics, art, love, and freedom illustrated by episodes from the lives of an engaging cast of characters. Its historical setting is the Prague Spring of 1968, an attempt to liberalize communism in Czechoslovakia, and its aftermath – the repression that followed a Soviet invasion.

A surgeon, Tomas, believes in the virtue of lightness, avoiding sexual or political commitment, but on both fronts he is trapped into commitment by a woman's love. Sabina is an artist who practises freedom both in her personal life and by rejecting the false art of political idealism. Although Tomas and Sabina are persecuted by the Czech Communist regime, the book maintains its lightness of tone, but Kundera makes his dedication to individual freedom plain.

WHITE NOISE

DON DELILLO, 1985

Delivering a savagely satirical view of consumerist modern America, *White Noise* is the breakthrough novel of American author Don DeLillo (b.1936). First-person narrator Jack Gladney teaches Hitler studies at the College-on-the-Hill. He lives with his fifth wife, Barbara, in a household of children and stepchildren, in which family life is ruled by television, advertising, and supermarkets. Just below the surface runs a paranoid obsession with death.

DeLillo weaves his text out of a hip parody of colloquial dialogue stuffed with product names and references to pop culture. His academics are cynically aware of the degradation of scholarly values, which have sold out to a commercialized populism. A semblance of plot appears when everyday life is interrupted by a major pollution event. This stimulates the characters to pursue a chemical cure for death, and eventually seek a resolution of their fears in violence.

In many ways deliberately "unrealistic", the novel expresses DeLillo's vision of a contemporary world in which reality has been usurped by the commercialized imagery fed to consumers.

THE JOY LUCK CLUB

AMY TAN, 1989

Author Amy Tan (b.1952) drew on her own experience as an American-born daughter of Chinese immigrants to create her bestselling first novel, *The Joy Luck Club*. In a linked set of 16 stories, it explores the lives of four mothers and their daughters. All first-generation Chinese immigrants, the mothers meet regularly to play *mahjong* (a tile-based Chinese game) and reminisce about the past. Their daughters are all American-born and oriented away from their Chinese origins. The characterization is sharp and complex, each of the mothers and daughters standing out as individuals.

Writing with humour and sensitivity, Tan delineates the gulf between the two generations with sympathetic understanding. The mothers' hair-raising anecdotes of life in pre-communist China contrast with their daughters' evocation of growing up in immigrant families, restive under the unbearable pressures of parental expectation. One daughter, who is the book's most prominent character, eventually travels to China to contact lost relatives in a partial reconciliation across the cultural divide.

◀ A SUITABLE BOY

VIKRAM SETH, 1993

Written in English by Indian author Vikram Seth (b.1952), *A Suitable Boy* is one of the longest novels ever published. Set in 1951, shortly after Indian independence, it centres around Mrs Rupa Mehra's search for a husband for her 19-year-old daughter Lata, a rebellious student who does not intend to submit to an arranged marriage.

Vikram Seth is pictured here in 1994, a year after the publication of *A Suitable Boy*.

Resolving this family situation allows Seth to field a huge cast of characters from diverse strata of Indian society, ranging from the anglicized elite to the impoverished in slums and villages. Digressions and sub-plots engage with political corruption, social change, and the often violent conflicts between Muslim and Hindu communities.

Despite its epic scale, the book is easy to read, light in style, and often humorous. It is also moderate in its attitudes – Seth is a gentle believer in domestic virtues. Obeying the narrative conventions of the novel as practised in the 19th century, *A Suitable Boy* invites identification with credible characters embedded in a solidly realized social world.

➤ PARADISE

ABDULRAZAK GURNAH, 1994

The Nobel Prize-winning author of the historical novel *Paradise*, Abdulrazak Gurnah (b.1948) was born of Arab parentage in Zanzibar. The book is set in East Africa around the start of the 20th century, when combined Arab, African, and Indian populations were feeling the mounting influence of German colonialism.

The family of Yusuf, a 12-year-old boy of unusual beauty, give him as a servant to a rich Arab merchant in payment for a debt. Travelling deep into the continent with a trading caravan, Yusuf finds landscapes and people that are exotic to him – both alluring and frightening. Through the characters that Yusuf meets, Gurnah skilfully conveys the ways of thought and behaviour of complex societies that have been threatened by modern colonialism. Yusuf comes of age during the novel, and this is complicated by his being attractive to both sexes. The book offers a refreshingly Afrocentric view of the past, and Europeans only take centre-stage at the end.

INFINITE JEST

DAVID FOSTER WALLACE, 1996

A demanding novel that tests its readers, *Infinite Jest* is not for the faint-hearted. American author David Foster Wallace (1962–2008)

created an encyclopaedic novel of more than 1,000 pages, in which stylistic parody and virtuosity take precedence over narrative clarity. The text is annotated with 388 endnotes that in turn have their own footnotes.

Setting his fantasy in the US in the near future, David Foster Wallace imagines a movie entitled *Infinite Jest*, which is so amusing that it fixates its viewers until they die. This deadly movie is sought both by Quebecois terrorists and US security agencies. Much of the action revolves around a tennis academy and a rehab centre, both of which represent destructive compulsions. Clever ideas abound: years are no longer numbered, for instance, because the right to name them has been sold off to corporate sponsors.

Although the novel itself is often wildly funny, depression haunts its characters, who are threatened at every turn by addiction and alienation. The hyperactive intelligence behind the writing never lets up.

THE FEAST OF THE GOAT

MARIO VARGAS LLOSA, 2000

A powerful novel by Nobel Prize-winning Peruvian author Mario Vargas Llosa (b.1936), *The Feast of the Goat* is based upon a historical event, the 1961 assassination of Rafael Trujillo, dictator of the Dominican Republic.

The story follows Trujillo, a pitiful old man in physical decline, through his last day on earth. Meanwhile, his assassins prepare for their deed. Their backstories reveal the complex web of corruption that dictatorship has extended over a whole society. In another strand of the book, a Dominican woman returns to her home country from the US in the 1990s to confront her ailing father, who was once an associate of Trujillo. The terrible secret of her youth, revealed late in the novel, exposes the sexual exploitation at the heart of the dictator's power.

Seamlessly blending fact and fiction, the book achieves the page-turning pace of a political thriller. The author's unflinching descriptions of violence, torture, and sexual abuse carry the reader into a heart of darkness from which there is no redemption.

Abdulrazak Gurnah was awarded the Nobel Prize for Literature in October 2021.

ATONEMENT

IAN McEWAN, 2001

In his Booker-shortlisted novel *Atonement*, British author Ian McEwan (b.1948) combines the strengths of a traditional historical novel with the formal trickery and literary self-consciousness associated with "postmodern" fiction.

A long opening section, set in 1930s England, is written in a style that is almost a pastiche of novels from that period. In a leisurely fashion, the story unfolds of a terrible injustice visited upon a lower-class man by an observant, but innocent, young girl, Bryony Tallis, when she misunderstands a sexual situation. The repercussions of her actions have devastating consequences for the characters, which are felt all their lives.

Moving on to World War II, we find the same characters in a much-altered setting. Scenes of the evacuation from Dunkirk and of wartime nursing are presented in a stark prose matching the brutal reality it describes.

Eventually, we discover that the book has been written by Bryony herself, who is now grown up and is in search of "atonement". Each section of the novel gives McEwan opportunities to exhibit his powers of detailed description, minutely evoking historical time and place.

DRIVE YOUR PLOUGH OVER THE BONES OF THE DEAD

OLGA TOKARCZUK, 2009

One of the shorter works of fiction by Polish Nobel laureate Olga Tokarczuk (b.1962), *Drive Your Plough Over the Bones of the Dead* superficially takes the form of a murder mystery.

The story is narrated by Janina Duszejko, a retired teacher living in a rural area of southern Poland. Janina is devoted to animals, astrology, and the works of the English poet William Blake. She gives her acquaintances quirky names such as Oddball, Dizzy, and Big Foot, but Janina's engaging narrative voice draws the reader into accepting her various eccentricities without question.

When members of a local hunting club start to die under mysterious circumstances, Janina suggests they may be victims of the animals that they have killed, who have begun a collective fightback. The text is enlivened by Janina's subversive comments on issues such as animal rights and vegetarianism. She also contemplates human identity, free will and determinism, and people's demeaning view of older women. The resolution of the murder mystery reveals that Janina is a very unreliable narrator indeed.

Index

Page numbers in **bold** refer to main entries.

Acknowledgments

DK would like to thank the following for their help with this book:
Bonnie Macleod, Hina Jain, and Lucy Sienkowska for editorial assistance; Helen Peters for the index; Sourabh Challariya and Aanchal Singal for design assistance; DTP Designer Bimlesh Tiwary, and Managing Jackets Editor Saloni Singh; Roland Smithies and Liz Moore for picture research; Loretta Deaver in the Manuscripts Division at the Library of Congress, Washington DC, Dr Walter Fant at Klagenfurt Robert-Musil-Institut für Literaturforschung / Kärntner Literaturarchiv der Universität Klagenfurt, and Allison MacIntosh at Bauman Rare Books for help with picture research.

The publisher would like to credit the following for the text extracts in the book:

The relevant page numbers appear in **bold** before the writers' names:

9 **Milan Kundera,** *The Art of the Novel* (Faber & Faber, 2005), translated by Linda Asher
13 **Murasaki Shikibu,** *The Tale of Genji* (Penguin Classics, 2001), translated by Royall Tyler
15 **Wu Cheng'en,** *Journey to the West, Revised Edition, Volume 1-4* (University of Chicago Press, 2012), translated by Anthony C. Yu
16, 18 **Miguel de Cervantes,** *Don Quixote of La Mancha* (Thomas V. Crowell & Company, 1920), translated by John Ormsby
20, 21, 22 **Daniel Defoe,** *Robinson Crusoe* (Oxford World's Classics, 1983)
25, 26 **Samuel Richardson,** *Pamela* (Oxford World's Classics, 2001)
29 **Voltaire,** *Candide* (Penguin Classics, 1947), translated by John Butt
30, 31 **Laurence Sterne,** *Tristram Shandy* (Penguin, 1997)
33 **Johann Wolfgang von Goethe,** *The Sorrows of Young Werther* (Oxford World's Classics, 2012), translated by David Constantine
34, 35 **Pierre Choderlos de Laclos,** *Les Liaisons Dangereuses* (Penguin Classics, 1961), translated by P.W.K. Stone
40, 41, 42 **Jane Austen,** *Pride and Prejudice,* (Penguin, 1996)
43 **Jane Austen,** Letter to Cassandra Austen, Friday 29 January 1813, cited in *Jane Austen's Letters* (Oxford University Press, 2011), collated and edited by Deirdre Le Faye
44 **Mary Shelley,** *Frankenstein* (Colburn and Bentley, 1831)
46 **Stendhal,** *The Red and the Black: A Chronicle of 1830* (Modern Library, 2004), translated by Burton Raffel
49, 50, 51 **Honoré de Balzac,** *Father Goriot (Le Père Goriot) and M. Gobseck* (The Gebbie Publishing Co., 1898), translated by Ellen Marriage
53 **Alessandro Manzoni,** *The Betrothed* (Penguin, 1972), translated by Bruce Penman
54, 55, 56, 57 **Charlotte Brontë,** *Jane Eyre* (Oxford World's Classics, 1980)
59 **Emily Brontë,** *Wuthering Heights* (Oxford World's Classics, 2009)
61, 62, 63 **Herman Melville,** *Moby-Dick; or, The Whale* (Harper Brothers. 1851)
64, 66 **Gustave Flaubert,** *Madame Bovary* (Knopf, 1919), translated by Eleanor Marx Aveling
69, 71 **Charles Dickens,** *Great Expectations* (Penguin, 1996)
72, 75 **Fyodor Dostoevsky,** *Crime and Punishment* (Everyman's Library, 1992), translated by Richard Pevear and Larissa Volokhonsky
80, 82 **George Eliot,** *Middlemarch* (Penguin, 1994)
84 **Leo Tolstoy,** *Anna Karenina* (William Heinemann, 1901), translated by Constance Garnett
85 **Leo Tolstoy,** *Anna Karenina* (Oxford World's Classics, 2014), translated by Rosamund Bartlett
87 **Leo Tolstoy,** Letter to N.N. Strakhov, 25 March 1873, cited in *A Karenina Companion* (Wilfrid Laurier University Press, 1993), by C.J.G. Turner
88, 89 **Henry James,** *The Portrait of a Lady* (Penguin Modern Classics, 1978)

92, 93 **Mark Twain,** *Adventures of Huckleberry Finn* (Charles L. Webster & Company, 1885)
94, 95, 96, 97 **Émile Zola,** *Germinal* (Penguin Classics, 1954), translated by L.W. Tancock
98, 99 **Benito Pérez Galdós,** *Fortunata and Jacinta: Two Stories of Married Women* (University of Georgia Press, 1986), translated by Agnes Moncy Gullón
100, 103 **Thomas Hardy,** *Tess of the d'Urbervilles* (MacMillan & Co., 1930)
104, 106, 107 **Thomas Mann,** *Buddenbrooks* (Penguin Books in association with Martin Secker and Warburg, 1924), translated by H.T. Lowe-Porter
108, 109 **D.H. Lawrence,** *Sons and Lovers* (Penguin, 1973)
113 **Marcel Proust,** *The Way by Swann's* (Penguin, 2003), translated by Lydia Davis
119 **Edith Wharton,** *The Age of Innocence* (Penguin Modern Classics, 1974)
120, 122 **James Joyce,** *Ulysses* (Penguin, 1972)
124, 125 **Jaroslav Hašek,** *The Good Soldier Švejk* (Penguin Classics, 2005), translated by Cecil Parrott
127 **F. Scott Fitzgerald,** *The Great Gatsby* (Vintage, 2010)
128, 129, 130, 131 **Franz Kafka,** *The Trial* (Penguin Modern Classics, 1953), translated by Willa and Edwin Muir
132 **Ernest Hemingway,** *The Sun Also Rises* (Scribners, 1926)
135, 136, 137 **Virginia Woolf,** *To the Lighthouse* (Penguin Modern Classics, 1964)
138 **Alfred Döblin,** *Berlin Alexanderplatz* (New York Review of Books, 2018), translated by Michael Hofmann
141 **William Faulkner,** *The Sound and the Fury: Norton Critical Edition* (W.W. Norton and Co., 1987)
143 **Robert Musil,** *The Man Without Qualities* (Vintage International, 1996), translated by Sophie Wilkins and Burton Pike
144 **Louis-Ferdinand Céline,** *Journey to the End of the Night* (New Directions, 1983), translated by Ralph Manheim
147 **Zora Neale Hurston,** *Their Eyes Were Watching God* (Virago Press, 2007)
148 **John Steinbeck,** *The Grapes of Wrath* (Modern Library, 1939)
151 **Albert Camus,** *The Outsider* (Penguin, 1961), translated by Stuart Gilbert
152, 153 **Yasunari Kawabata,** *Snow Country* (Penguin Modern Classics, 2011), translated by Edward G. Seidensticker
155 **George Orwell,** *Nineteen Eighty-Four* (Penguin, 1968)
160 **J.D. Salinger,** *The Catcher in the Rye* (Penguin Modern Classics, 1969)
163 **Ralph Ellison,** *Invisible Man* (Penguin Classics, 2001)
164, 165 **James Baldwin,** *Go Tell it on the Mountain* (Vintage International, 2013)
167 **Jack Kerouac,** *On the Road* (Penguin Modern Classics, 1972)
169, 171 **Giuseppe Tomasi di Lampedusa,** *The Leopard* (Collins & Harvill Press, 1960), translated by Archibald Colquhoun
173 **Chinua Achebe,** *Things Fall Apart* (Penguin Modern Classics, 1996)
174 **Günter Grass,** *The Tin Drum* (Penguin, 1965), translated by Ralph Manheim
176 **Harper Lee,** *To Kill a Mockingbird* (Penguin Books, 1973)
179 **Joseph Heller,** *Catch-22,* (Everyman's Library, 1995)
181 **Aleksandr Solzhenitsyn,** *One Day in the Life of Ivan Denisovich* (Penguin Modern Classics, 1963), translated by Ralph Parker
182 **Doris Lessing,** *The Golden Notebook* (Harper Perennial, 1999)
184, 185 **Kenzaburō Ōe,** *A Personal Matter* (Charles E. Tuttle Company, 1985), translated by John Nathan
187 **Gabriel García Márquez,** *One Hundred Years of Solitude* (Picador Pan Books, 1978), translated by Gregory Rabassa
189 **Mikhail Bulgakov,** *The Master and Margarita* (Penguin Classics, 1997), translated by Richard Pevear and Larissa Volokhonsky
190 **Philip Roth,** *Portnoy's Complaint* (Vintage, 2016)
192, 193 **Elsa Morante,** *History* (Aventura, 1984), translated by William Weaver

199 J.M.G. Le Clézio, *Desert* (Atlantic Books, 2010), translated by C. Dickson

201 Salman Rushdie, *Midnight's Children* (Everyman's Library, 1995)

203 Isabel Allende, *The House of the Spirits* (Everyman's Library, 2005), translated by Magda Bolin

205 José Saramago, *The Year of the Death of Ricardo Reis* (Vintage, 1999), translated by Giovanni Pontiero

206, 207 Margaret Atwood, *The Handmaid's Tale* (Vintage, 1996)

208, 210, 211 Toni Morrison, *Beloved* (Picador Macmillan, 1988)

212 Mo Yan, *Red Sorghum* (Arrow Books, 2003), translated by Howard Goldblatt

214, 215 Javier Marías, *A Heart So White* (The Harvill Press, 1997), translated by Margaret Jull Costa

216 Haruki Murakami, *The Wind-Up Bird Chronicle* (Vintage, 2003), translated by Jay Rubin

219 Arundhati Roy, *The God of Small Things* (Flamingo, 1998)

220 Michel Houellebecq, *Atomised* (Vintage, 2001), translated by Frank Wynne

222 J.M. Coetzee, *Disgrace* (Secker and Warburg, 1999)

225, 226 W.G. Sebald, *Austerlitz* (Penguin, 2002), translated by Anthea Bell

228 Orhan Pamuk, *Snow* (Faber, 2005), translated by Guneli Gun

231 Kazuo Ishiguro, *Never Let Me Go* (Faber, 2005)

232 Chimamanda Ngozi Adichie, *Half of a Yellow Sun* (Fourth Estate, 2007)

235 Marilynne Robinson, *Gilead* (Farrar, Strauss, and Giroux, 2004)

236 Karl Ove Knausgård, *A Death in the Family* (Vintage, 2012), translated by Don Bartlett

239 Hilary Mantel, *Wolf Hall* (4th Estate, 2019)

241 Elena Ferrante, *My Brilliant Friend* (Europa Editions, 2012), translated by Ann Goldstein

243 Colson Whitehead, *The Underground Railroad* (Fleet, 2017)

Picture Credits

The publisher would like to thank the following for their kind permission to reproduce their photographs:

(Key: a-above; b-below/bottom; c-centre; f-far; l-left; r-right; t-top)

1 Alamy Stock Photo: Album (cl). **Bauman Rare Books. 2-3 Getty Images:** GraphicaArtis. **4-5 Bridgeman Images:** Herbert Art Gallery & Museum, Coventry. **6-7 Alamy Stock Photo:** Randy Duchaine. **8 DNP Art Communications Co., Ltd:** Tokugawa Art Museum (bl). **Wisbech & Fenland Museum:** Townshend Collection (br). **9 Bibliothèque nationale de France, Paris. Günter und Ute Grass Stiftung:** Steidl Verlag / (br). **10-11 Liu Nan:** Liu Ji You. **12-13 DNP Art Communications Co., Ltd:** Tokugawa Art Museum. **12 DNP Art Communications Co., Ltd:** Tokugawa Art Museum (bl). **The New York Public Library:** Charles Stewart Smith collection of Japanese prints (tl). **Wikimedia Commons:** Wise Personages Past and Present 1868 (br). **13 Alamy Stock Photo:** Chronicle of World History (bl). **14 Alamy Stock Photo:** Makota Sakurai (tl). **Bridgeman Images:** Pictures from History (bl). **Liu Nan:** Liu Ji You (br). **15 Alamy Stock Photo:** CPA Media Pte Ltd (tr). **Library of Congress, Washington, D.C..** 16 **Dreamstime.com:** Whpics (l). © **MECD. Archivos Estatales (España).:** (bl). **17 Alamy Stock Photo:** Universal Art Archive (br). **Bridgeman Images:** Photo Josse (cla). **Getty Images:** (cra). **18 Alamy Stock Photo:** Universal Art Archive (cr). **AWL Images:** Matteo Colombo (bl). **19 Getty Images:** Heritage Images / Fine Art Images. **20 Getty Images:** Stock Montage (cla). **20-21 Bridgeman Images:** Christie's Images. **21 Alamy Stock Photo:** Chronicle (br). **Bridgeman Images:** British Library (cr). **22 Alamy Stock Photo:** Visual Arts Resource (tl). **23 Bridgeman Images:** Look and Learn (bl). **Getty Images:** Buyenlarge (br). **Sotheby's, London:** Private Collection (t). **24 Alamy Stock Photo:** Universal Art Archive (cla); Universal Art Archive (bl). **24-25 Bridgeman Images:** Victoria & Albert Museum, London, UK (c). **25 Bridgeman Images:** British Library (crb). **26 Alamy Stock Photo:** Universal Art Archive (br). **27 Bridgeman Images:** British Library (tr). **President and Fellows of Harvard College:** (l). **28 Alamy Stock Photo:** Universal Art Archive (br). **Bibliothèque nationale de France, Paris:** (cr). **Getty Images:** Corbis / Leemage (cla). **29 Bibliothèque nationale de France, Paris. 30 Alamy Stock Photo:** Svintage Archive (cla). **30-31 AF Fotografie. 31 Getty Images:** Universal Images Group / Sepia Times (bc). © **The Metropolitan Museum of Art:** The Elisha Whittelsey Collection, The Elisha Whittelsey Fund, 1959 (cra). **32 Alamy Stock Photo:** Ian Dagnall Computing (t). **32-33 akg-images:** Heiner Heine. **33 Alamy Stock Photo:** Lebrecht Music & Arts (tr, br). **34 Alamy Stock Photo:** Heritage Image Partnership Ltd (cla). **Bridgeman Images:** The Stapleton Collection (bl). **35 Bibliothèque nationale de France, Paris. Getty Images:** Fine Art Images / Heritage Images (br). **37 British Library. 38-39 Getty Images:** Heritage Images. **40 Bridgeman Images:** British Library (r). **Jane Austen's House:** (bl). **41 Bridgeman Images:** NPL - DeA Picture Library (tl); The Stapleton Collection (br). **42 Alamy Stock Photo:** Universal Art Archive (tr). **Bridgeman Images:** British Library (bc). **43 Bridgeman Images:** British Library Board. All Rights Reserved (br). **Jane Austen's House.** **44 Bridgeman Images:** Birmingham Museums and Art Gallery (bl); Fine Art Images (cla). **45 The Bodleian Library, University of Oxford:** (l). **Getty Images:** Universal History Archive. **46 Alamy Stock Photo:** AF Fotografie. **47 Bridgeman Images:** Giancarlo Costa (tl); Russell-Cotes Art Gallery (bl). **Getty Images:** Heritage Images (br). **48 Alamy Stock Photo:** AF Fotografie (tr); Heritage Image Partnership Ltd (tl). **Bridgeman Images:** Leonard de Selva (bl). **49 Alamy Stock Photo:** Universal Art Archive (b). **Photo Scala, Florence:** RMN-Grand Palais (t). **50 Getty Images:** Bettmann (bc); Sepia Times / Universal Images Group. **51 Bridgeman Images:** Archives Charmet (tr, br). **52 Alamy Stock Photo:** Universal Art Archive (tl). **Bridgeman Images:** NPL - DeA Picture Library (bl); The Stapleton Collection (br). **53 Biblioteca Nazionale Braidense:** (c). **Bridgeman Images:** Veneranda Biblioteca Ambrosiana / Mondadori Portfolio (br). **Getty Images:** DeAgostini (cl). **54 Alamy Stock Photo:** Granger Historical Picture Archive (bl); Painters (br). **Getty Images:** Apic. **55 Alamy Stock Photo:** AF Fotografie (tr). **Bridgeman Images:** British Library (tl). **56 Bridgeman Images:** British Library. **57 Alamy Stock Photo:** Martyn Williams (tr); Vintage Archives (cr, br). **58 Bridgeman Images:** Bronte Parsonage Museum (br); Stefano Baldini (tl); Look and Learn (bl). **59 AF Fotografie. Bridgeman Images:** British Library Board. All Rights Reserved / Clare Leighton (tl). **60 Alamy Stock Photo:** Universal Art Archive / Houghton Library, Harvard University (tl). **Yale University Library:** Beinecke Rare Book and Manuscript Library (bc). **60-61 Getty Images:** GraphicaArtis (b). **62 Alamy Stock Photo:** Universal Art Archive (br). **63 Raptis Rare Books. 64 Getty Images:** Heritage Images (tl, bc). **65 Musee Rouen. 66 Bridgeman Images:** Fototeca Gilardi (bl). ©**Tate, London 2022:** (t). **67 Alamy Stock Photo:** Universal Art Archive (t). **Bridgeman Images:** Giancarlo Costa (br). **68 Wisbech & Fenland Museum:** Townshend Collection. **69 Alamy Stock Photo:** Kentish Dweller (bl). **Bridgeman Images:** Charles Dickens Museum (tl). **Getty Images:** DEA / ICAS94 (br). **70 Alamy Stock Photo:** Neil McAllister (br). **71 Alamy Stock Photo:** Album (tl). **Wisbech & Fenland Museum. 72 Alamy Stock Photo:** Alexeyev Filippov. **73 Alamy Stock Photo:** Signal Photos (bl); Universal Art Archive (tl). **Getty Images:** Fine Art Images / Heritage Images (br); Universal Images Group / Photo12 (tr). **74 Alamy Stock Photo:** Alexeyev Filippov. **75 Alamy Stock Photo:** BFA (cr); John Heseltine (br). **78-79 Bridgeman Images:** Herbert Art Gallery & Museum, Coventry. **80 Bridgeman Images:** Christie's Images. **81 Alamy Stock Photo:** Universal Art Archive (tl). **Bridgeman Images:** Herbert Art Gallery & Museum, Coventry (bl); The Stapleton Collection (br). **82 Bridgeman Images:** British Library Board. All Rights Reserved. **83 Alamy Stock Photo:** PBS / Courtesy Everett Collection (bl). **Bridgeman Images:** The Stapleton Collection. **84 Alamy Stock Photo:** ITAR-TASS News Agency (bl). **Bridgeman Images:** Look and Learn (cra). **Getty Images:** Fine Art Images / Heritage Images (tl). **85 Bookvica:** (tl). **Getty Images:** Fine Art Images / Heritage Images (br). **86 Alamy Stock Photo:** Chronicle (br). **Getty Images:** Victoria and Albert Museum, London / The Royal Photographic Society Collection (bl). **87 AF Fotografie. The State Museum of L.N. Tolstoy:** (tr). **88 Bridgeman Images:** National Trust Photographic Library (tl); Raffaello Bencini (br). **89 Alamy Stock Photo:** Photo 12 (br). **Raptis Rare Books:** (l). **90 Bauman Rare Books. 91 Alamy Stock Photo:** Universal Art Archive (tl). **Bauman Rare Books. Getty Images:** H. Armstrong Roberts / ClassicStock (bl). **92 Alamy Stock Photo:** The Granger Collection (l). **Yale University Library:** Randolph Linsly Simpson African-American Collection (r). **93 Courtesy of the Library Foundation, BECPL. 94 akg-images:** (bl). **Bibliothèque nationale de France, Paris. Getty Images:** Imagno (tl). **95 Bibliothèque nationale de France, Paris. Getty Images:** UIG / Prisma (br). **96 Bibliothèque nationale de France, Paris. Bridgeman Images:** Giancarlo Costa (bl). **97 Bibliothèque nationale de France, Paris. 98 Alamy Stock Photo:** Album (br); The Picture Art Collection (tl); Heritage Image Partnership Ltd (bl). **99 Alamy Stock Photo:** UtCon Collection (br). **Biblioteca Nacional de España:** (l). **100 Dorset**

Museum 2022: (br). 101 Getty Images: Hulton Archive (tl). Thierry Gregorius: (br). Shutterstock.com: Renn / Burrill / Sfp / Kobal (cr). 102 Bridgeman Images: British Library (br); The Stapleton Collection (bc). 103 Bridgeman Images: British Library. 104 S. Fischer Verlag: (l). Thomas-Mann-Archiv an der ETH-Bibliothek: S. Fischer Verlag (r). 105 Alamy Stock Photo: Art Collection 4 (bl); Heritage Image Partnership Ltd (br). Getty Images: Culture Club (tl). 106 Alamy Stock Photo: imageBROKER (bl). Thomas-Mann-Archiv an der ETH-Bibliothek: (t). 107 Mary Evans Picture Library. 108 Getty Images: Bettmann (tl); Heritage Images (bl); Photo 12 (br). 109 Bridgeman Images: Fry Art Gallery Society (br). University of Nottingham Libraries, Manuscripts and Special Collections: (l). 110 Bauman Rare Books. Sotheby's, London: (cr). 111 Getty Images: Hulton Deutsch (tl); iStock (tr); Jean-Francois Monier / AFP (bl). Wikimedia Commons: Eric Houdas (br). 112 Bauman Rare Books. Bibliothèque nationale de France, Paris. 113 Bibliothèque nationale de France, Paris. Bridgeman Images. 114 National Diet Library, Japan. 115 Getty Images: Bettmann. 116–117 Getty Images: Universal History Archive. 118 Beinecke Rare Book and Manuscript Library, Yale University. 119 Alamy Stock Photo: Everett Collection Inc (tl). Library of Congress, Washington, D.C.: Detroit Publishing Company Photograph Collection LC-D4-13619 (bl). 120 Alamy Stock Photo: AF Fotografie (tl); Chronicle (bl); Album (br). 121 Bridgeman Images: Luisa Ricciarini (cr). The Charles Deering McCormick Library of Special Collections and University Archives: (br). The Rosenbach Museum and Library: Estate of James Joyce (l). 122 Alamy Stock Photo: Lebrecht Music & Arts (br). Bauman Rare Books: Shakespeare and Company (bl). 122–123 Getty Images: Lorenzo Ciniglio. 123 Alamy Stock Photo: AF Fotografie (br). 124 AF Fotografie. akg-images: Fototeca Gilardi (br); SNA (tl). 125 Getty Images: DEA / A. DAGLI ORTI (br). LA PNP: Jaroslav Hašek Fund (t). 126 Bauman Rare Books. Princeton University Library: Department of Special Collections / Manuscripts Division / F. Scott Fitzgerald Papers, 1897-1944 (r). 127 Alamy Stock Photo: Everett Collection Inc (tr). Getty Images: Corbis / Minnesota Historical Society (tl); Popperfoto / Paul Popper (br). 128 Alamy Stock Photo: Glasshouse Images (bl); Uber Bilder (tl). Getty Images: Paule Saviano (br). 129 Bridgeman Images: Paule Saviano (br). Deutsches Literaturarchiv Marbach. 130 Alamy Stock Photo: Album. 131 Alamy Stock Photo: Shim Harno (tr). BFA: StudioCanal (br). Getty Images: Heritage Images (bl). 132 Bauman Rare Books. 133 Alamy Stock Photo: INTERFOTO (tr). Getty Images: API (tl); Fotosearch (bl); Paul Popper / Popperfoto (br). 134 Alamy Stock Photo: Helen Dixon (bl). Bridgeman Images: Prismatic Pictures (tl). Getty Images: Hulton Archive / George C Beresford (br). 135 Bauman Rare Books. 136 Bridgeman Images: Bradford Museums & Galleries / © Estate of Vanessa Bell. All rights reserved / © DACS 2022 (bl). Getty Images: Ralph Partridge / Frances Partridge (tr). 137 Bridgeman Images: The Bloomsbury Workshop, London / Vanessa Bell / Hogarth Press / Penguin Random House UK (br). The New York Public Library: Berg Collection / © Virginia Woolf Estate / The Society of Authors (l). 138 Galerie Bassenge: S. Fischer Verlag. 139 akg-images: Erich Lessing (br); Sammlung Berliner Verlag / Archiv (bl). Deutsches Literaturarchiv Marbach: (cra). Getty Images: ullstein bild (tl). 140–141 (c)The Board of Visitors of the University of Virginia: Curtis Brown and Penguin Random House UK and W. W. Norton & Company. 140 Bauman Rare Books. Getty Images: Bettmann (bl); Carolyn Cole (tl). 141 (c)The Board of Visitors of the University of Virginia. 142 Alamy Stock Photo: ARCHIVIO GBB (tl). Getty Images: Imagno (tr, b). 143 Dominic Winter Auctioneers Ltd (br). Getty Images: Photo 12 (tr). ÖNB/Wien: Der Mann ohne Eigenschaften. Zur Ausarbeitung Ulrich-Agathe in Bd. II:: Mappe VII / 17, Nachlass Robert Musil, Literaturarchiv der Österreichischen Nationalbibliothek, Wien. Sign.: LIT 479 / Cod. Ser. n. 15113 / VII / 17 / 20 (l). 144 Bridgeman Images: © Denoël, 1982. 145 Alamy Stock Photo: World History Archive (bl). Getty Images: adoc-photos (t); Boyer (b). 146 Alamy Stock Photo: AF archive (tr); Randy Duchaine (br). Getty Images: Historical (tl). 147 Alamy Stock Photo: INTERFOTO (cr). Beinecke Rare Book and Manuscript Library, Yale University: Joy Harris Literary Agency, inc. (t). 148 (c)The Board of Visitors of the University of Virginia. 149 Getty Images: Bettmann (br); Hulton Deutsch (tl); Universal History Archive (bl). 150 Alamy Stock Photo: Everett Collection Inc (br). Getty Images: Miller / Topical Press Agency (bl). Magnum Photos: © Henri Cartier-Bresson © Fondation Henri Cartier-Bresson (tl). 151 AF Fotografie. Getty Images: Fine Art Images / Heritage Images (br). 152 Alamy Stock Photo: CPA Media Pte Ltd (tl). 153 Getty Images: Hongki Lee / EyeEm (t). TopFoto: (b). 154 Alamy Stock Photo: Artyom Smirnova / Russian National Library (tr); Granger Historical Picture Archive (tl). BFA: Halas & Batchelor (br).

155 Bauman Rare Books. Brown University Library: Special Collections / Donated to the Library by Daniel G. Siegel '57 (cl). 156 Alamy Stock Photo: Pictorial Press Ltd. 157 Alamy Stock Photo: Granger Historical Picture Archive. 158–159 World of Photos: Oldnycphotos.com / Brian Merlis. 160 John Aster Archive: The Crowell-Collier Publishing Company (br). Getty Images: San Diego Historical Society (tl). World of Photos: Oldnycphotos.com / Brian Merlis (bl). 161 AF Fotografie: Little, Brown and Company / Little Brown and Company / Hachette Book Group (t). Getty Images: US Army Photo / AP (br). 162 Alamy Stock Photo: Everett Collection Historical (tl); steeve-x-art (bl). 162–163 Library of Congress, Washington, D.C.: The Ralph and Fanny Ellison Charitable Trust (b). 163 Getty Images: Buyenlarge (br). Library of Congress, Washington, D.C.: Dick de Marsico (tr). 164 Alamy Stock Photo: CSU Archives / Everett Collection (tl); Granger Historical Picture Archive (tr). Getty Images: Bettmann (b). 165 PBA Galleries. 166–167 Bridgeman Images: © Christie's Images / © Jack Kerouac Estate / CMG Worldwide (cr). 166 Alamy Stock Photo: Photo 12 (bl). Bridgeman Images: Prismatic Pictures (tl). Getty Images: Corbis / Allen Ginsberg (br). 167 Bridgeman Images: AF Fotografie / The Viking Press / Penguin Random House LLC (br). Getty Images: Corbis / Ted Streshinsky (bl). 168 Alamy Stock Photo: The Picture Art Collection (tl). Bridgeman Images: Abbott and Holder, London (b). 169 Getty Images: DEA / G. CIGOLINI (b). Courtesy Nicoletta Polo: The Wylie Agency (t). 170 Alamy Stock Photo: Pictorial Press Ltd (bl). Getty Images: Mondadori Portfolio (br). 171 Alamy Stock Photo: Massimo Buonaiuto (r). Bridgeman Images: (l). 172 AF Fotografie. 173 Algonquin Books: (br). Shutterstock.com: The LIFE Picture Collection / Eliot Elisofon (tl). TopFoto. 174 Alamy Stock Photo: Süddeutsche Zeitung Photo / Scherl (bl). Getty Images: Hulton Archive / Imagno (tl). NS Dokumentationszentrum: (br). 175 Alamy Stock Photo: PictureLux / The Hollywood Archive (br); Steidl GmbH & Co. OHG (tr). Günter und Ute Grass Stiftung: Steidl Verlag / VG Bild-Kunst R.V. / © DACS 2022 (tl). 176 AF Fotografie. 177 Getty Images: Bettmann (tl); Silver Screen Collection (tr); FilmMagic / Taylor Hill (bl); Bettmann (br). 178 Alamy Stock Photo: Photo 12 (br). Getty Images: Hulton-Deutsch Collection (bl). Magnum Photos: Inge Morath (tl). 179 AF Fotografie: Simon & Schuster, Inc. (br). Alamy Stock Photo: (cr). Brandeis University: Robert D. Farber University Archives & Special Collections / Used with permission of the Estate of Joseph Heller, via ICM Partners, New York. (bl). 180 Bridgeman Images: Effigie (tl). Getty Images: Fine Art Images / Heritage Images (bl); Laski Diffusion (br). 181 Alamy Stock Photo: CSU Archives / Everett Collection (br). University Archives: (tl). 182 AF Fotografie. 183 AF Fotografie. Bridgeman Images: Oswald Jones Archive (tl). Getty Images: Gamma-Keystone / Keystone-France (tr); Popperfoto (bl). 184 Roland Smithies / luped.com: Shinchosha Publishing Co, Ltd. 185 Getty Images: Galerie Bilderwelt (crb); The Asahi Shimbun (tl). Shutterstock.com: AP / Gunnar Ask (bl). 186 Alamy Stock Photo: Chronicle (br). Feria Inernacional del Libro: (bl). Shutterstock.com: Everett (tl). 187 Alamy Stock Photo: Album / Editorial Sudamericana / Penguin Random House UK (l). Harry Ransom Center, The University of Texas at Austin: (br). 188 Alamy Stock Photo: The Picture Art Collection (br). Getty Images: Universal Images Group / Photo 12 (bl). Soviet Orders: (c). TopFoto: Roger-Viollet (tl). 189 Bridgeman Images. Wikimedia Commons: Nkrita / (CC BY-SA 4.0) (br). 190 Alamy Stock Photo: Archive PL / Penguin Random House LLC (r). Library of Congress, Washington, D.C.: Philip Roth papers, MSS22491, box 183 / The Wylie Agency (l). 191 Alamy Stock Photo: AF archive (br). Getty Images: Truman Moore (cr); Bob Peterson (tr). TopFoto: Picture Alliance (bl). 192 Alamy Stock Photo: Lilly Pudding (tl). BFA: Rai 2 (cra). Bridgeman Images: Everett Collection (bl). 193 Bridgeman Images: Fototeca Gilardi (br). Roland Smithies / luped.com: Giulio Einaudi editore (tl). 194 Getty Images: INA. 195 Getty Images: Mondadori Portfolio. 196–197 Getty Images: Gamma-Rapho / Jose-Fuste RAGA. 198–199 Getty Images: E+ / hadynyah (t). 198 Bridgeman Images: Louis Monier (bl). 199 AF Fotografie. Getty Images: Gamma-Rapho / Patrick De Wilde (bl); Universal Images Group / Universal History Archive (br). 200 Getty Images: Bettmann (bl); Hulton Archive / Imagno / Nora Schuster (crb); Fine Art Images / Heritage Images (br). Magnum Photos: Gilles Peress (cla). 201 AF Fotografie. 202 Raptis Rare Books. 203 Alamy Stock Photo: Miguel Sayago (tl); United Archives GmbH (bl). Getty Images: Bettmann (br). 204 John Aster Archive: (br). Getty Images: Print Collector (bl). Magnum Photos: Micha Bar-Am (tl). 205 Alamy Stock Photo: Penrodas Collection (cr). Biblioteca Nacional de Portugal: Fundação José Saramago (l). 206 Alamy Stock Photo: BFA (b). Getty

Images: Fairfax Media Archives (tl). **207 AF Fotografie:** Nan A. Talese / Doubleday / Doubleday / Penguin Random House LLC (br). **Bauman Rare Books. 208 Bauman Rare Books. Princeton University Library:** Special Collections / © 1987 Toni Morrison / Curtis Brown / Reprinted by permission of ICM Partners (cr). **209 Collection of the Smithsonian National Museum of African American History and Culture:** (br). **Getty Images:** Jack Mitchell (tl); Stock Montage (bl). **210 Alamy Stock Photo:** Art Collection 2 (tr). **Getty Images:** Alex Wong (bc). **211 AF Fotografie. 212 The Wylie Agency:** © Mo Yan. **213 Alamy Stock Photo:** Photo 12 (tr). **Getty Images:** Ulf Andersen (tl). **© The Metropolitan Museum of Art:** John Stewart Kennedy Fund, 1913 (br). **214 Alamy Stock Photo:** Sueddeutsche Zeitung Photo (tl). **Getty Images:** DEA Picture Library (bl). **Penguin Random House UK:** Alfaguara, S.A., Madrid. (br). **215 Roland Smithies / luped.com. 216 Shinchosha Publishing Co, Ltd:** (cl). **217 Alamy Stock Photo:** Süddeutsche Zeitung Photo / Brigitte Friedrich (cla). **Getty Images:** Gamma-Rapho / Jose-Fuste RAGA (cra). **Magnum Photos:** Peter Marlow (bl). **Raptis Rare Books:** Kodansha (br). **218 Alamy Stock Photo:** Steve Davey Photography (bl). **Getty Images:** Gamma-Rapho / Robert Nickelsberg (tl). **The Hindu:** (tr). **219 Getty Images:** New York Times Co. / Neal Boenzi (br). **Reprinted by permission of HarperCollins Publishers Ltd:** 1997 Arundhati Roy (l). **220 Alamy Stock Photo:** Photo 12 (tr). **Éditions Flammarion:** (bc). **Shutterstock.com:** Sipa (tl). **221 Alamy Stock Photo:** Constantin Film / TCD / Prod.DB. **222 AF Fotografie. Harry Ransom Center, The University of Texas at Austin. 223 Alamy Stock Photo:** Niday Picture Library (tr); Photo 12 (bl). **Bridgeman Images:** Basso Cannarsa / Opale (tl). **Getty Images:** Afro American Newspapers / Gado (br). **224 akg-images:** ullstein bild (tl). **Alamy Stock Photo:** INTERFOTO (bl). **Getty Images:** Bettmann (br). **225 Carl Hanser Verlag GmbH & Co. KG:** (bl). **Getty Images:** Imagno (br). **226 Alamy Stock Photo:** Hemis (br). **Library of Congress, Washington, D.C.:** https://lccn.loc.gov/2017659130 (bl). **227 Carl Hanser Verlag GmbH & Co. KG. 228 İletişim Yayınları. 229 Alamy Stock Photo:** Asar Studios (crb); dpa picture alliance archive (cla); Levent Karaoglu (bl). **Getty Images:** Bloomberg / Kerem Uzel (br). **230 Alamy Stock Photo:** sjbooks / Faber & Faber Ltd (cra); TCD / Prod DB © Fox Searchlight Pictures - DNA Films - Film4 (b). **Getty Images:** David Levenson (cla). **231 Faber & Faber Ltd:** Heritage Auctions, HA.com. **232 HarperCollins Publishers:** 4th Estate. **233 agefotostock:** Igor Lubnevskiy (clb). **Getty Images:** Bettmann (cra); David Levenson (cla); Evening Standard (br). **234 Alamy Stock Photo:** Kathy deWitt (tr); The Granger Collection (br). **Shutterstock.com:** AP / Brian Ray (tl). **Hank Zaletel:** (bl). **235 Beinecke Rare Book and Manuscript Library, Yale University:** Marilynne Robinson Papers. Yale Collection of American Literature / © Marilynne Robinson / Trident Media Group, LLC (tl). **Heritage Auctions, HA.com:** Farrar, Straus and Giroux / Pan Macmillan (cr). **236 Forlaget Oktober. 237 AWL Images:** Mauricio Abreu (cra). **Forlaget Oktober. Getty Images:** Lengemann / WELT / ullstein bild (cla). **Valiant Asbjørn Jensen:** © Asbjørn Jensen (bl). **238 Alamy Stock Photo:** IanDagnall Computing (br). **Getty Images:** Fine Art Images / Heritage Images (bl); David Levenson (tl). **HarperCollins Publishers:** Fourth Estate (c). **239 Alamy Stock Photo:** Ben Molyneux / Fourth Estate / HarperCollins Publishers (fbr); sjbooks / Henry Holt and Co. / Pan Macmillan (br). **The Huntington Library, Art Collections, and Botanical Gardens:** © Hilary Mantel / A. M. Heath Literary Agents (tl). **240 E/O Edizioni Srl:** Roland Smithies / luped.com. **241 E/O Edizioni Srl. Getty Images:** Mondadori (cr). **242 Bridgeman Images:** Basso Cannarsa / Opale (cla); Peter Newark American Pictures (cra). **© The Metropolitan Museum of Art:** Harris Brisbane Dick Fund, 1929 (bl). **Wikimedia Commons:** Gilbert Studios, Washington, D.C. (C. M. Gilbert); restored by Adam Cuerden / Public Domain (br). **243 Bauman Rare Books:** Penguin Random House LLC. **244 Alamy Stock Photo:** Independent. **245 Shutterstock.com:** Matt Dunham / AP

All other images © Dorling Kindersley
For further information see: www.dkimages.com

More Great Books from DK

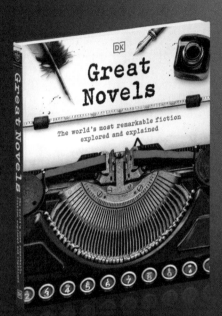

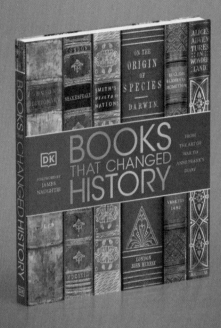

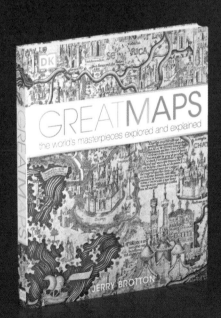

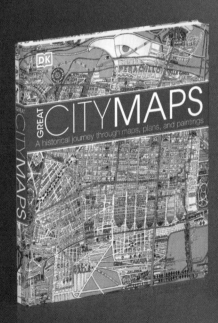